ISABELLA DE' MEDICI

CAROLINE P. MURPHY

Isabella de' Medici

*The Glorious Life and Tragic End
of a Renaissance Princess*

faber and faber

First published in 2008
by Faber and Faber Limited
3 Queen Square London WC1N 3AU

Typeset by Faber and Faber Limited
Printed in Great Britain by TJ International Ltd, Padstow, Cornwall

A CIP record for this book
is available from the British Library

ISBN 978-0-571-23030-3

FSC
Mixed Sources
Product group from well-managed
forests and other controlled sources
Cert no. SGS-COC-2482
www.fsc.org
© 1996 Forest Stewardship Council

2 4 6 8 10 9 7 5 3 1

to Brian Murphy
1934–2007

ISABELLA AB ETRVRIA
COSMI I. MAGNI DVCIS ETRVRIAE FIL.
PAVLI IORD. VRSINI DVCIS BRACHIANI VXOR

Contents

CONTENTS

Map of Florence and Medici Family Tree

View of Florence with Medici emblem

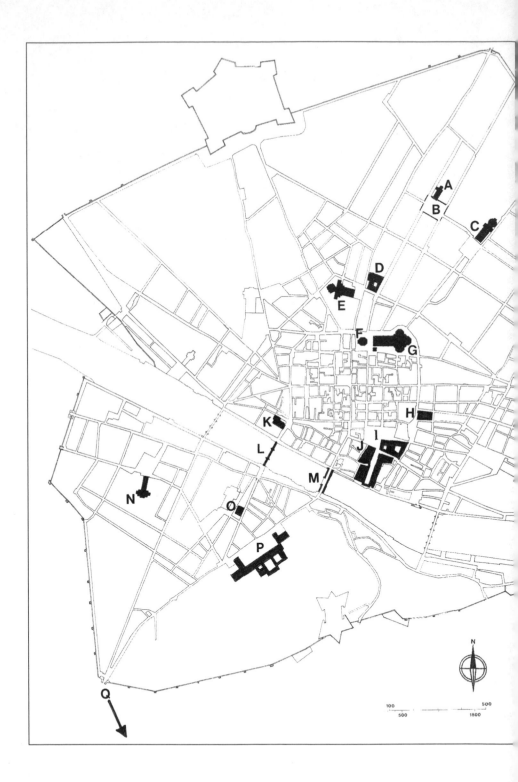

ISABELLA'S FLORENCE

A Church of San Marco

B Piazza di San Marco

C Church of Santissima Annunziata

D Palazzo Medici

E Church of San Lorenzo

F Baptistery

G Cathedral of Santa Maria del Fiore (Duomo)

H Bargello

I Palazzo Vecchio

J Uffizi

K Church of Santa Trinità

L Ponte Santa Trinità

M Ponte Vecchio/Vasari Corridor

N Church of Santa Maria del Carmine

O Palazzo of Bianca Cappello

P Palazzo Pitti

Q Direction of Baroncelli Villa

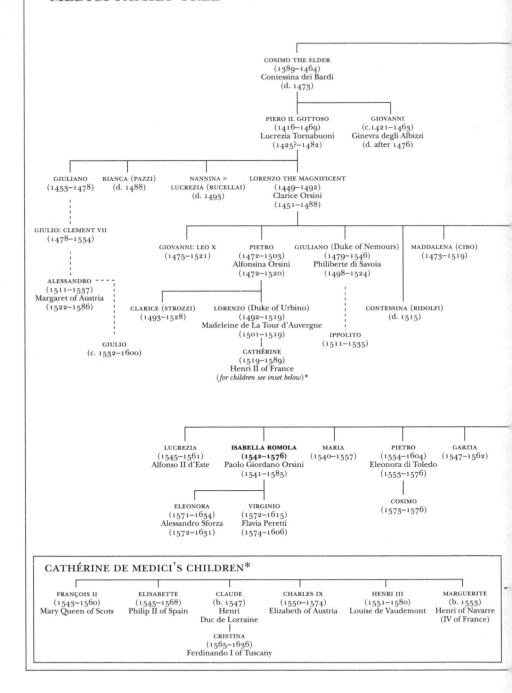

MEDICI FAMILY TREE

COSIMO THE ELDER
(1389–1464)
Contessina dei Bardi
(d. 1473)

PIERO IL GOTTOSO
(1416–1469)
Lucrezia Tornabuoni
(1425?–1482)

GIOVANNI
(c.1421–1463)
Ginevra degli Albizzi
(d. after 1476)

GIULIANO
(1453–1478)

BIANCA (PAZZI)
(d. 1488)

NANNINA =
LUCREZIA (RUCELLAI)
(d. 1493)

LORENZO THE MAGNIFICENT
(1449–1492)
Clarice Orsini
(1451–1488)

GIULIO: CLEMENT VII
(1478–1534)

GIOVANNI: LEO X
(1475–1521)

PIETRO
(1472–1503)
Alfonsina Orsini
(1472–1520)

GIULIANO (Duke of Nemours)
(1479–1546)
Philiberte di Savoia
(1498–1524)

MADDALENA (CIBO)
(1473–1519)

ALESSANDRO
(1511–1537)
Margaret of Austria
(1522–1586)

CLARICE (STROZZI)
(1493–1528)

LORENZO (Duke of Urbino)
(1492–1519)
Madeleine de La Tour d'Auvergne
(1501–1519)

CONTESSINA (RIDOLFI)
(d. 1515)

GIULIO
(c. 1532–1600)

CATHÉRINE
(1519–1589)
Henri II of France
(*for children see inset below*)*

IPPOLITO
(1511–1535)

LUCREZIA
(1545–1561)
Alfonso II d'Este

ISABELLA ROMOLA
(1542–1576)
Paolo Giordano Orsini
(1541–1585)

MARIA
(1540–1557)

PIETRO
(1554–1604)
Eleonora di Toledo
(1553–1576)

GARZIA
(1547–1562)

ELEONORA
(1571–1634)
Alessandro Sforza
(1572–1631)

VIRGINIO
(1572–1615)
Flavia Peretti
(1574–1606)

COSIMO
(1573–1576)

CATHÉRINE DE MEDICI'S CHILDREN*

FRANÇOIS II
(1543–1560)
Mary Queen of Scots

ELISABETTE
(1545–1568)
Philip II of Spain

CLAUDE
(b. 1547)
Henri
Duc de Lorraine

CHARLES IX
(1550–1574)
Elizabeth of Austria

HENRI III
(1551–1580)
Louise de Vaudemont

MARGUERITE
(b. 1553)
Henri of Navarre
(IV of France)

CRISTINA
(1565–1636)
Ferdinando I of Tuscany

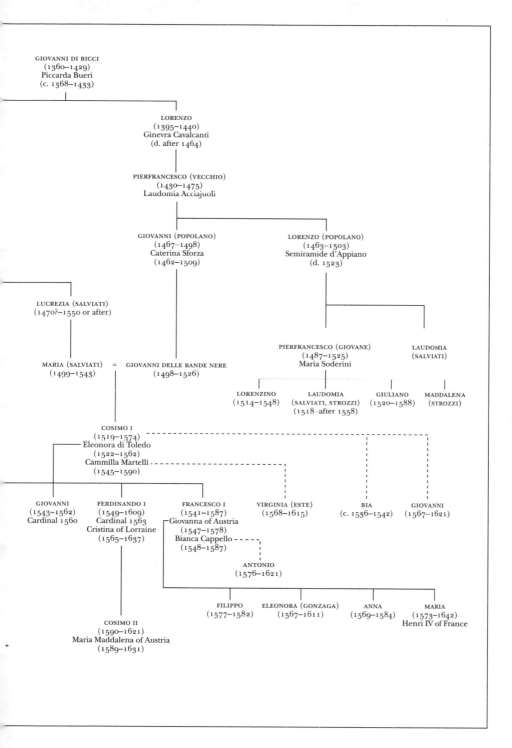

GIOVANNI DI BICCI
(1360–1429)
Piccarda Bueri
(c. 1368–1433)

LORENZO
(1395–1440)
Ginevra Cavalcanti
(d. after 1464)

PIERFRANCESCO (VECCHIO)
(1430–1475)
Laudomia Acciajuoli

GIOVANNI (POPOLANO)
(1467–1498)
Caterina Sforza
(1462–1509)

LORENZO (POPOLANO)
(1463–1503)
Semiramide d'Appiano
(d. 1523)

LUCREZIA (SALVIATI)
(1470?–1550 or after)

PIERFRANCESCO (GIOVANE)
(1487–1525)
Maria Soderini

LAUDOMIA
(SALVIATI)

MARIA (SALVIATI)   =   GIOVANNI DELLE BANDE NERE
(1499–1543)   (1498–1526)

LORENZINO
(1514–1548)

LAUDOMIA
(SALVIATI, STROZZI)
(1518–after 1558)

GIULIANO
(1520–1588)

MADDALENA
(STROZZI)

COSIMO I
(1519–1574)
Eleonora di Toledo
(1522–1562)
Cammilla Martelli
(1545–1590)

GIOVANNI
(1543–1562)
Cardinal 1560

FERDINANDO I
(1549–1609)
Cardinal 1563
Cristina of Lorraine
(1565–1637)

FRANCESCO I
(1541–1587)
Giovanna of Austria
(1547–1578)
Bianca Cappello
(1548–1587)

VIRGINIA (ESTE)
(1568–1615)

BIA
(c. 1536–1542)

GIOVANNI
(1567–1621)

ANTONIO
(1576–1621)

FILIPPO
(1577–1582)

ELEONORA (GONZAGA)
(1567–1611)

ANNA
(1569–1584)

MARIA
(1573–1642)
Henri IV of France

COSIMO II
(1590–1621)
Maria Maddalena of Austria
(1589–1631)

PROLOGUE

A Summer's Day at Cerreto Guidi

At first glance, Cerreto Guidi is not the most inviting of Tuscan towns, and certainly one of the least accessible. To reach it without personal transport is to be dependent upon an irregularly scheduled blue 'Fratelli Lazzi' bus on the Empoli–Pistoia route. The bus rattles along narrow country roads dotted with advertisements for the ubiquitous Co-op supermarkets or *agriturismi* – farmyard bed and breakfasts. Yet another hoarding invites visitors to the Fattoria Isabella de' Medici, which produces its own wine and olive oil. Its sign is adorned with a Renaissance portrait of a beautiful young woman with a generous mouth and dark hair and eyes. On arrival at Cerreto Guidi, the bus drops its passengers off at an architecturally undistinguished street corner. The town does not appear to expect many tourists; there are no Tuscan speciality shops selling *panforte* or *cantucci e vin santo*, and its only restaurant does not open for lunch. One store, for hunting gear and fishing tackle, reveals the chief pastime of Cerreto Guidi's residents, and also provides a clue to the town's place in the distant past. Although much of the surrounding land is now planted with vines, if you travelled back to the sixteenth century you would find a very

Villa of Cerreto Guidi

different Cerreto Guidi, surrounded by dense forest, home to wild boar, fallow deer and pheasants. Back then, the ruling family of Tuscany, the Medici, passed ordinances prohibiting the cutting down of trees and clearing of the woods. Deforestation might have improved the rural economy but would have spoiled the hunting, the sport that brought the Medici to this remote corner in the first place.

For the Medici, Cerreto Guidi functioned as a private country club. In 1566, Duke Cosimo I, founder of the dynasty that would rule Tuscany for two centuries, built a two-storey, seventeen-room villa up high on the site of a medieval fortress. Turn the corner from today's hunting shop and you will encounter the villa's grand entrance, a *cordonata*: a ramped double staircase, paved in red brick, designed by the Medici court architect, Bernardo Buontalenti. Ascend the stairs, on foot rather than the horseback of the past, and you can look out from the villa's terrace over the impressive stretch of terrain below. Cosimo, his sons Francesco, Ferdinando and Pietro and his daughter Isabella would ride out here from Florence, a distance of forty-two kilometres, with their retinues, servants, spouses, friends and lovers to spend a few days enjoying the thrill of the chase. As testament to the villa's past, it now serves as a museum of *la caccia*, the hunt, replete with displays of weaponry – bows and arrows, knives, flintlocks – designed to pursue, slaughter and claim the local wildlife as kills.

Although games, parties and carousing were part of the entertainment, hunting was always Cerreto Guidi's principal attraction, and the Medici family deemed trips here unsuccessful if it rained too hard or the sport was poor. Cosimo's Isabella spent much of her life on a quest for pleasure, and she was always the first to complain if the weather at Cerreto was *brutissimo*, as she would say, or the game elusive. Yet such potential vexations never deterred her from pursuing a favourite pastime. In any hunting party, Isabella always held her own and more, outriding many of her male companions and claiming her own personal haul. As much a Diana in the field as an Isabella, nobody could ever accuse the princess of displaying feminine weakness. But on a trip to Cerreto on 16 July 1576, in the company of her husband, the Roman lord Paolo Giordano Orsini, Duke of Bracciano, the possibility of inclement weather and poor sport were the least of the nearly thirty-four-year-old Isabella's problems. Indeed, if she turned her thoughts at all to hunting, it might have been to ask herself what form the intended quarry was to take. Was, in fact, a human being replacing the forest fauna as prey?

PART I

A Medici Childhood

Ludovico Buti, Child at a doorway

CHAPTER 1

The New Medici

On 10 January 1542, almost thirty-four years before that day at Cerreto, the Florentine cleric Ugolino Grifoni, who served the Medici family as one of their court secretaries, was busy presenting letters to the reigning duke, Cosimo de' Medici, in his chambers. The duke's wife Eleonora di Toledo was also in attendance. The ducal couple were young: Cosimo was not yet twenty-three, his wife two years his junior. As Cosimo perused his correspondence, Eleonora, who had recently announced her third pregnancy, began to 'vomit in such a great fashion, or I should say in such a quantity, that it seemed to me she flooded half the room', Grifoni recalled. The secretary searched for the right response to this rather unexpected interruption to proceedings. 'It is a sign you will bear a male child,' he eventually declared. Only a baby boy could have such control over a mother's body and cause such violent illness. But, to Grifoni's surprise, 'the duke replied to the contrary'.[1] Cosimo believed that his wife would produce a daughter.

Cosimo de' Medici's response was an unconventional one because he lived in a world in which every man was supposed to expect that his wife bear him sons. A daughter would be a poor substitute. True,

Baptistery of San Giovanni, Florence

Cosimo already had an heir, for his second child by Eleonora, Francesco, had been born the previous March, yet surely the duke would hope for the arrival of more boys? But Cosimo de' Medici both loved and liked the opposite sex. He had grown up fatherless, with the dominant force in his life being his mother, Maria Salviati, who was described as 'utterly wise . . . She would never let herself be won over by praise, as is usual at court.'[2] He had played the role of gallant lover for the first time at the age of fourteen, with a woman he referred to as 'my lady' and for whom he bought fine handkerchiefs. At sixteen, he had fathered an illegitimate daughter, Bia, whom he adored. At the age of nineteen, when the time came for him to choose a bride, he selected the Spaniard Eleonora not purely on the grounds of political expediency, as would have been normal for a man in his position, but because he had made specific enquiries to determine that she was beautiful. He was a young man who was perfectly prepared to welcome more females into his family, and he did not perceive a daughter as little better than a consolation prize if no son was produced.

It is appropriate, then, that Cosimo can be seen as a new man because in many ways he was new Medici. Indeed, he saw himself that way and had chosen as his personal device the *brancone*, a laurel tree, apparently dead and bending towards the ground but with 'an exuberant new shoot coming out of the old stump, completely renewing the tree'.[3] That old stump symbolized the old Medici, the line descended from Cosimo the Elder, the Medici *pater patriae*, the banking genius who in the first half of the fifteenth century had set the family on the path to such extraordinary financial and political success. Cosimo the Elder and his grandson Lorenzo the Magnificent are synonymous with the spectacle that fifteenth-century Florence still presents to this day. Their Medici hallmark is on so much: the Palazzo Medici on what is now Via Cavour, then Via Larga; the adjacent church of San Lorenzo, built and embellished with Medici money by Brunelleschi; the Dominican convent of San Marco, adorned with Fra Angelico's jewel-like frescos, which was Cosimo the Elder's handy spiritual retreat; the Uffizi art gallery containing works by Botticelli that were commissioned by these fifteenth-century Medici; the Bargello, the sculpture museum, boasting such works their *David* by Donatello, that exquisitely lascivious bronze. In Cosimo the Elder and Lorenzo the sharpest business and political acumen was combined with a strong recognition and support of humanist activities, characteristics still deemed as worth aspiring to by today's entrepreneurs. It is these Medici who are evoked in a recent self-help manual for aspiring businessmen, *The Medici Effect*.

Yet the direct descendants of this pair proved largely to be a disappointment. The Medici might, in the first decades of the sixteenth century, have produced two popes, Leo X and Clement VII, but there had been no secular Medici leader of real distinction and ability since Lorenzo the Magnificent. The family had even been expelled from Florence on two occasions, between 1492 and 1512 and 1527 and 1530. By the 1530s, the sole remaining legitimate Medici child was Cathérine, the daughter of Lorenzo the Magnificent's grandson Duke Lorenzo, who had gone to France as bride to François I's younger son Henri. Otherwise, the last male descendants of Cosimo the Elder were all illegitimate. Alessandro, made Duke of Florence in 1531 by the Holy Roman Emperor Charles V, was Pope Clement VII's illegitimate son, whom he fathered when he was still Cardinal Giulio de' Medici. Alessandro's mother was a Moroccan slave girl, and portraits of him show he was unquestionably black. Yet his dark complexion had proved no obstacle to his selection as Florentine ruler, for his Medici name trumped skin colour. However, in January 1537, Alessandro was assassinated in the Palazzo Medici on the Via Larga by a jealous cousin, Lorenzino de' Medici, who believed he would be elected in Alessandro's place. Lorenzino miscalculated his popular appeal as a new Brutus killing a tyrant and went into exile, followed by his younger brother. He was eventually assassinated.

That left only one Medici male remaining as a viable candidate for leader of the family and ruler of Florence: seventeen-and-a-half-year-old Cosimo. He had lived his life as the poor Medici relation, even though his parentage was distinguished. Through his mother Maria Salviati, Lorenzo the Magnificent's granddaughter, Cosimo could claim a bloodline back to the great Cosimo himself, and it was Maria's uncle, Pope Leo X, who had suggested her son be named after his illustrious ancestor. On his father Giovanni's side, he was part of the so-called cadet branch, the same as that of Lorenzino, which descended from Cosimo the Elder's brother Lorenzo. But Cosimo's father had been the greatest Medici of his generation. He was known as Giovanni delle Bande Nere, after the name of the company of crack mercenaries he led, whose insignia was the black armband they adopted in the wake of the death of Pope Leo X in 1521. Arguably the last great *condottiere* of the Renaissance, a specialist in guerrilla warfare, Giovanni was renowned for his audacity and great daring, for military manoeuvres which seemed 'marvellous and superhuman' to many.

Cosimo saw little of his father, who was often absent from Florence on military expeditions. However, the tale of an alleged encounter between father and son became a part of the story of Cosimo's *fortuna*. Returning home from an expedition, Giovanni caught sight of his son in the arms of his nurse at an upstairs window. 'Throw him down to me,' he instructed the nurse. After hesitating, the nurse complied. Giovanni caught the baby, who had made not a sound during his perilous descent. Proud of his son's apparent bravery, Giovanni decreed: 'You will be a prince. It is your destiny.'4

In 1527, at the age of twenty-eight, Giovanni de' Medici died. Surgeons had found it necessary to amputate his leg after he was hit by heavy artillery fire in a battle against the invading Holy Roman Emperor's troops in the bleak Po Valley on 24 November 1526. Gangrene set in, and five days later the young warrior was dead. Cosimo, reported his tutor, received the news with the same stoicism with which he had been tossed from the window. 'In truth, I guessed it,' the small boy said of the father he had so rarely seen.5

Maria Salviati was only twenty-seven when her husband died, and both the Medici and Salviati families were eager to see her remarry. But she refused, for a new marriage would force her to relinquish guardianship of Cosimo, and as she explained to Pope Clement VII, 'my son shall not be abandoned by me'. She was cognizant that the main Medici branch was wary of potential support from Florence for the boy who was the son of the city's modern hero. Pope Clement angered the young teenager when he tried to force him to wear the long gown of the ordinary Florentine citizen and not the military costume he preferred, with Cosimo refusing to alter his dress. His cousin Duke Alessandro was kinder to him but showed his bad judgement by favouring his eventual assassin, Lorenzino. With no real allies behind him, Maria made sure to instil self-reliance in her son. She issued instructions such as 'He should not expect my father [the wealthy Jacopo Salviati] or others to act for him, but rather he should act for himself, and be ready to ask for what he wishes.'[6] Occasionally, Cosimo did participate in courtly functions; otherwise, he lived quietly in a country villa at Trebbio, where he spent his time hunting. He was there when word came of Alessandro's assassination, so this apparently rustic existence became part of his mythology: 'As David by the will of God was called from pasturing sheep, so Cosimo was summoned from hawking and angling to the *principato*.'[7]

Nobody had groomed Cosimo for his new position, but his lack of a sense of entitlement served in his favour. Every Medici who had risen to prominence over the previous half century had suffered from self-indulgence and complacency. They were too secure of their place in the world to achieve the extraordinary. By contrast, Cosimo possessed little he could take for granted. Moreover, it seemed that the old Medici instinct arose in the seventeen-year-old, the mercantile, competitive sense that had made his ancestor Cosimo the Elder who he was. The new Cosimo had become Medici *capo* by default, and he knew, not least because his mother told him so, that the anti-Medicean Florentines would try to take advantage of his youth and inexperience to oust him. They were the republicans, who wanted to take Florence back to the time when there was no Medici 'duke' and government was by a mercantile oligarchy. But Cosimo was quite determined to hold on to his new position, and his intentions as to how he would do that soon became very clear. A significant number of these *fuorusciti* – 'outsiders' – the anti-Medici republicans who had been in exile during the reign of Alessandro – were convinced that they could overthrow this inexperienced teenage boy and reclaim Florence. By the summer of 1537, they had assembled an army to march on the city. Cosimo, in response, assembled his own and the opposing sides met on 1 August, at Montemurlo, outside of Pistoia. The *fuorusciti* suffered a spectacular defeat at the hands of Cosimo's soldiers.

It was an equally spectacular way for young Cosimo to begin his reign. In celebration, his servants threw a constant supply of bread from the windows of the Palazzo Medici, and 'from two wooden pipes they continually pour out a quantity of wine'.[8] Shortly afterwards, Cosimo, who had just turned eighteen, showed absolutely no mercy to a significant number of the captured *fuorusciti* ringleaders, having them beheaded in a public display in the Piazza della Signoria, right outside the Palazzo Vecchio. If Lorenzino had believed himself to be Brutus, with Alessandro as Julius Caesar, then Cosimo was the new Octavius, who as the young Emperor Augustus had dealt with his enemies in an equally ruthless fashion. Cosimo, like Augustus, earned himself any number of enemies from his actions. Anti-Medicean sentiment was always an undercurrent throughout his reign, and he had to work to keep it in check. During his life, Michelangelo had often done well by the Medici. However, he refused to return to Florence from Rome to serve Cosimo, a man whom he felt had qualities akin to a tyrant and who embodied the antithesis of the republican, autonomous city-state spirit upon which Florence was founded.

Cosimo's own personal history as the marginalized underdog meant that he never really felt a bond with the other members of the Florentine elite and always nursed suspicions and mistrust of them. It was his immediate family, not cousins and their satellites, with whom he wanted to surround himself. But all that Cosimo had was his mother and an illegitimate baby girl. He wanted to make a family and create a dynasty of his own, and for that he needed a wife.

Cosimo had hoped he could marry Alessandro's widow Margaret, Emperor Charles V's illegitimate daughter. In declaring his interest in Margaret, he sought to maintain imperial ties and to further distance himself from the traditional Medici–France alliance. Although Cosimo's cousin Cathérine de' Medici had married Henri, the son of François I, in 1533, François had thought a Florence not governed by the imperial-leaning Cosimo would be more to France's advantage. As such, he had given military backing to the most significant anti-Medici exile, the banker Filippo Strozzi, who headed up the exiles' ill-fated enterprise which ended at the battle of Montemurlo and in Strozzi's eventual execution. Undeterred, François continued to shelter any anti-Medici Florentines who found their way to France. So not only did Cosimo not feel any instinctive ties to France, he both wished for and needed an alliance with Emperor Charles V. He was worried that if he distanced himself from the Habsburgs, Charles might otherwise act upon a clause in Alessandro's marriage contract stating that were he to die without issue from Margaret, Charles could claim the fortresses in Florence, Livorno and Pisa.

However, although Charles V had officially sanctioned Cosimo being given the title of Duke of Florence, he decided he would be better served now by marrying his daughter Margaret into the reigning papal family, the Farnese. But the new Duke of Florence was dogged in his pursuit of an imperial alliance. 'What I want more than anything is to have the opportunity to demonstrate to His Imperial Majesty that I do not have any other lord and master in the world but him,' announced Cosimo. He commissioned the Florentine ambassador to Spain, Giovanni Bandini, to start looking for a suitable bride, one who was not only politically connected but also 'beautiful, noble, rich and young'. Bandini duly proposed a sister of the Spanish Duke of Alba and, perhaps more surprisingly, '*la principessa d'Inghilterra*', Henry VIII's daughter Mary Tudor, whose mother Catherine of Aragon was Charles V's aunt.[9] Nothing came of either royal match.

Then, late in 1538, another offer reached Cosimo: a marriage to one of the daughters of Don Pedro di Toledo, the Spanish Viceroy of Naples. Don Pedro, a member of one of Spain's great noble families, the Álvarez, had governed the Italian city on behalf of Charles V since 1534, when he had arrived in Italy from Spain with his wife and family. Don Pedro expressed interest in this proposed union with the Medici, and he offered as a bride for Cosimo Isabella, the elder of his two daughters, complete with a substantial dowry of 80,000 gold ducats. But despite the fortune, Isabella was hardly a catch. A Florentine agent down in Naples sent a warning up to Cosimo. 'She is incredibly ugly,' he informed Cosimo in January 1539, 'and her brain makes her the laughing stock of Naples.'[10]

As anxious as Cosimo was to cement his ties to Charles V, an unattractive and dull-witted bride was a price he was unwilling to pay. Moreover, Cosimo knew that Don Pedro had a much more appealing prospect: his younger daughter, the seventeen-year-old Eleonora, whom he had once seen himself a few years earlier, when he had travelled to Naples as part of Duke Alessandro's retinue. She was universally acknowledged as a beauty, 'beautiful, fresh, with a rosy complexion . . . with a graceful gait, reverential stance, a sweet voice, full of intelligence, a clear face, an angelic gaze'.[11] Eleonora's portraits suggest she actually, and unusually for these hyperbolic times, lived up to such description. With dark hair and eyes, a pink mouth, creamy skin and delicate features set into a face which was a smooth oval, she looked like the Virgin Mary personified.

Small wonder Eleonora was the Álvarez sister Cosimo, active since the age of fourteen as a lover of women, desired as his lifelong companion. But Don Pedro would not relinquish his beautiful younger daughter without a struggle. On learning of the unprepossessing nature of Isabella, Eleonora's sister, Cosimo immediately fired off a letter to his marriage broker Giovanni Bandini: 'I hear that the Viceroy of Naples is trying to convince his Majesty to make me accept his oldest daughter. I can't believe that he will allow something so inappropriate and disagreeable. I would be very dissatisfied with such a thing, and so I think you *must* get the Viceroy to give me his second daughter.'[12]

The wily Don Pedro used Cosimo's anxiety to wed his daughter Eleonora rather than her sister Isabella as part of the bargaining process. He agreed to exchange Eleonora for Isabella, but the dowry that he offered for his younger daughter was 30,000 gold *scudi* – coins that were minted primarily in Rome and Florence – 50,000 less than what Don Pedro had proposed would accompany Isabella. Nonetheless, Cosimo accepted his terms in order to have Eleonora. The marriage took place by proxy in Naples on 29 March 1539.

On 11 June 1539, chosen because it was the eve of Cosimo's twentieth birthday, Eleonora departed Naples to embark upon her new life in Florence, arriving at the Tuscan port of Livorno at dawn on 22 June. Traditionally, the groom awaited his bride at his home, but Cosimo could not wait that long to meet the young woman he had been so anxious to acquire and rushed on eagerly to meet her. 'That very day, at the same time, which was about 2 pm,' the Florentine Pier Francesco Giambullari recorded, 'Her Ladyship the Duchess left Livorno and His Lordship the Duke left Pisa, accompanied by many noble Florentines and by his whole court. Just about midway on that road the two Excellencies met, a most noble and beautiful couple.'[13] Shortly afterwards, Cosimo wrote separate letters to his new in-laws. He informed Don Pedro of Eleonora's safe arrival from Naples, 'of which I am as content and joyful as Your Excellency could imagine. I need say no more as there is nothing in the world that I have so longed for and desired.' To Eleonora's mother Doña Maria he wrote: 'I can only imagine how deeply Your Excellency must feel on the departure of the Signora Duchessa, for such is consonant with the love of a mother. Yet, since this is a woman's destiny, that they do not stay in those houses in which they are born, nor with those who gave them birth, I am sure Your Excellency will set against your grief the Signora Duchessa's happiness and well-being.'[14]

Cosimo de' Medici was quite remarkable for a Renaissance potentate in that he wanted a wife who was not only a politically advantageous match but one with whom he could fall in love as well. Such a desire made Cosimo very different from, for example, his cousin Catherine's new husband, Prince Henri of France, who had already given his heart to his mistress, Diane de Poitiers, and had no interest in attempting to love Catherine. Henri would never have done what Cosimo did – accept a beautiful bride for 50,000 *scudi* less than her ill-favoured elder sister – and his father François I would never have allowed him to do so. Nor would Henri have broken with decorum, as Cosimo did, and rushed to be by her side the minute she arrived in his land.

Their marriage consummated shortly after her arrival in Florence on 29 June, Eleonora willingly responded to her new husband's ardour. There seems little question that this was one royal couple who actually fell in love, apparently remaining so throughout their married life. Their remarkable devotion to each other was so striking it could not pass without comment. 'He loves her so well that he never goes abroad without her (unless it be to church) and is reputed to be a very chaste man,' observed the English traveller William Thomas.[15] A cousin of Cosimo, Caterina Cibò, told the Duchess of Urbino: 'The Duke and Duchess are so much in love with one another, that one is never without the other.'[16]

What Cosimo loved in Eleonora, other than her beauty, was not always readily apparent to those outside their immediate circle. Eleonora's upbringing in Spain, a world marked by rigid ceremony, ensured her determination to keep her private and public personae very separate. She probably spoke better Italian than she claimed, but she made it very clear to those around her that Spanish was her language and it was she who should be accommodated, and not the other way around. In fact, aside from her husband, she was not particularly keen on Italians, or anyone who was not Spanish. 'She has no affection for anyone from any other nation,' commented a Spanish Jesuit.[17] Eleonora was almost constantly by Cosimo's side, and because of that she wrote him few letters. In fact, she disliked and distrusted the practice of letter writing. 'I might write many other things I have to tell you,' she informed Cosimo on one of his rare absences. 'But since they might be spread around, it is better I keep them back, and tell you them in person.'[18] Eleonora did not share her husband's intellectual and cultural interests, but she liked money. She was a shrewd agricultural investor and she liked risk. These two enthusiasms came together in her passion for gambling, an activity also enjoyed by Cosimo, and husband and wife were keen on hunting, an activity not without its own risks either. But their greatest common interest was the family they were destined to raise together, whose interests and well-being the Medici Duke and Duchess were to prize above all else.

If Cosimo's love for his wife was an unusual aspect of their arranged marriage, what was expected of Eleonora in the partnership was very much the norm. When she entered Florence for the first time, she passed through an ephemeral triumphal arch erected in her honour. The arch displayed a sculpture of the figure of Fecundity, a woman surrounded by no less than five children and with a choir exhorting her to be 'fruitful in excellent offspring'.[19] And over the next fourteen years, Eleonora was to oblige Cosimo and her adopted city over and over again. In fact, she was to outdo that figure of Fecundity, who could apparently only manage five children. She would give birth eleven times, and of those eleven babies eight survived childhood, an astonishing record for the period. Small wonder, then, that Eleonora was not known simply as 'La Fecunda' but as 'La Fecundissima', 'the most fertile one'.[20]

Eleonora became pregnant soon after her wedding night, and on 3 April 1540, a little girl was born to her and Cosimo. They named her Maria, the name of both Cosimo and Eleonora's mothers. The following year saw the birth of Francesco, on 25 March 1541. Cosimo now had a son, to be known as *Il Principe*, the prince, in deference to his status as heir apparent. Eleonora had done what no Medici wife had done in more than half a century: she had produced a legitimate male heir. When she became pregnant for the third time at the end of that year, she felt sure she was carrying a boy again, her severe morning sickness confirming her belief in the opinion of others, if not that of her husband. Such was her conviction that Eleonora, the gambling enthusiast, made an enormous bet with a merchant, Niccolò Puccini. If she had a boy, he was to supply her with 'a piece of cloth of silver of 152½ *braccie* [about 97 yards]'. If she had a girl, Eleonora would pay him the impressive sum of 780 *scudi*.[21]

On 31 August 1542, Eleonora delivered her baby, and Niccolò Puccini became 780 *scudi* richer. Cosimo had been right all along, and the couple gave their daughter the names Isabella, after Eleonora's sister, and Romola, the feminine of Romolo, the patron saint of Fiesole. But Isabella was to be more than just a younger daughter. Five months before her birth, on 1 March 1542, Cosimo's first child, his illegitimate daughter Bia, died, aged about six years old. While he might have discarded her unknown mother long ago, Bia had been very precious to Cosimo. She was the firstborn to a man who was instinctively paternal and for whom children, the closest ties of blood, mattered more than anything. His mother Maria adored her too, and for her Bia 'was the comfort of our court, being so very affectionate'.[22] Maria was more than *nonna*, grandmother, to Cosimo's children; she was the one who supervised their care from their chief residence, the villa in Castello, to the immediate north of Florence. Even Eleonora took to the child Cosimo had fathered long before she arrived in Florence and, as others observed, 'brought her up very lovingly'.[23] After her death, Cosimo had his chief portraitist Bronzino make a posthumous image of Bia, which counts amongst the finest of his works. The artist immortalized the little girl's doll-like features, white complexion and reddish-blonde hair. And he emphasized Bia's bond with her father, for Cosimo's portrait hangs around the little girl's neck.

When, six months later, another little girl appeared, Cosimo's correspondents knew exactly the right thing to say to the father on an occasion when otherwise their tone might be marked somewhat by condolence that she was not a boy. From Rome, the celebrated scholar Paolo Giovio wrote to Cosimo to 'congratulate you on the beautiful baby girl God has conceded to you in recompense for the one he has taken to join him in paradise'.[24] Cosimo was soon to show his partiality for Isabella, pronouncing her more beautiful than her elder sister Maria. For Cosimo, if Isabella, born so soon after Bia's death, was not the reincarnation of the daughter he had so recently lost, she was to be the recipient of all the love he had once given to Bia. And the Medici duke, who could be so brutal a politician but so tender a husband and father, had no intention of ever letting Isabella go.

CHAPTER 2

'I Have Never Seen a More Beautiful Baby Girl'

While the birth of Isabella was a delight and a cause for celebration, her coming into the world was not without its attendant anxieties. At only forty days old, the infant fell very sick, and with the loss of Bia so fresh in the minds of those closest to this newest Medici arrival, every effort was made to monitor her illness and restore her to health. On 10 October 1542, Maria Salviati sent a report from Castello to Isabella's parents in Florence to let them know that 'the Lady Isabella has been coughing up black phlegm. I blame the passage of the moon, but last night we watched her carefully and I have not lost hope. She coughed up a great deal, but this morning seems much improved.'[1] A week later, she had regained 'flesh and colour, and her *balia* [wet nurse] has mentioned nothing of her illness'. But a few days later, the black phlegm had returned, and this time Maria did not blame the passage of the moon. Instead, she blamed 'excessive feeding' by the wet nurse, whom she was convinced was eating the wrong things, which affected Isabella when she fed from her breast and caused her sickness.[2] November saw Isabella suffering from a mixture of symptoms: one moment the baby girl had 'coughing fits, shivers, then she recovers,

Villa of Castello

then her flesh grows livid, in such a way that it renders one compassionate to see her'.[3]

Yet Isabella held on. By 15 November, Pier Francesco Riccio, who had been Cosimo's faithful boyhood tutor and was now his chief secretary, reported triumphantly that she had made a full recovery. 'I have never seen a more beautiful baby girl,' he declared.[4] It was Riccio who noted that Cosimo showed his partiality for Isabella when, comparing his two daughters, 'the duke affirmed that the Lady Isabella is more beautiful than the Lady Maria'.[5]

After these alarming incidents in her early months, Isabella suffered no more than her fair share of childhood ailments. She had periods of fractiousness and teething troubles, and at least one bout of the condition which plagued children with no respect to their status, especially if they lived in the country and were in contact with animals: worms. As Riccio reported to Cosimo and Eleonora, when the Lady Isabella was seventeen months old:

> I found the Lady Isabella asleep in the arms of Madonna Domenica, who told me that her nurse had informed the lady that around four or five she had begun to cough and be restless, and the same thing had continued this morning. As her anus [which Riccio delicately referred to as *bocchina*, 'little mouth'] felt like it had worms, they had given her stomach remedies and then the doctor, Francesco da Gamberaia, came, who in Lady Isabella's presence interrogated the nurse on all that had happened in the night, of the signorina's coughing and disturbance, and every other thing that he felt it necessary to ask. He concluded that he could not find a fever, but that her stools and her teeth showed the effects of the pain of worms, and recognized that her restlessness and fractiousness were a result of the condition of her *bocchina* and recommended giving her a draught of couch grass and unicorn horn.[6]

Unicorn horn was an expensive and precious cure-all. Sold by merchants and apothecaries, it consisted of the tusk of a rhinoceros, elephant or narwhal ground up into a powder and served as a drink.

Such minute attention to Isabella's health set the tone for her existence at the Medici court for her entire life. She was always cosseted;

there was always a team of doctors to attend to any ailments, to take careful note of any symptoms and to proffer remedies. Undergoing purges and bleedings to restore the balance in the body's humours was a way of life for the Florentine elite, as it had been for many patients since the time of Galen in the second century AD.

Isabella did not remain the youngest Medici for very long. A second Medici son, Giovanni, named after Cosimo's father, arrived just thirteen months after Isabella, meaning that Eleonora had thus far produced a child for every year of her marriage to Cosimo. Then there was a lag of two years, before the birth of Lucrezia in 1545. After Lucrezia, only three of the six children Eleonora produced survived infanthood: Garzia, born in 1547, and Ferdinando and Pietro, born in 1549 and 1554 respectively. Nonetheless, there was no larger ducal family in Italy, and the Medici children's world functioned as a kind of mini-kingdom. This kingdom had its own rules, its own mode of government, its own bureaucrats, courtiers, expenditures, fiscal crises, system of alliances and favourites. It can be seen as a microcosm of the court led by Cosimo and Eleonora, sometimes intersecting, sometimes separate from that of their parents. Its chief seat at Castello, Cosimo's father Giovanni's childhood home, was the very first Medici residence Cosimo chose to renovate. There, 'to please the Lady Maria', as the artist, writer and loyal Medici servant Giorgio Vasari would later chronicle, 'the court painter Jacopo Pontormo adorned the villa's loggia with portraits of herself and her son'.[7] In addition, in the vaults he painted the alignment of stars believed to have brought Cosimo to power. It was renowned for its *vivaio*, fish pond, which also translates, appropriately considering Castello's function, as nursery. Castello was where Cosimo ordered many of the exotic plants arriving from the New World to be planted. For instance, at the bottom of Castello's gardens was a field of maize, or 'Indian corn' as it was known, whose tall green shoots and enormous ears of corn were vastly different to any crop planted in Italy. As such, there was a correlation between such rare shoots in the gardens and the even more precious young blooms in the 'kindergarten' indoors.

Initially, the governess of this universe was Maria Salviati, who was then a more consistent presence in the life of baby Isabella than was her own mother. It was Maria who took care of Isabella from the moment she was born, nursing her through her first serious illness and reporting on her well-being in the same affectionate terms as she had with her first grandchild, Bia. That is not to say that Eleonora was neglectful of her children. In November 1542, she had Maria informed that she felt 'not a little displeasure that Her Ladyship [Maria] and her children are at present in Florence, where she knows the air to be very bad for them, and has taken not a little pleasure of her resolution to take them to their rooms at the Badia in Fiesole, and rejoices that they will be found in a place so salubrious for their health'.[8] However, Eleonora felt that Maria overreacted to potential dangers. Hearing a rumour in June 1543 of a potential invasion from the north by the anti-Medici, pro-republic exiles who still remained, Maria decided to take the children from Castello into the better-protected environs of Florence. This cautious behaviour irritated Eleonora, who was with Cosimo in Pisa. As court secretary Lorenzo Pagni described, she found it 'impossible to believe that there could be any danger at Castello, and she is convinced that the citizens and exiles will hear of it, and will mock us and declare us cowardly and fearful. So Her Excellency has decided to leave tomorrow for Poggio and send a manservant to Signora Maria, begging her to leave with the children, as this will show that there is no cowardice nor fear on our part.'[9] Such a statement on Eleonora's part shows the more political side of her existence, making decisions for the good of Medici public relations rather than being guided by maternal anxiety.

But Maria would not be able to protect her grandchildren from real or imagined dangers for much longer. In fact, Isabella would be the last grandchild Maria would be able to care for. In 1541, when Maria was forty-two years old, the court doctors began to send regular reports to Cosimo that she was experiencing bouts of rectal bleeding. However, Maria was hesitant to have such an intimate part of her body examined by a doctor. 'She says she would sooner die than show anybody,' Dr Andrea Pasquali explained to Cosimo.[10] Her condition worsened, and two years later Maria was being afflicted by frequent evacuation of 'watery blood'. She was continuously feverish, she could not sleep and she could not keep food down. She died at Castello on

12 December 1543. 'In her extremity', a courtier at Castello wrote to Pier Francesco Riccio, 'she asked twice to see His Excellency, moved by that desire more than any other.' Cosimo was not, however, summoned in time to say goodbye to his dying mother, who had been a constant and valuable presence in his life. Now the critical matter to arrange was the transportation of Maria's body to the church of San Lorenzo in Florence, to join the other dead Medici in the family tomb. The well-being of Maria's former charges remained of paramount importance: 'The children are being attended to with every care,' the courtier assured Riccio, 'and they are ready to leave [for Florence] as soon as the litters arrive to take them.'[11] Litters – narrow, boxy carriages drawn by mules – were still the most prevalent form of transportation for the Medici at this time.

Those attending to the children still felt Maria's presence in the aftermath of her death. When Isabella had her bout of worms, the initial stomach remedy given to her was one made 'according to the usual orders of the blessed soul of Signora Maria'.[12] Nobody ever replaced Maria as the authoritative figure in the hierarchy governing the Medici children's early lives. For their immediate needs – being fed, washed and dressed – they each had a *balia*, a nurse, who was overseen by noblewomen of Florentine families, with Isabella Rainosa the leader of this group. They monitored the nurses' diet, which would have an impact on the quality of the milk the Medici children sucked, and made sure they received whatever substances would ensure its quality. Pier Francesco Riccio's response to one such request from Castello was: 'Signora Isabella has asked for rose sugar for the nurses and so we will you send a big block.'[13] But these ladies-in-waiting lacked the authority to inform Cosimo and Eleonora directly of their children's needs and well-being. Instead, it was the Medici secretaries, such as Riccio and Lorenzo and Christofano Pagni, who travelled back and forth between parents and children. It was they who conveyed all matters concerning the Medici children to their parents, and others at court would supply their wants, which became more plentiful as the children grew older. The secretaries were privy to all that went on in the youngsters' lives and were never hesitant about sharing any intimate details. 'The children are very well,' reported Christofano Pagni to Riccio in December 1550. 'Except that worms are causing Don Garzia some trouble, who this morning started yelling "Worms, worms!" and two or three dropped out.'[14]

The Medici children were not apart from their parents all of the time, and indeed spent more time with the duke and duchess following the death of their grandmother. Sometimes their parents joined them at Castello. 'His Excellency wishes to dine tomorrow [at Castello],' a servant wrote to Riccio in Florence one day in August 1547. 'We will need to supply a table for the Duke, the children and Don Luigi [Cosimo's brother-in-law].'[15] Unlike most rulers, Cosimo did not keep his sons and daughters at a remove. Instead, he would sit down to eat with his children, another affirmation of his belief in the importance of the closeness of family. In so doing, he emulated the practice of Lorenzo the Magnificent, who also ate with his family. The young Michelangelo, resident at this time with the Medici, would sit down to eat next to Lorenzo's son, the young Cardinal Giovanni, the future Pope Leo X. Some fifty years later, in the late 1540s, all of Cosimo's children were seven and under, and so were hardly the most sophisticated dining companions for a Florentine duke. Still, Cosimo abandoned matters of state in order to spend time with them. Isabella and her siblings also sometimes joined Cosimo and Eleonora at one of the Medici country villas in relatively close reach of the city, such as at Careggi, in the hills behind Fiesole, at La Petraia, on the road to Bologna, or at Poggio a Caiano. On occasion they even made the long journey with their parents to Pisa, a distant outpost of Cosimo's duchy, but one it was important he visit in order to maintain it within his control.

Nor was Florence, despite Eleonora's belief that the city air was often bad for her children, off limits to them. Isabella and her siblings had the distinction of being the first Medici children to be raised in what we know as the Palazzo Vecchio or Palazzo della Signoria. In early May 1540, news rapidly spread through Florence that 'the duke, with all his family and court, is leaving the Medici home to go and live in the Palazzo Pubblico, once the seat of the Signoria [the city council]'.[16] To leave the Palazzo Medici on Via Larga, built in 1444 by the architect Michelozzo for Cosimo the Elder, and occupy the fourteenth-century seat of Florence's former republican government indicated to all that Duke Cosimo had firmly taken up the reins of power. Moving into the Palazzo Vecchio was not, in geographical terms, an ambitious move for Cosimo and Eleonora. In Florence's compact city centre, it is just a short distance from the Palazzo Medici to the Palazzo Vecchio. All the same, it was a clear demonstration of Cosimo's political will.

The move placed Cosimo and his family at the heart of Florence's historic centre. The route from his former residence on Via Larga to his new one takes in a significant portion of Florence's art and history. One moves from the Piazza del Duomo, with the cathedral and baptistery, and up the Via dei Calzaiuoli. One goes past the church of Orsanmichele, the medieval granary cum church with its magnificent decorations paid for by Florence's guilds, the niches on its ornate facade filled with sculptures designed by Donatello, Verrocchio and Leonardo. Via dei Calzaiuoli lets out into the Piazza della Signoria, a square that has witnessed many executions, including the 1498 burning of the Dominican preacher Girolamo Savonarola and the more recent beheadings by Cosimo of the anti-Medicean exiles. On the far right of the Piazza is the partially covered terrace then known as the Loggia della Signoria, built in the fourteenth century for civic ceremonial displays. Cosimo was to change its name to its present one, the Loggia dei Lanzi, for it was here he stationed his German bodyguards, *landsknechts* or *lanzinecchi*.

Facing the Loggia, one sees to its left the imposing fortress-like Palazzo Vecchio. Built in the early fourteenth century, its 311-foot-high bell tower made the palace the tallest building in Florence, until the construction of Brunelleschi's dome on the cathedral. At the Palazzo's main entryway stood another towering figure, Michelangelo's colossal *David*. Originally designed in 1501 to adorn the cathedral's rooftop buttresses, the great marble statue had arrived at the palace doorway in 1504, positioned there during the period of Medici exile to signify the triumph of Florentine republican government over Medicean tyranny. But now the tables were turned once again and it was a Medici who was appropriating *Il gigante*.

Cosimo marked his move with a dispatch to his father-in-law. 'The Lady Duchess is healthy and happy. Today, she and I, in the name of our Lord God, have taken possession of this greater palace where there are regal rooms. May it please his Divine Majesty that this marks a meaningful occasion, and that ourselves and our children shall prosper and grow, as shall the peace and tranquillity of the subjects in this dominion.'[17]

When they still numbered only three or four, the Medici children could easily be accommodated in a chamber or two at the Palazzo Vecchio. Cosimo now had a vast team of builders and painters labour to convert the palace into an appropriately royal residence. In addition to such state rooms as the Sala delle Udienze, the audience hall, Cosimo had supplied himself and Eleonora with a suite of six rooms each, on separate floors. But by the time Isabella was seven years old, her siblings had grown to such a number that Cosimo had apartments especially designated for his offspring constructed in the palace. Situated several floors above Cosimo's own suite of rooms, the *stanze dei signorini*, as they were described, could be reached by way of a narrow corridor and a short flight of stairs from Eleonora's rooms. Above them was a loggia, the Terrazzo della Duchessa, which was connected via a spiral staircase all the way down to Cosimo's apartments, which meant all the family could take fresh air conveniently and away from the prying eyes of the public.

The views of Florence that the Palazzo Vecchio affords still leaves an indelible impression upon its visitors, and it was from its windows that Isabella grew to understand her city. From the nursery quarters she could see up across the Arno to the eleventh-century Romanesque church of San Miniato, or look straight down at the Loggia dei Lanzi. From the other sides of the palace could be seen the red-tiled dome of the Old Sacristy of her family's church of San Lorenzo, designed by Brunelleschi and the smaller cousin of the Duomo. Isabella could see the latter's bell tower, designed by Giotto, as well as that of the medieval Bargello, which housed the magistrature and prison, and the tall Tuscan Gothic facade of the church of Santa Croce. Even today, these monumental buildings appear larger than life. Less visually prominent, but no less vital to the city, were the multitude of shops and businesses which lined the narrow medieval streets. Florence was, above all, a city of materials, and merchants and manufacturers of every kind – wool and linen, silk and velvet, leather and fur – were to be found here. There were guild offices and market squares and streets lined with tabernacles of the Virgin Mary to protect the inhabitants and the buyers and sellers who walked down them. Where the city ended, the ever verdant sloping hills began, nestled into which were the Medici villas. There are few more breathtaking vistas in the whole world.

At the back of the palace more exotic creatures lurked, for there, as the English traveller William Thomas recorded in the 1540s, was 'the house wherein the wild beasts are kept, lions, tigers, bears, wolves, apes, eagles, gripes [vultures]'.[18] Undoubtedly, then, the occasional roar and howl might have reverberated throughout the palace, along with the cries of the crowds in the piazza outside and the shouts of the soldiers who protected the family inside. The loudest sounds of all would have been the bells of Florence. Although the Palazzo Vecchio's enormous bell, the so-called 'Leone', had been dismantled by Isabella's time, the big bell of the Duomo still rang out, as did other church bells. They rang to mark the hour, to commemorate specific feast days, to announce the start of the working day and to mark the coming of night, when all respectable people should be safely indoors.

If the view was magnificent, conditions at the Palazzo Vecchio were still somewhat crowded for the Medici children, accommodated as they were in five rooms, with one reserved for 'the ladies-in-waiting and nurses'. Isabella da Rainosa acted as superintendent for these *stanze*, and her reward was a private room, albeit one simply furnished with '*un letto sulle panchette*', or trestle bed. But everybody else, the servants and children, shared their bedroom space and even their beds. The maids' room contained eight bed frames and fourteen mattresses. Moreover, according to an inventory from 1553, the children's rooms contained only three bedsteads in all, which suggested that these little princes and princesses were accustomed to doubling up at night.[19] Originally the walls were painted with a decoration of floral trellises. However, the wall hangings covering them to keep out the damp and draughts were frayed and old, as was the seating. Their parents may have been dukes, but they were still thrifty enough not to waste new luxury goods on the wear and tear of daily childhood existence.

Despite access to an open terrace, life was still rather restrictive for the Medici children when they were in Florence. It was in part a desire to allow her children more open space, while still living within the security of the city walls, which prompted Eleonora's acquisition in February 1549 of yet another residence for the Medici family. She bought the Palazzo Pitti on the 'Oltr'arno', the side of Florence divided from the main part of the city by the River Arno and most easily accessible by way of the Ponte Vecchio, the medieval bridge on which the Florentines had built shops and houses. The merchant Luca Pitti had built this palace in the mid-fifteenth century, based on a design which Giorgio Vasari claimed was by Brunelleschi, a belief in which he was probably mistaken but which enhanced the prestige of the property. With its heavy, rusticated facade, the palace (substantially enlarged later in the sixteenth century) was remarkable for the amount of land it commanded, rendering it more country villa than urban residence, yet still very close to the city centre. It was this terrain which had so attracted Eleonora to the Pitti in the first place. From her time in Naples she remembered the now destroyed Poggio Reale, the fifteenth-century royal villa overlooking the bay of Naples, the site of many festivities and receptions at the Neapolitan court. Poggio Reale was remarkable in its day for its magnificent gardens, unsurpassed anywhere in Europe, and in particular for the water system which fed the landscape, thus permitting the creation of lakes, fish ponds, fountains and the planting of fruit trees.

Eleonora authorized the purchase of land from the Pitti's neighbours. Here, Medici gardeners planted orange and lemon trees, as well as vines of muscatel grapes which, with their sweet and heavy odour, could make Florence's sometimes dank and humid atmosphere more inviting. Engineers quickly went to work on creating a hydraulic system for the Pitti which brought water from a spring outside the city gates. The new water system allowed the installation of the kinds of features witnessed at Poggio Reale. There was a large fish pond, which served as a reservoir as well as a source for fresh fish, not to mention such edible water fowl as ducks and swans. The first of the magnificent aquatic displays which embellished the gardens was begun in 1553. It was a grotto dedicated to Eleonora herself, the 'Grotticina di Madama', replete with the playful humour so important to such installations. Its main sculptural feature was a she-goat with swollen udders – chosen as emblematic of Eleonora's own fertility – whose 'milk' flowed into the basin below. The gardens became known as 'I Boboli', the name of the hill on which they were laid. Small wonder, though, what with these watery displays, that some English travellers believed them to be called 'Bubley'.[20]

From the moment of its acquisition, the Pitti, as the Medici always referred to the palace, never abandoning the name of its original owner, played a continuous role in the life of Isabella and her family. As Isabella grew up, she would see the gardens amplified, made more splendid by the addition of further grottos and fountains. The Pitti would become the site of receptions for visiting dignitaries, as well as more intimate family gatherings, parties and, eventually, scenes of discord.

Both Eleonora and Cosimo were keen to augment the orchards at the Pitti. By doing so they increased their own access to highly sought-after fruits, for their own table and that of their children, and expanded the range of gifts they could send out. Baskets of peaches, plums, pears, apples and figs always met with an appreciative audience. Moreover, rounded fruits evoked *palle*, the balls that were a Medici emblem, a symbol derived from the way *medicina*, medicine, was sold in sphere-shaped packages at this time. Of course, the Medici children had a much more varied diet than the vast majority of the populace, for whom plain bread could be a precious commodity. Two years before Isabella's birth, a drought in Tuscany had ruined the crops and brought famine, and Cosimo had personally ordered religious processions to take place to 'implore for divine help' to feed his people.[21] Cosimo's own interest in bread was such that he once sent a letter to a Medici court official on the island of Elba explaining to him that if the island's bakers were to 'combine two thirds of wheat flour and a third of rye flour to the mix you will get a much better bread'.[22] The Medici court consumed copious amounts of bread, in addition to asparagus, eggs, crabs, trout, eels, pigeons, chickens, milk-fed veal, pork, beef, ricotta cheese, olives and almonds. Wild boar, stag and game birds were the fruits of court hunts. Mortadella and salami were imported from Bologna, and while the Medici gardeners grew cucumbers, they had

trouble with artichokes, which had to come from Genoa, as did cauli-
flowers, until Cosimo received a packet of seeds as a gift. All the same,
vegetables were not the primary nutritional choice for the elite. They
were, in Aristotelian terms, 'cold', and thus associated with causing
negative reactions in the body. So, although the first tomatoes to arrive
in Italy from the New World were at Cosimo's court, they were no
more than a curiosity, and it would take over two hundred years for
them to become the staple ingredient in Italian cooking they are today.
While Florence had its own reservoirs, the bringing of 'barrels of water
from the spa at Montecatini' indicates that the drinking of mineral
water is no modern fashion.[23]

Ingredients for meals at this point in history were by necessity sea-
sonal and not a lifestyle choice. All the same, the wealthy still had
access to an extremely varied diet, as a cook book by the Florentine
Domenico Romoli indicates. Compiled in the 1540s, as Isabella was
growing up, it includes recipes for every day of the year. An *antipasto* in
March might include stuffed Damascene prunes and a salad of rose-
mary flowers, followed by red lentil soup, salted eel in white almond
sauce, snails in green sauce and artichoke pasties. Meat does not feature because it is Lent. Later in the spring, a meal could see the serving of 'baked veal liver, veal tongue covered in peppercorns, meatballs
alla Romana, young capon with salted meat'.[24] Stuffed pigeon with peas
might feature, or *animelle dorate*, sweetbreads in batter. The summer
brought lighter, cooler fare; aspics (*gelatini*) with prawns and eels were
popular. Quails and hares appear in the autumn menus. What would
be served at breakfast time was certainly eclectic. In addition to serving the more usual *ciambelle* – essentially doughnuts and sweet breads
with mortadella or salami – there might be '*crostate* of the eyes, ears and
brain of baby goats'.[25]

Sweets and sweeteners were still important and Eleonora, along
with Maria Salviati shortly before her death, arranged for the establishment of an apiary at Castello. As such, the children and their sweet-
toothed *balie* would have the pick of the honeycombs produced. What
Italians today call *granite* – fruit-flavoured ice – Isabella's world knew as
neve, snow. Since ancient Roman times, ice had been cut from the
mountains in winter and stored in ice houses. *Neve* was a great

favourite of Isabella's, who as an adult was recorded as falling ill on account of overindulging on the icy treat.

If Eleonora had been anxious to provide her children with an alternative Florentine residence, as well as a varied diet, another area of their life to which she personally attended was the matter of their clothes. Her love of fabrics – cloth of gold and silver, damask, brocade, cut velvets – was almost as great as her love of gambling. Nonetheless, she exhibited thriftiness, only ordering what befitted the occasion, not to mention the status of the wearer. For example, when ordering trappings for her and her ladies-in-waiting's horses, she made it clear that those of her ladies 'should be made of cloth, not velvet'.²⁶ At their christening, the Medici children would be wrapped in robes, such as one made of 'gold gauze with gold trim, and swaddling bands of gold patterned tabby, lined in red damask'.²⁷ But gold gauzes and damasks were not for the everyday. During daily life as an infant, Isabella was dressed much more simply: 'Madonna Caterina Tornabuoni says the little smocks should be trimmed in white, and both are to serve little "Isabellica",' Lorenzo Pagni wrote to Pier Francesco Riccio in December 1543 in a letter which also dealt with the problems of the protocol for welcoming the king of Tunisia to Florence, given that he was 'an infidel king'.²⁸ As Isabella grew older this linen smock, or *camiciotto*, would serve as the basic undergarment and foundation for other outerwear. Still, Eleonora continued to keep her daughters comparatively modestly dressed in everyday life. The item she most frequently ordered for Isabella when she was a child was a *sottana*, a loose petticoat, worn over the *camiciotto*, and she usually chose ones of sky blue made from velvet in winter and lighter silk damask in summer.²⁹ New clothes were not automatically provided for the Medici children. One month Don Garzia's nurse had to ask several times for new shoes for the boy, and one October Lorenzo Pagni wrote that Signora Pimentella, one of the girls' ladies-in-waiting, 'called me in today and ordered that I write to the Duke and Duchess to ensure that they are willing to confirm that the Ladies Maria, Isabella and Lucrezia are provided with new clothes for this winter'.³⁰

For special occasions, Eleonora would outfit her daughters more elaborately. In June 1550, the Medici accounts list the purchase of a length of white *mucajarro*, a mock velvet made from wool, to make a 'dress with a train' for the soon-to-be-eight-year-old Isabella.[31] Isabella's elder sister Maria appeared, for the christening of her brother Garzia in the Florentine baptistery, in a dress of the same silver cloth that her mother was wearing for the occasion. This fabric was the same kind as that which Eleonora had hoped to win from the cloth merchant Niccolò when she wagered Isabella would be born a boy. For the christening, Maria's hair was dressed with a few jewels, but in everyday life the Medici girls had much plainer styles. Isabella would wear a tight centre parting, her hair at the front braided to keep it off her face and gathered up at the back into a *scuffia*, a net. This coiffure was one Eleonora had introduced when she first arrived in Florence, and subsequently she ordered her daughters' hair to be dressed in the same way.

The young Isabella's everyday appearance is captured in a bust-length portrait painted when she was about seven or eight years old by Bronzino. She is wearing a white *camiciotto* with a high collar under a deep blue *sottana* with slashed sleeves. Her hair, taken back in the simple style her mother favoured, is reddish brown, the same colour as her father's and her half-sister Bia's. Indeed, had Bia lived beyond the age of six, she and Isabella would have looked very much alike. But Isabella is no longer a baby. Unlike Bia, she has survived the perils of early childhood and two of her distinguishing features have evolved: her high forehead and a mouth that turns up at the corners. In Bronzino's portrait of Bia, the five-year-old's face is a pale white, for he had portrayed her from her death mask. By contrast, Isabella's complexion is 'as fresh and pink as a rose', the expression the Medici secretaries regularly used to assure Cosimo and Eleonora of their children's good health. Most striking is the sense of alertness, life and intelligence she projects. In her ears hang earrings in the shape of cornucopia, promises of a fruitfulness to come.

Attention to her health and well-being from a devoted team of caregivers, with shelter, sustenance and clothing supplied by her parents: these were the structures of support that maintained Isabella de' Medici's childhood existence. But while all were of a far grander nature than experienced by almost every other child of her time, there were other important facets to the life of the girl who was called by such diminutives as 'Isabellica' and 'Isabellina'. There was also the training of her mind, her expectations of life and her place within the society into which she had been born. These were all critical issues which were to contribute to the formation of the woman Isabella de' Medici would eventually become.

CHAPTER 3

Growing up Medici

Cosimo and Eleonora's brood of children lived in extremely close proximity to one another, even to the point where they shared beds. Reared together, there was no divide between the sexes. Still, it is hardly surprising that as they grew older different kinds of bonds formed between the Medici siblings. They might be closer to one than the other. For example, the favourite sister of Francesco seems not to have been his older sister, Maria, nor Isabella, a year younger than him. Instead it was Lucrezia, the youngest Medici daughter, four years Francesco's junior. Maria, the eldest, appears to have been a little aloof from her younger brothers and sisters. For the elder children, the very youngest, Ferdinando, born in 1549, and Pietro, in 1554, were almost like a separate family. Giovanni and Francesco seemed fond enough of one another; Giovanni and Garzia, younger than Giovanni by three years, less so. Isabella's own love and loyalty went to Giovanni, only thirteen months her junior. The feeling was mutual, from infancy they were drawn towards each other as playmates.[1] 'Yesterday', Cosimo's secretary Riccio reported on 7 May 1545 from Castello, 'I passed an hour with the greatest contentment, as Signor Don Giovanni and

Donna Isabella danced together to the sound of a lyre, and playing now at one thing, and then the other.'[2]

Together Isabella and Giovanni formed the mid-section of the Medici children. Like other middle children in large families, they could learn from their elder siblings what behaviour they could get away with, while those taking care of them attended to younger siblings' needs, thus leaving them free to do more of what they pleased. Not that Isabella or Giovanni lacked attention from their parents. Giovanni has been seen as Eleonora's favourite son, while as Eleonora grew older she and Isabella may not have been as close. Nonetheless, Eleonora still wanted to ensure good care was taken of her middle daughter. 'My Duchess', Lorenzo Pagni wrote from Pisa to Pier Francesco Riccio at Castello in 1545, 'wants me to tell you that when it is time to give Signora Isabella a bath, do not forget to do it, and make sure she is watched.'[3] But there is no question that Isabella was closer to her father, or, as she called the man all others referred to as 'His Highness', '*babbo*' – the word used specifically in Tuscany for 'daddy'. Cosimo, in turn, always exhibited a great deal of care and concern for Isabella, sending these specific instructions via Riccio to Castello when the seven-year-old's baby teeth were coming loose: 'In regard to the Lady Isabella's loose tooth, His Excellency wishes you to extract it gently, causing her as little pain as possible.'[4]

There was certainly more pleasure than pain in Isabella de' Medici's childhood, although she was not necessarily spoiled in the modern sense of the term. For example, the children's rooms at the Palazzo Vecchio had rather shabby appointments, and Eleonora was careful in what clothes she ordered for her children. Nor were the Medici children universally showered with toys and gifts. Instead, it was the eldest two, Maria and Francesco, who were usually the recipients of such items as dolls, wooden horses, spinning tops and toy boats, and not the younger ones. These were evidently to be passed down the line when outgrown and discarded, and there is no sense from the secretarial correspondence that this strategy created any discord.

The Medici children were encouraged to engage in play, games and jokes, activities that mirrored adult life among the Italian elite. Like many children, they did not always sit quietly in church. Riccio describes three-year-old Francesco's behaviour as he attended Mass with Maria and Isabella in the church of Santa Trinità's magnificent Sassetti chapel, whose decorations by Ghirlandaio contained depictions of their Medici ancestors as children: 'When the priest was chanting *kyrie*, His Lordship responded "*eleison, eleison*", and sprinkled his sisters with holy water. I thought I would die laughing.'[5]

At Christmas and New Year, Eleonora had treats purchased for Isabella and her siblings, such as fruit and animals made out of sugar, and little animals – *animaletti* – made from glass. One Christmas list from 1546 also notes an unusual item: two '*uomini selvatichi*' – wild men.[6] The courts of Renaissance Italy had long exhibited an obsession with possessing what they perceived as strange and deformed. The Gonzaga family of Mantua had special small-scale apartments built in their family palace for the court dwarves. By the mid-sixteenth century – 'the age of the marvellous' – the fascination with all that was exotic grew, encompassing inanimate objects such as misshapen 'baroque' pearls, pieces of coral and flora and fauna of all kinds. 'Wild men' could include members of tribes brought from the New World or children abandoned in the woods who, without human contact, had grown up feral and been subsequently captured. Alternatively, they might be the mentally ill, sold by their family to provide entertainment at court with their antics – in this instance, at the Medici children's Christmas.

Despite the addition of such new creatures as *uomini selvatichi*, it was dwarves who were the enduring feature of Medici court life, and one dwarf in particular, named Morgante. In fact, Morgante came to be regarded as such a necessary presence that when one Morgante died, dwarves being short-lived, he was replaced by another, also given the name Morgante. The original Morgante was painted around 1550 by Bronzino, naked, rotund and with a bellicose stance that matches the disposition for which all the Morgantes were renowned. In 1544, there was a fight staged at court between Morgante and a monkey during which, as a spectator described, 'the dwarf sustained two injuries, one in the shoulder and the other in the arm, while the monkey was left with his legs crippled. The monkey eventually gave up and begged the dwarf for mercy. The dwarf, however, didn't understand the monkey's language and having seized the monkey by the legs from behind, kept beating his head on the ground. If My Lord the Duke had not stepped in, the dwarf would have gone on to kill him. The dwarf fought naked, having nothing to protect him except a pair of under-shorts that covered his private parts. Suffice it to say that the dwarf was the victor and he won ten *scudi* in gold, which had been secured by pledging the ring of the Bishop of Forlì.'[7]

It seems unlikely that Cosimo's children were present at this brutal spectacle. Nonetheless, Morgante was very much a part of Isabella's childhood and, indeed, her adulthood. Morgante spent a lot of time with the children, with garments for the dwarf being dispatched to Castello along with the children's clothing, and he would put on less violent entertainments for them – or at least ones which did not involve almost beating a monkey to death. On 2 November 1544, Lorenzo Pagni described Morgante's activities at the Petraia villa outside Florence: 'This evening the Duke stayed in the garden for more than an hour. The dwarf stretched big cloths on those boxwood trees outside the maze and put his owl there and thus succeeded in catching six or eight birds. This greatly pleased His Excellency, but pleased Don Francesco and Donna Maria even more.'[8]

Life at the Palazzo Vecchio could be a bit overcrowded for the Medici children, and until Eleonora bought the Palazzo Pitti their access to the open air in Florence was confined to the palace's terrace high above the Piazza della Signoria. However, the sprawling grounds at Castello were a different environment entirely. Here there were fountains with nymphs and *putti* pouring water, a rambling series of paths, a vast labyrinth with a path of white marble running through it, and grottos fed by water, stuccoed with shells and containing statues of such mythical, magical creatures as unicorns. The adults of the court marvelled at the artifice, while for the children such a landscape would have seemed like something out of a fairy tale, complete with the strange plants at the bottom of the garden.

Notions of magic-making were ever present in the lives of the Medici and the Florentines. Magic certainly had its dark side, with the witch, the *strega*, lurking in the fringes of the imagination to scare children at appropriate times. The fifteenth-century Florentine humanist Poliziano described how Florence's grandmothers would threaten their charges into good behaviour with tales of 'witches who lurk in the woods to eat crying children'.[9] But there were tales of other mysterious, and far more seductive, magical creatures who also infiltrated their lives.

At not quite three, Isabella's younger brother Giovanni 'is always telling stories, and loves to tell the tale of the Fata Morgana', as Christofano Pagni proudly reported.[10] The Fata Morgana was Morgan Le Fay, the Fairy Queen and sometime sister to King Arthur. She had emerged out of Celtic legend, but by the time the Medici children were born, Fata Morgana was well entrenched in Italian folklore. She was also the enemy of the heroes in the epic poems written in the early sixteenth century by Boiardo and Ariosto, *Orlando Innamorato* and *Orlando Furioso*. Both poems derived from the Carolingian *Song of Roland*, and their heroes, heroines and villains captivated the courts of Italy, who saw in these characters their legendary counterparts. In *Orlando Innamorato*, the hero, Orlando, comes upon Fata Morgana at a grotto on an island in the middle of an enchanted lake, asleep by a fountain. It is the hero's task to rescue the young knights and princes whom the fairy, 'a lady of a lovely aspect, dressed in white and vermillion', has imprisoned in her crystal dungeon, and to evade her trickery.[11] Even the dwarf Morgante was named in irony for an *Orlando* character: his counterpart in the story was a giant.

Just as Morgante, even if he was not the same one she knew when she was a child, would be a part of Isabella's adult life, the Fata Morgana and her cohorts would also follow her out of childhood. As seemingly charmed as life was for her and those around her, the lure of another world, one replete with chivalrous knights, beautiful and sometimes lovelorn princesses, fairies, magical creatures and supernatural feats, would always bewitch her.

Growing up Medici meant more than entertainments by dwarves and wild men and the telling of fairy tales. The Medici children were subject to the same programme of spiritual, physical and intellectual development as other children of the Florentine elite. Some aspects of their growth were perhaps more successful than others. Although they attended Mass regularly, those tending them did not necessarily frown overly upon any misbehaviour in church, and none of the Medici children, Isabella included, grew up to be renowned for their piety. Perhaps unsurprisingly, they were far more enthusiastic about physical activity. Because they spent so much time in the country, they engaged from an early age in all kinds of sport: hunting, fishing and horse riding, which they learned almost as infants. Maria Salviati describes three-year-old Maria's 'pleasure for riding on her pony', and her younger siblings followed suit.[12]

Other physical activities included dancing, an essential part of a young Medici's training for courtly activities, receptions and balls, and one which, as a Medici dancing master, Fabritio Caroso, would later write, 'renders beautiful any prince or princess, lord or lady'.[13] Although dances were a centuries-old established component of courtly society, at the time the young Isabella was learning to dance in Florence styles underwent a dramatic transformation. Steps and formations became more intricate, and dances could come into and go out of fashion. Isabella learned from the Medici dancing master how to greet her partner with the *riverenza*, long or short, depending upon the pace of the dance. She performed *passi minimi* – quick little steps in the air; *fioretti* – flourishes of little foot kicks; *pirlotti* – turns; *zurli* – twirls; *balzetti* – little bounds; as well as *tremolanti* – shakes, in which she would raise her 'foot and move it extremely fast three times, shaking it both left and right, and put it down on the ground the last time'.[14] The simpler and slower steps were integrated into more stately dances such as the *allemande* and ubiquitous pavane, performed all over the courts of Europe, in which contact between the partners was limited. The more advanced and modern dances were faster and also more flirtatious. There was the jumping *saltarello* and the quick-moving *corrente*. The leaping *gagliardo* was an opportunity for male virtuosity, while the *canario* – so named as it was believed to have been first danced in the exotic Canary Islands – with its flamenco-like steps allowed both dancers their individuality. Some dances were performed in a group, but increasingly popular were those in which partners were removed from interaction with others on the dance floor and focused only on each other. What Isabella could not yet know, as she practised with her siblings in the Medici nursery, was what else could evolve between herself and her male partner during the dance, as they touched hands, swayed their hips and performed their *fioretti* and *zurli* together.

Isabella's mother Eleonora did not have extensive scholarly interests and did not greatly concern herself with her children's intellectual education. Cosimo, on the other hand, wanted to give all of his children academic training, mirroring the environment he had taken pains to establish at court. For him, it was important that his world was a reflection of his great Medici ancestors, Cosimo the Elder and Lorenzo the Magnificent. As such he invested significant amounts of time and money in establishing and promoting literary academies whose members included Florence's keenest intellects, men such as Benedetto Varchi and Anton Doni. They would convene for debates on rhetoric, poetry, the foundation of language, philosophy and theology. Of great significance was the foundation of the *Accademia Fiorentina*, the Florentine Academy, formed the year Isabella was born for the study and propagation of Florentine history and culture. *Toscano*, the language of Florence and Tuscany, was the *volgare*, the vernacular of the Italian peninsula, and the Florentines took increasing pride in their language taking precedence over all other Italian dialects. Cosimo promoted a revival of Dante, the greatest of Florence's poets and writers, and had Benedetto Varchi write a lengthy history of Florence, the *Storia Fiorentina*, which culminated in Cosimo's own exploits. Moreover, intellectual activity was not the sole province of men. In late 1545, the poetess and courtesan Tullia d'Aragona arrived in Florence. She formed her own literary circle, took Varchi as her lover and won the patronage of both Cosimo and Eleonora, to whom she dedicated sonnets and entire books of poetry. Laura Battiferra, married to Bartolomeo Ammannati, the court architect and sculptor, became one of the primary composers of poetry extolling the virtues of the Medici court and its members.

In this culture of lively intellects, it was only right that Cosimo's children should be given the means to participate in this aspect of the Medici world sponsored and cultivated by their father. The Medici children had a movable schoolroom, set up wherever they were in residence. The *stanze dei signorini* contained '*deschi per la scuola dei signorini*', suggesting flat boards that could be attached to a chair and then folded up for greater portability. Some of the children were more able pupils than others. Isabella's younger sister Lucrezia appears to have been the least intellectually gifted of the three sisters. By contrast, although Isabella might have been named for her mother's elder sister, who was described as 'the dunce of Naples', she was very far from a dunce herself. She was multilingual, with Spanish (her mother's tongue), French, Latin and Greek, and she became very keen on the precise speaking and writing of Tuscan. As for her elder sister, the children's tutors would set Maria to help her brother Francesco, younger than her by one year, when he struggled with his Greek.[15] Francesco was *Il Principe*, the heir to the Medici throne, but in the Medici home that did not mean he had to be viewed as cleverer than his sister if he actually was not.

The Medici children's initial tutor was the very same one who had taught their father as a boy, Pier Francesco Riccio, but Cosimo soon had specialist teachers replace the already overburdened Riccio. They included Antonio Angeli da Bargo, the brother of the celebrated philologist Piero, and the prolific classicist Piero Vettori, who was highly celebrated for his work on Aristotle and Cicero. Thus, the Medici children received significant humanist training.

If classical learning was a major part of these children's education, so was the necessity of understanding what it meant to be a Medici. For Cosimo, such an issue was an important one due to the complexity of his lineage. He and his children were only descended from the main branch of the Medici through his maternal, not paternal, side, giving Cathérine de' Medici, the last remaining legitimate descendant from that line and now Queen of France, reason to look down upon him and his family. The need, then, for him to underscore his relationship with the Medici of the past for political purposes is in part what drove Cosimo's vast programme of artwork related to the Medici dynasty and genealogy. Pontormo and Bronzino and his workshop produced portrait after portrait of long-dead family members, and later Giorgio Vasari embellished the Palazzo Vecchio with frescos of great moments in Medici history. Vasari became the composer of many of Cosimo's visions of Medici past and present, and was the author of the *Lives of the Artists*, in which he gave primacy to those artists who came from Florence and ensured the Medici featured centre stage as patrons. If such work was political propaganda, designed to impress visiting dignitaries, Cosimo also intended that this imagery ensure that his children took pride in their Medici ancestry. Compared to other titled Italian families, such as the d'Este of Ferrara or the Gonzaga of Mantua, the Medici were a very young royal family. Only the previous century they were still merchants, but Cosimo was determined that his children not see themselves as inferior to anyone.

To elucidate his work on the Palazzo Vecchio, Vasari would compose the *Ragionamenti*, an imaginary discourse with Francesco, the young *principe*, which was arguably based on real-life conversations. Together, the two stroll the palace, Vasari indicating to Francesco where and how he has represented the great deeds of the Medici as protectors and promoters of Florence. In the *Sala di Cosimo Vecchio* (Cosimo the Elder), Francesco saw images of Brunelleschi and Ghiberti presenting a model of San Lorenzo to Cosimo the Elder, and a depiction of the Medici patriarch surrounded by artists and writers. He could also view 'Cosimo's departure into exile', which naturally prompted Francesco to ask Vasari why Florence would do that to such a 'good, wise and experienced citizen'.[16] The next room was dedicated to the deeds of Lorenzo the Magnificent, seen with his artists and writers. Francesco and Vasari dwelled long upon the scene of Lorenzo's political bravery, his dangerous mission in 1479 to Naples out of the 'pity he felt towards his town' in order to plead with the Aragonese to cease inciting war against Florence. And so the prince and the artist moved chronologically through rooms embellished with scenes from the lives of Leo X and Clement VII, through to a room dedicated to the deeds of Giovanni delle Bande Nere. There, as he looked at the paintings, Francesco confessed that while he 'could recognize the Lady Maria Salviati, mother of the Duke my lord, I can't make out who that young boy might be', to be told by Vasari: 'That is Cosimo, Your Excellency's father, and son of Signor Giovanni, at the age of six years old, before he became Duke.'[17] In this way, for Francesco, Isabella and their other siblings family history came to life on the walls of their home.

Isabella willingly absorbed all the instruction given to her. She grew up to love riding and sportsmanship in general, dancing and humanism, and she was always fiercely proud of her Medici identity. However, the part of courtly training that moved her the most was music. Music was an integral part of life at the Medici court. Cosimo employed a team of musicians – lutists, violists, trombone players and singers – and Isabella had heard musical performances for as long as she had lived. 'His Excellency', Pier Francesco Riccio was informed when Isabella was two years old, 'wishes to have a comedy performed here at Castello next Saturday. He would like a music of viols and Corteccia to come here with four boy singers.'[18] Francesco Corteccia was Cosimo's choirmaster and the chief composer of music for Medici festivals.

However, Isabella was not expected simply to listen; she should know how to perform as well. Musical accomplishment was an essential part of courtly training for both men and women. Castiglione, in his treatise on *The Courtier*, noted that the noblewoman should have a knowledge of 'letters, music and painting', although he cautioned against the un-ladylike comportment of 'playing and singing too vigorously' or 'playing drums, pipes, and trombones'.[19] Such instruments as the lute and the virginal, however, were thought suitable.

The great passion at the Florentine court was for the madrigal. This secular song form, with parts for as many as five voices, offered unparalleled opportunities for self- and collective expression. The madrigal could tell a tale, one made all the more evocative by being set to music. Its stories could evolve from the verses of the great fourteenth-century Florentine writer Petrarch or celebrate political and civic events. The Frenchman Philippe Verdelot had produced a series of madrigals for the wedding of Cosimo to Eleonora extolling the magnificence of Cosimo's domain. Primarily, the madrigal came to be associated with love and the invocation of a chivalric world. Not surprisingly, it was *Orlando Furioso*'s poetical domain, as described by Ludovico Ariosto, that became the madrigal's most popular subject matter. As Isabella's contemporary Gioseffo Zarlino would write: 'Music induces in us various passions, in a way that it has always done, but reciting some beautiful, learned and elegant poetry to the sound of some instrument, we

43

are even more greatly moved, and incited to do various things, such as laugh, cry, or other similar things. And it is so that the beautiful, learned and exquisite compositions of Ariosto can be experienced.'[20] It was against this musical background that Isabella herself learned to play the lute, sing and compose music. Music was to become a device which she could use to express her feelings or to create an ambience against which she could tell stories, sometimes taken from fantasies and fictions, sometimes from true life.

CHAPTER 4

Approaching Adulthood

Isabella's world was one in which, as a general rule, boys took precedence over girls. On some levels, her family upheld that tenet. Eleonora, for example, posed for individual portraits with each of her three eldest sons, Francesco, Giovanni and Garzia, but never with her daughters. It was her ability to produce sons that had earned her her reputation as '*La Fecundissima*'. Cosimo, on the other hand, was apparently never painted with a child of either sex, and it was he who had had his sons and daughters educated and brought up together, giving them intellectual parity. The Medici boys had no obvious dominance over their sisters.

Certainly, such an attitude was at odds with how other young girls in Florence lived their lives. Of all sixteenth-century towns in Italy, Florence seems to have been the most restrictive in regard to what women were allowed to do and where they were permitted to go. Florentine women were discouraged from venturing outdoors into the public sphere, which was deemed to be the world of the males. 'The Florentines' wives are nothing so gay as the Venetians,' commented the English traveller William Thomas in 1549. 'And they keep their maidens so strait that in manner no stranger may see them.'[1] In 1546, when

Battle of Marciano

Isabella was four years old, Juan Luis Vives, author of the international-al best-seller *Institutes of a Christian Woman*, thought Eleonora was the appropriate dedicatee for the Italian edition. The book was a conduct manual for women, advising on the most appropriate decorous and chaste behaviour from cradle to grave. But many aspects of Isabella's youth differed from what Vives recommended. 'Let her only play and have pastimes with maids of her own age,' instructed the pedagogue. 'Keep all male kin away from her and do not let her learn to delight among men. For naturally, our love continues the longest towards those with whom we have spent our time in youth.' Isabella, in flat con-tradiction to such prescription, spent as much time with her brothers as she did her sisters. And Vives wanted parents to ensure they tem-pered a young girl's disposition, for 'affectionate love is strongest in women, because they are more disposed towards pleasure and dal-liance'.[2]

Vives championed that girls be taught to sew and spin, as Queen Isabella of Castile had instructed her own daughters. These were activ-ities that Isabella de' Medici loathed. Occasionally in later life she would attempt to make a chemise, which would end up 'blackened from her efforts'. Vives decried dancing, which Isabella had loved from the moment she twirled as a toddler with her brother Giovanni. 'What learning should a woman be set to?' Vives asked rhetorically. 'The study of wisdom, which informs their manners, and ensures that they live and are taught the ways of a good and holy life. As for eloquence, I have no great care. A woman does not need it, but she needs good-ness and wisdom.'[3] And although Vives did endorse the training of the female mind and the reading of certain classical authors, he urged pro-hibiting a young woman from reading such 'foul and filthy songs' as the Arthurian myths and legends, in which courtly love and romance abounded, unfettered by matrimony.[4] These tales were, of course, very much a part of the young Medici household.

As Isabella grew up, it was evident that she was somewhat removed from the ideal of Renaissance womanhood, which extolled modesty and obedience. At the Medici court, Isabella's serious and intellectual sister Maria earned praise for her graciousness, her 'rare beauty, and regal ways'.[5] Lucrezia, less gifted than her sisters, attracted little comment. Observers of Isabella, however, commented upon her irrepress-ibility: 'Her liveliness never leaves her, it is born within her,' was the judgement of the Ferrarese ambassador on the teenage Isabella.[6] Such courtly comment seems more appropriately directed towards a boy than a girl, and perhaps explains why Eleonora, when pregnant with Isabella, who was boisterous even as an embryo, had been so con-vinced that the child in her womb was a male, not a female.

Her departure from childhood in the mid-1550s marked a signifi-cant step forward in Isabella's life. Indeed, the four eldest Medici chil-dren, Maria, Francesco, Isabella and Giovanni, were all growing up and were now ready to play a more active role in the Medici family's fortunes. Over the fifteen years that had passed since Cosimo had become ruler, the duke, once a Medici outsider, had laboured tremen-dously to consolidate his kingdom, to enhance its political and eco-nomic security. In marrying Eleonora he had garnered the valuable support of Charles V, Holy Roman Emperor and king of Spain, and he had been instrumental in engineering the election of Cardinal del Monte as Pope Julius III in 1551, thereby ensuring favour at the Vatican from the new pope. Over a number of ensuing papal elections Cosimo would prove himself adept at establishing his chosen candi-date on the papal throne.

Cosimo also scored what could be perceived simultaneously as both a domestic and an international coup. Since Cosimo had declared him-self for the Habsburg empire, the king of France had sought ways to needle him, if not oust him. François I had transferred the support he had given to the anti-Medici exile Filippo Strozzi, executed by Cosimo, to his son Pirro Strozzi in his attempts to overthrow Cosimo. In 1544, Cosimo defeated the younger Strozzi in battle in Piedmont, northern Italy, where Strozzi had been backed by French troops. In 1553, the French sent him to defend Siena, which was rebelling against the rule of Philip II, who had succeeded to the Spanish throne on his father Charles V's abdication. The French, ruled now by Henri II, were embroiled in the so-called Italian wars, which were really battles between the Valois and Habsburg houses, the French intent on regaining more than a foothold in Italy in order to establish political dominance over the empire. Cosimo went into battle against them, supposedly on behalf of Spain but really on behalf of Medicean Florence. Strozzi was joined not only by the French and the Sienese but by a certain number of the anti-Medici faction in Florence, who saw fighting with Siena as an opportunity to bring down Cosimo and end Medici supremacy. But Cosimo took this as his opportunity to launch an all-out campaign against Siena. A long siege of the city eventually led to the Battle of Marciano in August 1554. Marciano was as decisive a victory for Cosimo as the battle of Montemurlo seventeen years earlier. After his defeat of Strozzi and the Sienese, Cosimo manoeuvred Philip into letting him annex Siena to his own state and, in 1557, he was officially declared Duke of Florence and Siena, a humiliating blow for a town that had once rivalled Florence as an independent city state. But neither Florence nor Siena were city states any longer; they were both subject to Medici rule. Moreover, in his way Cosimo had vanquished the French once more. He contributed to their increasingly weak position in their war on Italian soil with the Habsburgs, culminating in 1559 in the Treaty of Cateau-Cambrésis, in which the French relinquished their Italian claims.

Although the Sienese war was an extremely costly enterprise, Cosimo did make significant improvements to the Florentine economy, in particular by promoting the tapestry industry, previously a monopoly of northern Europe. In 1549, he hired a northerner, Jan Rost, to teach the foundlings in Florence's Ospedale degli Innocenti 'the arts of tapestry weaving, and the secret of dyes [so that they can] be learned and acquired, and established in the city of Florence, and in such a way without the support or training of any foreigner whatsoever'.[7] Cosimo's initiative proved successful and Florence became the dominant city for tapestry production in southern Europe for the next two centuries.

With Florentine foundlings part of the city's workforce, it was now time to consider the contribution his eldest children could make to the Medici regime. Francesco's path was the clearest cut. He was son and heir, destined one day to rule in place of his father. Some attention was paid as to his betrothal. At the age of nine, the possibility arose that he might marry the sixteen-year-old daughter of Henry VIII of England, Elizabeth. Despite the age difference, the accomplishments of

Elizabeth were of great interest to the Medici court, but Cosimo's agent in England did confess he 'found only one fault, she is very inclined towards, greatly favours, and observes the new religion [*ordinazione*] in her kingdom'.[8] There was to be no such Tudor–Medici alliance.

Oddly though, given that he was *Il Principe*, it is hard to find a great deal of attention being paid towards Francesco during the 1550s, and he did have a disposition that seemed to discourage interaction. 'He is always pensive, with a strong propensity towards melancholy, the complete reverse of Don Giovanni, who is always very happy, and from whom any anger quickly comes and goes,' was the assessment of Lorenzo Pagni to Pier Francesco Riccio when Francesco and Giovanni were six and four years old respectively.[9] Even as a young boy, there is a brooding quality to Francesco's thin, dark features, in contrast to those of Giovanni, who if he did not remain the angelic blond seen at his mother's side in Bronzino's famous portrait did retain the same kind of charm his sister Isabella possessed. Francesco spent his teenage years developing what was to be a lifelong passion for alchemy and other chemical investigations, something he shared with his father. Cosimo originally had a foundry installed in the Palazzo Vecchio – later removed because it blackened the walls – and Francesco spent long hours installed there in pursuit of his desire to turn base metal into gold. His siblings came to mock his obsession, younger brother Giovanni suggesting Francesco 'not dwell too deeply in the pleasures of the Foundry'.[10]

There was, in fact, more discussion at this time as to what Giovanni's future should be, and this matter was one in which Eleonora took a very active and aggressive interest. 'What do you think?' she apparently asked her confessor, Diego Lainez, of her six-year-old son. 'Should we have little Don Giovanni made a cardinal?'[11] Lainez was appalled at the duchess's worldly calculation and responded that it was inappropriate to consider consigning someone to holy orders who was not yet of sufficient 'age, virtue, learning and will' to comprehend the undertaking.[12] But Eleonora was determined to secure that all-important cardinal's hat for her younger son, which could potentially result in the Medici seeing a third family member as

49

pope in the same century. In March 1550, Cosimo was equally resolved to make his son 'a man of the church'. Two months later, the duke had contrived to arrange for his son, not yet six and a half, to obtain the Archbishopric of Pisa, along with all its attendant benefits. Meanwhile, Eleonora cultivated Pope Julius III, whom her husband had campaigned to have elected. She had Bronzino dispatched to Pisa 'because she wants him to make a portrait of Signor Don Giovanni, to send to the Pope, which she wants dispatched as soon as possible'.[13]

Clearly, by virtue of their sex, neither Maria nor Isabella were destined to become either Medici ruler or their family's insider at the Vatican. Their prescribed role as Medici was to participate in marriages which would advance the family agenda. For Maria, Cosimo chose to betroth her to Alfonso, the son and heir of Duke Ercole d'Este of Ferrara. The Medici and the d'Este were to some degree rivals. They were the pre-eminent ducal families of northern Italy, and the Ferrarese and Florentine ambassadors at foreign courts always fought over precedence. Nonetheless, a matrimonial alliance could serve the political interests of the two families on both the national and international stages, one which would allow Ferrara and Florence to appear united, even if that was not actually the case. Learned, elegant and decorous, Maria would be an appropriate bride for the prospective Duke of Ferrara.

And what would be the destiny for the second-eldest Medici girl? Isabella had come into this world viewed as recompense from God, and she evolved into a teenager who was accomplished, healthy, lively and intellectually curious. Her Medici childhood was behind her and womanhood lay ahead, a time when she should take the name of another and relinquish the name of Medici. What husband would Cosimo choose for Isabella to accompany her on this next step of her journey?

PART II

A Medici Princess Grows Up

View of Florence

CHAPTER 1

A Bridegroom for Isabella

As the Medici rose to wealth and prominence in the fifteenth century, their need to consolidate their position within the city of Florence became increasingly pressing. Not only did they want to marry into Florence's most powerful families, such as the Tornabuoni, Salviati and Rucellai, they also sought matrimony with families who could bring political connections and protection from outside. Such families could also add a noble lustre to the Medici, who not so long ago were dairy farmers in the Mugello. In 1467, Lorenzo the Magnificent's parents took advantage of the family's presence as bankers in Rome to pursue an alliance with one of that city's illustrious families, the Orsini. In contrast to the Medici, the Orsini could trace their roots back to the eighth century, when they served as warriors for the last of the Roman emperors, whose western capital had moved from Rome to Ravenna. Lorenzo's bride was Clarice, from the Orsini branch known as the Monterotondo, named for the fiefdom they governed. Clarice came well connected, with popes, cardinals and *condottieri* numbering among her ancestors and living relatives, associations the Medici lacked, and these Florentines were willing to take her pedigree in lieu of a substan-

Rider in a rainstorm

tial dowry. Twenty years later, in 1487, Lorenzo and Clarice married their eldest son, Piero, to another Orsini girl. This time the bride in question was Alfonsina, whose father was from the Neapolitan branch of this vast family, and so she also brought with her the favour of the Aragonese who ruled that city.

When, in the early 1550s, Cosimo turned to the issue of a husband for Isabella, he chose to revive this bond with the Orsini. He was always keen to evoke his relationship to the Medici of the past, and a husband from the same family as Lorenzo the Magnificent's bride would serve that very purpose. On a more practical level, Cosimo was nervous about security in southern Tuscany. His territory had increased since the taking of Siena. Bandits – *banditi*, named for the bans passed against them from entering into cities – often unemployed soldiers who still bore their weapons, were becoming a major concern in those parts. The Orsini family's northern lands bordered upon those of the Medici. From Cosimo's perspective, an alliance with them could help improve territorial security and, subsequently, economic prosperity in these more removed parts of his dukedom.

In 1553, when Cosimo decided to betroth Isabella, almost eleven, to twelve-year-old Paolo Giordano Orsini, he cited both these points as reasons for the match: 'We have chosen to make such a match for these reasons: This Lord, has, with his estate, many beautiful and important lands close to our own; the other is the antiquity of the relationship between his house and ours in making other matches.'[1] Paolo Giordano was a member of the Orsini of Bracciano, who commanded the greatest amount of terrain of all the Orsini family branches. His father was Girolamo Orsini, son to Gian Giordano and Felice della Rovere, the illegitimate daughter of Pope Julius II. The prospective groom sent the following words to Cosimo, undoubtedly written on his behalf by his elders: 'When I learned this morning of the match which has been made between your daughter and myself, I thought a grave mistake had been made, and I am very much in your debt, and these few lines cannot do sufficient reverence to Your Excellency.'[2]

Despite the antiquity of the house of Orsini and the 'many beautiful and important lands' over which he was lord, Paolo Giordano's family background and upbringing greatly contrasted with that of Isabella.

The Orsini property and economy had suffered enormous damage in the 1527 Sack of Rome, when the Spanish and German troops sent down by Emperor Charles V during his conflict with Pope Clement VII all but decimated the city. Then, in 1534, Girolamo Orsini was sentenced to death for the murder of his hated half-brother Napoleone, and the Medici pope Clement VII confiscated the family estate. Girolamo's widowed mother Felice succeeded in petitioning the Pope to have Girolamo's sentence lifted, and she managed to raise enough money to pay the huge fine and have the Orsini estates restored. Before her death in 1536, she negotiated a politically advantageous marriage for Girolamo to sixteen-year-old Francesca Sforza, the granddaughter of Pope Paul III.

The marriage, which took place in 1537, seemed to mark the return of the Orsini, rescuing Girolamo from the shadow into which fratricide had cast him. The wedding itself was a splendid affair. The celebrated, if pathologically boastful, Florentine goldsmith Benvenuto Cellini recorded in his autobiography that it was he who 'had to supply all the ornaments of gold and jewels for the wife of Signor Girolamo Orsino . . . I employed eight work-people, and worked day and night together with them, for the sake alike of honour and of gain.'[3] Cellini produced exquisite pieces for Francesca: her family gave her belts of gold and silver, gold bracelets embellished with enamel or amber, gold buttons in the shape of Orsini roses, a square-cut diamond worth 300 *scudi*, an emerald ring worth 600, and many other items.

Girolamo took up the Orsini family profession, that of *condottiere*, and began to make a name for himself fighting the Turks. The first child he and Francesca had together was a daughter, whom they named Felice for Girolamo's mother. In the late spring of 1540, Francesca became pregnant again with their second child. Then, in November, twenty-seven-year-old Girolamo, who had cheated death by execution only six years before, died suddenly. Two months after his father's death, on 7 January 1541, Paolo Giordano, Girolamo's son and heir, was born.

Girolamo's untimely demise threw the Bracciano Orsini into complete disarray. Initially, governance of the estate and Girolamo's children was divided between their nineteen-year-old mother and their uncle Francesco. The teenage Francesca was completely out of her depth, helplessly admitting that she had no idea 'what she was supposed to do' when Orsini servants and subjects came to ask for help and judgement. As for Francesco, although he was a year older than his brother, his mother Felice had long ago recognized her eldest son was profoundly mentally unstable, if not downright psychopathic. Believing him incapable of successfully governing the vast estate, she had made Girolamo his father's heir. Her doubts about her eldest son proved justified. As Orsini governor, Francesco embarked upon a dissolute and diabolical path, sanctioning robbery, murder and the ensuing anarchy on the estates. He ran up vast debts and reneged on the payments of dowries and inheritances for family members. In not much more than a year, Francesco had succeeded in almost bankrupting the Orsini estate, despite its vast land holdings.

It was Francesca's family who intervened to save the Orsini family from complete ruin. In 1542, her grandfather Pope Paul III excommunicated and forced Francesco into exile under pain of death. As for Francesca, her family decided it was in their best economic interests to have her remarry. In Renaissance Italy, a woman rarely took her children with her into a second marriage, and Francesca abandoned Paolo and his sister Felice. She herself died only six years later, leaving Paolo and Felice orphaned before either reached their tenth birthday.

In Francesco's place Pope Paul III installed Francesco's brother Cardinal Guid'Ascanio Sforza as Orsini governor and guardian, or *tutore*, of the children. Cardinal Sforza sought to alleviate some of the debt his nephew, the juvenile Orsini lord, had incurred through his uncle's profligacy. As a means of raising money, he arranged for the Bracciano Orsini to vacate their Roman home, the palace of Monte Giordano, which he then rented out to Cardinal Ippolito d'Este, uncle of Alfonso d'Este, who was betrothed to Isabella's sister Maria. Paolo Giordano and his sister Felice came to live with him at the nearby Palazzo Sforza Cesarini, the same palace in which their grandmother Felice had married their grandfather many years before.

Cardinal Sforza's major concern for his niece and nephew was to secure advantageous marriage alliances for both. In 1552, Felice married Marcantonio Colonna, who was Paolo Giordano's counterpart in the other great Roman family. The Orsini and Colonna were instinctively rivals and enemies, and had been for several centuries. The marriage of Felice and Marcantonio was a means of ensuring peace between the two families. Moreover, as Cosimo himself noted, this marriage proved a further incentive for him to consider Paolo as Isabella's bridegroom, since Marcantonio's mother was the Neapolitan Giovanna d'Aragona, who provided a further connection to Spain.

Cardinal Sforza was an apparently able administrator and marriage strategist, but he was less than attentive to other matters of his nephew's upbringing. He did not provide Paolo with the rigorous academic training that the Medici children received. Paolo grew up with a fondness for music but with less interest in and understanding of the world of humanism into which Isabella had been indoctrinated. His handwriting, even as an adult, was very poor. Nor did the cardinal instil in him a sense of his responsibilities as a feudal lord, and Paolo had no innate talent for the attention to bureaucracy such positions demanded. Cardinal Sforza did attempt to send him out as a soldier, like so many of his Orsini ancestors had been before him. However, the cardinal vacillated between having him fight for France, whom the Orsini had traditionally supported, or Spain, now in the political ascendancy, and so Paolo lost out on gaining military experience and discipline at a critical age.

What Paolo did do was naturally gravitate towards the more pleasurable aspects of life afforded by his status as Orsini lord. He was an inveterate partygoer, and his greatest passion was for horses and riding. Paolo grew up in a new age of the horse, the moment when improved roads in Rome made coaches more feasible and the sure-footed mule less of a necessity, leading to a fashion for more streamlined, faster horses. In 1550, when Paolo was nine years old, Federico Grisone published his enormously influential riding manual *Gli ordini di cavalcare*, a personal favourite of Paolo's, which promoted the art of dressage and riding for show. These were the skills in which the young Orsini excelled. It is often difficult to ascribe a modern-day persona to a sixteenth-century individual as matters such as morality, religious faith, life expectancy and life expectations were so very different then than they are today. All the same, Paolo Giordano, as a type, is recognizable among the young rich today, essentially a playboy, defined by his keenness on horses, parties and socializing.

What was most dangerous of all about the absence of pastoral care and discipline in Paolo's life is that he was left to his own devices in Rome, a city which offered many distractions and temptations for an unsupervised adolescent. He might have grown up as a Roman noble in a cardinal's palace, but his neighbourhood was full of taverns frequented by brigands and gambling dens filled with card sharps. Moreover, unlike the hierarchic court at Florence, in which the elite associated only with the elite, in Rome lords and ecclesiastics mixed with pimps, criminals and other disreputable characters. And in a big city there were always those keen to take advantage of a young man of apparent wealth and a lack of guidance.

It was not only anti-papist sentiment that earned Rome the title of 'city of whores'. Rome had a preponderance of single men in the form of clergy, soldiers and itinerant workers, so the city had an especially high demand for sex workers. 'Rome wanteth no *jolie dames*, specially the street called Julia,' commented the Englishman William Thomas of the street built by Paolo's great-grandfather Pope Julius II right in the neighbourhood where he lived, 'which is more than half a mile long, fair builded on both sides, in manner inhabited with none other but courtesans, some worth 10, and some worth 20,000 crowns.'[4]

The world of prostitutes, pimps and their cohorts became one in which Paolo readily moved. His literary skills might not have been remarkable for a nobleman, but they were still such that Rome's courtesans sought him out to 'write a letter to a beloved', as one prostitute later recounted.[5] Some of the undoubtedly coarse and crude exchanges that took place within these circles made their way into the letters Paolo sent Isabella in the time after their betrothal. It was customary for a betrothed couple to engage in epistolary exchange; however, the manner in which Paolo sometimes wrote to Isabella was inappropriately intimate. 'My Lady Sister has just produced a baby girl,' Paolo wrote to his thirteen-year-old fiancée, 'just as she did the time before, so don't learn from her, because she only knows how to make girls.'[6] A year later he informed Isabella: 'Every hour, I would give a thousand years to find myself sleeping one night with you. I desire you so much. The first thing I desire is to speak with you of many things, the second, I do not wish to say, but I will leave it with a smile to you, and I kiss both your hands, and your mouth.'[7]

Such personal missives, alluding to the time when their match would be consummated, would certainly have elicited surprise, if not downright disapproval at the Medici court. Isabella's letters to Paolo from this time do not survive. However, if not actually composed by the Medici secretaries and tutors, the nature and tone of the young princess's correspondence to her fiancé would have been regulated by them, as was the case elsewhere at the courts of Italy. But there was nobody regulating Paolo's correspondence, and he wrote as if unaware just how many would be reading his letters to the young Isabella. A letter at this time was rarely a private thing: it might be dictated to another individual, read aloud to the recipient or passed around, the very reasons why Isabella's mother Eleonora disliked letter-writing so much. It was likely that these kinds of letters never reached the young Isabella at all. As for Isabella herself, her own perception of Paolo, who did make some visits to the Medici court, was coloured by the context in which she met him. She spent all her time with her brothers and sisters. She already had one elder brother, Francesco, and a favourite one, Giovanni, and at that time in her young life Paolo Giordano was not all that necessary to Isabella's requirements for male companionship.

Paolo's sexual activities and the not entirely acceptable tone of his letters to Isabella could be overlooked. However, there were other ways in which his behaviour raised alarm bells at the Medici court. When it came to his personal spending habits, he took after his uncle Francesco. As a young man he was physically personable enough, tall and well built. But his most defining characteristic was that he was 'extremely inclined to profuse spending'.[8] Paolo loved fine clothes, furnishings, horses, coaches and the accoutrements for the hunt, such as dogs and falcons. Moreover, he bought not only for himself but also for the entourage of paid hangers-on he had about him. Like many a Roman baron, he was not enormously cash rich, as his wealth was his land. By the age of sixteen, he was deep in personal debt, which only exacerbated the fragile conditions of his estate's economy. Although usury was a cardinal sin, there was a burgeoning culture of debt in sixteenth-century Italy. Even the Catholic Church had entered into the world of making loans. In the late fifteenth century, the establishment of the Monte di Pietà would allow good Christians to circumvent Jewish moneylenders, 'those enemies of the cross of Christ', as the Florentine Marco Strozzi described them when putting forward the case for a Monte in Florence.⁹ An English traveller to Florence in 1598, Sir Robert Dallington, translated the Monte di Pietà quite literally as 'the Bancke of Pitty; a palace where any poore man may pawne his household stuffe or cloathes'.¹⁰ But the elite came to use the Monte as well. Paolo, with his desire for a lavish lifestyle, combined with his possession of hundreds of square miles of land, was a prime target for creditors. He blithely borrowed money and was indiscreet enough to let it be known that he intended to repay his debts upon his marriage, when he would have access to his wife's 50,000 ducat dowry.

It was not long before word of Paolo's activities reached Cosimo. Cosimo would have seen his future son-in-law's amorous activities as outside the realm of his concern. This world was one in which male fidelity, such as Cosimo's apparent constancy to Eleonora, was the exception rather than the rule. But what Paolo planned to do with Isabella's dowry, and how his out-of-control spending would affect Isabella's life, was a matter which Cosimo, as both concerned parent and as a Medici with sound instincts for business, could not ignore. In October 1557, the duke sent Paolo a lengthy, stern letter, one which highlighted Paolo's numerous personal failings: 'I would be lacking in my duty as a good father if I did not freely tell you things that will not please you to hear,' wrote Cosimo. 'You are not behaving as one born from such an honourable house, and from such rare personages as were your ancestors.' Instead, Paolo was in danger, deemed Cosimo, of becoming the same figure of fun as his uncle Francesco, for 'what opinion should be had of you, you who are turned and moved by your servants according to what accommodates them?' He told Paolo he should learn to 'recognize your qualities and take counsel from those who do not think to profit from you, but who only desire your honour'. Cosimo warned him: 'You are a ship blown about on the winds, on the brink of being broken on the rocks, and the winds are those unloving servants of yours, who are consuming you little by little, the rocks are your creditors, who will break you up with the interest they are charging you.'

Cosimo even gave Paolo advice on how to manage his household and cut down his expenditure. 'You should reduce your entourage in this way: You do not need more than four gentlemen companions, of which one should be a cavalier, four gentlemen of the bed chamber, four or six pages, and four footmen.' He promised Paolo that if he changed his ways, 'I will not admonish you any further, and stop smacking you over the head.'

But the words that must have caused Paolo the greatest alarm were the following: 'I have heard that you have promised my daughter's dowry to the merchants . . . Do not think that you will be able to take care of your affairs and escape debt in such a way. I do not want to consign my daughter's dowry to you, because spending and frittering away everything, you will then condemn Donna Isabella to bartering with merchants.' Cosimo's apparent fears were that Paolo Giordano would turn Isabella from Medici princess into a common Tuscan housewife. 'When I see that you do not wish to ruin yourself, and wish to attend to your well-being, I will not fail to help you in any way that I can that is not damaging to my daughter. You are of an age to know right from wrong, and truth from falsehood.'[11]

It might seem strange why the Medici duke would wish to endow a beloved daughter with a husband of whom he had apparently profound and well-founded misgivings. Paolo was a spendthrift, and his weak and pleasure-loving character allowed him to be swayed by those around him. Yet it was clear that despite his reservations, Cosimo planned to let Paolo's marriage to Isabella go ahead. This Orsini bridegroom still had his uses. His house was still large and venerable, and Cosimo still wanted to ensure security in his southern lands. Moreover, Pope Julius III had died before making young Giovanni de' Medici a cardinal, and his successor, Paul IV, from the Neapolitan Carafa family, was not so malleable. Instead, Paolo's uncle, Cardinal Sforza, had become the Medici duke's inside man at the Vatican. He now personally attended to Cosimo's requests from the Holy See, such as his demand for greater personal control regarding the disbursement of the ecclesiastical offices of Tuscany and their attendant financial worth.

Nonetheless, Cosimo's letter made it clear to Paolo that he had no illusions about his qualities, and he voiced his concerns in words that are astonishingly strong and harsh in a world that delivered barbs and rebukes in honey-coated phrases. Cosimo let Paolo know that he recognized him for what he was, a man of noble and heroic ancestry who had the potential to be destroyed by his associates and by his compulsive spending. Cosimo was not going to let Paolo take his daughter down with him. However, although he might have been Medici duke, Cosimo still had all the instincts of a Medici businessman and was more than prepared to exploit Paolo's weaknesses to his own end. And what the father thought about his son-in-law would come to influence how the daughter felt about her husband.

CHAPTER 2

Medici Weddings

The summer and early autumn of 1558 was to be the season for the weddings of the Medici princesses. However, Isabella's elder sister Maria, betrothed to Alfonso d'Este of Ferrara, was destined not to be a bride. She died on 19 November 1557, aged seventeen. Cosimo mourned for her, the first of his adult children to die. 'She was of the same disposition as myself,' he was heard to say, 'and she was deprived of fresh air.'[1] He was to keep his eldest daughter's portrait in his room until his dying day. However, paternal grief notwithstanding, Cosimo could not afford to let the opportunity of a marriage to the future Duke of Ferrara pass the Medici by. He quickly entered into negotiations with Ercole d'Este, Duke of Ferrara, for his son Alfonso to take, in Maria's place, Cosimo's third daughter, twelve-year-old Lucrezia, a substitution Ercole and Alfonso were willing to accept. The families had a marriage contract drawn up by April 1558, and Alfonso arrived in Florence on 19 June, received in person 'with the greatest honour' by Cosimo at Florence's Porta di San Gallo.

The marriage between Alfonso and Lucrezia took place on 3 July, the wedding Mass being celebrated in the chapel in the Palazzo

Church of San Lorenzo, Florence

Vecchio, 'with all the court and [Lucrezia's] father and mother present'.[2] The entertainments for the wedding also took place at the
Palazzo Vecchio that evening, with the presence of 'one hundred and
ten Florentine ladies, all noble and beautiful, almost all married,
bedecked in dresses with gold, pearls and other jewels. That evening
there were five most beautiful masques, with players dressed in gold
and silver velvets. There were twelve Indians, twelve ancient
Florentines, twelve Greeks, twelve emperors, twelve pilgrims, accompanied by the most exquisite music, and all night long there was dancing, music and other pleasing entertainments.'[3]

Paolo Giordano Orsini, who had yet to celebrate his own marriage
to Isabella, insisted on making a contribution to the wedding entertainments. He could thereby indulge his taste for display and, he hoped,
establish his own position within the Medici family and demonstrate
his own *magnificenza* to Alfonso d'Este, an elite male three years his senior whom he was anxious to impress. Paolo chose an appropriately
masculine spectacle: a game of Florentine *calcio*, football. Now known
as *calcio storico*, and still played in Florence in period dress, *calcio* was a
game that dated back to the Middle Ages and had been played enthusiastically by Medici of the past. The objective of the large teams of
twenty-seven men each was to get the cumbersome ball to the goal at
the end of the field by any means necessary. Essentially battlefield
strategy re-enacted on a piazza, *calcio* was rough and violent, and it
thrilled the crowds. It also fed the deeply partisan Florentine sense of
competition, with two major matches being played each year between
the rival districts in the city: one on the piazza in front of the church of
Santa Maria Novella, the other in front of Santa Croce.

But like any Renaissance tournament, there was far more to the
game than the competition itself. The competitors themselves might
have ended up shirtless as they endeavoured to battle their way to victory, but the game's opening ceremonies necessitated parades in the
most festive of liveries which were of greater interest to some
Florentines than the game itself. Certainly it was the costumes that
seemed to be the principal attraction of the football match sponsored
by Paolo following a previous game at Santa Croce. As one diarist
recalled: 'On July 2, there was a game of *calcio* at Santa Maria Novella,

thirty a side, one side were dressed in cloth of gold on a red background, the other in silver. They called it the rejects' game, because the players were those who were not accepted to play in the first match on the day of St Peter's at Santa Croce.'⁴ The game, it was reported, was sponsored by Signor Paolo Giordano, entirely at his expense. Cosimo de' Medici might have warned Paolo a year earlier about excessive expense, but he did not prevent him from spending money he did not have on uniforms of cloth of silver and gold. The match enhanced the celebrations for Alfonso, and thus reflected well on the Medici and the vaunted Florence, always Cosimo's primary concern.

If Paolo was hoping that by contributing to the sumptuous festivities celebrating the Medici–d'Este union he would see a return contribution at his own nuptials to Isabella, then he was to be mistaken. Cosimo did not need to invest in lavish celebrations, as there were no critical Orsini relatives to impress in the way the Florentine duke had to make an impact upon the Ferrarese duke, Alfonso d'Este's father. However, relics of the regalia commissioned for this Medici–Orsini wedding, again probably paid for by Paolo, do survive: two plates, perhaps part of a larger set, made from Venetian murano glass. They are remarkable for their finely wrought engraving, produced by a new technique that incised the design with a diamond point. The borders contain a design of Orsini roses intertwined with fantastical animals. At the centre is a new coat of arms, the Orsini rose and shield, intertwined with the Medici *palle*, which both Paolo and Isabella were meant to adopt as their personal device.

If Cosimo had no intention of paying for enormous banquets and theatrical entertainments, he did commission songs and poems to celebrate Isabella's union with Paolo and he spared no expense making sure his daughter appeared as a beautiful bride, authorizing the purchase of almost thirteen metres of white damask, taffeta, velvet and satin for Isabella's wedding gown. The wedding took place not in the city of Florence itself but at the villa at Poggio a Caiano, where the family had retreated following Lucrezia's marriage in order to avoid the brutal heat of Florence in August. The wedding was a family affair, its intimate tone suggesting that the event was simply part of the daily life of the Medici rather than a momentous occasion signifying the imminent departure of one of their girls into the house of another family.

On 3 September, the Medici gathered at the villa, the air perfumed by the ripening of the fruits on the trees planted in Poggio's grounds. They listened to words and music composed to welcome the Orsini into the Medici family, a reversal of the norm in which it was the bride who was welcomed into her husband's family. 'The strongest of Rome, the wisest of Florence and the most beautiful, Paolo and Isabella, heaven united here on earth' went one celebratory madrigal performed at the wedding, composed by Filippo di Monte. 'Now who can adorn this fair head and that other, since pearls, gold and diamonds are worth nothing to these twin virtues, that surpass every honour.'[5] Filippo emphasized the qualities of Paolo and Isabella that seemed obvious to all: the Roman groom's great physical strength; the Florentine bride's good looks and great intelligence.

The chief court musician, Francesco Corteccia, who had composed songs for the marriages of Cosimo and Eleonora and, most recently, for Lucrezia and Alfonso, also wrote a madrigal for the wedding of Isabella and Paolo: 'Oh, Paolo,' sang the company of singers, 'pinnacle and glory of the Orsini Family, favourite and son-in-law of the magnanimous Cosimo. You who practise with unbeatable strength, and retain in your mind the arts of both powerful Mars and chaste Pallas. Rejoice immensely now that a bride is given to you, for nowhere is there anyone more beautiful or better than she. And promptly beget numerous offspring like yourself to rule over Latium and the land of the Tiber.'[6]

These words, sung in Latin, sound stately, even pompous, yet the tune was that of a popular song, making it seem more light and lively than solemn.[7] Significantly, this tone contrasted with that of the songs Corteccia had composed in honour of Alfonso d'Este on his marriage to Lucrezia, a subtle way for Cosimo to remind his Roman son-in-law of his standing within the hierarchy of Medici bridegrooms.

Another courtier who produced a composition for the event was the poetess Laura Battiferra, who envisioned Rome weeping at 'strong, wise and just' Paolo's departure for Florence. In her poem, Paolo was like those 'ancient heroes who once so triumphed. You have come as a god to us fortunate ones. Here is Rome, whose dear children turn to her, asking, "Is it true our Quirinus is preparing to leave us?"'[8]

Certainly Paolo could not fail to have been satisfied at listening to such a eulogistic description of himself as magnificent and godlike.

Although there were readings of poetry and music that had been specially commissioned for the event, as well as festive decorations, the marriage of Isabella and Paolo was clearly a much more low-key affair than that of Lucrezia and Alfonso. No reports leaked out to the public of lavish entertainments, as was the case for the Medici–d'Este union. Instead, all that Florence seemed to know about the marriage of Paolo and Isabella was that on 'Saturday evening, Lord Paolo Orsini, son-in-law to Duke Cosimo, consummated his marriage with the Lady Isabella. The next day he rode back to Rome, and they say that he will go to Spain, to the court of Philip II, the King of Spain.'[9]

One of the ways Cosimo intended to assist Paolo financially was by ensuring he secured diplomatic commissions with Spain. This move was to Cosimo's own advantage in more ways than one, for it meant he did not have to give his new son-in-law money out of his own pocket. Cosimo was also ensuring Paolo's loyalty to his liege lord, the king of Spain, whereas Paolo might have preferred allegiance to France, the traditional Orsini ally. Moreover, the secondment allowed Cosimo to send Paolo away and let Isabella stay in Florence. Twenty years previously, Cosimo had consoled his mother-in-law, far away in Naples, on losing Eleonora to Florence: such 'is a woman's destiny', he wrote, 'that they do not stay in those houses in which they are born, nor with those who gave them birth'. And he was right. A bride, especially one from a noble family, had always left her father's home to go that of her husband.

But what was the experience of her mother and conventional practice for her peers was not going to apply to Isabella. Cosimo had decided that she was not to take up residence in Rome with Paolo. He decreed that Paolo would live by himself in Rome and would come to Florence when he wished to see his wife. Cosimo's decision was partly financial, for if Isabella left Florence, and her dowry went with her, Cosimo would be placing her fiscal well-being in the hands of Paolo, whom he did not trust to make wise decisions. Paolo was heavily dependent upon Cosimo's largesse and was not in a position to object to his father-in-law's decision. Yet Cosimo's desire for Isabella to remain in Florence was not solely a monetary issue. He did not want to let his favourite daughter go. With this decision, Cosimo was about to give Isabella, only just turned sixteen, a rare gift, one worth more than the 5,000 *scudi* worth of wedding jewels she received: a particular kind of independence that would give Isabella all the protection of a married woman, combined with the kind of freedom from spousal authority experienced by very few women of her day.

Venetian glass plate commissioned for the marriage of Paolo and Isabella

CHAPTER 3

Zibellini and a Hat Full of Musk

Around the time of her marriage to Paolo Giordano, Isabella sat for her nuptial portrait, produced once again by Bronzino's studio. Most bridal portraits present their subjects either modestly averting their eyes from those of the viewer or else gazing back with a serene, often opaque expression, young women as objects and possessions rather than subjects in their own right. But not Isabella; the same quizzical, amused expression one could see upon her face as an eight-year-old has intensified, added to which is now a greater degree of self-awareness and confidence. The viewer has the slightly discomfiting sense of being appraised by Isabella as much as they might be appraising her. As rosy as Isabella's cheeks might be, she is no blushing bride.

She still wears as her undergarment the high-necked *camiciotto*, worn since childhood. However, now it is covered with a *sopravestita*, an overgown, which a maiden put on once she had reached adulthood. Isabella's slashed dark velvet overgown and sleeves was the costume she would wear on a daily basis, and in the portrait it is embellished with pearls, applied in the shape of Medici *palle*. Her pearl necklace and girdle are threaded with jewels fashioned in the shape of Orsini

Young Florentine noblewoman

roses, an indication that she now unites two houses. Most significant of all, attached to the girdle and threaded through Isabella's hand is what a modern viewer might mistake for a fox fur, worn for warmth or pure decoration. But the animal, with its gilded head, is in fact a *zibellino*, an ermine or marten. They are members of the weasel family, the animal into which Juno turned Lucina, the infant Hercules's midwife, after she managed to foil Juno from preventing Hercules's birth. These animals had long had associations with childbirth, but it was only more recently that their bejewelled pelts had become popular accessories for brides as talismanic fertility aids. Isabella's mother Eleonora owned at least four.

However, despite the consummation of her marriage to Paolo, Isabella's ownership of the furry talisman at this time was largely symbolic, as her husband was not there in person to get her pregnant. After his departure on 4 September 1558, Isabella's life went on very much as it had done before. She continued to live alongside her siblings, including Lucrezia, who did not move to Ferrara until February 1560, for her husband Alfonso d'Este was fighting in France. The Medici family, Cosimo, Eleonora and their children, continued to move as one. 'I went to dinner with the duke and duchess, and the children,' ambassadors would report home, or 'The duke and duchess and all the children are about to go to Pisa,' or 'The duke and duchess and all the children have returned home to Florence.'[1] Even though they were now adult, Francesco, Isabella, Giovanni and Lucrezia appeared yet to have separate public identities.

In contrast to the celebrations of the previous year, 1559 was a relatively quiet one for the Medici. They limited their entertainments to more private ones for the family and court. When the family was in Pisa in the spring of 1559, Francesco's personal secretary Antonio Serguidi sent instructions for new dances for them to practise: 'the hunt', which involved chasing down and swapping partners during the dance; 'the wheel of fortune', with lots of leaps and twirls; 'the battle', with plenty of stamping of the foot and aggressive movements between the partners; and the slow and dramatic 'the unfortunate one'.[2] A more sober event was the transferral of the bodies of Lorenzo the Magnificent and his brother Giuliano from the Old Sacristy, designed by Brunelleschi in the church of San Lorenzo. They were relocated to a tomb in Michelangelo's adjoining New Sacristy, a space stunning in its sense of harmony and peace, which derived from the harmonious and tranquil decoration of the soft grey Tuscan stone, *pietra serena*, against the white plaster. The body of Lorenzo was still intact, while that of Giuliano was 'almost entirely consumed and transfigured', although the wound to his head that had killed him during the Pazzi conspiracy of 1478 was still visible. Honouring the Medici of the past was always an important part of Medici family existence.

On a more public level, Cosimo, feeling pressure from the severe Pope Paul IV, who had formerly been a friar of the Dominican order – fanatical leaders of the Inquisition – found himself forced to engage in acts that were contrary to his intellectual instincts. The Pope had issued ordinances mandating the burning of heretical books, and Italy's rulers had to respond if they were not to run the risk of appearing to have heretical sympathies themselves. Cosimo tried a compromise, as one of his servants explained in March 1559: 'The duke has ordered that we have to destroy the books that deal with religion, conforming to the order of His Holiness, but we should leave alone other books which are not on it, even if they are prohibited and on the Index, because His Excellency wants the burning to be more of an ostentatious demonstration to satisfy the orders of Rome than an efficacious act, in order that we can keep safe our poor booksellers, as otherwise this will be their ruin.'[3]

These token burnings did take place in Florence very soon after this decree: 'They have begun to burn books, one part in the Piazza of San Giovanni [in front of the Baptistery], the other in the Piazza of Santa Croce,' recorded Florence's chroniclers.[4] However pragmatic Cosimo tried to be, to the eyes of many of the onlookers it must have appeared as if the spectre of another Dominican, Savonarola, and his infamous Bonfire of the Vanities had returned to haunt the city. Nonetheless, as the Counter-Reformation, the Catholic response to the Protestant Reformation, took hold in Italy, Florence was a more tempered environment than many. Cosimo would not let the Inquisition take hold, the papal nuncio could not interfere in matters of faith in Florence, and books were the only heretical objects burnt, not people. At this time,

Cosimo also resisted attempts by the church to persecute Tuscany's Jewish community. When Paul IV wanted a rule enforced across Italy that Jewish men wear yellow, Cosimo's secretary Lelio Torelli scoffed: 'What a ridiculous notion! His Holiness will have to let His Excellency's subjects dress and shoe themselves according to his own fashions.'[5]

In the meantime, Paolo Giordano, back in Rome, was apparently attending to the running of his estate. In the summer of 1559, he solicited Cosimo's help in acquiring a particular garden in Rome, but Cosimo informed him its owner refused to give it up. Paolo continued to write to Isabella, using the same terms of endearment he had used over the previous years: 'I love you more than life itself . . . I feel so bad at not being with you.' However, that May, indications of how he really spent his time came to light.

In May 1559, Paolo played a part in the events leading up to the trial of Camilla the Skinny, a Roman prostitute living in Paolo's neighbourhood charged with burning the door of a rival, Pasqua. Camilla's pimp was called Paolo de' Grassi, a good friend of the Orsini lord's, with whom he spent much of his time. In court on 16 May, Camilla described how the previous Saturday

> I rode off to Signor Paolo Giordano . . . when we went into the house I couldn't find Signor Paolo, and I went looking for him. I found he was behind the bed with a woman in fur trim whom I didn't recognize. The Signore came toward me and I began to say, 'Oh, what stinks?' because the Signore was wearing a garland of musk in his hat. At this point, that woman got up, and I saw it was Pasqua the courtesan . . . She began to say, 'What do you mean, "stink"?' The Signore came over to put his arms around my neck and Pasqua began to call me a slut and wanted to throw a candlestick, but the Signore held her back and gave her a big shove. Those gentlemen who had come with me had their spurs on their hands, and when they tried to intervene, so they've told me, they touched her a little in the face with their spurs, and gave her a big scratch. I wanted to leave. The Signore didn't want me to. I sat down. Pasqua began to say insulting words again, I told her I didn't want a slang-

ing match and I did not care a bit about what she said. And then the Signore, who wanted nothing better than for us to have it out with our fists, and seeing that I did not want to, said, 'Now you've satisfied me. Be off with you.' So I left.[6]

That Camilla, a common prostitute, could cite Paolo, one of Rome's most important noblemen, so freely in her deposition suggests how unsurprising his presence in this sleazy and unpleasant debacle was to the magistrates listening to her case. Also of interest is the apparent contempt of Camilla for this supposedly great lord as she mocks the overabundance of musk in his hat. Along with his insatiable sexual appetite, Camilla's account reveals something else about Paolo: he was not averse to hurting women, and he liked to see them get hurt.

If Rome was not surprised at such testimony to Paolo Giordano's behaviour, Isabella's husband was clearly nervous about Medici reaction to the news, which was quickly disseminated from the law court. If the family understood that marital fidelity was not a part of their contract with Paolo, they certainly did not expect him to become involved in situations that were so degrading and insulting to Isabella and, by extension, to the rest of her family. On 22 May, Paolo sent Isabella these cautious words: 'I beg you to let me know if you have received news of me, and if you are angry about such sinister information. But soon you will be able to see me in order that I can explain everything, await my arrival in eight days at the most.'[7]

Whatever explanations Paolo gave to Isabella and her family for his conduct, one thing is for sure: he did not alter his Roman lifestyle.

In August, he sent word to the Medici of a more positive situation: the prickly and difficult Pope Paul IV had died. As the conclave to elect the new pope began, Cosimo promised the d'Este family that he would support the candidature of Cardinal Ippolito d'Este, the brother of Cosimo's son-in-law Alfonso, but in reality he had no intention of doing so. He wanted a pope whose primary interests would be closer to his own, not those of his Ferrarese rivals. If there was no Medici candidate to be had from his own family, Cosimo was willing to endorse another Medici, one who was no relation but whose comparatively humble background meant he would be happy to claim ties with the

Florentine Medici. As such, Cosimo backed the candidacy of the Milanese Cardinal Giovanni Angelo Medici, elected Pope Pius IV after a lengthy conclave on 25 December 1559.

Immediately after his election, Pope Pius IV began immediately to repay his debt for Cosimo's support of his successful candidature. On 31 January 1560, Paolo Giordano's uncle, Cardinal Guid'Ascanio Sforza, the new papal chamberlain, paid a visit to Florence. He brought with him the prize for which sixteen-year-old Giovanni de' Medici's parents had schemed for almost a decade: a cardinal's hat for their son. The Medici had had no cardinal since the death of Ippolito de' Medici almost three decades before. With Giovanni's election, the ecclesiastical aspirations of the Medici were renewed, as expressed in this celebratory poem written by the court poet Laura Battiferra in his honour:

> Terrestrial Jove, for you in your budding
> Years the lofty mover who never errs reserves the
> Keys and reins of heaven and earth to gladden our
> Anguish-filled world;
> Hence in your sacred unripe bosom He locks
> Mature, ever wider wisdom, and after such long war
> He sows sweet peace in your face
> Serener than sky.
> He sees your just, unvanquished and bright
> Saturn, to whom you will be faithful and pious, as
> Much as are his deserts and your constant duty.
> And bountiful Berecyntia measure for
> Measure matches hope with desire yet to see you a
> New young Leo.[8]

This last line is the poem's most revealing. The last Cardinal Giovanni in the Medici to transform Ovid-like into a lion had become Pope Leo X at a remarkably young age.

In March 1561, young Giovanni went to Rome for an extended visit. Giorgio Vasari described how in some of the Tuscan towns Giovanni passed through en route the townspeople called '*Papa, Papa*' when they saw him, instead of '*Palle, palle*', the traditional cry when greeting the Medici.⁹ While the latter evoked a Medicean symbol, shouting 'Balls, balls' as a Medici man processed by certainly paid his masculinity compliments as well.

While it was the seasoned Florentine prelate Alessandro Strozzi who performed the real work, the cardinal's position entailed constant political and bureaucratic negotiations, the jovial Giovanni networking at dinners, hunts and parties. Paolo Giordano was at that time in Florence with Isabella, but in his absence Giovanni got to know Paolo's relatives better: his uncle Cardinal Sforza, his sister Felice and brother-in-law Marcantonio Colonna. 'I kissed the hand of Signora Felice in your name,' Giovanni wrote to his brother Francesco, 'who is indeed worthy of the gesture, a most noble woman, extremely affectionate to our house, and she sends her same respects back to you, and the Lady Isabella.'¹⁰

It is by way of Giovanni's letters from Rome that one learns that, by April 1560, Isabella had become pregnant for the first time. In early May, Giovanni wrote to Paolo, who was in Florence, to let him know that 'I have the greatest contentment that the Lady Isabella's pregnancy goes so well, as you have written to me, and again I congratulate everyone on this, which is our communal joy, and I beg you to give Isabella my most affectionate recommendations.'¹¹ Then Giovanni added some words which Isabella would hear several times in her life. He asked Paolo to 'beg her to take care, as it is so important for her health, and the health of others'. Isabella's love of dancing and hunting were not activities deemed to promote the well-being of an unborn child.

However, later that month, Isabella lost her baby. Giovanni asked Paolo 'to comfort her, and get her to take every means to safeguard her health, so that in time, we can, with God's help, see from her and Your Excellency those fruits which we all so desire'.¹² For most young women, transplanted after marriage to their husband's home, the shame of a miscarriage would have been immense, given that her purpose in the house was to bear an heir. But for Isabella, who had never left her family, the impetus and emphasis upon her having children seemed not nearly as intense, thus diminishing any subsequent distress or sadness she might feel. When Giovanni wrote to her towards the

end of May, he mentioned nothing to her about the end of her pregnancy. All he told her was that he was sending her 'these few little
things that priests ordinarily send out from Rome [rosaries, holy
medals or *agnus dei*] along with the love that I bear you, and which I
know will please you'.[13]

Whatever the pleasures of Roman society, Giovanni soon grew
homesick for his own kind. When Francesco told him he had been
spending time in the company of Isabella, Paolo and their uncle Don
Luigi di Toledo, Giovanni grew wistful. 'I learned with infinite pleasure of the wonderful activities in which you have been participating
with the Lady Isabella, Signor Paolo, Don Luigi, and I envy you such
sweet company. I am praying to God that the terms of my departure
will come soon.'[14] In June, Giovanni finally returned to Florence for the
rest of the summer, and the Medici family was reunited once again.

That summer, Cosimo turned his attention to further embellishment of Florence. In June 1560, the artist Bartolomeo Ammannati
began work on creating a grander courtyard for the Pitti Palace, which
would widen the palace's scope for entertainments. Cosimo wanted to
see the Piazza della Signoria made more spectacular by the addition of
statues depicting heroes and gods which would not only beautify the
square but also speak of the greatness of the Medici. In 1554,
Benvenuto Cellini had completed the exceptional bronze statue of
Perseus holding the head of Medusa – the head of the gorgon reputedly based upon that of his mistress – which had been placed in the
Loggia dei Lanzi. Now Cosimo desired another colossus to accompany Michelangelo's *David*. On 22 June 1560, 'a beautiful piece of marble' arrived in the city, which, like the *David* before it, was already designated to be transformed into a colossal statue, this time a figure of
Neptune, before even a sculptor had been selected. Then, on 7
October, 'the marble designed to represent Neptune was raised up in
the great loggia of the piazza, so that work could be begun on it by the
hand of Bartolomeo Ammannati, whose design pleased Duke Cosimo
more than that of Benvenuto Cellini'.[15]

On this occasion, Cosimo's artistic judgement proved to be sadly
lacking. Even today, *Neptune*, while impressive in size and enlivened by
the fountain in which he is placed, clearly lacks the wit Cellini would

have brought to the work, and is rendered even more lumpen in its place next to Michelangelo's *David*. '*Ammannati ruinati*' was the eighty-seven-year-old Michelangelo's assessment of the damage Ammannati had done to a once beautiful and flawless piece of marble.

That same October, as Ammannati chiselled away in the Piazza della Signoria, Cosimo made an unprecedented decision in the life of his family. He was going to leave Florence in the hands of Francesco, the nineteen-year-old *principe*, and make a trip to Rome, taking Eleonora, Giovanni, Garzia and Isabella with him.

CHAPTER 4

The Duke and Duchess of Bracciano

Since making Giovanni de' Medici a cardinal, Pope Pius IV had bestowed even more honours on his family. In October 1560, the Pope gave Cosimo's third son Garzia the title of Commander of the Papal Fleet. Given that Garzia was thirteen years old, nobody had any intention of sending him away to sea, but of course income accompanied the position which the Medici would find useful. Moreover, if the eldest son would one day be ruler of Florence and the second a cardinal, it made sense to put the third on the path to a military career. Pius also hoped that in due course Garzia would be betrothed to his niece, although Cosimo was disinclined towards marriages with papal families due to the likely brevity of the value of the union.

Over the summer of 1560, Cosimo had also been at work to secure benefits for Paolo and Isabella. 'The Archbishop of Rozzano will for the love of you do all that you ask of him in the matters of Signor Paolo,' Giovanni wrote to his father prior to leaving Rome in June of the Lombard who had particular influence with the Pope.[1] In October, Pius IV issued a four-page proclamation in which he announced that 'we create, constitute and deputise Paolo Giordano as Duke and

Pitti Palace, Florence

Bracciano as a duchy with all honours, titles, prerogatives, privileges, and upon his successors'.[2] As Paolo Giordano's lands were in the Papal States, it was only Pius IV who had the ability to make him a duke, and in so doing make Isabella a duchess in her own right. The occasion was marked by the casting of a commemorative medal designed by Domenico Poggini, head of the Florentine mint. Isabella's profile appeared on one side and Paolo's on the other, with both rendered as static, solemn weighty figures.

His elevation could help Paolo Giordano receive higher-paid commissions from Spain. Moreover, it would bring him, at least in terms of title, parity with the Medici, d'Este, Farnese, della Rovere, Gonzaga and, most importantly, with his great Roman rival Marcantonio Colonna, who was the Duke of Paliano.

With these new honours bestowed upon the family, Cosimo decided that a visit by his family to the Eternal City to pay their respects to the Pope was fitting. Furthermore, the visit could also coincide with the celebrations for the opening of the Council of Trent, which was meeting to discuss reforms to the Catholic Church and to ensure no further encroachment by Protestant heretics. Cosimo's presence in Rome could underscore his identity as a good Catholic ruler.

On 7 November 1560, 'Duke Cosimo made his solemn entrance into the city of Rome around seven in the evening, where he was received with great honour by the papal court, and a great number of lords, barons and gentlemen.'[3] That same evening, Eleonora, accompanied by Isabella, was received by Pius IV out at the Vatican's Villa Belvedere, the traditional site at the palace where the Pope could formally entertain women from the elite. These rooms would serve as the apartments for the Medici family during their stay in Rome. Cardinal Giovanni had his own rooms in the papal palace also. Paolo Giordano, with much of his own palace still rented to Cardinal d'Este, had nothing of sufficient magnificence to offer his wife and in-laws while they stayed in Rome.

There was plenty of entertainment to be had in Rome for the Medici. On 25 November, they watched a great ecclesiastical procession, in which the entire papal court paraded from St Peter's to the church of Santa Maria sopra Minerva to commemorate the opening of the

Council of Trent. Isabella had never in her entire life left Tuscany, and there were many sights to visit that would appeal to a young woman well versed in ancient studies. As for modern works, not least among them were those by the former Medici protégé Michelangelo. He had refused to return to Florence – his way of protesting at Cosimo's harsh treatment of the anti-Medici exiles twenty-three years before. Still, this breakdown in relations between the family and the greatest living artist did not lessen the appeal of seeing this native son of Florence's contributions to the cityscape of Rome. Under Michelangelo's direction, denied him for so many decades, the building of the new St Peter's no longer languished and was now making rapid strides towards completion. The basilica's walls, gigantic columns and piers were now finished, and work had begun upon the vast drum on which the immense dome would eventually sit. Michelangelo had also contributed to the newly built church where the Florentines worshipped in Rome, San Giovanni dei Fiorentini, initiated by Cosimo's great-uncle, Pope Leo X. The church, built on the Via Giulia, faced out onto the Tiber River, whose waters, when the river rose, lapped at the church's foundations, immersing it like the Baptist himself.

Also of interest to Isabella was the burial chapel her uncle by marriage Cardinal Guid'Ascanio Sforza had recently commissioned in his titular church of Santa Maria Maggiore. Remarkably, the cardinal had succeeded in convincing Michelangelo to produce the designs, whose unusual inflected walls brought remarkable life to the space (although exactly where the cardinal had found the money to hire Italy's greatest living artist was certainly an intriguing question).

Cardinal Giovanni de' Medici was extremely pleased to have his family accompany him to Rome this time, and particularly happy to have his sister and brother-in-law's youthful company. He wrote home to Francesco describing the times they had come to dinner. 'Today,' he reported on 17 December, 'we have been hunting up towards La Storta [wooded land to the north-east of the Vatican Palace], Signor Paolo, Lady Isabella and I. And even though I was unused to the country, we did not do badly at all.'[4]

All the same, Giovanni was anxious for a return to his native home. Like every Medici ecclesiastic before him, his heart was in Florence, not in the centre of the Christian world. Rome might offer the Medici sights of things they had never seen before, but it lacked Florence's neatness and cohesion, not to mention an instinctive familiarity for Giovanni and his family. By contrast, Rome sprawled, its stupendous sights, palaces and villas divided by pockets of ruined areas that were dangerous no-go zones. Giovanni's desires notwithstanding, the family's departure from Rome was delayed due to Cosimo suffering from a severe bout of food poisoning, and the family did not move north again until late December.

Heading north meant that they would pass through Bracciano, Paolo Giordano's titular fiefdom, now a dukedom. The new Duke of Bracciano was enthused at the idea of the Medici visiting his terrain, and he began to prepare for the event as best he could. He was particularly anxious to impress his wife and her family with his castle at Bracciano, which had been in his family since the fourteenth century, an antiquity to which the Medici could not lay claim for any of their residences. The problem with Bracciano was that it was very shabby. It had not undergone serious renovation and repair in several decades; the village at its foot was medieval in every sense, its housing and streets in equally dire need of updating. Still, Paolo was determined to *fare la mostra*, put on a show, an expression that the Elizabethan traveller Sir Robert Dallington learned was extremely important to the Italian way of life. Paolo hired the latest fashionable painter in Rome, Taddeo Zuccaro, to fresco the castle's most prestigious room, known as the 'Camera Papalina' for its occupancy by Pope Sixtus IV in 1481. In December, this small chamber was also a lot warmer than the stately but draughty halls, and as such was where Paolo's visitors would be spending much of their time. Zuccaro decorated the room with an allegory of Peace and Victory, the signs of the zodiac, little figures of pagan gods, impish creatures and fanciful design. Such images are known as grotesques, the word deriving from *grotto*, cave, for they were first seen in Nero's Golden House, which when it was discovered in Rome at the end of the fifteenth century was buried underground, the rooms appearing like caves. Interspersed were depictions of the Orsini coat of arms and, above the door, a shield emblazoned with the Medici *palle* borne by two *putti*.

Paolo was also concerned that his servants were not trained to the exacting Medici court standards, so he asked if good-natured Giovanni would lend him some members of his household. Giovanni did his best to be accommodating, sending out the decree: 'In regard to Signor Paolo's request concerning the trip to Bracciano with Isabella, tell him that I need my *credenziero* [steward] but I will willingly lend him my under-steward and my cook.'[5]

'Now we find ourselves at Bracciano,' Cosimo wrote to the Duke of Ferrara on 29 December 1560, without making any comment on his opinion of his son-in-law's castle.[6] He needed to move on. He had arranged for Giovanni to become the Archbishop of Pisa, and together they would progress through eastern Tuscany prior to Giovanni officially receiving the mitre. His absence from Florence made Cosimo more disposed to cede to a request from his son-in-law that he let Isabella stay at Bracciano for the New Year. For the first time in her married life, Isabella was alone with her husband in his titular castle.

While Bracciano was a far more ancient residence than any of the palaces or villas Isabella had ever occupied, age did not necessarily compensate for comfort and familiarity. Isabella was accustomed to Florentine homes which gave out onto the city's streets, which were filled with people speaking Tuscan, her own language as well as the common language for much of Italy. Now what she mostly heard was the foreign dialect of the Lazio. She spent a lot of time in the countryside, but the Medici villas were surrounded by lush fields and gardens and neatly cultivated rolling hills with olive groves. Bracciano had no such gardens. It was a fortress, enclosed by a castle keep, closed, forbidding and alien to her, made all the more so by the departure of her family. She hated being cold and damp, never wanting to venture out into muddy streets and railing one December in Florence about 'the greatest cold, and even though we wear lined dresses, it is still not enough to heat us up, so we stay as close to the fire as we possibly can'.[7]

In many ways, it was this moment at Bracciano which marked eighteen-year-old Isabella's real passage into the realities of womanhood, more so than the moment when she lost her virginity or became pregnant or miscarried. She was very far away from her familiar Tuscan world, and now she was far from her parents and siblings, who had been with her throughout her time in Rome; she 'parted very unwillingly from her father'.[8] If Isabella had ever wondered why her father had been so insistent she remain in Florence following her marriage, all was clear to her now. The life in Rome and in this seemingly godforsaken fiefdom that her husband offered her, a Medici princess, was simply not good enough. Paolo might come from a venerable family, but even his recently acquired dukedom would not have been bestowed upon him, she might reason, were it not for his relationship to her family and her father's negotiations with the Pope. As for Paolo's feelings towards her, his letters might be full of terms of endearment, but Isabella had not spent two months in Rome without learning something of how Paolo really liked to spend his time. The standard for married life set before Isabella was a high one: the marriage of her parents. It was by now evident that hers was not to come close.

But like every woman in the early modern world, Isabella understood that marriage was rarely about love. It was a business transaction designed to benefit both families. She knew that despite his shortcomings, Paolo was of use to her father, and that it was her job, as a Medici, to ensure he fulfilled that role. For his part, Paolo recognized Isabella's role in his life as a facilitator, a line to her father, on whose goodwill he depended. If he had no more real love for her than she for him, he might appreciate her intelligence and vitality. If the miscarriage was a disappointment, he reckoned there would be more pregnancies and she would soon bear him the sons who would carry on his new title of Duke of Bracciano. Cosimo's insistence that Isabella remain in Florence might be somewhat insulting to Paolo's honour, for it was apparent to all that he did not control his wife. On the other hand, the arrangement gave him free rein to pursue his other sexual pursuits. And if, reckoned Paolo, Cosimo did release Isabella into his command, he would make sure she spent plenty of time away from Rome out here at Bracciano, and thus far from his friends such as Paolo de' Grassi the pimp, Camilla the Skinny and Pasqua of Padua. That was precisely what Isabella feared, to be stuck away in what seemed to her a dreadful place, far from everything she knew and loved. Isabella's adherence to Florence was not only the wish of her father, it was her own fervent desire as well.

Nonetheless, the appearance of a loving marriage had to be maintained, as it was essential to the credibility of both the house of Orsini and the house of Medici. They could not write a single letter to one another without expressions of affection for fear of interception and the word then spreading of conflict between the Orsini and the Medici. There were plenty of factions keen to take advantage of any such discord, not least of whom were the French, who had lost long-standing support from the Orsini when Paolo, in accordance with Cosimo's wishes, began to stand for Spain. For the Orsini lord to take such a position could involve him, in times of war, potentially gathering an army and fighting for Spain against France, his family's traditional liege lord. Even in times of peace, it would be known in Rome that the leader of one of the city's most powerful families was pro-Spanish and, if need be, a voice for Spain.

As representatives of both houses, united by their marriage, Paolo and Isabella had to engage constantly in business negotiations, advancing their personal or mutual interests. In January 1561, Paolo, who was turning twenty, and eighteen-year-old Isabella stood face to face in the castle of which they were both now duke and duchess. They sat down to discuss a pressing problem, one of many which would acquire their collective attention over the years. Paolo had taken into his house a former Medici servant, Carlo Fortunati, who five years previously had committed a murder in Florence and fled into exile. He wanted to return to Florence and serve in the Medici–Orsini household. Isabella was willing to agree to this, as Carlo's mother already served her, so she picked up her pen and duly wrote to her father. Her tone is one that will grow increasingly familiar, a little bit playful, prone to hyperbole, and quite certain that her *babbo* would give her whatever she wanted: 'This letter is to appeal to Your Excellency to grant a safe conduct to our servant Carlo Fortunati. As this is the first favour I have ever asked of you, I really hope you won't deny me it, and I am asking you with all the humility I could possibly have.'[9] Cosimo granted her request and sent out a safe-conduct pass for Carlo for the duration of two months.

Isabella's letter to her father concluded: 'I am praying to God that I see you really soon.' The Duchess of Bracciano had seen enough of her titular home. It was time for Isabella to return to where she really belonged, and she would do everything in her power to ensure she would never have to visit Bracciano ever again.

CHAPTER 5

'My Brother and I'

———

By mid-January 1561, Paolo and Isabella had left Bracciano and were on their way back to Florence. They stopped in Pisa to meet up with Cosimo and Giovanni, and stayed there a few days. There was some disturbance at the Pisan court. Morgante the dwarf had been getting into fights and exchanging verbal abuse with one of Cosimo's gentlemen of the bedchamber, Antonio Vega. Vega turned for assistance to 'Signor Paolo, as he quiets Morgante down'.[1] Paolo Giordano evidently had some rapport with the dwarf and it was thought best that Morgante spend more time in Isabella and Paolo's retinue, where he would be less inclined to fight with the duke's high-ranking staff.

On the family's return to Florence, Cosimo turned his attention to the construction of the building which would come to define his reign, one which at a price of 400,000 *scudi* ranks among the costliest of the late sixteenth century. The Palazzo degli Uffizi degli Magistratura, the 'palace of the offices of the magistrates' – to be known as the Uffizi – was designed to house and thus centralize Florence's administrative agencies. They included the merchants' and bankers' guild and the guilds for the silk trade, medicine, spices, wood workers and carriage makers. Other offices

Boboli Gardens, Florence, early seventeenth century

included those of the ducal militia, the Tribunale di Mercanzia, the commercial court, the Magistrato dei Pupilli to protect the rights of minors, as well as the Ufficio dell'Onestà, which supervised public morality and the prosecution of prostitutes and homosexuals. Given that the building was to extend from the Palazzo Vecchio down towards the River Arno, such centralization also gave Cosimo greater control over these agencies, who instinctively flinched from ceding to greater authority.

The project was one that Cosimo had long nurtured. In 1546, he ordered the demolition of the rows of medieval houses and shops that led down towards the river to create space for the Uffizi. Consequently, for the following decade and a half a messy gash, hugely muddy from its proximity to the river bank and frequently overflowing, blighted the Florentine landscape while an architect was chosen for the proposed offices. Cosimo eventually selected Giorgio Vasari as the designer. As the artist himself later wrote: 'I never built anything more difficult, nor more dangerous, as I had to put foundations in the river bed.'[2] Nonetheless, the completed building is indisputably the highlight of Vasari's architectural career. He created two long, three-storeyed galleries with a loggia on the ground floor, each flanking a rectangular piazza. The design of each bay, dressed in the grey Tuscan stone *pietra serena*, was repeated over and over again, creating a clean, sharp, corporate look and becoming the benchmark for office design throughout Europe over the subsequent centuries.

The building of the Uffizi was yet another symbol of Medici dominance over the city of Florence. However, in April 1561, news arrived from Ferrara which struck a blow to Cosimo's carefully planned strategies to secure external alliances. His daughter Lucrezia had been severely ailing for about a month, to the extent that Cosimo sent the family doctor, Andrea Pasquali, to attend to her and to send detailed reports back to him. Her symptoms – fevers, severe weight loss, constant coughing and a permanently bleeding nose – have led to a modern diagnosis that Lucrezia was suffering from tuberculosis. On the night of 20 April, Pasquali wrote to Cosimo: 'We have reached the end. If God does not help her, we doubt that she will last the night.'[3] Lucrezia was dead the next day. There had been no children resulting from her marriage to Alfonso d'Este.

Neither Lucrezia nor her sister Maria had lived out their seventeenth year. Isabella, not yet twenty, was now the last remaining Medici princess, and as such she became an increasingly precious commodity in the eyes of her father. In the last few months, she had shed the remaining vestiges of girlhood. She was a duchess in her own right and was gaining both an increasingly independent voice and habits, not all of them especially rigorous, about which she was quite candid. For example, she did not like to get up early. 'I thought Niccolò would bring you one of my letters,' she told Paolo in Rome, 'but unfortunately his diligent early rising meant that I was not up in time to write to you prior to his departure.' She complained about having to write too many letters: 'You are going to find a wife with a broken finger,' she warned her husband.[4] Nor did she seem to have inherited the Medici banking gene. Cosimo gave Isabella an allowance, but she had a lot of trouble staying within a budget, as she herself makes all too clear: 'I am putting in order a sale of certain of my jewels in order to pay those who would have things of me, and I'm afraid it's like throwing them in the river because they are worth one thousand ducats, and I'm only getting two hundred from the Venetians,' she told Paolo in a letter of 10 May 1561.[5] Chances were good that Isabella received more than two hundred ducats for her jewels, which were probably pawned, not sold outright, but she was not going to let her husband know that for fear the always-short-of-cash Paolo might ask for some of the money. Cosseted all her life, she would fret about any symptoms of ill health, and indeed, in the wake of the demise of her sisters, was encouraged to do so by those around her. 'I am waiting to be able to take some exercise, to see if I can finally shake off this feeling of biliousness,' she announced out at Poggio a Caiano in June, but not bilious enough not to be pleased that the 'hunting is good'.[6]

Hunting had now become one of Isabella's great passions, as it was for other members of her family, and it was undoubtedly her greatest common interest with her husband. 'I am not a huntress of birds,' Isabella declared, and if that was the only sport to be had on an excursion, she would announce that she had not had any pleasure.[7] On the other hand, she would participate in the more leisurely sport of catching in nets *becaficchi*, little warblers that were a table delicacy and which as a child she had watched the dwarf Morgante hunt with his owl.

And she liked fishing a great deal. When it came to hunting, for Isabella the thrill of the chase was not enough, as on the occasion when 'we had the most bumbling hunt . . . we took nothing but one miserable boar who died in the net'.[8] Trapping a wild boar in a net was much less satisfactory than bringing the animal down outright. A good day's hunting for Isabella would be like the one out at the remote villa of Artimino, when 'we killed 42 wild boar, 10 stags and perhaps 12 hares with great enjoyment', and she even walked 'three miles on foot' in pursuit of the prey.[9] She also kept and bred her own hunting dogs, a breed still known as the Bracco Italiano, a white and tan pointer first recorded in Italy in the fourteenth century. She was particularly proud of her bitch Signora Anna, whose puppies, she was proud to report, 'have supplied the entire province'.[10]

Isabella's disdain for early rising, her extravagant declarations of tiredness – 'I am dead from fatigue' – and carelessness with money might make her seem like any spoilt rich girl with few preoccupations other than herself.[11] But even at nineteen she was playing her part as a Medici and assisting in organizing the society over which her family reigned. In between hunting excursions at Poggio, Isabella assessed a situation regarding the high-ranking Medici courtiers the Capponi, an old Florentine family who resided in Oltr'arno on the other side of the river: 'There are always girls to marry here in Florence, and now that I have gained a bit in years I have begun to take part in making the best arrangements. In the past few days a sister of Gian Battista Capponi has died, leaving three thousand *scudi* to be redistributed. His parents are now tormenting him to make a decision about who he wants to take as a wife, and I am certain that Capponi will do whatever I command him.' Isabella had now become the Capponi family patron. On 18 August 1561, she explained to her husband: 'I cannot write at length, I am expected at dinner by Madonna Lisabetta Capponi, who is marrying off one of her daughters.'

On other occasions, the very transport of her letters to her husband in Rome could afford the Medici an opportunity for political exchange. 'I do not want to miss the opportunity of kissing your hands and giving you news of my well-being, and so I hope to hear the same of you,' Isabella wrote to Paolo, not long after she turned nineteen.

And then she turns to the real import of her missive: 'The bearer of this letter will be a Spaniard called Scalantese who will request certain favours of Your Excellency that I hope you will deign to perform for love of me.'[12] Clearly Scalantese's requests were ones of a politically sensitive nature that could not be put into writing. Presented as the bearer of his wife's letter, Paolo would know that he had arrived in Rome under the authority and protection of the Medici.

Isabella was now performing the kind of role in Florence that should have been her mother's. She brokered marriages, liaising and negotiating in different ways with the Florentine nobility and ensuring their allegiance to the first family, and even corresponded with other Italian rulers on behalf of those who had been servants to the Medici. At the end of 1561, the nineteen-year-old sent this letter to the Duchess of Mantua, regarding a soldier banned from that city for having committed a murder:

> With that confidence that the courtesy and goodness of Your Excellency promises me, I come to beg with every efficacy that I know and possess, that I wish to ask you about doing me the favour of lifting from Gian Paolo Donato the ban he has from your city for having killed a certain Magrino, who had priorly mistreated and clearly provoked the said Gian Paolo, and having the knowledge that his relations are willing to ensure that he keeps the peace, he would also desire the benignity of Your Excellency. I again turn to beg you with all of my soul that it would please you in doing me the first favour I have ever asked of you. I will remain with so much obligation to Your Excellency, as much as my person can ever do for you, I will do whatever you want of me, and with all of my heart I offer myself to you and kiss your hand. Yours as a daughter, Dognia Isabella Orsina.[13]

Cosimo also wrote a letter to the Duchess of Mantua about the matter, using much more prosaic language and explaining that Gian Paolo had had to 'defend his honour as a soldier'. Clearly he had a hand in Isabella's more fervent outburst. Its appropriately, if not calculatedly, more girlish tone might sway the duchess and make her more disposed to assist in the lifting of the ban from Cosimo's Florentine subject.

Even the bestowing of the smallest of favours could be significant. 'Mutio Frangipani', wrote Isabella from Poggio a Caiano in reference to a Roman noble, 'has sent a missive to me requesting a pair of flowered gloves, and I will send him some at the first opportunity.'[14] She might not have been very good with money, but Isabella instinctively understood the importance of goodwill and reciprocity to the governmental system. Her mother, brought up in a Spanish world in which her family answered only to the king and having made no effort to become Florentine, did not possess such ability, refusing to make concessions and taking rather than giving. Moreover, Eleonora had recently become even more remote from Florence and the Medici court, spending her time with her youngest children. She was no longer in the best of health and was probably suffering from tuberculosis. It was noted, in 1561, that she was 'always ill and every morning she throws up her food'.[15] A portrait from the late 1550s shows the duchess with a drawn and rather cadaverous face, very different from the blooming Madonna depicted not much more than a decade previously.

In fact, Eleonora, who had been a strong presence in Isabella's childhood, appears to have played hardly any role in her life by the time Isabella was nineteen. It was as if she had only one parent, Cosimo. In late July, Isabella wrote: 'The Duke my Lord and the Cardinal together have begged me to come and stay for three weeks at the Pitti, and so I am here, and we are all well, and they have caressed me so many times I could not say, and here we will avoid the heat together, in such company that I think the time will pass very well.'[16] These days in the stifling heat of July and August were spent with little exertion, with no hunting or lively dances. Instead Isabella, Giovanni and Cosimo would stroll by the cooling waters of the fountain and fish pond of the Boboli Gardens, and in the evenings dine in the then open loggia of the Pitti Palace, interspersed with games of *tarocchi*, the card game that had been popular for centuries at Italy's courts. Even so, by the end of the month, Isabella, who disliked extreme weather conditions, found herself 'most troubled by the incredible heat in these parts. I have dealt with it the best I can by staying at the Pitti. However, I think that in six to eight days we will go to the hills surrounding Pistoia.'[17] Among Isabella's possessions were *infrescatori* – portable cooling devices, pots with handles which could contain ice to provide a chill in such sweltering times.

Cosimo could relax in the presence of Isabella and Giovanni, free, to some extent, from the pressures of dukedom. For him, the paths in life of his last remaining daughter and his clergyman son were set. He obviously wanted Isabella to have a son as soon as possible, to see some fruit from this Medici–Orsini union. A tremendous desire he nursed was to live to see Giovanni made pope, an ambition less far-fetched than it seems. The last Cardinal Giovanni de' Medici had become Pope Leo X at only thirty-seven years of age, and Cosimo was only twenty-four when his own son Giovanni was born. Thus, he could be in his sixties if his son were made pope.

Cosimo's eldest son Francesco did trouble him. At the age of twenty, Francesco was still prone to the bouts of melancholy, gloominess and anti-social behaviour he had exhibited as a child, which hardly made him the best of company. These qualities were now combined with a lack of atten-tion to the duties of prince, excessive spending and an unnecessary entourage – not exactly the man of *virtù* Cosimo hoped to see. In August, Cosimo wrote a letter to Francesco, very similar in length and content to the one he had composed to his son-in-law Paolo Giordano four years earlier. As with Paolo, Cosimo addressed Francesco's tendency to be 'managed and turned by his servants, making yourself ridiculous in front of other men'. He counselled him to 'leave behind the adulators, know the limitations of people, things, and money, but never your own honour'. He was also concerned about Francesco's disrespect and 'lack of gratitude' towards his mother, 'who thinks of little else but of your greatness, even if you do not desire it yourself'.[18] Cosimo also instructed his secretaries that this letter be copied out several times, just in case Francesco lost his own copy and Cosimo needed to remind him of its contents.

Cosimo's harsh words to his eldest son were an attempt to make sure that the son who would one day take his place would be a man of firm, resolute and virtuous character, one who would be a beloved and popular duke. Still, Francesco felt injured by his father's attitude towards him and was certain that his place in his father's affections ranked below that of his sister and brother Giovanni. Certainly Isabella's and Giovanni's characters and temperaments made for more harmonious company, but Francesco seemed to avoid them both, rarely joining them or the rest of his family.

Isabella was often in the company of her brother Giovanni alone.

Giovanni did not like being apart from his sister for too long. 'I know that you keep me always in mind,' he wrote to his sister from Pisa early in 1561. 'The pastimes here are those according to these parts, but you should not envy me, because if you think that you have no one to enjoy things with in Florence, think how much more I would enjoy things with the concession of your company, without which I find life truly imperfect.'[19]

Just as the circumstances of Paolo and Isabella's marriage were unusual, so was the adult relationship which evolved between Isabella and her brother. It might be said that Isabella had more of a marriage with Giovanni than she did with Paolo. She certainly spent more time with him, and the bond between them, forged in blood and, more importantly, in real love, was far deeper than the one Isabella had with Paolo. Practically twins in terms of age, neither could remember a time without the other, and the longest they had ever been separated was during Giovanni's three-month trip to Rome the previous year. Rarely did Isabella write a letter to her husband without it being plain that her brother was never very far away: 'The *signori* at court send you their greetings, and especially the cardinal,' was the usual way in which she would sign off.

The interests of brother and sister – music, hunting, antiquities – grew in sympathy with one another. They were both interested in collecting small sculptures of marble or bronze, either antiquities or copies. Giovanni used his status as a cardinal to acquire such artefacts as 'a beautiful little marble figure of a little boy riding a dolphin, plumbed for a fountain', a Laocoön or to commission a copy '*al'antica*, of the torso of the Bacchus that Luca Martini gave to our mother the Duchess'.[20] Isabella, for her part, would inform Paolo in Rome that 'I desire that Your Excellency do me the favour of having made for me eight marble figures – the greatest favour in the world.'[21] Together, then, Isabella and Giovanni could compare their growing collections.

The two siblings were good-looking in their late adolescence, and they resembled one another. One can compare portraits of Isabella, with her reddish-brown hair, dark eyes and sensual mouth with the face of the semi-naked John the Baptist in a painting by Bronzino, believed now to be Giovanni in the guise of his titular saint. Their temperaments fitted well too: Isabella was playful; Giovanni a bit more good-natured than his sister, who at the age of eighteen knew how to put a sting in the tail of her comments. Not that Giovanni was beyond teasing his relatives. 'Let's hope that on my return [from Rome] we will see some new and beautiful invention,' he wrote to Francesco, referring to the obsessive amounts of time his brother spent in the Palazzo Vecchio's laboratories.[22] Alone together, Isabella and Giovanni could mock the peculiarities and singularities of their family and courtiers, not to mention their own foibles. Giovanni was no better with money than his sister, admitting that his 'household is in disarray, due to so many expenses' at the same time as Isabella was selling her jewels to pay her debts.[23] He also gently refused Paolo Giordano's request that he find room in his entourage for one of his associates, explaining to his brother-in-law that 'it is hard enough for me to maintain the *famiglia* I have already, let alone availing myself of even more servants'.[24]

Isabella and Giovanni spent more and more time alone with each other. They took hunting trips to some of the more remote Medici residences, such as at Monte Paldi, twenty kilometres to the south-west of Florence. The villa there was little more than a farmhouse, a place of seclusion in which the retinues Isabella and Giovanni brought with them were minimal. 'The cardinal and I are here for eight days. The hunting is excellent, big partridges and hares, which is an enormous pleasure,' Isabella informed Paolo on 30 June 1561.[25] Hare coursing was Isabella's favourite sport, an indication of her serious interest in hunting, for hares were considered the hardest of animals to catch. Yet however good the hunting at Monte Paldi, Isabella did not wish for her husband to share the sport she and her brother were enjoying. She took some steps to dissuade Paolo from joining them. 'In fact,' Isabella told her husband, 'we are here escaping the plague that they say has already arrived at Bologna. In Florence there is a huge guard at the gates and nobody can enter the city without a clean bill of health, so if you wish to come, you should come healthy.'[26] Isabella's tone might be playful, but it certainly contained the warning that, with plague lurking, Paolo might wish to stay away. Despite this apparent threat, a few weeks later Isabella and Giovanni were back in the city, at the Pitti with Cosimo, and with Paolo nowhere in sight.

CHAPTER 6

Overcome by Sorrow

────

On 4 January 1562, Isabella, who had spent the festive season apart from Paolo Giordano, wrote to him to say that 'the duke my lord and Cardinal de' Medici send you their greetings. The duke my lord who has said he intended to lend me money now says it will not be for another four months.' All the same, Isabella was well enough provided for her to tell Paolo that 'I am sending you a crystal cup and a very fine diamond.'[1] The highlight of winter 1562 in Florence was Carnival, the time when 'Florence's women are at their most beautiful,'[2] as Ridolfo Conegrano, the new fun-loving ambassador from Ferrara who was to become a fixture in Isabella's life, described it. His 20 January 1562 report to the Duke of Ferrara noted that 'the Lady Isabella together with Signor Paolo are coming tomorrow to make Carnival'.[3] Paolo Giordano thus made a point of timing a visit to Isabella to coincide with these days of festivities, parades and parties leading up to Lent. He was gone from Florence by the early spring. 'I thank you for the truffles,' wrote Isabella of a gift of the precious fungi he sent her after his departure. 'I haven't had any because I am still on a diet and I do not wish to succumb, but I have stored them away

Catching songbirds

really well. So I kiss your hands, and so does the cardinal.'[4]

Diet and exercise were important to Isabella's sense of well-being. All the indications are she was not possessed of a deep sense of spirituality, but she was conventionally religious and, like many of her contemporaries, willing to turn to the veneration of relics or miraculous images if that could keep her healthy. One such image in Florence was in the basilica of Santissima Annunziata. The church was in fact named for its painting of the Annunciation, produced by a friar in the Middle Ages with the assistance of an angel. As such, a whole host of miraculous cures were attributed to adoration of the painting: the healing of the blind and the lame; even a woman whose baby was born black turned white after she prayed to this Annunciation. The painting itself was not actually visible, concealed as it was within an elaborate tabernacle designed by Michelozzo and commissioned by Lorenzo the Magnificent's father Piero back in the mid-fifteenth century. Isabella, however, wanted to see the miraculous picture with her own eyes, as she explained to her father in November 1561:

> This letter is to petition Your Excellency to pardon me for the presumption I am using, but Your Excellency must know that when I was sick I went to the 'Nuntiata to pray, and finding myself there on All Saints Day, I resolved to go again to satisfy this *voto*, and so I just went with lots of noblewomen to speak with the friars to ask if they would show us the icon, and they replied 'Only with the permission of His Excellency,' and without that, they denied me access, so I beg you to grant it, and wish you pardon me my presumption which I know should prevent you from giving me such grace.[5]

It must be said that despite Isabella's apparent desire to venerate the sacred image, her appearance at the church with a crowd of her girl-friends suggests that she was turning the opportunity to pray to the icon into a social event. And her appearance at Santissima Annunziata, unannounced, to solicit a view of the precious image from the undoubtedly scandalized friars, who were unused to such requests from young women, is an indication of her boldness and disregard for decorum.

Towards the end of May, the Medici family waved goodbye at the port of Livorno to Francesco, 'not without tears from the Lady

Duchess', as Ridolfo Conegrano remarked.[6] Francesco was going to spend some time at the court of Philip II of Spain as his family's representative. Desirous of receiving acclaim on a distant shore, he had been asking his father to let him go for some time, and Cosimo had long been considering the benefits of such a trip for this less than model *principe*. He did warn Francesco, 'You cannot behave as you do in Florence' at this strict protocol- and etiquette-obsessed court. Francesco's request granted, on Wednesday, 6 May 1562, 'Prince Francesco held a most wonderful meal for a great number of the Florentine noblewomen at the Pitti Palace, as a sign of the benevolence and gratitude to the city of Florence prior to his journey to Spain' – a public-relations exercise undoubtedly initiated by his father.[7] Despite his petitions to be allowed to leave, the always contrary Francesco now felt that he was being sent away, banished from his family's presence. He kept in touch with them, asking Giovanni to send him a selection of straw hats and straw shot balls, and sending a separate letter to Isabella to ask her to remind him when his brother did not comply 'as he promised he would do'.[8]

Giovanni and Isabella spent the summer of 1562 in very much the same way as they passed the previous year's. They moved from villa to villa to escape the heat, seeking out whatever sport they might have together. Later in the season, Paolo joined them again for a while. He left in his wake a rather poorly Isabella, whose condition Giovanni described in detail in a late September letter to Francesco in Spain: 'I kiss your hand, and can give you the same news of the well-being of Their Excellencies, and the rest of us, and a bit more news on the health of the Lady Isabella, who has now been several days all clear of a fever. On Sunday she took a little medicine, just to conclude the course of her purge, rather than for any other reason, and she will stay a while longer in the rooms at Poggio, as Signor Paolo has returned to Rome to take care of business.'[9]

Giovanni himself was obliged to leave on business soon after. Cosimo wanted his son, as Archbishop of Pisa, a role to which Giovanni had thus far paid only nominal attention, to accompany him on an inspection of the towns of the Maremma coast – Livorno, Grosseto and Rosignano. Eleonora and her younger sons Garzia and

Ferdinando were also part of the party. Isabella stayed behind. Her sickness had turned out to be another pregnancy. She was by herself in Florence, which did not seem to concern her greatly and she carried on alone quite happily. She wrote to her father in her usual hyperbolic terms shortly after his departure for Pisa, with no mention of her own well-being: 'I wish to ask a favour for my old servant Francesco Taruga, who has a carnal brother who for many years has greatly desired to go to study at the University in Pisa, and could now this year begin his studies, so I beg Your Excellency to grant this favour, for love of me, your most humble and most obedient servant Dognia Isabella Medici Orsina.'[10]

It was Giovanni, rather than Isabella, who seemed particularly anxious about her pregnancy. He had one of his servants, Titio, keep an eye on his sister, whom he was clearly convinced was not going to alter her habits if there was no one around to take care of her. 'We have received your letter', wrote Giovanni to Titio on 25 October, 'and seen what you have written of the state of Lady Isabella, and we hope for every success in regard to her condition. However, I do lack any hope for her pregnancy if there isn't anybody to go around hand in hand with her, so I am pleased you will serve and attend to her with your usual faith and diligence.'[11] Evidently Paolo Giordano was not especially concerned about his wife's well-being. Giovanni wrote to him that same day regarding his brother-in-law's 'prompt return, as you promised', although whether it was Isabella or Giovanni who wished for Paolo's presence in Florence is rather hard to tell.[12] Giovanni began to fret a little less when Isabella agreed to move into his apartments in the Palazzo Vecchio, from where he could receive daily reports of his sister's health from his servants. On 27 October, he wrote to his chamberlain Ugolino Grifoni (last seen witnessing Eleonora, pregnant with Isabella, vomiting copiously) to express his delight at 'the pleasing news you have conveyed to me of the well-being of Lady Isabella'.[13] But in the end it was not the health of Isabella that should have been the object of Giovanni's concern.

The causes of most illnesses in Renaissance Italy were as undetermined as they had been since the days of ancient Rome. The disease which came to be known as malaria acquired its name from the belief it was caused by *mal'aria*, or 'bad air', the vapours and mists emanating from swampy lands and marshes of the very kind that bordered the Maremma coastline. There was as yet no understanding that malaria was caused by a parasite carried by the mosquitoes which bred in such waters. Indeed, the sickness was not even referred to as malaria. Instead, malaria was *la febbre* – 'the fever' that could bring about sudden death. Over the centuries, malaria had claimed amongst its victims in Italy St Monica, the mother of St Augustine, who himself managed to recover from the disease. Pope Gregory V died of malaria, as did Innocent III, who had previously complained unknowingly about the mosquitoes at the coastal town of Subiaco. Malaria also took the lives of Pope Alexander VI and his son at the end of a hot summer in Rome. Still, even in those times, malaria did not always kill. Paolo Giordano's brother-in-law Marcantonio Colonna had made a recovery from an outbreak in Rome in 1557, as had Duke Cosimo himself during an earlier episode of the disease.

Cosimo was aware of the problems of *la febbre* in the Maremma region. In June 1560, he had one of his galleys, stationed in the waters around Livorno, moved further south, for its sailors were beginning to fall ill. He also sacked the ship's doctor, to be replaced by one who would be more 'attentive and more caring' to his nautical patients.[14]

Since malaria appeared to be only prevalent in the summer, the Medici tended to avoid the Maremma coast during those months and restricted their trips to the winter – hence Cosimo scheduling a late October/November trip to these parts. However, the winters of the late 1550s and early 1560s had been unusually warm, so that mosquitoes that ordinarily would be dead by then were still thriving. Several spring floods, causing the Arno to rise and burst its banks, also meant the land was particularly swampy.

On Sunday, 15 November 1562, Cardinal Giovanni de' Medici was at the small town of Rosignano, having gone hunting on the wooded coastline. He began to feel that he had a fever, but he decided not to say anything about it and rode on to Livorno the following day to join his parents and two brothers, 'happy and full of goodwill', as Cosimo described Giovanni in a letter to Francesco. On Tuesday morning, the family was due to return to Pisa, only Giovanni's fever had grown worse, to the extent that he could not get out of bed. On the Wednesday, Cosimo explained: 'They took three ounces of blood from his veins, and it seemed that he began to be easier, but in a few hours he was worse again.' On Friday morning, 'They applied leeches, who took a good two pounds of blood, along with all the other remedies they could possibly employ.' But on the night of Friday, 20 November, at twelve o'clock, having received the last rites Giovanni de' Medici died in his father's arms. Cosimo, struggling to reconcile himself to the death of his beloved son, told Francesco that he took comfort from the fact that Giovanni 'has passed from this life with such goodness, and a recognition of God, which makes a real Christian. And your mother, persuaded by me, remains similarly content and comforted.'[15]

But the depth of Cosimo's pain was evident to all who knew how much he loved his son. Benvenuto Cellini describes the event in his autobiography: 'The poison from the bad air of those marshes first attacked the Cardinal, who was taken with a pestilential fever after a few days, and died at the end of a brief illness. He was the Duke's right eye, handsome and good, and his loss was most severely felt. I allowed several days to elapse, until I thought their tears were dried, and then I betook myself to Pisa.'[16] This entry happens to be the last in Cellini's autobiography. A tale which encompasses the Sack of Rome, accounts of plague and pestilence, boys dressed as girls, and praise and blame for the artist from dukes, kings and Michelangelo ends with the death of young Giovanni de' Medici.

Two days after his death, the body of 'the lord Cardinal was carried back to Florence in a box covered with gold embroidered black velvet, drawn by mules, and accompanied by all of his household'.[17] But tragedy for the Medici was not at an end. Cosimo concluded his letter to Francesco by telling him that his brothers, fifteen-year-old Garzia and thirteen-year-old Ferdinando, were also suffering from 'a bit of fever, but they are being well cared for, and I believe that it's not truly dangerous'.[18] However, Cosimo's optimism was largely misplaced. Although the younger Ferdinando did begin to make a recovery, Garzia grew worse. On 10 December, he was 'in such a way that the doctors have resolved to bleed him'.[19] Two days later came the report that 'Don Garzia has gone to a better life, the doctors say the illness was in his head, because he always had pain there.'[20]

News of the deaths of both Giovanni and Garzia made their way back to Florence and beyond, either through official channels – court couriers and ambassadorial dispatch – or via below-stairs tales carried by word of mouth by merchants, soldiers, muleteers. There was shock and surprise because the deaths of the boys were so close together. Despite the fact that there were outbreaks of *la febbre* throughout northern Italy, the idea that Giovanni and Garzia had both met much more sinister ends began to spread, although the stories did not reach printed form until long after their deaths. In 1576, one Venetian correspondent described a scenario in which Giovanni and Garzia were out hunting together, got into a quarrel and drew their swords. Then Garzia 'wounded the cardinal in the side in such a way that he was dead in a few hours. He was then felled by a blow from one of the cardinal's servants.'[21] Even later versions of the story saw Garzia killed by Cosimo in revenge for the death of his favourite son.

All the contemporary documents disprove this story, and there were clearly many at the bedsides of both Medici sons to observe the brothers dying from malaria. Moreover, recent investigations into the disinterred corpses of the two brothers revealed that neither had apparently died of foul play. However, the fictitious dispute does mirror one which had occurred between the brothers four years previously and which had found its way into ambassadorial dispatches, as the Ferrarese ambassador recounted back in 1558: 'Fooling around together after dinner, Don Garzia threw a fork at Don Giovanni, two prongs of which struck him in the leg, and caused a great quantity of blood to gush forth. With this great injury, Don Giovanni staggered out to Their Excellencies, who had the injury doctored, and they put him to bed.'[22]

What the Medici were actually contending with in Pisa was not fratricide but the apparent obliteration of their family by epidemic. In the aftermath of the death of Garzia came the news that 'the duchess is with the fever, which is accompanied by these sorrows'.[23] Such sorrows were, of course, the death of two of Eleonora's sons, just three weeks apart. In the last five years, she had lost also two of

her adult daughters, but the death of her sons had a particular reso-
nance. It was upon their existence where her identity as '*La
Fecundissima*' rested. Eleonora had been portrayed with her sons over
and over again, never with her daughters, and she had, as Cosimo told
Francesco, thought of little else but her sons' greatness, investing her
energy in securing honours for them. After the death of Giovanni, 'she
did not eat or sleep for three days', noted Cosimo.[24] As Garzia went
into a decline, despite her own malarial symptoms, 'she would not let
herself be governed by the doctors, as was her usual custom', her husband recounted. After Garzia's death, she suffered from 'incredible
anxiety, and could not sleep, she was so desperate and afflicted'.[25]

The combination of her own burgeoning malarial fever, tuberculosis and the mental anguish she was suffering after the deaths of
Giovanni and Garzia were too much for Eleonora. She lost the will to
live. On 16 December, five days after Garzia's death, the Ferrarese
ambassador Ridolfo Conegrano wrote home, informing the d'Este
duke: 'It is believed that the Duchess will pass from this life. The doctors have lost all hope.'[26]

Eleonora died at three in the morning. Her body was prepared to be
transported back for a funeral in Florence, dressed in an embroidered
yellow satin dress with a red velvet bodice underneath and red silk
stockings. In life, Eleonora had ruled her orbit. Events occurred at the
time and pace she dictated. But now, fear of contagion from her corpse
caused those who dressed her and laid in her coffin to rush: 'One
string of her bodice was haphazardly laced, skipping eyelets: one
stocking was put on inside out; crude silk strips cuffed her wrists and
ankles as she lay in her coffin.'[27]

Cosimo stoically told Franceso that he was taking comfort for the
sacrifice of 'two dear sons, and your most rare mother' in the fact that
he still had 'yourself, your two brothers [Ferdinando and eight-year-
old Pietro] and the Duchess of Bracciano, who is with me'.[28] It was true
that having four adult children was still a significant achievement in
Renaissance Italy. But what comfort was there for the young Duchess
of Bracciano for the death of her brother the cardinal?

Giovanni's funeral on 24 November at the church of San Lorenzo
was an especially stately occasion, as befitted the young man who had

been Medici cardinal, although the family members sick with malaria in Pisa were unable to attend. Nonetheless, there was a funeral procession, with all the Florentine clergy, the extensive retinue of Paolo Giordano, 'all clad in mourning', and the household of the cardinal himself, including Giovanni's dwarf Barbino, 'struggling under a long mourning veil six times his size'.[29] Giovanni's coffin followed, carried by the canons of Santa Maria del Fiore. Directly behind the coffin came Paolo Giordano and other members of the Medici court, including Alessandro de' Medici's son Giulio. Inside San Lorenzo, Piero Vettori, the scholar who had once been tutor to the young Giovanni, gave an oration in Latin, extolling the dead boy's virtues and undoubtedly overexaggerating his piety and commitment to the church.

Being a woman, Isabella was not a part of the all-male funeral cortège. Instead, she sat with the congregation in San Lorenzo. All around her was beauty: Brunelleschi's harmonious arcaded church design in *pietra serena* and Donatello's bronze pulpits, symbols of Medici magnificence and seeming but illusory omnipotence. They could not cheat death. Isabella listened to Vettori's eulogy, the man with whom she and Giovanni had once sat to study Latin and who had taught them about the world of antiquities that so fascinated them as adults. She heard what her brother had done and what he would have gone on to do. Isabella could not contain her grief. Ignoring decorum, she got up and rushed out of the church, an action that was noted by some, if not all. 'As the service was celebrated,' one observer noted, 'one of the gentlemen of Signor Paolo came up to tell him to let him know that the Lady Isabella, overcome by sorrow, had gone outside, and immediately the Signor left the church in order to go and console her.'[30]

But it seems that Isabella was inconsolable. Word of the extent of her grief reached her brother Francesco in Spain, and he took it upon himself to write to her. The letter certainly makes clear the extent of the Medici family's understanding of the depth of feeling between Giovanni and Isabella. 'I know most certainly that nobody feels the loss of the cardinal our brother more deeply than you,' Francesco told Isabella, 'because I know the love between you was infinite.' Then his words to his sister take a harsh turn. 'At the same time,' he went on to say, 'I do believe that after you have paid your debt to the things of the flesh, you should be able to give way to reason, which ought to persuade you that in adversity we can find recourse in Christ, and can congratulate ourselves that in this way we are different from beasts, who are guided by sex alone. Humankind has the use of reason, and you should have no desire to degenerate from that. You have the example of the duke who goes about things in his usual way, and I hope soon to learn that you will have succeeded in conquering your grief.'[31]

Francesco wrote this letter to Isabella in the aftermath of the deaths of both Garzia and Eleonora, yet he makes no mention of either in his missive. It seems he knew that for Isabella the deaths of a mother from whom she had become increasingly distant and a brother with whom she spent little time were of little consequence in comparison to the loss of Giovanni, her constant companion. Nor, apparently, had the death of her sister Lucrezia the previous year affected her greatly, for Isabella was writing in light-hearted spirits to Paolo Giordano just a couple of weeks later. It was Giovanni who was special to her. Also of significance is the fact that Isabella's elder brother does not urge her to turn to her husband for comfort, an appropriate suggestion to a woman needing to assuage her grief, as if he knew such a measure would mean little to his sister. Nor does he remind her of the child she was supposed to be carrying; in fact, Isabella may well have had another miscarriage by this point in time.

Instead, Francesco took an admonitory tone with her, in which he made it clear he found something bestial in her anguish at Giovanni's death, beyond the realms of how a good Christian man or woman should behave – 'different from beasts'. One is left with the underlying sense that Francesco felt the relationship between his younger brother and sister had gone beyond the realm of simple fraternal affection. 'Keep all male kin away from her and do not let her learn to delight among men. For naturally our love continues the longest towards those with whom we have spent our time in youth' was the counsel of the Spaniard Juan Luis Vives in his *Education of a Christian Woman*. There is nothing to suggest Giovanni and Isabella were physically intimate with one another; nonetheless, there was a profound intimacy in their love for one another. In Giovanni, Isabella had a dancing partner, a hunting partner, a soulmate, a mirror, a twin. He was the reason why she really had no need of her husband, and she was equally secure of her place in her brother's life: because he was a cleric, he was not going to take a wife. At twenty years of age, Isabella could not envision an existence in which she and her brother were not always together. Paolo Giordano might make appearances in her life in order to impregnate her, to let her fulfil her family obligations, but Isabella had no reason to suppose that the centre of her world would ever be anybody other than Giovanni. However, now Giovanni, just turned nineteen, had been taken from her, and a desolate and devastated Isabella had as yet no idea how she was going to fill the void his departure from this world had left in her life.

PART III
The First Lady of Florence

Florentine noblewoman with one from Parma

CHAPTER 1

After Eleonora

According to his son Francesco, Cosimo's stoic response to the deaths of his wife and two sons was to go 'about things in his usual way'. The attendant responsibilities of ruling a dukedom denied Cosimo the option of losing himself in grief the way that Isabella did in the aftermath of Giovanni's death. For Cosimo, Giovanni's demise meant not only the loss of a beloved son but the loss of the only Medici cardinal. Cosimo was determined to see the position restored to the family as quickly as possible. On 23 December, less than a week after the death of Eleonora, he began negotiating with Pope Pius IV to have the cardinalate transferred to his thirteen-year-old son Ferdinando, who, recovered from the malaria that had claimed his brothers' lives, was now the second-eldest Medici boy. Exactly two weeks later, on 6 January 1563, the Pope had complied with Cosimo's request, the remarkable rapidity of the conferral on so young a candidate perceived as a gesture of sympathy on the part of the duke's papal ally. The death of his mother had hit the young Ferdinando very hard, 'but he really will rejoice at getting the hat', pronounced Isabella.[1] She knew that her younger brother's formerly more marginal position in the Medici hierarchy had

Uffizi, Florence

now improved stratospherically. Cosimo made sure his Italian counterparts knew exactly what had occurred, informing the Duke of Mantua
just five days later of His Holiness's generosity in 'reigniting the splendour of the cardinalate in our house'.[2]

Cosimo did more than behave as normal; he demonstrated an
extraordinary spurt of energy and activity. Throughout 1563, he over-
saw projects old and new throughout his domain, micro-managing to
a degree unusual even for this detail-oriented duke. By 3 February, he
was corresponding with his architect Bartolomeo Ammannati regarding the progress on work at the Pitti Palace, instructing him to config-
ure the entrance to the Boboli Gardens in such a way that access
would be denied to 'curs, only let gentlemen enter'.[3] The next day he
had a court official, Raffaello Vacchia, attend to the vaulting of a large
room in the villa at Poggio a Caiano, prepare Castello for a visit and
oversee work on the hydraulics at the villa at La Petraia. A month later,
he took Vacchia off the Poggio a Caiano project due to his dissatisfac-
tion with his progress. That same day in early February, Cosimo wrote
to Giorgio Vasari for a progress report on the Uffizi, and at the same
time instructed him to work on the New Sacristy at San Lorenzo.
Shortly afterwards, Cosimo corresponded with him about making a
chimney piece for the chapel, as 'I am displeased at the blackening of
the figures' by smoke from candles burning during the saying of Mass.
He had no desire for a sooty *Day and Night* or *Dawn and Dusk*, those
exquisitely rendered opalescent statues by Michelangelo that rested on
the tombs of his Medici ancestors. At the same time, he also wanted
scouting reports from Vasari for an appropriate location for the burgeoning artists' academy, the Accademia del Disegno.[4] The following
week, the duke was concerned with having old silver plates melted
down to make new ones and the disbursement of Eleonora's old
clothes.

In April, Cosimo decided he needed the bridge leading to the bowl-
ing alley at Poggio a Caiano improved, and to save money, he proposed to Ammannati that he use old paving stones left over from the
resurfacing of the roads near the Pitti for that palace's extension. He
also authorized the transportation from Elba of a block of granite for
'the great cup, 35 braccia [about 12 metres] in circumference, to be

placed in the Pitti' to serve as the fountain basin that still stands there.[5] Another gigantic granite piece that made its way to Florence that year was an ancient column from the ruined Roman baths of Caracalla, a gift from Pius IV. This column Cosimo chose to have erected by the church of Santa Trinità as a monument to connect Florence with the grandeur of the ancient world. Cosimo kept Vasari as busy as ever. In addition to all the other Medici projects, the artist also began decorating the largest of the halls in the Palazzo Vecchio with a scheme that would endow the room with the name Salone del Cinquecento, as he illustrated it with Medici deeds of the present century. Here was Cosimo's opportunity to shine, as he was depicted, for example, 'planning the war of Siena'. Moreover, the duke informed the artist, he was to be depicted alone, without any advisers surrounding him, 'because it was I who planned it all by myself'.[6]

Cosimo also engaged in some legal tussling with Cathérine de' Medici. Since the death of her husband Henri II in 1559, Cathérine was no longer the scorned wife obliged to secede power to the king's mistress Diane de Poitiers. She was now a powerful queen mother. Yet although they shared the same year of birth and surname, not to mention blood, relations between Catherine and Cosimo were never warm. Having left for France at the age of fourteen, never to see Florence again, Catherine regarded Cosimo as her inferior for having been born into the 'cadet' branch of the Medici. Now they entered into litigation regarding the estate of the long-dead Alessandro, acknowledged as her half-brother but really her cousin. Nonetheless, despite the animosity, Cosimo also sent Catherine word that he was expediting 'the drawings, plans, together with the gardener Your Majesty desires'.[7] Plans and gardener were presumably intended for Chenonçeau, where Catherine's formal Italian garden was to stand in contrast to the French-styled one of her now defeated rival Diane. All the same, Italian-style garden or no, Catherine was a French queen mother first and foremost.

Cosimo even took the time to send personally a recipe for a remedy described as 'olio di caravita', the 'oil of dear life', to the Prince of Piombino. The duke explained to the prince that for the potion to be effective 'you have to soak scorpions in the oil for forty days'.[8] At the other end of the social spectrum, Cosimo also informed the welfare office, the Ufficio di Carità, that he thought their programme to dispense bread to the poor should be changed from early morning to early evening. 'The reason', he explained, 'is that many of the poor come from far away to get this, their only bread, and travel through the night to arrive there through bad streets and wicked times, which often lead to their deaths.'[9] Such a broad range of issues were claiming Cosimo's attention that he absolved himself from work for a while in October to undergo treatment for his passing of a kidney stone 'the size of a fennel seed'.[10]

While the Medici duchy was far from impoverished, its outgoings were considerable, and funding for Cosimo's new slew of projects was provided for at least partly by the considerable inheritance left by Eleonora. Although she made various bequests to religious institutions and to her relatives in Toledo, and even left Isabella 4,500 *scudi*, it was Cosimo who received the bulk of her estate, which was substantial. 'I understand', the Ferrarese ambassador Ridolfo Conegrano wrote to Alfonso d'Este, who was very interested in such matters, 'that Her Excellency had 600,000 *scudi* worth of jewels, 200,000 in liquid assets, 50,000 in livestock, 9,000 in grain.'[11] There were additional properties in her name, such as a castle and estate in Spain. Eleonora might have only come to Cosimo with a modest 30,000 *scudi* dowry, but she left her husband a much richer man.

Cosimo began immediately to fulfil the terms of his wife's will. He had work started straight away on designs for the Benedictine convent SS Concezione, intended for nuns from noble families, which Eleonora had wished to found. This attentiveness to her wishes and the burst of activity following her death can easily, and perhaps even rightly, be seen as the response of a widower working to escape his grief. Yet in his own life he began to erase the presence and influence of the woman to whom he had been married for twenty-three years in ways that were quite obvious to courtly observers. 'His Excellency keeps the same table with the same companions as he did in the time of the Duchess,' reported Conegrano in the year after Eleonora's demise. 'That is to say, Signor Paolo is there, the Lady Isabella, Don Pedrino, but the table is better served, and is more intimate. He keeps it in the morning as well as the evening, and many enter in order to see him.'[12] In other words, Cosimo allowed his courtiers a greater degree of familiarity and accessibility than Eleonora had permitted. Moreover, dining service was better now that Cosimo had abandoned his wife's Spanish protocol and its attendant onerous delays, which often resulted in cold and unpalatable food. As a dutiful and loving husband during his wife's lifetime, Cosimo had observed customs that had chafed at him. Now that she was gone, he could relinquish them.

As for Isabella, on 14 January 1563, a little less than two months after her brother Giovanni's death, the Ferrarese ambassador Conegrano was able to report to the d'Este duke: 'Lady Isabella has much improved, even though she remains somewhat afflicted. Every day she goes out hunting with His Excellency.'[13] The distractions of hard riding and the pursuit of a quarry were beneficial for both father and daughter. At the end of that month, Isabella assured Francesco that she had come to terms with Giovanni's loss. 'I am now most totally resigned to God's will,' she wrote to her elder brother. Still, the memory of Giovanni lingered. In April, Isabella sent her father the following petition: 'I find myself so obligated to the blessed memory of my brother the cardinal that it appears to me that I should take the opportunity to do something of benefit to his creatures [servants], many of whom have offered me consolation. Carlo Ceccharelli was once the Monsignor's head groom, and he would like to continue this position with the cardinal [Ferdinando]. For my love, please accept him into this position. He will serve with love and fealty.'[14] However, a court secretary wrote upon her note that 'the cardinal does not require the services of a head groom'. Ferdinando might be a cardinal, but he was still only a thirteen-year-old boy, presently suffering from the measles, and as yet had no need of his own 'creatures'.

Still, even if she could not find places for Giovanni's former servants, Isabella's position in Florence had changed. Conegrano informed his master: 'I have made appropriate gestures to receive her blessing, and she has replied with the most loving words that I could possibly desire, and she kisses Your Excellency's hand, and thanks you infinitely for your continuous affection.'[15] Such a passage, the first in Conegrano's dispatches which would now regularly report upon

Isabella's activities and well-being to the Ferrarese duke, is of particular significance. In the political spectrum Isabella was now more than Paolo Giordano's wife, more than her brother Giovanni's playmate and companion. She was now by default the first lady of Florence, and consequently her favour and goodwill were highly desirable because she had her father's ear. Conegrano took pains to cultivate her, assuring his duke that 'whenever she finds me, I always have the first place at table after herself and Signor Paolo'.[16]

One family member who seemed less than enthused about Isabella's own advancement in the family hierarchy was her brother Francesco. He had already made it clear to his younger sister on how he expected her to comport herself following their brother's death. In late February 1563, an appropriate period for mourning having passed, he sent Isabella a letter from Madrid regarding the role he thought she should appropriate in the aftermath of their mother's death: 'I ask that you keep safe Don Hernando [as his siblings called Ferdinando], whose promotion to the cardinalate has given me the greatest pleasure, as it has renewed the splendour of our house. With Don Pietrino I know that you will perform the office of the most loving of mothers.'[17] Francesco appeared to envision Isabella as a kind of governess, retreating into the nursery the way his mother had done during her last years.

But surrogate motherhood was not a role to which his sister took readily, nor does it seem to be one that, contrary to her brother's expectations, her father intended Isabella to fulfil. Cosimo wanted Isabella's company, but it was clear that he had no interest in replicating in its entirety the kind of family life that had existed during Eleonora's reign. And the changes he planned went far beyond offering a more informal table at meal times.

Thus far in its history, Florence did not have the same reputation for sexual licence as either Venice or Rome. Unlike these two cities, it had not sponsored a courtesan culture which had produced the likes of Venice's Veronica Franco or Rome's Fiammetta. True, both Cosimo and Eleonora had welcomed Tullia d'Aragona, the poet and courtesan, to the court of Florence, but Tullia had performed primarily the former rather than the latter role. More scandalous was the behaviour of her lover, the scholar Benedetto Varchi, who almost found himself in prison after sexually abusing a nine-year-old girl. Cosimo intervened on his behalf, but the penalty he extracted from Varchi was the composition of the lengthy *History of Florence*, a panegyric to the Medici family and Cosimo himself.

Even if the skills of its prostitutes were not internationally renowned, Florence still had its share of brothels. The 1562 census, '*la descrizione delle bocche* (mouths) *della città*', accounted for the professions of many of the 59,216 individuals living in the city, listing the homes and establishments of the practitioners of 310 separate professions. They ranged from ambassadors and accountants to barbers, saddlers, street vendors, money changers and gardeners, and were as specific as the *peduccaio* who specifically sold pigs' trotters and other animal hooves. Amongst the business enterprises are '*case di meretrice* [brothels]', located primarily in the central quarters of San Giovanni and Santa Maria Novella.[18] *Puttane* who worked on the streets would not have been counted. The majority of the *case* supported only one or two working girls, such as '*Orsolina, meretrice, Bolognese*', '*Lucretia, meretrice, Florentine*' or '*Marherita, meretrice, Lucchese*'. The largest ones housed around twelve, with the workers not listed by name. One of these larger houses was described as the property of Chiarissimo de' Medici, a distant cousin of Cosimo's, who was a Florentine senator and the overseer of the Monte di Pietà, the bank and pawn shop endorsed by the Catholic Church. Chiarissimo's brothel was in the fashionable Santa Trinità neighbourhood, where the homes of members of such illustrious families as the Strozzi could be found, indicating it catered to the pockets of Florence's elite and to wealthy outsiders.

Nevertheless, as long as Eleonora presided over the Medici court, there was a profound separation between these aspects of Florentine life and the world she ruled, and she made her influence felt in different ways. In Venice, for example, Titian and his cohorts produced painting after painting of beautiful and inviting blonde Venuses and Floras. Modelled on the city's famous courtesans, their painterly warmth promises the pleasures of seduction, as they caress themselves at their toilette or listen to the dulcet music played by a devoted admirer. By contrast, one of the relatively few erotic works of art painted by the Medici court artist Bronzino, kept busy with portraits of the Medici and their courtiers, is the painting in London's National Gallery known as *Venus, Cupid, Folly and Time*. Painted in 1545, the body of Bronzino's Venus is glacially white, a stark contrast to the honeyed skin tones of her Venetian counterparts, and projects what was once described as an icy obscenity. She leans in to embrace her son Cupid, her mouth open, tongue flickering to bestow what will emphatically not be a chaste maternal kiss. For his part, Cupid's projecting buttocks were once deemed so scandalous that a seventeenth-century painter covered them with some ivy leaves, painting out Cupid's mother's tongue at the same time. Behind the illicit lovers are symbols of the dangerous effects of their love: Father Time reminds the viewer of how fleeting such pleasures are; a child acolyte of Cupid, throwing rose petals at the couple, has a bleeding foot from stepping on thorns scattered on the ground; a pretty little girl is holding sweet, alluring honeycomb, but she has the lower body of a griffin. Most alarming of all is the maddened figure clutching his face in despair with decaying fingers and nails, recognizable as symbols of syphilis, a disease which took hold in Florence at the end of the fifteenth century, following the invasion by the French. In fact, Cosimo eventually decided to send Bronzino's picture to François I. The golden apple Venus holds is both her own symbol and a Medici *palla*, its symbolic double duty reminiscent of the baskets of fruit the Medici liked to send out as gifts. But in this instance, this gift of diplomacy is tinged with a perhaps not so subtle undercurrent of malice.

However, by 1563 such outward concessions towards morality were fast on the wane at Cosimo's court. A role he chose not to play was that of the celibate, grieving widower. He had always liked women, having been sexually active since the age of fourteen. In the aftermath of Eleonora's death, a report from the frequently sharp-tongued Venetian ambassador regarding the once faithful Cosimo observed that 'he loves women liberally, and leaving decorum aside, publicly makes love to many'.[19] Clearly, a new age had arrived, in which the Medici court was no longer staid but libertarian. Florentine noblewomen were no longer remote paragons of virtue but potential sexual partners for their duke.

It was not only Cosimo's wooing of the women at his court which captured the attention of the citizens of Florence, however. Stories began to spread about the true nature of the relationship between Cosimo and his own daughter Isabella. The two had always spent a great deal of time together, but it was in the company of others; in recent times, particularly with Isabella's other constant companion, her brother Giovanni. Now there were no mediating presences. Suspicions began to be aroused about what exactly the duke and his grown, married daughter, whose husband was so frequently absent, were doing together on excursions such as their solitary hunting trips. Such companionship was far from normal.

Rumours began to abound that Isabella was 'loved by the Duke Cosimo in a way that some voices say is carnal'.[20] Another story placed Vasari as an unwitting witness to a very startling scene: 'When Giorgio Vasari was painting the great hall of the ducal palace, one day after dinner he discovered the duke together with his daughter in that hall. Having seen the prince with his daughter from a distance, he quickly retreated, and decided not to do any more painting in the room that day.'[21] The alleged incident could thus be dated to 1563, when the artist began work on the Sala del Cinquecento in the wake of Isabella's mother's death.

Not surprisingly, this story would find great favour in guides for the English aristocracy on the Grand Tour. Mark Noble's *Memoirs of the House of Medici* recounts the incident with an enthusiasm that is somewhat alarming for an eighteenth-century curate. Cosimo, he reported, 'was amorous to a more criminal length than his predecessor Alessandro ever could. That one defiled the beds of his subjects and violated the cloister. Cosimo robbed his daughter Isabella of her purity.'[22] Alexandre Dumas made sure to include it in his colourful account of the history of the Medici family: 'He saw Isabella enter, around midday, she had an ardent air,' imagined Dumas. 'She drew the curtains and lay down on a couch, and dozed. Cosimo entered in his turn, and made his way to his daughter. Isabella let out a cry but at this cry Vasari saw no more, for in his turn he closed his eyes and pretended to sleep.'[23] He feared, Dumas explained, a dagger or poison were it revealed he had discovered the Medici duke had such a dreadful secret.

There is nothing in Vasari's archive that suggests he ever observed such a scene. His presence as witness in its recounting was perhaps purely to add further colour and authenticity to a salacious tale. Painting the Sala del Cinquecento in the Palazzo Vecchio in the aftermath of Eleonora's death, the artist was in the right place at the right time to serve as the observer in this tale. For the eighteenth-century English traveller, already convinced of the depravities of Italian papists, and the intrigue-loving Alexandre Dumas, an incestuous relationship between Cosimo and his daughter added piquant spice to the story of the Medici. Certainly it turned a visit to the Palazzo Vecchio from a tour of a staid hall of government, decorated with sometimes inscrutable scenes of Medici achievement, into a look at a much more exciting seat of familial scandal.

Nor is there anything to prove that what passed between Cosimo and Isabella was anything more than paternal and filial love, albeit one that was unusually intense for this time. Isabella always attended her father whenever he wanted her. As she makes clear in one letter, 'I did not really want to go to Cafaggiolo,' referring to her lack of desire to go that villa. 'But now I have received a request from the duke my lord to attend him there, I must immediately depart.'[24] In October 1563, when Cosimo was suffering from kidney trouble, word went out around Italy that 'the duke cannot urinate'. Isabella, out at Poggio a Caiano, 'came into Florence for a night, at the announcement of the duke's illness, and returned the next day having ascertained that His Excellency was out of danger and doing well.'[25]

Still, for those outside of the inner Medici circle, increasingly mystified by what they knew of the terms of the relationship between Isabella and her husband, this scenario might help to explain a lot. Paolo and Isabella had been married for five years now. Why, asked some, was the Duchess of Bracciano not fulfilling her marital duties from her titular home, far away in Rome? Why was her father insisting she remain in Florence, were it not for the fact that he wished to make his daughter first lady of Florence in more ways than one? It mimicked what many believed about another unnatural father/daughter relationship: that of Lucrezia Borgia and her father the Pope, who had also wanted to prevent his daughter leaving home after her marriage. 'This is what happens when a woman goes about without her husband' was the conclusion reached by many with regard to the lifestyle of the Medici princess.[26]

CHAPTER 2

At Home with Paolo and Isabella

Although Paolo Giordano only spent a certain period of each year in Florence, in 1563 he and Isabella began to maintain their own residence in the city, apart from the rest of her family. The building of the new Uffizi had rendered vacant a prime piece of real estate – the Palazzo Medici on the Via Larga, which had been housing several of the bureaucratic offices now moving to the new address. Despite his irregular presence in Florence, Paolo was keen for himself and Isabella to take over the Palazzo Medici, for the occupancy of a separate 'Orsini' residence would make him appear less dependent upon the Medici family than might actually be the case. He campaigned quite hard for the privilege. Real estate was always at a premium in Florence's small city centre. Even the illustrious might share rooms, and there were plenty of ambassadors, foreign officials and dignitaries willing to pay dearly, in more ways than the purely financial, to be the old Medici palace's tenants. Paolo petitioned Cosimo, who took his time making up his mind. Frustrated, Paolo turned to Giovanni prior to his death, who proved to be no more helpful. The cardinal wrote to Gianozzo Cepparello, the agent Cosimo had appointed to act on

Palazzo Medici on Via Larga, Florence

Paolo's behalf in Florence: 'We have spoken to the Duke our father about the old house on the Via Larga, whose rooms Signor Paolo would desire for his own person. His Excellency has replied that it depends, and so we cannot say otherwise, as we need to do whatever His Excellency orders.'[1] Giovanni, it seems, was not particularly anxious to see his father allow his brother-in-law a headquarters in their town, one which his sister would be expected to occupy and so be apart from him.

Eventually, Cosimo acquiesced to Paolo's demand and allowed his old family palace to be set aside for the use of his daughter and son-in-law. Furthermore, in the aftermath of Giovanni's death, Isabella became much more interested in maintaining a home of her own, whereas previously she was content to reside wherever her brother was. She might be close to her father, but now she wanted a residence of her own. The Palazzo Medici became associated specifically with Isabella, especially during Paolo's long absences from Florence. Moreover, Isabella had become increasingly interested in her Medici heritage, and so to reside in the original family palace allowed her a special and privileged connection with her family's past.

Isabella's new home had been designed in the fifteenth century in such a way as to assure Florence that Medici ambition was not overreaching and that the family would never think of competing with the official seat of government, the Palazzo Vecchio. When Cosimo the Elder had initially commissioned the Medici palace in 1444, he had turned to Brunelleschi to produce the design. The architect presented his model to Cosimo at a gathering of the Florentine elite. Cosimo the Elder complimented Brunelleschi on his work, and then added: 'But it's too magnificent and sumptuous for me.'[2] Cosimo's Florentine compatriots were relieved to see that his ambition did, apparently, have its limitations. They therefore uttered no protest at the hardly diminutive, barely modest, rusticated palace, emblazoned with Medici *palle* and resembling a banking house, that the architect Michelozzo went on to produce as the Palazzo Medici. Comparatively speaking, it seemed like a lesser building to the one Brunelleschi had proposed.

The Medici patriarch proceeded to create an environment which dazzled its visitors, who would gasp at the 'studies, little chapels, living rooms, bedchambers and gardens, all of which are constructed and decorated with admirable skill, embellished with gold and fine marbles, carvings and sculptures in relief, pictures and inlays done in perspective by the most accomplished and perfect of masters, down to the benches and all the floors of the house . . . then a garden all created of the most beautiful polished marbles with various plants, which seems a thing not natural but painted'.[3] Cosimo the Elder's grandson Lorenzo the Magnificent continued his grandfather's work, notably turning the garden into a sculpture courtyard in which the young Michelangelo studied. The Palazzo Medici certainly stood as a symbol of Medici power, and was a target for the Florentines when they ran the family out of town in 1494. They stripped it of many of its magnificent decorations: Donatello's statues of a stunningly sexual bronze David and a militant Judith, whom the republicans moved to the Palazzo Vecchio to stand as a triumph against tyranny.

In the subsequent decades after the return of the Medici, the family decided for reasons of security to wall up the open loggia originally created on the ground floor of the palace facing out onto the Via Larga. They used a design by Michelangelo, produced by the artist around 1517, to fill in the open space with windows of 'extraordinary beauty'. Inflated hyperbolic volutes employed under the window sills suggested they were carrying an especially heavy load, a symbol of the gravitas of the Medici family. As such, the windows, anthropomorphically kneeling, became known as *finestre inginocchiate*, 'kneeling windows', and came to be used in designs all over Florence to signify loyalty to the Medici.

Not long after Isabella moved into her family's old palace, Michelangelo's windows came to be endowed with even greater value and prestige. On 18 February 1564, their architect, in his eighty-ninth year and in failing health, died in Rome, irritating Isabella's father for having concealed his plans for the facade of the church of San Lorenzo, unfinished to this day. Nonetheless, the duke authorized a magnificent funeral procession for the artist, who had wished to be buried in Florence, that was attended, it seemed, by the entire city, 'who appreciate him much more now than they did when he was alive'.[4] When the coffin was opened at its final destination, the church of Santa Croce, those present marvelled that the body had not decomposed. 'It is a divine sign', some said, 'that the body was not decayed.'[5] Michelangelo had indeed become the *Il Divino* he had believed himself to be. And what Isabella now saw as 'her' windows, a rare piece of secular architecture from their creator's hand, became increasingly sacred.

Paolo and Isabella took on not only Isabella's ancestral residence. Close to the Palazzo Medici was the Palazzo Antinori, whose owners, the Antinori family, were loyal supporters of the Medici and had modelled their own home on their neighbours' palace. They rented a considerable part of it to Paolo Giordano to accommodate the substantial retinue he always brought with him to Florence. Needless to say, this expense, as well as those associated with the Palazzo Medici, all came out of Paolo's own pocket, all year round, even when he was absent from the city.

The expenses for Paolo and Isabella's life at the Palazzo Medici were recorded in *Libri di entrate e uscite* – the double-entry book-keeping system the Medici bankers had helped pioneer over a century ago. This task was the responsibility of their accountant, Gian Battista Capponi, whose family were loyal supporters of Isabella. It covered a myriad of expenditures, beginning with improving the fabric of the palace itself, described as the '*amigliorando* [improvement] *del Palazzo Medici*', which included tasks such as the repointing and whitewashing of Isabella's personal suite of rooms adjoining the palace's cortile and garden.[6] Also under the heading '*amigliorando*' was payment to 'Alberto Fiorentino, *natapharo*', a diver called in 'to clean out the kitchen well, where a cat had fallen in'. Other aquatic expenses included the barrels of water regularly brought from the River Arno 'for the Signora's bath'. In addition, 'Francesco della Camilla *scultore*' was hired to revive the courtyard's fountain.

When Paolo and Isabella moved into the Palazzo Medici, they required new furnishings, mostly chosen by Isabella, such as canopied beds. Under 'the expense of seats' came 'benches for la signora' and four low chairs upholstered in turquoise velvet. Dining sets for thirty-two people were also purchased, giving a sense of the number of guests who would come to dinner. At the same time, costs were incurred from moving belongings in and out of the palace, as when Isabella travelled to spend periods at one of the family villas, she took with her her own bed linen, folding chairs and wall hangings. Another category of expenses was the '*spesa d'arme*' – weapons to protect the establishment, such as crossbows, harquebus, lances and swords. The Palazzo Medici had been built to resemble a strongbox, but it was only as secure as those protecting it were armed, as a former resident, Alessandro de' Medici, had learned to his cost.

The '*spesa di vestire*' – clothing expenses – listed such items as yellow silk purchased to clothe 'His Illustrious Lordship', red silk shoes or a hat 'made with peacock feathers and silver tassels, lined in taffeta, from Andrea Cortesi, known as the rich merchant'. Paolo liked extravagant hats, as Camilla the prostitute had recounted in her trial. His shirts were bought from the Dominican nuns at the convent up the street, Santa Caterina da Siena. The Orsini account also paid for the servants' clothing – a livery for the footmen, for example – and no expense was spared on the quality of these fabrics. Lengths of red and yellow silk and velvet and red taffeta shot with yellow were purchased to dress the household. The palace's ever-growing number of pageboys were dressed in costly blue velvet. These were the teenage sons of Florentine nobles, and there was a great deal of competition among the families to have them placed in the household of one of the Medici, as it was an invaluable means of entrance into, and advancement at, court. For Isabella and her family, it was a means of securing the loyalty of this younger generation. Nor was it cheap to feed and clothe this army of teenagers, not to mention the washing of their clothes. The washerwoman, Caterina *lavanderia*, was kept busy at this task. But while the expenses incurred by pages, these boys from good families, regularly feature across the account books, there was another army of servants who are quite invisible. These were the slaves, some from eastern Europe, others African blacks like the mother of the late Alessandro de' Medici, who lived high up in the Palazzo Medici's attic. Even with such indentured labour, another listed expense was that of *staordimani* – extra pairs of hands – to supplement workers in the kitchen or dining room when needed.

Although the Palazzo Medici had been stripped of many of its original objects, others had come to take their place. A gilded Mercury adorned the fountain in the small cortile, while a bronze horse's head was displayed in the larger courtyard. There were small tables of mother of pearl or alabaster, and silver candelabra. Isabella kept precious objects in the *studiolo*, small study, which she now claimed as hers, such as pieces of ebony or the the skin, complete with head and tail, of an animal only identified as a 'great golden cat', perhaps a puma or a jaguar, 'from the Indias'.[7] Other items would include nautilus cups, elaborately embossed vessels made from the vast sea shells of the same name found in the Pacific and Indian oceans and a fan made from red parrot feathers. There were ancient cameos, figures carved from two-tone onyx, or pieces of agate or coral, all items the Medici family collected avidly. Isabella commissioned some pictures too, including a '*Noli me Tangere*', the dramatic scene where Christ first reveals himself to Mary Magdalene after his resurrection.

Isabella also used Orsini funds for the '*spese di limosine*' – alms giving. These were never vast sums, but they were donated to a variety of institutions and individuals, including 'the poor company of orphans', 'Anna, the poor widow', and nuns from the convent of the Murate. Isabella also paid for the novitiate meal when one Caterina Zoppetta entered the convent of Santa Chiara. '*Le spese di limosine*' also encompassed the cost of the wine 'ordered by the Signora to give to Captain Saldano, who came before the Illustrious Signora on Good Friday to beg for charity', as well as 'two bottles of wine' for her confessor. Isabella also ordered that the troubled Carlo Fortunati, the son of her maidservant and a murderer once banned from Florence, be given money as 'alms' as well.

A large proportion of funds were directed towards 'the expense of hunting', 'the expense of the stable' and 'the expense of the coach'. Hunting required the purchase of dogs and hawks and payment of the salaries of those who looked after them, such as 'Moretta da Melia, who governs the dogs' – the chief kennel man. Both canines and birds of prey were heavy consumers of meat, and the birds needed hoods, made from beautifully tooled leather, the hounds collars and leashes. The sport also necessitated the procurement of further weapons, not to mention the horses. These animals were like a court unto themselves, with their own litany of servants, groomsmen and stable boys to take care of them. A stable boy was described as a *famiglio*, a familiar of the stable, and there were around fifteen of them in number, several of them from further north, such as Cesare da Modena and Geronimo Piacentino (from Piacenza). Paolo and Isabella still stabled mules, primarily for the use of Isabella's ladies-in-waiting, but whereas mules might have once outnumbered horses in a stable, it was now the other way around. All the animals required tack: bits, bridles, velvet trappings. Pisicotto the saddler was paid the substantial sum of 126 *scudi* to make saddles for the mounts of Isabella and her ladies.

The kings of this stable were two stallions: an Arabian, described as '*il cavallo turcho*', and a black one, '*il morello*', whom Paolo liked to use for his travels between Rome and Florence. Copious correspondence passed between Paolo and his stable manager as they looked for appropriate additions to his *equipe*. One had 'good form, but is a little bit capricious', another had 'a beautiful face, and is a sincere horse, but is coldly melancholic'. Such descriptions give a good sense of Paolo Giordano and his associates' understanding of, and obsession with, the relationship between equine personality and performance. There was also a hunter and a *chinea*, a hacking horse, in the stable specifically for Isabella's use, but her real pride and joy were the four white coach horses she had secured, who were perfectly matched. She had tried and failed to get her brother Francesco to part with a chestnut horse who would match one she already had in her stables. She became equally jealous of her white ponies, which she hated to loan out. 'Tell your coachman he had better be careful with my little white horses,' she warned her husband when he persuaded her to let him borrow them.[8]

Sourcing identical equines was a by-product of what had become only quite recently the latest, most luxurious and expensive status symbol in Italy: the coach, or *cocchio* or *carrozza*. Up until the mid sixteenth century, the Italian carriage had changed little since the times of ancient Rome. Not much more than a covered wagon, it had little to protect a passenger from the jostles and jolts of the road. It was a slow and unglamorous form of transportation, not one the fashion-conscious Italian elite would willingly seek out. However, in the early sixteenth century the Hungarians devised a spring suspension system for carriages. This new invention provided a much faster and smoother ride in coaches described by the Italians as *carrozza all'ongaresca*. And as roads further improved, the coach became an ever-greater object of desire.

As fashionable young nobles, Paolo and Isabella were first in line for a coach, wanting at least one for themselves at the Palazzo Medici. The cost of the vehicle was such that Cosimo actually advanced Paolo 105 *scudi* to pay for its red leather upholstery alone. More money was spent on painting the frame in red and gilt.

Riding the streets of Florence in a coach painted red and gold and drawn by four white horses would certainly have created a dashing sight. The Florentine writer Lionardo Salviati boasted of the time Isabella actually sent her grand coach to bring him to her house. She also procured a more stately but no less eye-catching means of transportation: a *lettica*, or litter, which she had outfitted in peacock-blue velvet and brocade. Litters had traditionally been employed by pregnant women or by the sick, as being carried through the streets was certainly more comfortable and less bumpy than riding a horse or going by coach. Isabella was always prone to exaggerate her ailments and to discuss them in detail – descriptions of an ear infection she suffered featured regularly in court dispatches – but her illnesses never prevented her from attending hunts and parties. Consequently, one might suppose that what Isabella, in her early twenties, found appealing about a litter was appearing in public raised up on such an opulent platform, as if this Medici princess was the Queen of Sheba, first lady of Florence, if not, in her mind, the entire world.

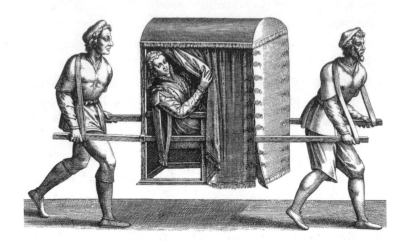

CHAPTER 3

Debt

All of the expenses associated with the maintenance of the Palazzo
Medici – horses, dogs, servants, food – were the responsibility of Paolo
Giordano. These were the *uscite*, outgoings, which always outstripped
any income, *entrate*, recorded in the account books. Paolo was accustomed to living with debt; in fact, he could barely remember a time in
his life without it. By the age of fifteen he had already been obliged to
turn over the rents from part of his estate to the Florentine merchants
the Bandini in order to satisfy an outstanding account of 14,000 *scudi*.
Accepting debt as a way of life meant Paolo never hesitated to engage
in more and more spending. It is true that for the nobility there was a
certain prestige associated with debt, in that it was a recognition that
one's name and personal worth were such that one could be granted
easy credit. But Paolo saw no shame where others would in parting
with portions of his land to pay off the creditors from whom he had
purchased golden spurs, not just for himself, but for those in his retinue. Other precious items he was obliged to sell included the jewellery
Benvenuto Cellini had designed for his mother's wedding. He would
sacrifice such exquisite items to finance his continued acquisition of

Lady in a litter

jewels of lesser worth. A pendant 'set with an emerald, a little ruby and a pearl' from his inheritance was estimated at 12,000 *scudi* when it went on the market.[1] His biggest expense by far, however, was the horses, which he seemed unable to stop purchasing. One of his accountants back in Rome told him frankly that the Orsini estate would not be so badly in debt 'were it not for the superfluous and damaging expense at Bracciano, of which the major part, or in fact almost all, result from the blessed stable. However, things might be resolved if it would please you to restrict yourself to five or six horses, and to send away the others which cause such superfluous and damaging expense.'[2]

Paolo also frequently ignored such necessary expenses as feeding his servants in favour of more exotic outgoings. As one Orsini servant wrote gloomily back home to Bracciano in December 1563: 'There are triumphal arches, jousts, hunts and such costumes that you could not imagine the money spent on them, but as for us courtiers we cannot touch any funds for household management or to put the palace in order.'[3] Still the debts accumulated, exacerbated by the mismanagement of the Bracciano estate by its *fattore* Giulio Folco, who was subsequently imprisoned for embezzlement. But for his own private reasons that were never made clear, Paolo insisted upon Folco's release, declaring his name had been unjustly blackened, and rehired him. However, Isabella certainly did not trust him, as she made very apparent in a letter she wrote to Folco regarding some important items he was supposed to have acquired on her behalf:

> Everything I have ever seen from you makes me feel as if my stomach is suffering from bad digestion. Let me tell you that I am not one to be played about with, and do not think that you can show me white for black just because I normally deal with people who tell me things clearly and not with a thousand lies and strategies as you have shown me. I saw what you wrote to Gianozzo Cepparello [her business manager] regarding those provisions coming from Naples, to which I say to you that you had better immediately remit the money to me, and do not give me any more excuses, and don't imagine that these few little words will be all from me. I strongly

recommend that you immediately put a copy of that contract in the post to me, and tell me exactly where my jewel is.[4]

Folco had been the appointment of Paolo's uncle, Cardinal Sforza. The Medici family became increasingly certain that he too had not resisted the temptation to appropriate funds from his nephew's estate, which might explain why he had been able to afford Michelangelo as the architect of his chapel in Santa Maria Maggiore in Rome. When he died, Isabella told her husband quite bluntly: 'I cannot say anything other than that I wish to say that his sins do not merit any lesser punishment. I could make infinite more comments, but I will stop for now as fatigue assassinates me.'[5]

Isabella was never ever thrifty. She knew her father Cosimo would ensure her outstanding debts were paid before too long. In February and April 1567, Cosimo released a total of 4,000 *scudi* 'to be paid to the creditors of the Lady Isabella, daughter to His Excellency'. Among those listed were: 'Marco Giachini, merchant [a total of 750 *scudi*], Costanzo Gavezzini, velvet maker, 200 *scudi*, Giovambattista Bernardi and company, *battilori*, 200 *scudi*, and maestro Vicenzo di maestro Carlo, *tiraloro*, 100 *scudi*.' Both these last were specialists in the weaving of gold thread. The list of creditors also included 'Agnolo Alessandrini and company, linen workers, 100 *scudi*, Bartolomeo da Filichaia and company, silk merchants, 100 *scudi* [and another half a dozen silk merchants too], Soldo del Cegia, furrier, 24 *scudi*, Maestro Berto Cino, slipper maker, 50 *scudi*.' It might seem surprising that a Medici princess might owe 200 *scudi* to 'Francesco Gaburri and company, *rigattieri*' – second-hand dealers.[6] However, during the Renaissance there was no social stigma attached to the second-hand market in clothing and precious textiles; indeed value could be added dependent upon the provenance.

Cosimo also gave Isabella a personal allowance, although she frequently spent it before the next one was due. She was thrilled to learn that he was going to advance her 4,000 *scudi*. 'I can pay my debts, and then I can live like a queen,' she crowed to Paolo.[7]

Despite this apparently breezy attitude and the certainty that her father would always come to her assistance, Isabella would take action if she thought the household finances were really out of control. 'I have had Gian Battista Capponi come over with the books so I can go through them. The house is going into the greatest ruin,' she wrote frankly to Paolo in Rome in July 1566.[8] By contrast, Paolo seems to have never voluntarily called upon a bookkeeper to try to ascertain the extent of his financial problems. He was always keen to see what sums of money Isabella could advance him. His response to her news of her pending 4,000 *scudi* was to ask if she would be able to let him have 500, and Isabella was forced to backtrack on her boasts of queendom: 'It's all promised to the merchants with the exception of 300 *scudi*,' she told him in reply.[9]

To raise money Paolo would also pawn items as collateral. He went to Jewish moneylenders, such as Daniello Barocco '*hebreo*', where he received 115 *scudi* for three silver candlesticks, and Gian Battista Cossetti, from whom he got 215 *scudi* for an assortment of silver plates and flasks.[10] He pawned cloth as well, with some silk hangings raising him eighty-two *scudi*. Other items made their way to the Monte di Pietà, including a carpet from the Levant, a gilded cup and a silver bed warmer. Even if pawning was an established means of raising money among the Italian nobility, they preferred that the transactions took place away from their native cities so as to disassociate themselves from any potential stigma. Isabella as a nineteen-year old had negotiated with Venice, while Paolo did business in Florence rather than his native Rome.

It is a sign of the extent to which Florence's Monte di Pietà had become an extension of the Medici domain, staffed by Medici officials, that Isabella also took loans on her own behalf from the Monte. She offered jewels as collateral for such sums as 2,000 *scudi*, but the proximity of the Monte meant she would get them back much more quickly. Cosimo, true to his banking blood, had turned the institution once designed to protect the poor from '*gli ebrei*', the Jews, into one designed to benefit his family, offering low-interest loans such as the following, which Isabella signed: 'It pleases Her Illustrious Excellency to promise and irrevocably pay to the Office of the Monte di Pietà 12,000 ducats in cash and interest over three years at the rate of 5% a year, from the assignment given by the Lord our Duke . . .'[11]

Isabella would pawn some jewels or arrange loans to tide her over, if necessary. Paolo Giordano, however, was willing to continue to sell parcels of his land and other property to meet his creditors' demands, and such action made Cosimo very uneasy. He had arranged Paolo's marriage to Isabella in part to safeguard Medici terrain in the south. If his son-in-law's patrimony fell into the hands of others, it rendered the marriage almost pointless. Consequently, Cosimo decided to take the step of advancing Paolo an enormous loan, using as cash some of Eleonora's inheritance. 'Signor Paolo has told me that His Excellency will lend him 100,000 *scudi* to pay off his debts, in return for the rights to the estate's income, to be returned in five years' time,' Ridolfo Conegrano informed Alfonso d'Este in February 1563.[12] The Orsini duke had exaggerated: the loan was actually 30,000 *scudi*, and Cosimo did more than secure the estate's income against it. A year later he bought back two Orsini fiefdoms, Isola and Baccano, from the Florentine merchants the Cavalcanti, to whom Paolo had sold the land to pay off yet another debt. But the land was then made into an irreversible donation to Isabella, thereby guaranteeing her some income from this precarious spousal source.

This 30,000 *scudi* loan was still not enough, however. Three years later, Paolo would announce once more: 'Being resolved to get certain annoyances off my shoulders, that is to say those debts I have, for the sake of expedience, taken the decision to sell some of my property.'[13] And the cash loans from the Medici continued as well. By 1568, the Monte di Pietà had financed a loan so vast they had to break it into separate accounts. Moreover, because it went way beyond their ordinary terms, they kept the recipient's identity something of a secret, only identifying him by his initials. But the initials inscribed against this 40,000 *scudi* loan were easily recognizable: 'P.G.O.'

CHAPTER 4

Conflict

Despite the extra financial burden of maintaining a Florentine residence for himself and his wife, Paolo Giordano had made some profit through his association with the Medici. Benefits had come to him by way of the warm relationship between Cosimo and Pope Pius IV, who had, among other things, raised the Orsini lord to the exalted position of duke. Pius's successor, Pius V, the Lombard Michele Ghislieri, was inclined to be similarly well disposed towards him, and in 1566 he nominated Paolo as governor general of the Catholic Church, in charge of the papal troops. As a soldier of the church, the newly nominated governor general felt an appropriate change in demeanour was necessary. Paolo told his wife: 'I have taken the way of Christ, that is to be a good Christian, and every morning I hear Mass, have the table blessed and overall I live like a Christian whereas before I was a dissolute and a wretch.'[1]

Isabella was profoundly sceptical of her husband's pious conversion and responded in sarcastic tones: 'So now that you have become a good Christian I have begun to be read to when dining in order to become accustomed to the ways of monks, and as I see you taking such a way may God let you persevere, as Our Lord commands that you wish only for one wife, and you do not desire the women of others, and I would be the happiest woman in the world if you were to observe these two things. But let me leave off the teasing, because I am greatly pleased about this favour from our lord [the Pope].'² Significantly, in her apparently affectionate banter she did not allude to another point Paolo had made to her in his letter: that if he were the governor general of the Catholic Church, it would be 'best that you come to live with me in Rome'. He needed the dignity of an attendant wife, as he informed Cosimo: 'I am writing to Your Excellency to allow me the favour of having my wife come to Rome, as I am in service to His Holiness, who every day does me a thousand favours, and as I desire to continue in such service, I believe that Your Excellency will give your consent to my request.'³

But Isabella was not going to Rome, and in any case Paolo ruled himself out of this coveted position before even taking it up. Notwithstanding his newly declared piety, and ever enamoured of pomp and admiration, he had immediately availed himself of all the attendant regalia of the Pope's governor general, including a standard embossed with the papal symbol of the keys of St Peter. This he rashly displayed to the French ambassador before Pius V had officially announced his appointment, a breach of decorum that shocked all at the Vatican. The Pope was said to be so appalled by Paolo's inability to observe protocol that he withdrew the offer of the position – 'a most strong rebuke', as some commented.⁴ But protocol had been breached before without such drastic consequences. The possibility that Cosimo had played a part in persuading Pius V to rescind the post cannot be ruled out. Certainly, this diminution in Paolo's status rather negated the necessity of Isabella being by his side in Rome.

Cosimo was also displeased by the fact that it was the French ambassador Paolo had been attempting to impress. Cosimo did make occasional apparently friendly gestures towards France, sometimes as a means of playing that country off against the Habsburgian Spain and the Holy Roman Empire in order to ensure he was not taken for granted as some imperial pawn. But as far as he was concerned, Paolo lacked the ability for that kind of political finesse and so was meant to follow the imperial path Cosimo had laid down for him. Paolo had begun to chafe at being held to this prescribed fealty. The Orsini were historically soldiers and supporters of France, and Paolo found himself further seduced by the flattering overtures from the French as they attempted to persuade him to return his loyalty to their side. From the French perspective, Paolo, as head of Bracciano, brought with him support and soldiers from other members of the vast house of Orsini as a matter of course. With the Wars of Religion, the ongoing battles between the Catholic French crown and the country's Huguenots, not to mention increasing hostilities between France and the Habsburg crown, the vast manpower of the Orsini was something worth securing.

Paolo, excited about the prospect of fighting for France, was equally resentful of the lack of lucrative military commissions from the Spanish, who were understandably reluctant to give him a post requiring good management and strategic skills when he administered his own lands so poorly. He wrote to Isabella telling her he believed he had lost the position of governor general because he had been maligned by the Spanish ambassador, and he only acted as a servant of Spain due to the 'dependence and relationship I have' with Cosimo. He also mentioned his pleasure at receiving the French ambassador in Rome, who he explained was prepared to offer him a commission with France. Isabella perceived immediately what was happening and told her father. Medici father and daughter decided that the renegade husband had to be finessed to a certain degree, his pride already severely wounded at having been denied the governor generalship. In this instance, Cosimo would not directly intervene to redirect his son-in-law's allegiance. Instead, Isabella sent her husband a response using the same kind of blunt language her father adopted when dealing with the wayward:

> It seems strange to me that you wish to abandon the certain for the uncertain and that you would wish to present to the world a malleable brain, as would be the case if you were to do such a thing . . . I wish you to take account of the fact that if the French ambassador comes with this commission, that I do not believe it, because if it were real the King would have written you a letter and not sent him

just to simply tell you by word of mouth. However, let us suppose that the ambassador has such a commission, then I beg of you to take to heart the example of those others who have served France, but have not had anything they have been promised, and they will lead you in such a way, they will promise you oceans and mountains, and you will get absolutely nothing. You can stay with King Philip of Spain without any obligation and I wish to suggest to you that he has more need of you. In times of peace, King Philip has given more to you than any other Italian cavalier, and if you wait he will give you more . . . Give caresses to every one, but know the difference between those who are your real friends and those that would do you damage . . .

Isabella softened her directives by claiming that ultimately these were her husband's decisions to make. 'If you wish to be French, then I will be French, if you are Imperial, then I am Imperial. You being much more wise than I, I will leave you to decide for yourself.'[5] But such wifely subservience was the literary rhetoric with which Isabella invariably decorated her letters to her husband. Paolo Giordano understood the message. The Medici wished him to remain with Spain.

Isabella was thus charged with managing Paolo in such a way as to ensure that he followed the path of her father's interests, as well as her own. As they grew older, the challenges and the tensions of their relationship multiplied. Paolo recognized that contrary to a custom that united societies the world over, his wife was not his to command; Isabella was her father's creature, not his. His requests, for he could never demand, that she come to Rome to his domain had little to do with genuine affection on his part for Isabella and more to do with his sense of honour, pride and masculinity. This was the era in which the codpiece as fashion accessory grew to outsize proportions, an indication of the supposed giant within, but a wife beyond Paolo's reach made such trappings an idle boast.

And Isabella, having spent that dreary December trapped up at Bracciano, was determined never to repeat the experience. Her line of resistance against her husband's petitions was to claim that despite her eagerness to come to Paolo in Rome, she would need to ask her father for permission. Cosimo would turn out to be indisposed and not ready to acquiesce, and then other matters would intervene until Paolo was eventually overwhelmed by other matters. At other times, Isabella would apply more subtle tricks, as she reveals in this letter to her husband: 'I promise you that I am completely set on coming to Rome. I do desire to have the certainty confirmed, because my brother the cardinal has told me that he would want to come stay with us, and he too wants to know the certainty and the exact date.' Then Isabella segues into the following news: 'Cardinal Farnese has arrived here and the duke and cardinal have given him a thousand caresses, God remains satisfied that he is lodged in the prince's [Francesco's] palace, and my brother never leaves him alone.'[6] Cardinal Alessandro Farnese was Paolo's cousin and a personal enemy of the Bracciano duke. Isabella knew that the thought of the cardinal in Florence as a Medici favourite would certainly distract her husband from thoughts of whether she was coming to Rome. Even if Cosimo told Paolo Isabella could go to Rome, he had no hesitation on going back on his word. 'From Signor Latino Orsini', wrote Paolo to Isabella one time, 'I received news that has put your coming here in doubt for not having had permission from the Duke my lord, and I take infinite displeasure from this news as he has gone back on his promise.'[7]

Although Paolo and Isabella's letters often read like the correspondence of a most loving couple, conflict between the pair manifested itself in different ways. Isabella showed considerable disregard for the Orsini name. While she would sign herself as 'Isabella Medici Orsini', she rarely appended 'Duchess of Bracciano' after her name, and those around her simply referred to her as 'Signora Isabella'. Her significance, influence and position rested on the fact that she was a Medici by birth, not an Orsini by marriage, as can be seen in the design of the dedication to her of a little book of poetry. 'Isabella de' Medici' occupies a single line in block capitals and her married name and title appear on the next line, in fainter typeface, almost as an afterthought. Whenever Isabella referred to 'the duke my lord', she always meant her father, not her husband. She was a Medici first and foremost, she did not think of herself as an Orsini. For Paolo Giordano, if there was one thing of which he had reason to be proud, it was the antiquity of his house. He had no interest in putting its financial business in order, but he is credited with creating 'the archive' of his family papers, thus creating a record of his family history. He knew that the venerability of his name once so appealed to the mercantile Medici that they were willing to acquire an Orsini bride without a dowry – Clarice, Isabella's great-great-grandmother – and now Paolo did all he could to remind the world of the fame of his line. He commissioned the Venetian writer Francesco Sansovino to produce *The History of the Orsini Family*, for which he gave the writer the rental income of a slaughterhouse and attendant butcher's shop in the Orsini domain of Cerveteri. Given the Orsini history as soldiers for hire, such a payment has a certain symmetry.

In this dense tome, which appeared in 1565, Sansovino underscored the length of the family's history, lauded the brave deeds of Orsini warriors of the past and, not surprisingly, concluded with a panegyric to the book's patron himself. For this last task, the author had rather limited material with which he could work, the worthy activities of the Orsini duke being rather limited. Sansovino praised his 'handsome, large and well-formed stature, a face which alters between laughter and seriousness, and with a benign aspect which mirrors the excellent qualities of his generous heart'. Cosimo and Isabella would have been surprised to read his conclusion, an explanation of how the Medici duke had come to choose Paolo as his daughter's bridegroom:

> Having earned a supreme title of excellence, a fine soul, and infinitely valorous, which have made him like a king . . . having maintained his estate through the dangerous wars of the kingdom, and shown military prowess, Lord Cosimo de' Medici, estimated by all as the most prudent and fortunate prince, recognizing with exquisite judgement the virtues of this lord . . . made him his son-in-law, giving him the Lady Isabella as his wife, a woman whose incomparable goodness, courtesy and worth make her in no way dissimilar to her excellent consort.[8]

If this book, with its manifestly false account of the reasons why Cosimo selected Paolo as her husband, was designed to impress

Isabella, then it failed. She might have had an Orsini for an ancestor, but that mattered very little to her. All that concerned her was the Medici name. She had grown up in a world surrounded by emblems of the greatness of her family. She believed in nothing but Medici primacy, which she cited in a fight between herself and her husband that reportedly took place in the wake of the composition of the Orsini family history. In the midst of the row, Paolo told her: 'Ultimately, I am of greater standing than Your Excellency.' In retort, Isabella scoffed: 'The Medici, for greatness and magnificence, are the first princes of Italy, after His Holiness the Pope, and you, ultimately, are no more than a feudatory of the Holy Church.'⁹ Paolo did not make a verbal reply to Isabella's taunt, which alluded to the manner in which he had acquired the dukedom. Instead, he slapped his wife's face. As one knows from the trial of Camilla the Skinny, in which the prostitute recounted Paolo shoving her around, this incident would not have been the first time Paolo physically assaulted a woman.

Isabella, in a rare letter revealing a more brutal reality of the relationship between herself and her husband, may have alluded to this event or perhaps another similar incident after which the couple had parted ways. In February 1565, she wrote to Paolo in Florence from Pisa, to where she had evidently retreated: 'I am finally writing to you because I was, and with reason, of the same opinion that first I should tell the duke my lord of the injuries I have received from you, but I am now resolved that it is better for us if I do not speak of this to anyone as it is so very prejudicial. You should better know your error, which is so very great . . . to come to be my husband is to bear my honour, as well as yours. I am content in pardoning you as long as you take some remedy . . .'¹⁰

Although Isabella does not specify the nature of the 'injuries' Paolo dealt her, it seems most likely they were verbal and physical. She would not be so offended by adulterous behaviour on his part because that she would take for granted. However, violence against her person was an astonishingly injurious assault upon her honour. Nobody hit a Medici princess as if she were a common prostitute. Moreover, although Isabella claimed she was keeping this matter a secret between them, she knew full well that by putting into writing an allusion to injuries she had received from her husband they were now on record. She might say that she had not told her father, but Paolo knew the chances were good that Cosimo had learned of his transgressions. Isabella might not be able to strike her husband with her fists, but she had another, much stronger weapon: she possessed Cosimo, against whom Paolo, so deeply in debt, was powerless. As long as Isabella had Cosimo there was no battle Paolo could triumph in against his wife, no argument he could win, nothing he could make her do that was against her will. On this occasion, as perhaps on others, he had resorted to his only remaining means of dominating her: his physical strength. Yet Paolo knew that as long as Isabella had her *babbo*, laying a finger on his daughter was very ill-advised indeed.

CHAPTER 5

The Baroncelli

With work on the Uffizi nearer to completion, Cosimo de' Medici charged Giorgio Vasari with yet another architectural project. His task this time, which he began in early 1564, was to design and build the covered raised walkway known today as the Vasari Corridor. The corridor connects the Uffizi with the Palazzo Pitti on the other side of the River Arno, using as part of its support one side of the most ancient of Florence's bridges, the Ponte Vecchio, and exiting into the Boboli Gardens. The new structure allowed Cosimo, his family and his court to pass securely and privately between these two establishments, turning them into one massive monolithic Medicean institution. Beneath them, literally and figuratively, the rest of Florence went about its business, using the Ponte Vecchio to cross from one side of the city to the other or to purchase items in one of the small shops which had spanned the bridge since its inception in the thirteenth century.

The building of the Vasari Corridor marked Cosimo's connection with the Arno and the land on either side of the river. The following year he had the level of the river banks from the Ponte Vecchio to the Ponte Santa Trinità raised, 'pleasing everyone with the beautiful view

The Baroncelli villa, circa 1550

it allowed of the waters of the Arno'.[1] The raised banks also reduced, although never eliminated, the perennial risk of the Arno flooding the city. The Santa Trinità bridge itself, originally built in 1252, had suffered major damage in a great flood in 1557, and Cosimo had hoped that Michelangelo would undertake the restoration of this important conduit. While Il Divino did produce some sketches, it was the ubiquitous Ammannati who would eventually bring the design to completion in 1567. Nonetheless, the bridge, connecting the wider thoroughfares of the Oltr'arno with the rest of Florence, clearly bears the mark of Michelangelo. The graceful elongated lines of the three elliptical arches define the bridge, and it has the same elastic quality as the bracket details of that other Michelangelo Medici project, the Laurentian Library vestibule. One has to be reminded that what stands today is actually an exact replica of the sixteenth-century Santa Trinità bridge, blown up by German mines in 1944 to prevent Allied troops from crossing over. The more idiosyncratically charming Ponte Vecchio, which could not have withstood the tanks, was spared, and it so happened it was the Vasari Corridor which provided the line of communication between the Tuscan resistance and the Allied troops.

Isabella was also very interested in what lay on the other side of the river, for she had decided she wanted to establish her own presence there. However, such a negotiation was one that required the support of her brother Francesco. He had returned home to Florence from Spain in the autumn of 1563. His personality seemed not much improved. Rather it had worsened, for now complementing his original lack of charm was the dourness and aloofness of manner which was the signature of many Spanish courtiers. Cosimo wished to keep his potentially wayward son occupied. Feeling that the twenty-two-year-old *principe* was in need of further training for the role he would one day occupy as Medici ruler, he gave him greater responsibility in the running of the state. He was careful to ratify Francesco's role in the eyes of other Italian rulers, sending out this message to the Duke of Mantua, among others: 'As it is my custom to communicate with friends in whom I trust, I am pleased to deposit into the hands of the Prince my son the care and government of my estates . . . the peace that exists today in Italy permits me to do this, and the knowledge that

I have of my son's inclination for intelligent negotiations which satisfies me.'² As such, when in January 1565 Isabella had a particular request, Cosimo instructed his daughter to address it to her brother: 'Because for so many years', explained the twenty-two-year-old Isabella, 'I have desired a villa near to Florence, I wish to beg Your Excellency to grant me the Baroncelli. In doing so you would be granting me not only the comfort I would obtain from having the villa, but it would be the most singular favour because it would be from the hands of Your Excellency . . .'³

The villa of the Baroncelli, later known as Poggio Imperiale, after the Habsburg Maria Maddalena d'Austria, Cosimo II de' Medici's wife, acquired it in the seventeenth century, radically altering and enlarging it, now functions as a school. On the Arcetri hills near Florence's Porta Romana, its grounds met those of the Pitti Palace. The merchant Jacopo Baroncelli had originally built the villa in the fifteenth century as a simple rectangular sequence of rooms surrounding a courtyard. However, his family, facing bankruptcy in 1487, were forced to sell it to a creditor, Agnolo Pandolfini, who in turn sold it in 1548 to the banker Piero Salviati. He invested heavily in the property, remodelling and embellishing it with splendid and sought-after objects. Notably, these included a vast painting by Andrea del Sarto, the great painter of 1520s Florence, depicting the *Assumption of the Virgin*. The picture is beautiful in its jewel-like tones and Leonardoesque *sfumato* painterly technique, the brush strokes smoke-like, without beginning or end. It served as the altarpiece for the villa's adjacent chapel and can now be viewed in the Galleria Palatina in the Pitti Palace.

However, upon Salviati's death Cosimo confiscated the villa and its contents, along with the rest of the Salviati estate, exploiting a law he had passed recently in which the Florentine state was authorized to seize the property of all rebels. While Piero Salviati had been conspicuously loyal, or at least inconspicuously disloyal, to the Medici family, his son Alessandro had become an anti-Medicean rebel. In 1554, he had joined Pirro Strozzi's troops in Siena to fight against those of Cosimo. After his defeat and capture, Cosimo, a Salviati on his mother's side, offered him the opportunity to repent. Alessandro refused, and was executed in 1555. Cosimo waited for Piero's death a decade later to enact his revenge upon the rest of the Salviati family, who would pay the severest penalty for Alessandro's treachery – the loss of their estate. At the same time, Cosimo could turn a profit.

As part of his new duties, Francesco de' Medici was placed in charge of distributing the spoils of the Salviati estate, ensuring the Medici did not just benefit financially from the disbursement but politically as well. The Baroncelli was the jewel in the crown of the Salviati holdings. Like the Pitti, it was a suburban villa, with sufficient grounds to make one feel as if one was deep in the countryside, yet at the same time the centre of Florence was less than a mile away. Moreover, its new occupant would be the recipient of its original furnishings, courtesy of the Salviati, including the magnificent Del Sarto painting. Many were anxious for such a prize, but Isabella was determined that she would be its recipient.

Francesco had other ideas. 'I cannot really write about your desire for the Baroncelli,' he wrote to his sister a few days after her request. 'Everything in this confiscation has yet to be liquidated, but in any case, it seems to me that you do not lack for villas, as you can use any of our family's as if they were your own.'⁴ Isabella, not satisfied with this response, did what she would always do in such circumstances: she went to her *babbo*. Cosimo might have placed Francesco in charge of the Salviati confiscation, but his was still the ultimate power in the family, and he prioritized satisfying his daughter's desires over the authority he had given his son. 'Give it to her,' was the command he issued to Francesco, as if his two children were fighting over a toy. Francesco, undoubtedly irritated that Isabella had got her own way, not to mention the fact that she now had something he did not have – a villa which she did not have to share with anyone – was forced to give in.

It was not long before the Baroncelli was Isabella's very own – '*la mia villa*', as she referred to it to everyone, including her husband. There was no shared ownership of the Baroncelli, still the villa's official name, as far as Isabella was concerned, and she wasted no time in putting her personal stamp upon the property. To make sure that the villa could be associated with the Medici name from afar, she had the walls embellished with hundreds of round spheres, the Medici *palle*.

But that was not her sole contribution to its adornment and improvement. As one contemporary commented:

> When the villa of the Baroncelli was benignly given by the Most Serene Duke to his family, it was not the palace nor villa of the beauty, greatness and magnificence that we see today. For the palace was beautified and enlarged by the Lady Isabella, as one can see by the inscription of her name in many parts. She planned the rooms and the garden walls, and beautified it with fountains, and little gardens, and improved the houses of the workers . . . All of these improvements cost tens of thousands of *scudi*.[5]

On the farm lands beyond the formal gardens there was a vineyard, fruit and olive trees and an aviary. Isabella also acquired other pieces of property, such as the land belonging to the Medici court painter Santi di Tito. These allowed her to build an additional roadway going down into Florence past the church of San Felice, rendering easier access to her new possession.

Isabella's greatest pleasure was in turning the gardens into a fantasy world inhabited by the gods, like those she had grown up in at Castello and also mimicking those of the neighbouring Boboli Gardens. Sculptural pieces that arrived to embellish the villa's gardens included a marble statue of the female figure of abundance, Dovizia, a symbol always very dear to Florence, large lustrous marble heads and marble water basins. From Rome Isabella imported 'two modern granite panels, a pile of marble in the form of a sepulchre [probably an ancient Roman sarcophagus], and a similarly ancient head of a Roman woman'.[6]

From the sculptor Vincenzo de' Rossi, who was in her family's service, Isabella acquired two highly admired sculptures, still present in the Medici collections. Both works are bigger-than-life-size statues of naked male figures, which provide a significant clue to the kind of independence Isabella enjoyed. Noblewomen did not, as a rule, commission sculpture, and the artwork that they did purchase was invariably of a religious or moralistic nature, not overt erotica. In just about any other environment, it would have been unthinkable that a woman would select what Isabella was able to choose from Rossi.

One statue, a *Bacchus with Satyr* which now resides in the Boboli Gardens, gives a sense of the magic these sculptures would have wrought on Isabella's gardens. Bacchus, grapes entwined in his curly hair, stands, his strong legs firmly planted on the plinth, his muscular torso rippling, with a hand to his brow, his gaze directed out into the distance. The little satyr peers out from behind his legs. Originally situated on the hill on which Isabella's villa stands, the statue was positioned in such a way that Bacchus would appear to be looking out onto the terrain beneath him. The relationship between the verdant landscape and the grey stone sculpture was thus activated, bringing Bacchus and his companion to life.

The other sculpture Isabella procured from Vincenzo de' Rossi was a *Dying Adonis*. This work depicted the god lying prone, his beautiful face racked in agony, while the boar, sent by an angry Diana to destroy him, goring him and causing his demise, lies at his feet. Isabella chose such a subject at least in part to display her erudition, as in ancient times the cult of Adonis was one to which young women like herself dedicated themselves. But perhaps also embedded in her choice of sculpture is some part of the tale of herself and her brother Giovanni, who, like Adonis, was cruelly taken before his time. Isabella could recognize herself in Adonis's lover, Venus, and the goddess's devastated reaction to his death, as described by Ovid in his *Metamorphoses*, poetry which Isabella, schooled in the classics, knew so well: 'When looking down from the lofty sky, she saw him nearly dead, his body bathed in blood, she leaped down – tore her garment – tore her hair, and beat her bosom with distracted hands. And blaming Fate, she said, "But not everything is at the mercy of your cruel power. My sorrow for Adonis will remain, enduring as a lasting monument."'[7] And indeed, to accompany Adonis, Isabella commissioned another statue to stand in her garden: a 'life-like Venus in marble', also naked, whose downward gaze could be directed to the marble form of her dying lover.[8]

The statue of Adonis in her garden might, then, have reminded Isabella of Giovanni and how she had lost him. The pair, who loved spending time together at one of the family's many country residences, had perhaps talked of possessing a villa together. They could have embellished it with the antiquities that the brother and sister, not yet out of their teens, had begun to collect voraciously, fabricating a world of their own, exclusive to themselves. But now Isabella had had to set about this endeavour on her own.

For her, possession of the Baroncelli helped her realize the completion of the construction of her own domain. She boasted of its microclimate – 'the coolest place in summer', she claimed. She wanted to create her own world, which, while it might be a satellite of Cosimo's court, was one she ruled in her own right and could fashion in her own unique image. There was, indisputably, no other woman in Renaissance Italy quite like Isabella. She was young, in her early twenties, and she was childless, a state which would have caused any other married noblewoman shame and despair. But for Isabella, her childfree state, while it made others around her anxious, only served at this time to enhance the independence bestowed upon her by her father. Other women with the degree of autonomy she possessed, such as her husband's grandmother Felice della Rovere, were usually in a position of authority by way of serving as widowed regents of estates. As such, preoccupied with the attendant responsibility, they had little time for themselves and the pursuit of their own pleasures. Although Isabella played her part in Medici machinations, she was not overwhelmed by having to serve the needs of others. Pleasure played an important part in her existence. 'We are out seeking *spassi* [pastimes],' she might say, '*facciamo l'arte di michelaccio*' – 'performing the art of lazing around'.[9]

Still, there is an element of disingenuousness in such declarations. No woman who was single-minded enough to ensure that she got a villa of her very own was truly indolent. Some might see Isabella as a 'daddy's girl' whose possessions and lifestyle were only acquired by way of his authority. But it was Isabella's spirit and intelligence that had won her her father's admiration from an early age and made him want to bestow upon her whatever she desired. In that sense she did not take without giving back; her very existence enhanced the Medici world Cosimo had created. And Isabella was to use her newly acquired possession of the Baroncelli villa as ammunition in launching a new phase of her life. It was to be one in which her qualities and talents – her acknowledged power and influence in her city, her intelligence, love of learning, culture and sociability – truly came into their own. And it was one in which her passion for *spassi* also played a part, bringing not only pleasure but also risk.

CHAPTER 6

The Theatre of Isabella

Isabella's two properties, the Palazzo Medici and the Villa Baroncelli, now provided her with a stage upon she could enact her entertainments and performances: comedies, tragedies and melodramas. In Isabella's world, the line between what was fictive theatre and what was real life could sometimes blur; those around her could become both audience and player in her personal dramas. Small wonder, then, that her favourite holiday was Carnival, the very time when it was hard to distinguish between spectatorship and participation in the celebrations leading up to Lent. Parties and parades were the order of the day. Members of the city's elite sponsored fantastical floats, their name or corporate identity enhanced by these extravaganzas produced for public delight. One year the Capponi family produced a scene of Osiris surrounded by his court, and the corporation of Genoese merchants in Florence organized a *tableau vivant* depicting a bacchanal of Silenus and his merrymakers. No expense was spared, with the actors dressed in an array of silks, velvets, furs and cloth of gold and silver. It seems that it was Isabella's high spirits and love of festivities that spurred the court on to attain the highest level of entertainment

Florentine stage set, 1565

possible. Even Francesco admitted, one year when she and her father were in Pisa for Carnival, that without Isabella 'we don't do anything especially good'.[1]

If Isabella did not have especially maternal instincts towards her younger brothers, she did make sure that Ferdinando could attend Carnival too, as he testified enthusiastically at the age of thirteen: 'I received your letter in which I saw your wish to move me to Florence, which greatly conforms to my own as you can imagine, in order to enjoy the festivities of those few days of Carnival . . . and I shall not be amiss in making sure that I appear on my best behaviour.'[2] Such an assurance might suggest young Ferdinando had not always behaved so well in the past.

In 1565, Isabella commissioned a play for Carnival, *La Gostanza* (*Constance*), from the cleric and satirist Silvano Razzi, who published the work later that year with a lengthy dedication to her, his patron.[3] In keeping with the world-turned-upside-down theme of Carnival, *La Gostanza* was a burlesque farce. Its heroine, the beautiful and intelligent Costanza, was 'a mirror and example of a truly Christian life' who divided her time between a home in Florence and a villa outside the city. Despite a marriage to Leonardo, who has long since disappeared, she is believed to be a virgin and 'constant' to him; what is revealed is that Costanza has, in fact, married another in secret, Antonio. Matters grow complex when Leonardo turns up, but all ends happily when he agrees to marry Antonio's sister.

The audience at *La Gostanza* could not fail to see the parallels between the life of the play's patron and that of its heroine. Here were two young women, one seated among them, the other on the stage, both supposedly faithful to an absentee husband. However, this rather risqué commentary by the prelate Razzi on Isabella's life was sanctioned by the 'anything goes' nature of Carnival, in which nothing is meant to be real and such comments could go unchecked, and were even encouraged.

Isabella had always enjoyed the theatre. At the age of nineteen, she was the dedicatee of a five-act religious play. Beltramo Poggi's *The Finding of the Cross of Jesus Christ* was staged at La Crocetta, a Florentine convent of Dominican tertiaries, and the author dedicated his work when it was in manuscript form to the convent's abbess. Its perform-ance, like those of many others of its time, was aimed at providing both spiritual education and entertainment for the sisters, who also played the parts themselves. Their entertainment value was such that noble-women would pass through the supposedly impermeable convent wall to watch such plays, despite attempts by church authorities to forbid the practice. On the occasion of the staging of Poggi's play, Isabella was the highest-ranking woman in the audience watching the sisters re-enact the finding of the true cross, which had been initiated by a woman, the Emperor Constantine's mother Helena. When it came time to publish his script, Poggi abandoned the dedication to the worthy but less influ-ential abbess and made the Medici princess its dedicatee.[4] However, as was the case with the visual art she commissioned, Isabella did not actively seek to align herself with pious, religious work. Her real inter-ests revolved around the secular and profane.

More than the visual arts, more than theatre, it was music that Isabella loved above all other forms of artistic expression. It allowed her numerous identities: performer, patron, creator, subject, muse. Music was both entertainment and soundtrack, one she could control and manipulate, setting or altering on a whim the mood of the room. To a modern ear, the madrigals of Renaissance Italy can sound uni-formly stately, decorous and rigid in their sweet yet often melan-cholically sonorous harmonies. But for Isabella and her contempo-raries there was astonishing variation and nuance in their songs, mes-sages in the words of the verses and arrangements of the notes not readily perceived by a modern listener. What might also go unheard are the songs' sexual innuendoes. Seemingly chaste lines can be ripe with eroticism, rendering the experience of listening to them all the more seductive. But Isabella's world was not one in which music could be turned on at will. Although Florence had plenty of buskers – *cantam-banchi* – on the street corners, to listen to perfectly trained voices accom-panied by the finest musical instruments, which Isabella possessed, was another thing entirely. To attend a performance of '*belle musiche*' at Isabella's house was a privilege in itself, endowing the songs with further rarefied value. She sought out excellent performers. Paolo Giordano's Roman retinue contained a Neapolitan vocalist – the technique of singers from Naples was already renowned – and Isabella wanted him for herself: 'You would do the greatest favour', wrote Isabella to her husband, 'to send the Neapolitan who sings, because I am missing a vocal part.'[5]

The extent to which Isabella associated herself with the making of music is attested to by the portrait she had painted of herself around the year 1565. *Isabella with Music* depicts the Medici princess posed in a similar position and wearing clothing very much like that she was wearing when she was painted at the age of sixteen, just following her marriage. She is thinner now, but she still has the same smirk around her mouth, although her expression seems a bit more watchful. Isabella is manifestly quite different from her sixteen-year-old self, and as she herself would announce around this time: 'I am not a girl any more, and that which I did not know at that age I know now.'[6] One of her hands still clasps the chain to which her ermine, her fertility talisman, is attached, but the other holds a sheet of music. Isabella was extolled as a musician and poet, and one short composition believed to be by her survives, in which she professes that she would 'live happy and content, as long as my handsome sun shows me his bright rays'.

But then the song laments, 'I am so tormented when I see him fade away, that I would readily die.'[7]

Still, it is surprising that Isabella wishes to be painted with a sheet of music. Such an accessory is a departure from the usual images of young noblewomen, who are rarely accompanied by anything other than a small dog, child or prayer book. It is usually the courtesan who is depicted with a musical instrument or notation, designed to allude to her many talents in the art of seduction. Again, the confidence with which Isabella could appropriate such a symbol is further indication of the singularity of her place in the world, as well as the importance of music to hers.

Any other woman in her position would wish to avoid at all costs any association with a woman of less than impeccable moral conduct, or simply the association with a profession of any sort.

But to associate oneself with the world of the madrigal was to embrace one of romance and sensuality, the words themselves dictating its tone. And Isabella let the words dictate the tone of her own house, one filled, as her frequent guest Ridolfo Conegrano commented, with 'beautiful music'. Isabella's position of authority and influence in the musical sphere went beyond Florence. It was such that the first ever published female composer and singer, Maddalena Casulana, sought and received her patronage. Maddalena was a mezzo-soprano based in Vicenza in the Veneto. She accompanied herself on the lute while she sang, and her unusual life as an independent touring musician must have intrigued Isabella. At the age of twenty-eight she dedicated her first printed book of madrigals, designed for four voices, to the Medici princess with these telling words:

I would like, other than to give Your Excellency some proof of my devotion, to show also to the world (as much as is allowed me in this musical profession) the conceited error of men. They believe themselves so strongly to be the masters of the high gifts of intellect, that, in their opinion, these gifts cannot likewise be shared by women . . . I hope that these works will acquire so much light from the renowned name of Your Excellency to whom I reverently dedicate them, that from this light other, more elevated minds may be kindled . . .[8]

Maddalena indicated her recognition of the rarity of both herself and Isabella as female composers and *cognoscentae* in a profession dominated by male musicians and male patrons. The madrigals that followed in her book feature Isabella as subject, both directly and obliquely, and Isabella undoubtedly heard them for herself at performances at her house. One song, which opens the book and would perhaps have opened a night of music at Isabella's, is a *laude* – a song in praise of Isabella entitled 'How High Your Clear Light Ascends . . . to Isabella Medici Orsini'. Four voices rose to declare:

> Your bright splendour rises so High, O Lady,
> That you appear as a new Sun to our eyes,
> And so gracefully you shine
> That you inflame every soul to offer you praise sublime;
> So let the great, lovely name of Isabella proudly cleave the air.

While the audience might expect a paean of praise to their hostess, they would have been taken by surprise when they heard the name Isabella sung on a high note of B.[9] The high pitch correlated with Isabella's place in the song, an earthly princess turned into an unearthly goddess, a new sun rising higher than all else.

The songs by Maddalena that follow this opening invite the listener into a world of ardent passion, of undying, painful, inextricably entwined love. In another song, the singers proclaim: 'My heart cannot die, I would like to kill it, since that would please you, but it cannot be pulled from your breast . . .'[10] Elsewhere, 'Love engraved your image on my soul. It burns it constantly with such an ardent touch that it is dying.'[11]

Burning for love, dying for love. The audience could hear in these words and music voices ebbing, flowing, throbbing and rising to crescendos. They could perceive not-so-subtle relationships between these declarations of love and the act of making love, from foreplay all the way through to climax. Such musical eroticism was not the sole province of Isabella's court – similar madrigals were sung in Ferrara or Mantua, for example. Less usual was for a noblewoman to be the sole orchestrator of their performance, as Isabella was. Moreover, she knew how songs could be staged and interpreted to send messages and make carefully crafted statements about her life. She commissioned a court poet, Giovan Battista Strozzi, to pen the words for a series of madrigals around the theme of *lontananza* – distance. She instructed Strozzi, when he circulated them, to inscribe that he had written them 'by command of the Lady Isabella, her consort Signor Paolo being in Rome and she in Florence'. The verses declared, in tones similar to the song she herself composed, that with the departure of 'My ardent sun, do I not cry every hour? For it causes me such strong pain . . .'[12]

In such songs, Isabella seems to take on the role of the virtuous and melancholic heroine, lamenting the absence of her husband. One might assume, simply from listening to the words, that the hostess of the events at which these madrigals were performed was bravely enduring her enforced separation from her husband. As she counted the hours to his return, the audience to these songs were guests invited over for the evening to keep a desperately lonely woman company, and consequently they played a part, complicitly or not, in Isabella's theatrics. But the songs' messages were not solely for the benefit of those listening. Printed or passed around from court to court, they would travel beyond the walls of her house.

That is not to say that Paolo was always absent. He was sometimes the co-host, such as on 9 September 1564, when 'in the evening Signor Paolo and Lady Isabella gave a banquet, with a half dozen noble ladies, and there was music and dancing' in honour of the Spanish ambassador. The purpose of this event had a political dimension: to ensure conversation between Paolo and the Spanish ambassador to keep Isabella's husband loyal to Spain, while making sure that the ambassador promised him subsidies and honours. But Isabella gave plenty of parties in his absence, and she was never short of guests. 'Many beautiful noblewomen are coming to dine with me tonight,' she wrote to her husband in May 1566, suggesting a girls' night in in his absence.[13]

One might imagine the behaviour of the crème de la crème of society as decorous and genteel, but in fact Isabella and her cohorts were boisterous and rowdy. In the 1560s, there were many hard-working Florentine citizens deprived of a good night's sleep because 'it was during this time that the number of coaches multiplied in Florence, and with them noise that ruined Florence, and especially at night, when at around 2 a.m. Signora Isabella would be departing with her four coaches, singing, shouting, carousing because she was young, and without any mind for the scandal she was creating, knowing full well that in her company were some of the most dissolute young men in Florence'.[14]

The 'most dissolute young men' were, after all, the most fun, the ones without work to do the following morning, willing to stay up all night. Among them were ambassadorial retinues, young Florentine nobles, cavaliers and the adolescent pages who lived at Isabella's house. Quite a number of Isabella's male friends and associates feature, as she does herself, in Celio Malespini's *Duecento Novelle*. The *Novelle* is kind of a late Renaissance *Decameron*, filled with tales of carousing, seductions, tricks and mishaps, but based on actual events in Florence at which the Veronese Malespini was often present or of which he had been told. After the stories were published, safely far from Florence in Venice, in 1609, they became a source for Jacobean dramas, the English appetite ripe for tales of the outrageous behaviour of those Italian papists.

From Malespini one learns a little more of Elicona Tedaldi, 'loved greatly by Lady Isabella and who delighted in improvisatory singing, and attended to every little thing for her'.[15] A part of Isabella's retinue since at least 1561, she sometimes used him as a messenger to deliver letters for her, but she really kept him around because of his ability to entertain. Another character in Malespini's tales was the Ferrarese Ridolfo Conegrano, now a regular fixture at Isabella's house. In the stories he is the perennial buffoon with a one-track mind and an impressive knowledge of ribald Ferrarese drinking songs, and is the butt of plenty of jokes. There were no places Ridolfo liked to go in Florence more than Isabella's. 'Lady Isabella', he told the Duke of Ferrara, 'has a place [the Baroncelli] outside on the road to Rome where that lady grants much pleasure through music and dancing, and one passes the evening very agreeably.'[16] However, in this letter to his duke Conegrano does not mention something else he liked at Isabella's: the 'lovely games'.

Game-playing had long been an important part of Italian court culture, a way to pass long afternoons and evenings. There were card games, dice games, memory games and games to test one's general knowledge. It was this last variety which formed the backbone of the first published Italian compendium of games, Innocenzo Ringhieri's *One Hundred Games of Liberality and Ingenuity* of 1551, dedicated to Cathérine de' Medici. The games in Ringhieri's book were intended solely for female players. However, men and women did play against each other, and a frequent complaint of some of the top female gamers at Italian courts was that their male components 'allowed' them to win and would not make games into a real competition.[17]

A decade after Ringhieri's collection, the Sienese Girolamo Bargagli devised another compendium of games, *The Dialogue of Games,* for another Medici woman, this time Isabella. However, the games he compiled were very different from those for her cousin. Bargagli came up with one hundred and thirty in all, and there was no question that the participants were intended to be members of both sexes. All those described were party games designed for a large group, and interaction between the players, rather than the search for an outright winner, was their prime objective. Some are familiar: 'game of the ear', today's Chinese whispers; 'game of ABC', in which each player recited a line of verse beginning with the next letter of the alphabet; and 'game of devil's music', which was devoted to imitating animal sounds.

The majority of the games described were designed to encourage teasing and flirtation between the men and women present. Some did have highly intellectualized and literary components. The 'game of the portrait of beauty' and the 'game of painting' required the male participants to extol the physical and internal beauty of the women present using the language of the poets Petrarch and Ariosto. Others were intended to extract secrets from the players' pasts, such as 'the game of misfortunes', where one player had to recount an amorous misfortune from their past and a judge decided whether the misfortune was the player's fault or not.

But there were plenty of games clearly intended to be played later at night, when inhibitions were lowered. Picture, then, the Florentine elite at Isabella's house playing 'the game of slaves' and the 'game of servants', in which male and female players would be 'sold' into service to whoever wanted them the most. In 'the game of madness', those who declared themselves maddened by unrequited love would be 'locked up' in an asylum. Another game was 'the school master', in which the players would take childish names, such as 'little bit of sugar' or 'little horse', and be instructed by another taking the part of the school-master. There were even games that seem highly blasphemous in a church-governed society, where the players would pretend to be monks and nuns and enact religious ceremonies.

It should be clear by now that evenings at Isabella's home were not the staid affairs of a *salonnière*. A further component of her parties that her friend Conegrano enjoyed were the 'sweetest temptations' to be found at her house. Almost every part of the entertainments she offered involved the frisson of contact between the sexes, much of it physical. Glances and smiles were exchanged throughout theatrical performances; guests partnered up in dances; sharing a piece of sheet music to sing together meant hands would touch. Male and female guests selected which of the opposite sex they found the most appealing in the games Isabella proposed, games which got wilder as the evening progressed.

And as the night went on, was Isabella, her husband hundreds of miles away, simply a ringmaster? Did she merely enjoy the spectacle of her guests at play, while she maintained her virtuous solitude, anxious for her 'sun' to return so she might enjoy his rays again, as she was so keen to remind those around her through song? Was she really immune to the 'sweetest temptations' so enjoyed by her guests?

CHAPTER 7

Fidelities

———

When Giovanni de' Medici died, there was really no one left to curb
Isabella's more reckless abandon. Her brother was the one who had
had the most influence over her, the one who had fretted over her
health and made sure she took care of herself. Without Giovanni to
reel her in, Isabella was prepared to take on all kinds of risks. For
example, it seems unlikely that had her cardinal brother lived she
would have hired the Sienese Fausto Sozzini as one of her secretaries.
Trained as a theologian and lawyer, he was a part of the same intellectual circle as Girolamo Bargagli, who had provided Isabella with her
compendium of games. However, Sozzini was also the nephew of Lelio
Sozzini, who corresponded with Calvin and other northern heretics.
Fausto shared his uncle's sympathies and was working his way
towards becoming the founder of an anti-Trinitarian sect, later known
as the Socinians. Among their beliefs, they held that there was no
Trinity, that Mary was no virgin and that St Joseph was Jesus Christ's
real father. As court secretary, Fausto was obliged to perform innumer-
able mundane tasks for Isabella and Paolo, who used Fausto's legal
training to sort out some tricky affairs for him in Siena, thus diverting

Music making

him from his natural spiritual interests. Nonetheless, under Isabella's patronage, Fausto produced his first manuscript, *On the Authority of Holy Scripture*, which extolled the pre-eminence of Christianity among all faiths and the importance of the fact that it was supported by convincing historical evidence. Its content undoubtedly formed the basis of some of the discussions at Isabella's house, where intellectualism co-existed with hedonism. All the same, had Giovanni still been alive, with the Medici aspirations that he would receive the papal tiara, Isabella would have been much more wary about any association with one who had known heretical sympathies.

Isabella took greater physical risks as well. Many women of her station rode and hunted, but they were traditionally cautious, mindful of the bodies that acted as vessels for the bearing of children. Most women who went hunting would not have leapt the deep ditch that Isabella did while hunting near the abbey of Certosa on the outskirts of Florence in the summer of 1563, with disastrous effects. The accident she suffered was sufficiently serious for the court doctor, Andrea Pasquali, to be called out, and he subsequently wrote a report to her father:

> Our Lady Isabella, at around 12 o'clock, fell from her horse, down into a ditch, about five or six *braccie* [yards] deep, and knocked her head in such a way that there is a great bruise, mostly on the surface, however . . . Her chest is fine, as are her arms and legs. However, she moaned a lot, especially when she was moved. To make certain I took six or seven ounces of blood from her opposite side to make a diversion, and to allow evacuation. She ate some bread and milk and took some water, and I have left her to rest.[1]

However, another report indicated that 'while out hunting, the Lady Isabella's mount went flat out into a ditch about twenty *braccie* deep'. Dr Pasquali seems to have reduced the depth of the ditch to cause Cosimo less alarm. Nonetheless, it was clear there was nobody holding Isabella back, cautioning her as to what she should and should not do.

The void Giovanni's passing had left in Isabella's life was filled to a certain degree by the vast number of people with whom she was surrounded. From morning until night, she was never short of company. But what was still missing from her existence was the intimacy, the sense of closeness with somebody of her own age and sensibilities, which she had shared with her brother from birth until the time of his demise. Isabella could not replicate her relationship with Giovanni with any of her three remaining brothers. There was little affection between herself and Francesco: the gregarious, ebullient sister was a very different individual from the dour, misanthropic brother. Isabella's two younger siblings, Ferdinando and Pietro, were seven and twelve years her junior, still adolescents while she was in her mid twenties, and they could not become her confidants the way Giovanni had been.

Furthermore, even if Isabella and Giovanni were not physically intimate, the intensity of their relationship seems to have been such that it would have kept her faithful to Paolo Giordano. There would simply not have been room in Isabella's life for anybody else. Giovanni was virtually her twin; she could look at him, see herself in him and like what she saw. As the 1560s wore on, Paolo Giordano, by contrast, was becoming less physically appealing. In this period, comments on a man's physical appearance are rare, unless there was something remarkable about it. What was noticeable about Paolo Giordano was his increasing girth. The Venetian ambassador to Rome described him as 'of extreme size', although he was diplomatically careful to qualify it: 'but with that, extremely strong and healthy'.[2] Paolo's nickname in a literary academy to which he belonged was *largo*, the 'big one'. In her letters to him, Isabella would sometimes refer to her husband in supposedly affectionate terms as '*il mio grassotto*' – 'my big fat one' – or call him '*il mio orso*' – 'my bear' – a play on Orsini. Paolo himself was unhappy with his size. He would go to thermal baths in an effort to *smagrire* – thin down. By the time he was in his thirties he could no longer ride a normal size horse. It was this bloated individual for whom Isabella was meant to be pining when he was absent, racked with worry that he was not faithful to her.

Even if she had cared, Isabella did not expect her husband to be faithful to her. Male adultery was the norm in Renaissance society. In a contemporary book on conduct, Pietro Belmonte's *Institution of the*

Bride, the author counsels his female reader to be tolerant of her husband's 'weaknesses', while, of course, remaining chaste and virtuous herself. Still, Isabella liked to let her husband know that she knew of his extracurricular activities, such as on the occasion when she remarked that she hoped his newfound religiosity would curb his infidelity. In another letter, she made the romantic declaration that she would follow him as far as India. Then she turned the knife somewhat: 'Would you do me the favour', she asked sweetly, 'of sending me your portrait engraved on a ring, just the same as you gave that woman?'³ The woman in question is not specified, but she could be one of any number of women with whom Paolo was connected. They ranged from the courtesans of Rome to a Sienese woman 'most beautiful and amiable', on whose behalf Paolo had petitioned Francesco to allow her to break sumptuary law and wear clothes and jewels reserved for women of higher status.⁴

But whatever Paolo was up to, he would expect Isabella to maintain her chastity when apart from him. At stake was not only his sense of masculinity and honour but his patrimony. Any infidelity on the part of his wife meant he could not guarantee that any children she might bear as his heirs would be his own progeny. As long as Isabella lived on her own in Florence, with her father giving her licence to do as she pleased, there was nothing Paolo could do to patrol her sexual conduct – yet another reason why he wanted her to live with him in Rome. And there was no reason why Isabella, who very much desired the affection her late brother had constantly given her, would not choose to seek such attention elsewhere if she could. However, in her epistolary spousal existence, as in her literary and musical one, she preferred to play the role of the solitary and frequently wronged wife. 'Your wife, who sleeps alone in her bed' was one way she might end a letter to Paolo. Alternatively, she would underscore her apparently lonely existence at the Baroncelli Villa: 'I am returning to my villa, to my usual solitude.'⁵ Undoubtedly her most extravagant declaration of misery and loneliness is in this missive to her husband on 29 March 1566: 'I am completely lonely, and very discontented, and I am not very well, and this morning I found myself in bed with my usual headache, but I believe it is born out of the greatest solitude and affliction in which I find myself and in which I will find myself for many months. Excuse me if I do not write at greater length, but the pain in my body will not leave me.'[6]

Moreover, she was quick to react to any aspersions Paolo might cast on her behaviour. Having accused her, in June 1566, of 'making music with Signor Mario', Isabella returned a lengthy reply which skilfully deflected the issue at hand. She reminded Paolo of what she knew of his own behaviour, which he had attempted to hide: 'I am not that big a fool, having heard of the deeds, that I would believe the words, and I do not believe that you could imagine I would . . . It would appear', Isabella went on to say, 'that you have a wife of such little worth, such as myself . . . even though my father has always loved you like a son.'[7]

This last comment was, of course, a not so subtle reminder of Paolo's financial obligation to Isabella's father. And when she turned to the subject of Paolo's own accusations of her, Isabella became magnificently sarcastic: 'I am at the Baroncelli because I can better pass my miseries there than in Florence, and I wish to God that the music you claim I am making with Signor Mario would be often enough to distract my imagination from the little love you bear me.'[8] The lengthy letter, the core of which served to underscore the fact that her husband had neither the place nor the leverage to question her behaviour, would ensure Paolo would raise no objections to what she was doing, at least for a while.

There were a few Marios in the vicinity of Isabella, a couple of them Paolo Giordano's own cousins. One was Mario Sforza of Santa Fiore, given at least one military position coveted by Paolo. Another was a more distant cousin, Mario Orsini of the Monterotondo branch of the family. Like most of the Orsini men, this Mario made some form of a living as a soldier and spent time in Paolo's retinue and also at Cosimo's court. He was certainly the kind of young man who would easily find a place at Isabella's house in her husband's absence, singing, playing an instrument or participating in one of the games designed for entertainment. But there were plenty like him around Isabella. Was he one to whom she would show particular affection?

In December 1562, Mario was in Pisa, offering condolences to Cosimo on the deaths of his wife and sons. But he was much more excited about the possibility of entering into the new military order Cosimo had created: the Knights of Santo Stefano. Such an induction required money, which Mario was hoping his elder brother, Troilo Orsini, would supply. And it was Troilo who was the real reason why Isabella could defend herself from the charges Paolo had levelled at her. For it was Troilo with whom Isabella, by the mid-1560s, was making music, and not his brother Mario.

CHAPTER 8

Troilo

There was no question that Paolo Giordano Orsini was the most privileged member of his vast clan. Although he was unable to live within it, he had a guaranteed income from the vast estates that he controlled. He received pensions and benefits from individuals such as the king of Spain, without actually having to do anything, as Isabella had pointed out to him. And although Paolo claimed he was anxious for military service, 'he has seen very little action', as the Venetian ambassador remarked. The same ambassador concluded his summary of the Orsini lord with observations on his other chief characteristic – his profuse spending.

Life was not so easy for the majority of his Orsini relations. None had an estate anything like the size of the one Paolo Giordano ruled, and all needed supplementary income. A few entered the church, but the majority, if they wanted to make money as soldiers, had to actually go to war and fight. They were dependent upon the goodwill of courtiers and ambassadors who could advance their case and who were willing to promote them. Every quality such men possessed – guts, aggression, determination, wit, charm – was a marketable asset, and some possessed more of them than others.

Stag hunting

No Orsini of his generation was more determined to succeed on his own merits than Troilo Orsini, who was the same age as his cousin Paolo. His line, the Monterotondo, named for the feud they held twenty kilometres north-west of Rome, was the one to which Lorenzo the Magnificent's wife Clarice Orsini had belonged. She was Isabella's great-great-grandmother, which made Isabella and Troilo distant cousins as well.

One of the first things that many noticed about Troilo was his good looks. If Paolo's prodigious size was remarkable enough to be commented upon by his contemporaries, than Troilo's 'great beauty' also drew the attention of ambassadors. 'He was a man who was elegant in all his endeavours, extremely handsome, a great entertainer, a true courtier, the friend of all the ladies and gentlemen' was a contemporary summary of Troilo.[1] Although produced in the seventeenth century, some time after his death, a painting made at the French court by Anastagio Fontebuoni, depicting Troilo meeting Catherine de' Medici, gives some indication of how those in Troilo's world saw him. The courtly Troilo doffs his feathered hat and makes a deep bow to the French queen mother. His dark hair is curly and lustrous, his pointed beard neat and trim, his features refined, elegant and sensitive. He appears every inch the perfect *cavaliere*, cavalier, as any higher ranking soldier of his time was known. In this picture, even the famously unyielding Catherine de' Medici seems rather taken with him.

Moreover, the young Troilo had not got by on his looks alone. By 1559, he was trying to raise money to establish his own company to take to France to fight in the Wars of Religion, and he took part in several military campaigns over the next few years. It seemed evident to many that, of his generation of Orsini, as a warrior it was Troilo in whom the spirit of his ancestors lived on. The Venetian ambassador's assessment of him contrasts greatly with the one he gave of Paolo Giordano, describing Troilo as a young man 'who has seen a great deal of war in France, and of whom there are great expectations . . .'[2] The picture of Troilo as the able but merry cavalier is completed by the fact that, in addition to his horse and dog, he carried a violin with him on his campaigns, thus able to ensure all could enjoy singing and dancing in the evenings in the battle camps.

Still, Troilo's handsome face, apparent charm and abilities as a soldier had not earned him a worry-free existence. Like many Roman
noble families, the Orsini of Monterotondo had never really recovered
from the toll of the 1527 Sack of Rome and were struggling financially. Troilo's father was dead and so, as the eldest son, albeit unmarried,
Troilo was responsible for his younger brother Mario and his married
sister Emilia, who had financial problems of her own. He was not the
head of his branch of the Orsini clan; that was his uncle, Giordano,
who expected some parts of Troilo's earnings to go towards the
upkeep of the crumbling estate. However, in periods of ceasefire and
peace, there were no military assignments to be had and no money to
be earned. It was during such a period that Troilo inserted himself in
Florence into Paolo Giordano's retinue of extended family and hangers-
on who lived in the Palazzo Antinori. In this way, Troilo would to
some degree be able to live at the expense of his Orsini cousin, while
also keeping a foot in the Medici camp and being open to any potential offerings that might be had from Cosimo. To a certain extent he
worked for Paolo, obeying instructions from his cousin such as:
'Because you know the issues more clearly than I do, I am desirous
that you attend to the Pignatello [another Orsini fiefdom] negotiation
as soon as possible. I am sending Maestro Bartucci, who will let you
know fully what my wishes are.'[3]

At the other end of the spectrum, Troilo's relations back at
Monterotondo expected him to provide them with reports of Paolo's
activities, for anything that happened to Paolo Giordano, as head of
their entire clan, had some impact upon their own lives. 'I am happy to
hear', his uncle Giordano wrote to Troilo at the end of 1563, 'that the
financial affairs of Signor Paolo Giordano have improved . . . any honour and glory that comes to him, his relatives, servants and friends can
participate in also.'[4] Equally, anything shameful also reflected badly
upon Paolo's family. 'Now it would be sufficient if he were only to
have children,' mused Giordano to Troilo.[5]

All the Orsini were anxious that Paolo have an heir in order to
cement the relationship between themselves and the Medici. The following summer, Giordano wrote anxiously to Troilo: 'I beg you to let
me know if the pregnancy of the Lady Isabella is for real, and how

long along she is, and if it is certain, I ask you to take the opportunity to advise the illustrious Lord Paolo that it please him to ensure that he governs his wife, so that the pregnancy does not fail as it did the other time . . . '⁶ This comment was a reference to the widely held belief that it was Isabella's wild ways, her parties and her hunting that had caused her miscarriages in the past. It also gave a clear indication that the Orsini family felt that Paolo had no control over his wife.

Interestingly enough, in regard to this supposed pregnancy, Ridolfo Conegrano would tell the Duke of Ferrara: 'Everybody says that the Lady Isabella is pregnant again, but she says it is not true.'⁷ The Ferrarese duke might well wonder why this Medici princess would be so keen to deny the truth in such a rumour, when most noblewomen were only too anxious to proclaim their fecundity the moment they thought they might be pregnant.

The only concern Troilo was supposed to have for Isabella lay in her position as his cousin's wife, an instrument whereby his family at large could prosper. He might dance or sing with her, but if Troilo was playing by the rules, Isabella should be *intoccabile*, untouchable. She was Orsini property not to be sullied by his hands. But Isabella did not see herself in this way, and Troilo was personally ambitious. He could see that to prosper at the Medici court did not entail securing the favour of Paolo Giordano; one needed Isabella's. And Troilo very badly wanted, indeed needed, to prosper. Moreover, like others in his family, he had little respect for Paolo; that his uncle freely told him to advise Paolo to govern his wife indicates they saw Paolo's weaknesses quite clearly. Troilo would feel no compunction in exploiting them.

His interest in Isabella already ran deep in the months after her brother Giovanni's death, suggested by the fact that, absent from Florence in the summer of 1563, a friend sent him a detailed report of her hunting accident, when she fell into a deep ditch. This news is the letter's sole contents, and so was clearly the reason for the correspondence, his friend recognizing that Troilo would want to know what had happened to Isabella. That is not to say that Troilo saw Isabella only as a means of advancement. Her influence with her father aside, she was the 'star of the Medici court', the wittiest, most vivacious woman in Florence, an object of desire in her own right.

As for Isabella's reaction to Troilo, it is not difficult to imagine why she would be attracted to him and why she would allow that attraction to go further. He was handsome and charismatic; moreover, he had lived the life of a soldier and had carried out brave military deeds. By contrast, while Paolo Giordano talked incessantly of wanting to go to war, he never actually went. For Isabella, Troilo seemed more like her war-hero grandfather, Giovanni delle Bande Nere, or one of those chivalric heroes from the tales of Ariosto, which had informed her world since birth, come to life. His persona came automatically imbued with romance. The fact he was her husband's cousin – as well as her own – could only make an assignation with Troilo all the more pleasingly piquant for Isabella in its implicit danger.

As to how Isabella could facilitate such a relationship, she had everything she needed. She had her autonomy, and Paolo's own family members recognized he did not rule his wife. Her father had created an environment in which he permitted sexual licence and, most importantly, he was not going to stand in the way of Isabella pursuing such activity. Her husband was frequently absent and she possessed her own properties, meaning it was not difficult for Troilo to come to her bedchamber at the Palazzo Medici or for her to invite him to the Baroncelli, where Isabella claimed she stayed 'in her usual solitude'. There might have been any number of Signor Marios, Fliconas, charming pageboys and ambassadors with whom Isabella could dance, sing and flirt. However, they could not provide the kind of relationship with which she had grown up, somebody with whom she could connect on a deeper, more personal level. As such, Troilo Orsini was not simply Isabella's lover; he became, as much as was possible, the replacement for the role her brother Giovanni had once fulfilled. That reason perhaps explains why Cosimo allowed his daughter this relationship, he being the only one who had the power to put a stop to it. Both father and daughter knew the marriage could not bring her satisfaction, and Troilo went some way to filling the lacuna in Isabella's life that her brother had left and which her husband could not fill.

CHAPTER 9

A 'Clandestine' Affair

The relationship between Troilo and Isabella was one which any number of people might have known about, but the unwritten rule was not to speak, and certainly not to write, about it. So, for example, Celio Malespini has a story about Troilo and Isabella, but he cannot breach decorum by indicating that the married Medici princess is an adulteress, so in his tale he makes them partners in crime rather than lovers. Nonetheless, he tells a story which gives a good indication of what they might have liked about each other, beyond physical attraction or the lure of advancement. They both liked practical jokes, and not always ones of a particularly nice nature, especially when seen from a modern perspective. In Malespini's tale, Isabella is cross that Ridolfo Conegrano, the Ferrarese ambassador whom she regarded as her pet buffoon, is enamoured of a young lady who happens to be a girlfriend of Troilo's, so the pair hatch a plot to teach Conegrano a lesson.

They arranged for Conegrano to invite the girl to dinner at his home. 'After a while, Lady Isabella, dressed as a man, accompanied by Orsini and two other men who were their confidants, crept into the ambassador's stable, bringing with them a slave girl who had

Strolling couple

been brought up from the port of Livorno, ugly and dirty, like a monster, but very young and who did not understand our language.'[1] They accosted a stable boy, swore him to secrecy, and asked him how far through dinner were the ambassador and his guests. 'Almost finished,' was the response. 'Well then,' questioned Lady Isabella, 'can we go up into his bedroom without being seen?' The stable boy replied in the affirmative. They took the slave girl up to Conegrano's bedroom and deposited her, 'naked as the day she was born', in the ambassador's bed, where, 'finding it soft and delicate, she immediately fell asleep'.

Meanwhile, downstairs at dinner, the young woman excused herself and told Conegrano to join her in a little while in his bedroom. Instead, she went out to join Isabella and Troilo in the stable. Conegrano went upstairs to his unlit bedroom, saw a sleeping figure in his bed, crept in beside her and began to make love to her. At which point 'the slave girl woke up and cried out in her language, "I don't want to! I don't want to, God help me!"' Conegrano leapt out of bed, called for lights and was horrified to be 'confronted with the ugly slave girl, whom he had believed to be the beautiful young woman and whose lips he had kissed many times'.

Troilo and Isabella rushed upstairs, and Isabella told Conegrano that she hoped he had learned his lesson for his inconstancy to her: 'You really deserve a greater punishment,' she told him, 'disrespecting women as you do.' Conegrano was abject and admitted his shame. Troilo proposed that the slave girl be allowed to spend the rest of the night in the soft bed, with the provision 'that you do not ill-treat her, as you did a moment before'. Conegrano agreed to this, saw his visitors to the door and 'went to sleep in another bed, believing his own was now full of fleas'.

Although in Malespini's story the relationship between Troilo and Isabella appears to be platonic, it is, nonetheless, Troilo and not the ambassador with whom Isabella is roaming the streets of Florence in the dead of night, cross-dressing as Venetian courtesans did when they wished to go out on the streets. For a sixteenth-century reader, that element of the story – a Medici princess engaging in such behaviour – is equally if not more outrageous than the sexual exploits recounted therein. So the real story is Troilo and Isabella together, co-conspirators in this prank.

Isabella might never have openly declared her feelings for Troilo, but she did use other means to let her love be known, such as music and poetry. Officially, the songs performed at her soirées were supposed to reflect her longing for Paolo Giordano when he was gone from Florence, a means by which Isabella could garner good public relations as the dutiful wife. But the songs' words and sentiments become Janus-like when they are addressed not to an absent husband, but an absent lover, for Troilo would have to go away on missions and secondments. The madrigals in Maddalena Casulana's songbook for Isabella then take on much more passionate ramifications, ones in which 'A new love, a new fire, and a new order I feel inside my heart . . . my beloved peace has turned into cruel war . . .' Or, in the words of another, 'If you are my heart, my life, and my soul, now that I am deprived of you, who can keep me alive?'[2]

Isabella also commissioned a volume of madrigals from the composer Stefano Rossetti which took as their unified theme 'Olimpia's Lament', a tale from Ariosto's *Orlando Furioso*. She perhaps chose this story, out of many in Ariosto, because she saw it as providing her with a platform to justify her actions, as well as some wishful thinking as to how she hoped things might turn out.[3] Ariosto's Olympia has been abandoned by her unfaithful husband Bireno. However, her story ends happily when Orlando introduces her to Oberto, the king of Ireland, who falls in love with Olympia, then puts Bireno to death and marries her. Perhaps these very thoughts ran through Isabella's head. If Paolo Giordano were to die, what would stop her from marrying Troilo?

Other quasi-hidden expressions of Isabella's love for Troilo are to be found in the verses the court poet Laura Battiferra penned for Isabella. Only to be found in manuscript form, inscribed next to the stanzas are the instructions 'not to be published', as if the feelings they express are too private for public consumption. Their sentiments are very much like those of the songs Isabella commissioned, reflecting a mind and body tormented with desire and anguish at the thought of separation from the beloved:

As a miserable body abandoned
by its more noble soul
is wont to remain a gelid short-lived corpse
so I was left, alas, at your departure
sweet strength of my
life and beloved support
Holy Love, you who can do
what others cannot, bring me back to life
joined with my fair soul.[4]

Isabella might only make her requests for these kinds of poems and songs, reflective of her inner desires, very obliquely, recognizing the importance of discretion. She believed that whatever one put in writing and to which one signed one's name could be perceived as the truth, even if it was a lie, which explains the bombastic expressions of love she made to Paolo Giordano. Conversely, she would make no public announcement of her feelings for Troilo, even if their behaviour made clear to all who observed them the real nature of the relationship between them. She certainly would not send him a love letter she had penned personally, for no matter how secret its delivery might be, there was always the chance of the interception or discovery of such a missive. Omitting her signature was insufficient, as Isabella's distinctive sloping, confident hand was too readily identifiable.

But correspondence between lovers is often necessary in order to relieve and express their emotions and to communicate when they cannot speak in person. There is a cache of seven letters to Troilo from a woman who signs herself as his 'slave in perpetuity', held to be Isabella. The handwriting of the letters does not match hers, nor does its style belong to that of any noble, male or female. Instead, the even hand is that of a professional scribe, a secretary, somebody who writes for a living. It is likely that if Isabella wanted to send her beloved declarations of her feelings for him, she would shield her identity by using another – a trusted servant within her retinue – to write the words, which could not then be traced back to her.[5]

Other than not signing her name and disguising her hand, the author makes other efforts to conceal who she is. For example, she never dates a letter, mentions few names and places, and obfuscates her meanings. However, she reveals enough information to suggest that the writer really is Isabella, and the tone she often uses – hyperbolic, emphatic – is one Isabella frequently adopts. Some of the letters make clear that they cannot be together due to the presence of '*il maestro*', which appears to be the code word for her husband, who evidently is not with the writer all the time, as was the case with Paolo Giordano and Isabella. Thus she might write: 'The master returns and it will be the longest Sunday ever.' On another occasion, the language she uses to describe him is even harsher: 'You know that that animal has returned, and wants to go out to Pistoia, but you do not know my displeasure at this news, because you are there, and I cannot talk to you as is my desire.' Pistoia was one of the places where the Medici court regularly went out hunting.

She also alludes to Cosimo: 'I have written to the duke and you will see that everything is well in a way that I cannot say to you.' Such a statement might refer to the promise of some advancement for Troilo. One letter makes some negative references to Francesco, whose hand in governing the state, forcing her to ask him for favours, irritated his sister: 'I feel as if I've been knocked over into kneeling at the feet of the prince . . . it is so evident that everybody sees his miserable ways from morning 'til night.' In many ways, this proclamation regarding Francesco provides almost irrefutable proof that Isabella is the writer, for it is very difficult to imagine any other woman in Florence expressing such sentiments in so vigorous a manner.

The love and passion expressed in these letters are of a melancholic nature, in keeping with, and indeed perhaps informed by, the tenor of the poems and songs performed at Isabella's house. It is true that some of the sentiments are voiced in a similar manner to that used by Isabella when she addresses Paolo Giordano, but one must remember that Paolo and Isabella's letters were for public consumption, while those destined for Troilo were extremely private. The words thus take on deeper, more heartfelt meaning. Theirs is a relationship that comes with a certain degree of pathos, a love between two people who cannot express their feelings openly and who cannot always be together. To some degree, Isabella might have exploited this situation, giving her as it did the opportunity to play the part of the romantic heroines of the poems she so enjoyed. 'I received your letter,' Isabella would write, 'which gave me such great contentment, and more, it gave me the presence of him who is desired by me more than life itself. You did wrong in thinking I would leave you. I could never take the opportunity to lose a lord so desired by me, whose slave I am and on whom I am eternally intoxicated, and who has deigned in his kindness to offer me his love. You can be assured that I will not lose you for anything. Every hour seems like a thousand, and if it were not for the great hope I have of seeing you again, I would be finished at this time. And do tell me that your return will be the quickest possible, so dear is it to my life.'

Although there are references to letters Troilo has sent to her, only one such missive from him survives. He omits the name of the addressee, although he signs his own name. This letter is apparently in response to one in which Isabella had chastised him for having spoken too freely about their relationship. This issue is one she had addressed in one of the surviving letters. 'Watch out for him,' she had warned Troilo, in relation to his dealings with one Francesco Spina: 'he is a man who does not know how to keep secrets.' Given that Spina was her brother Francesco's treasurer, Isabella had good reason to wish that Troilo keep away from him.

The letter to which Troilo responded concerned Isabella's suspicion that he had not composed his last letter himself, as it showed him too well versed in Tuscan composition. Troilo was, after all, a native Roman. Isabella's mother tongue was not his own and she prided herself on being a keen judge of her language. Troilo wrote:

> Let me excuse myself and express my sorrow. I know very well it would be better to talk in person than to write, but I wanted to write to assure you of my servitude. I cannot believe that you would esteem it so lightly as to think that I would communicate with anyone as to what passes between you and me, I keep dear in my heart your honour as much as life itself . . . As for your assertion that my last letter was neither written nor composed by me, the only proof I can provide is in sending this letter, assuring you that my blamelessness is promoted by my love, and I can do no more than put

together these fifty Florentine words that you have, my dear benefactress, from your most faithful servant, although you have generated a little bit of suspicion in me that I am no longer loved by
you . . .

But whatever provisions for, and claims of, secrecy Troilo and
Isabella might make, they both knew their relationship was not a
secret. One Medici representative, Ciro Alidosi, writing from Emilia
Romagna, asked the court secretary Antonio Serguidi to pass on letters to Troilo and Isabella, as if knowing the two of them would be
together. Troilo would receive petitions from friends, family and
acquaintances asking him to assist them in securing Isabella's patronage, such as this request in August 1564 from the nobleman Sforza
Aragona of Appiano:

> Most Illustrious cousin: I am sending to your lordship a letter from
> my lady wife for Lady Isabella, which is in reply to one of hers, as
> Her Excellency has deigned to hold at baptism our baby girl who
> was born to my wife at 4 last night and thanks to God both are in
> good health. Perhaps you would be good enough to convey this
> information to her, and to procure a response.[6]

Troilo was only one of any number of relations of Sforza Aragona
in the Medici orbit. However, the Appiano singled him out to relay his
news to Isabella and to get her to reply because he knew that Troilo
had a special relationship with the Medici princess. The chances are
that it was Troilo who had initially persuaded Isabella to agree to serve
as his cousin's godmother in the first place.

Word spread to even the darkest corners that the line of influence in
Florence ran from Troilo to Isabella. In May 1564, Troilo received a letter from a man called Lepido Massarini, who reminded Troilo that he
had served with him as a soldier in France. Lepido had been imprisoned in a Sienese gaol for over a year for an unspecified crime 'which
has caused the greatest damage to my wife and children'. The prisoner
hoped that Troilo 'could say just one word to my lord Paolo Giordano,
who could then address himself to the Prince, and ask for my libera-
tion. I know it would take only one word from Signor Paolo.'[7]

But whether Signor Paolo only said one word on his behalf or not, it did not do Lepido any good. Nearly two years later, he was still languishing in prison. In April 1566, he tried Troilo again:

> Now that I have been imprisoned for thirty-seven months here in Siena, I am forced to send my wife to that most felicitous court [of the Medici]. I know that if she could come under your favourable, and most powerful arm, that she might be able to secure my liberation . . . My wish is this, that you might present my wife to the Lady Isabella, who, through her natural goodness and at her instance, might present my petition to the Prince, obtaining from you this most special favour from Her Excellency . . .[8]

Lepido might be in gaol, but he was sufficiently well connected to the outside world to have learned that he stood a much better chance of seeing the light of day if he asked Troilo to intercede with Isabella, and not her husband. Somebody had clearly told him that putting his wife under Troilo's patronage could procure an audience with Isabella. And if a miserable prisoner of no great consequence in a Sienese cell could be privy to such information, the odds were great that plenty of others were too. Isabella and Troilo's affair was clearly clandestine only in name.

Isabella's mother, the Spanish Eleonora di Toledo, 'la fecundissima' who gave birth to eleven children.

Isabella's beloved father, Cosimo, who started life as Medici underdog, and ended as the family's first Grand Duke.

Bia, Cosimo's illegitimate daughter, who died a few months before Isabella's birth. Baby Isabella was seen as 'compensation' for her loss.

Isabellina, aged eight, already self-possessed and confident.

ISABELLA'S BROTHERS: Cardinal Giovanni, Isabella's earliest love, portrayed in the guise of St John the Baptist.

'Liveliness is born within her.' Isabella at sixteen, around the time of her marriage to Paolo Giordano Orsini.

The cool and calculating Cardinal Ferdinando.

Her elder brother Francesco, an increasingly sinister presence in her life.

In her twenties, a Florentine beauty, enjoying an intellectual and romantic freedom experienced by few women of her era.

Pietro, the youngest, who would grow up even more disturbed than the rest of his siblings.

Paolo Giordano Orsini, Isabella's part-time husband, renowned for his reputation as a spendthrift and his predilection for violence

Isabella's lover, Troilo, much admired for his good looks, seen here charming Cathérine de' Medici.

A game of *calcio*, an early and rough version of football, seen here played in Florence's Piazza Santa Croce, where Paolo Giordano sponsored such a game.

Leonora di Toledo, Isabella's pretty cousin, and partner-in-crime, wife to her brother Pietro.

Cammilla Martelli, Cosimo's, blonde second wife, a commoner. The marriage scandalized every court in Europe.

Giovanna of Austria, Francesco's increasingly unhappy wife.

Bianca Cappello, Francesco's increasingly powerful mistress, supposed friend to Isabella.

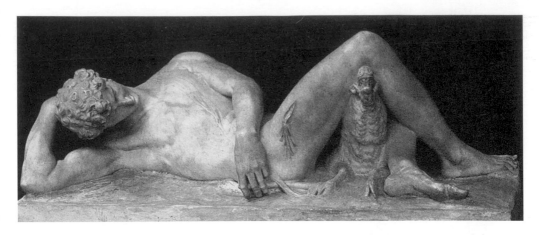

MEDICI PRIVATE LIFE, conventional and uncoventional:

A scene illustrating the betrothal of Isabella's sister Lucrezia, taking place in the family's sumptuous Palazzo Vecchio in Florence, witnessed by chosen courtiers, including an attendant dwarf.

Two of the statues in the gardens of Isabella's own villa, the Baroncelli. Although it was highly unusual for a woman to commission profane and erotic statuary of this kind, Isabella had created her own domain for personal pleasure.

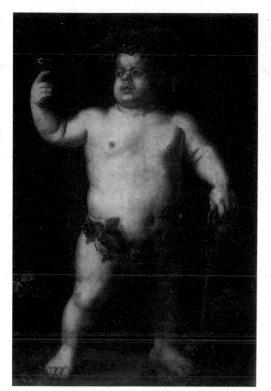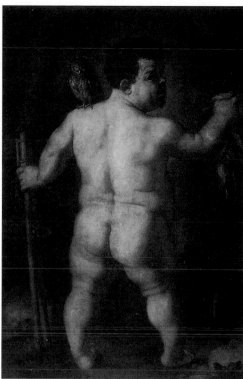

The dwarf Morgante, seen here portrayed as Bacchus, and with the owl he used to hunt small birds, one of the last to ever see Isabella alive.

A scene from Bocaccio's *Decameron* warning of the punishment meted out to inconstant women, where the ghost of a woman who spurned her lover is hunted down by him through eternity, his dogs ripping out her heart. The scene here is enacted in front of a banquet attended by Florentine families, the Medici coat of arms, balls against a gold background, displayed prominently in the background.

Isabella (bottom left), her father Cosimo and brother Ferdinando behind her, Francesco and Paolo Giordano on the right hand side, depicted as the saints they clearly never were in real life.

PART IV
Medici Machinations

Medici frontispiece

CHAPTER 1

The Imperial Sister-in-Law

In December 1565, a new addition to the Medici family arrived in the form of a bride for Francesco: seventeen-year-old Giovanna of Austria. Giovanna's status was an indication of the degree to which the Medici star had ascended during Cosimo's reign. His predecessor, Duke Alessandro, had been married to Margaret, an illegitimate daughter of the Emperor Charles V, and Cosimo himself married into Spanish nobility of the highest rank. But now Cosimo's son was taking a legit-imately born imperial bride, the sister of the Emperor Maximilian II, and she would bring with her a dowry of 100,000 ducats. The pres-tige of the match was such that when the engagement was announced, 'a Mass dedicated to the Holy Spirit was sung in the Duomo as a sign of happiness for the betrothal, and all the shops were shuttered'.[1] Isabella declared that 'no greater happiness could come to me in life' than the news of the imperial alliance.[2] Such a statement is typical Isabella hyperbole; nonetheless, as someone so fiercely proud of the Medici name, she knew the extent to which the marriage advanced her family on the international stage.

Much of 1565 was dedicated to readying Florence fit to receive an

German ladies

emperor's daughter. The Duomo was whitewashed, the Neptune fountain in the Piazza della Signoria finally put in place and Giorgio Vasari received yet another commission. This time he and his team were to fresco the Palazzo Vecchio's courtyard, painting scenes of Tuscany alongside the sort of grotesque decoration Paolo Giordano had commissioned for one of the chambers at Bracciano when Isabella and her family visited in the winter of 1560.

Cosimo also arranged for a delegation to travel to Austria with Francesco in order to pay their respects to the emperor, bring his daughter back to Florence and shower them both with gifts. He instructed Paolo Giordano to accompany his brother-in-law, entrusting him with a particularly magnificent diamond to give to the Habsburg princess. In so doing he created an opportunity for Paolo to engage in the pomp and magnificence he so enjoyed, and one for Cosimo to remind his son-in-law of his imperial obligations. His plan seems to have worked. Paolo wrote excitedly to Isabella from Vienna:

> I don't want to forget to tell you about the infinite favours His Imperial Majesty has shown me. This evening the emperor had me come up to his room and once again showed me infinite courtesy. This morning we were departing for Trent and His Majesty commanded that I not yet leave, and all the morning showed me *infinitissime* courtesies, in such a way that I was not able to leave for Trent until the afternoon.[3]

After her arrival in Tuscany and a few days' rest at the villa in Poggio a Caiano, the emperor's daughter made her first entrance into Florence on 16 December. The entire city was dressed in ephemeral triumphant arches appropriate for an imperial princess. Giovanna herself was wearing rich brocade and a crown upon her head. Prior to her entrance, Cosimo sent her a note requesting she not wear any other hair ornaments for fear they might 'break or cause any of the crown's jewels to fall and get lost', advice which reveals that the Medici duke's mercantile genes were still buoyant.[4] As other new Medici brides had done before her, Giovanna's entrance into Florence was designed so that as many citizens as possible could see her. They, in turn, had never seen anyone accompanied by so vast a retinue. It included

Cosimo, his son Pietro, Paolo Giordano and other important family members, thirty-four pages, sixty representatives of the religious military orders, a hundred and thirty from Giovanna's own lands and a further eighty-two 'qualified persons'.[5] She stopped at the newly whitewashed Duomo to receive a blessing before making her way to the Palazzo Vecchio, where she was met at the doorway by Francesco and Isabella, who officially welcomed her into her new family. Isabella would be Giovanna's constant companion at the breathtaking array of events that were to follow her entrance. Her documented presence was so ubiquitous as to earn her a place in a seventeenth-century tapestry commemorating Giovanna's marriage to Francesco, standing behind the new bride.

Isabella was with her two days later in the coach that took Giovanna to the Duomo, where the marriage to Francesco took place and a nuptial Mass was sung. There then followed two months of celebratory events. They included wild animal hunts, with bears and other more exotic beasts imported for the occasion, as well as the usual plays, parties and concerts. The celebrations culminated in the festivities for the 1566 Carnival, which were accordingly all the more opulent that year. Paolo Giordano took this opportunity to shine by staging an extravaganza designed to outstrip anything offered in commemoration of the marriage. He commissioned from the Florentine painter Santi di Tito, a young up-and-coming artist, a series of ephemeral decorations to be displayed in the Piazza San Lorenzo. Vasari later recalled how Santi, 'with great and incredible labour . . . painted in chiaroscuro, on several enormous canvases, pictures of the deeds of the illustrious men of the house of Orsini'.[6] While these temporary images, which were subsequently destroyed, were clearly worthy of praise, there can be no denying that Paolo was trying to shoehorn his own family history into a Medici/Habsburg celebration. He then had an enormous wooden theatre in the Piazza di San Lorenzo erected, producing a spectacle starring himself and his brother-in-law Francesco that was played out in front of an audience which included Cosimo, with Isabella by his side dressed in white silk. Another spectator, Ridolfo Conegrano, sent a report of the event back home to Ferrara:

Saturday was the day of Signor Paolo's tournament and it was extremely successful. The prince [Francesco] appeared as a star who came down from the heavens in human form into the centre of the theatre, and immediately music started up played by four young boys who were high up on one side of the theatre and who circled it. I can't find the words to describe how this was accomplished. When that was finished, Mount Etna opened up with a great number of flames, and out popped Signor Paolo and Pirro Malvezzi [a renowned soldier], both dressed in white armour, cloth of silver and white silk, and they had with them two pages dressed in the same way, six drummers, six trumpeters, six trombone players and two angels. They stopped at one end of the theatre, where they re-enacted the ship of the Argonauts with five cavaliers . . .

These spectacles were followed by jousts featuring Francesco, Paolo and the noble participants, culminating in 'a most sumptuous banquet with, at the end, three ladies and three cavaliers on the most beautiful horses, performing the "battle dance" which was a marvellous thing to see'. For all his foibles, Paolo was certainly at the cutting edge of equestrian matters. These kinds of horse ballets would become a staple of stupendous courtly entertainment during the coming centuries across Europe.

Everybody wondered at how much this event had cost, especially those who were aware of Paolo's financial difficulties. 'It stupefied everyone because of the great expense,' wrote one commentator. Conegrano was more precise: 'The expense was 15,000 *scudi*, but in my estimation it [the entertainment] was seven or eight, because the greatest expense was the theatre itself.'

The months-long series of entertainments in her honour over, Giovanna von Habsburg was now to settle down to the business of life in a land and in a style very different to the one to which she was accustomed. She had brought with her from her homeland a cortège of ladies-in-waiting, with whom she could converse in her mother tongue and who were collectively known in Florence as '*le tedesche*' (German women). Despite the comfort these women gave her, the Austrian princess also had to integrate with her new family members. By disposition, her new father-in-law, Cosimo, tended to be kindly towards his female relatives. However, from the start of their marriage, Francesco made it very plain he had little interest in her beyond her ability to produce children, an issue called into question by her 'very thin and small stature . . . for this respect there is the suspicion she is not well adapted for conceiving'.[7]

As for her new sister-in-law Isabella, it is true that she and Giovanna could not have been more different. The Venetian ambassador described Giovanna as of 'singular goodness and religious example, beautiful in soul but of scarce physical beauty, being small of stature, pallid and with a not very pretty face, with a mind that is placid and quiet, rather than lively and elevated'.[8] In other words, Isabella's sister-in-law was probably not going to participate enthusiastically in games of monks and nuns at two in the morning at the Baroncelli.

Nonetheless, Isabella was friendlier to Giovanna than was Francesco. Having retreated in the warm May of 1566 to the Baroncelli, Isabella wrote: 'I find myself again in Florence to visit with the princess and dine with her at the palace, and I have been with her all day and night.'[9] Giovanna was very fond of fruit, so whenever Isabella was away from Florence she made sure to send Giovanna whatever was to be found in the other Medici gardens. 'I did not want to be remiss in immediately on my arrival sending you some fruit,' Isabella wrote from Pisa in May 1568, 'and those few that I found I am dispatching.'[10] In October, Isabella was at Poggio a Caiano: 'wandering the gardens I found these few fruits, please accept them along with the good soul which accompanies them'.[11] Isabella always addressed Giovanna, six years her junior, in the most formal way possible. 'I wanted to write to remember myself to Your Highness as that most affectionate servant that I am and will be as long as live,' Isabella assured her, mindful of the etiquette and protocol which was a near religion to the Habsburgs.[12]

Giovanna, alone and isolated, as so many foreign brides were in their new homes, and not always treated very nicely by her new relations, seemed appreciative of Isabella's overtures. But it should be said that Isabella's gestures towards her were not entirely altruistic. Giovanna's personal sphere of influence was not immense, but nonetheless there were certain things she could do for Isabella. Isabella was pleased when one of her retainers, Luigi Bonsi, was 'accepted by the princess into her retinue for love of me, and he will serve her with all his heart'.[13] Bonsi could then serve as an extra source of information for Isabella from within the Palazzo Vecchio and could let her know anything that might be said about her within those walls.[14] Moreover, it was probably Giovanna who was instrumental, with Isabella's encouragement, in Troilo Orsini receiving a highly sought-after appointment. In 1567, Troilo travelled to Germany to serve as the Medici representative at the wedding of Giovanna's cousin, the Duke of Bavaria, who had been part of her escort to Florence little more than a year before.

This was the kind of commission Troilo had long been seeking, offering as it did excellent prospects for receiving gifts, for networking and for expanding his own profile and reputation across the European stage. Isabella also created opportunities for him where she could. In January 1567, he arrived in Mantua as her representative, bearing a letter in her name addressed to the Duchess of Mantua. 'I have commissioned him and rendered him with full testimony to kiss your hand in my name, as a sign of my singular observance to you,' Isabella wrote. 'I beg Your Highness to lend him your full confidence . . .'[15]

However, this new appointment to go to Germany was clearly far more prestigious and wide-reaching than any Troilo had received previously. It required a certain amount of contrivance for it to be secured for Troilo, who was not trained as a diplomat and was not even a Florentine. He certainly would not have been Francesco's first choice, whom Troilo was technically representing, which suggests that Isabella had persuaded Giovanna to indicate that Troilo was the man she wanted sent to her Bavarian cousin. Giovanna did have some sway on issues concerning her homeland, and she could have petitioned Cosimo on this matter. He would surely have seen Isabella's hand in the affair, and was willing to grant his daughter and daughter-in-law's apparently shared wish. Still, Francesco was clearly irritated that it was Troilo who was selected to go. He had the court secretary Bartolomeo Concino draw up a long list of instructions for Troilo as to what he was to do along every step of the way, addressing him in the condescending '*tu*' form to remind him of his subservience. However, the most important issue, according to Concino, was for Troilo to 'be aware above all that if there is a representative of the Duke of Ferrara, you do not cede to him in any way . . . so as not to prejudice the precedence that we have over that duke'.[16] All over the courts of Italy and Europe there were Florentine and Ferrarese representatives fighting over who should precede the other in a procession, at a meeting with the head of state or at the dinner table.

Troilo was evidently a success as the Medici representative at the German wedding, to the extent that two years later he was charged with more sensitive political matters. In April 1569, with instructions 'on the congratulation of His Most Christian Majesty for the victory against the Prince of Condé', Troilo was sent to the court of King Charles IX in France. Ostensibly the purpose of his journey was to offer Charles and his mother Cathérine congratulations on the defeat of the Huguenot force at Jarnac in the ongoing Wars of Religion between the French crown and the protestants. However, among the letters Troilo carried in his credenza was one from Cosimo, in which the duke did more than offer compliments, he pledged to lend his support to France: 'We shall send a subsidy of 2,000 infantry from our militia and 100 horsemen . . . so that we can shed blood, needing, as we do, the suppression and extinction of those seditious rebels and enemies.'[17] This is one of those instances when Cosimo decided it was in the Medici political interest as a Counter-Reformation ruler to be seen to support the French crown.

A few months later, the Huguenots suffered another defeat at the hands of the French crown at the battle of Moncontour. Once more Troilo was dispatched to Paris, with instructions to not only offer Medici congratulations on the victory but also felicitations on the recent marriage of Charles IX. The French king had married Elizabeth, the Emperor Maximilian's daughter and Giovanna's niece. Giovanna actually made a request to Cosimo on behalf of Elizabeth, asking if he would let his court doctor, Filippo Cauriano, serve her niece in France.

It was the scene of this last mission – Troilo bowing to Catherine, the real power in France, and offering nuptial congratulations –

which would later be captured as a pictorial symbol of Franco–Medici relations. Troilo was evidently popular with the French royal family, in particular with Cathérine and her favourite son Henri, and sometimes his visits to France were extended. If Isabella was unhappy at being parted from her lover for the periods of time when he went on such missions, she realized that this was the price she paid for his affections. It was, in fact, in part her doing that her Orsini lover appeared to be held in greater regard across parts of Europe than was her Orsini husband.

CHAPTER 2

Family Lives

Despite Isabella's separate residences, her night-time pursuits and supposedly clandestine relationship with Troilo Orsini, the Medici
princess still occupied a pivotal position at her father's court. Ridolfo
Conegrano's description of her role in the welcoming reception for
Giovanna's brother Karl, Archduke of Austria, in April 1569, under-
scores this point. Having been met at Florence's Porta del Prato by
Francesco, the ever numerous mounted nobles and the military com-
panies, the Archduke processed on to the Palazzo Vecchio, 'where His
Highness [Cosimo] was waiting for him, in a ground-floor room with
Lady Isabella and fifty noblewomen of the first families of the city, all
dressed in golden silk embroidered with jewels. His Highness wore a
vest of black velvet, embroidered with gold and silver. Lady Isabella
was dressed entirely in white and gold, of a cloth with infinite jewels
and embroidery and the most beautiful pearls at her neck, so richly
dressed and decorated that I cannot describe it any further.'

Giovanna's appearance merited no description whatsoever in
Conegrano's dispatch, even though she naturally took precedence
over Isabella at the meal which followed. The next day, the Medici laid

View of Ponte Vecchio with the Vasari Corridor, Florence

on further sights and entertainments. 'They went to Mass at San Lorenzo,' Conegrano reported, 'but first they took him to visit the chapel that Michelangelo made, with those beautiful statues, holy relics, the library, and all the things that should be visited in that church.' Then, 'at six o'clock in the evening, the archduke danced a *gagliardo* with Lady Isabella, and so they went on until bedtime'.[1]

Such days were big events in the life of the Medici, while others were quieter, such as when Isabella spent time with Cosimo at the Pitti, 'in tranquillity and without trouble to anyone', as she described it. Now that he was a bit older, Isabella also began to spend more time with Cardinal Ferdinando when he came up to Florence. Ferdinando's life as a cardinal was somewhat different from that of his predecessor Giovanni in that, although he was no more religious than his brother, Ferdinando spent a lot more time in Rome from an early age. Rome allowed him centre stage far more than did Florence, which was dominated by his father and elder brother and sister. Ferdinando had better social skills than Francesco, being more willing to appear to be on good terms with everybody, although he seems to have had difficulty concealing his feelings about Paolo Giordano. 'Cardinal Ferdinando had a bit more desire to see me than before,' sniffed Paolo to Isabella, in July 1566, suggesting he had felt Isabella's brother had snubbed him on previous occasions.[2] When he returned from Rome, Ferdinando often stayed in the Palazzo Medici with Isabella.

Other family members with whom Isabella got on very well were her mother's brothers Luigi and Garzia Álvarez di Toledo. Luigi, now Lieutenant of the Kingdom of Naples, like Isabella had deep-running intellectual interests and had spent time in Florence when she was a child while earning his doctorate at the University of Pisa, the duchy of Tuscany's primary seat of learning. He had later served as Cosimo's Procurator, formally receiving in Cosimo's name the city of Siena after the Medici victory. He often stayed with Isabella on subsequent trips to Florence. Garzia, five years older than Cosimo and appointed Viceroy of Sicily in 1565, was one of Spain's most admired military men, the naval commander-in-chief. It was in part due to his military career that he was persuaded, following the death of his wife, to leave his baby daughter in the care of her aunt Eleonora in Florence. The little girl, also named Eleonora, was sometimes called 'Dianora' as a pet name to avoid any confusion, but came more commonly to be called Leonora.

Leonora was born in 1553 and spent her infancy very much in the background of Medici court life, largely cared for out of sight by the Medici *balie*. As she passed out of childhood, it was evident that she possessed considerable charm. She was extremely pretty: her portraits show a fawn-like redhead, with huge dark eyes, 'like two stars in her head', as one writer would later describe them. Leonora was also extolled as gracious and genteel, charming and affable.

Isabella had not been especially interested in the infant Leonora, who at the age of five liked to attach herself to Isabella's younger sister Lucrezia. But she did later take the blossoming Leonora under her wing. An expense in Isabella's household account book for 1565 reads: 'By order of the Illustrious Signora, three golden *giulios* for Madonna Leonora as alms to give to Anna the poor widow woman.'[3] Such an entry gives a picture of Isabella engaged in a kind of virtuous pedagogy, instructing her twelve-year-old cousin in the practice of Christian charity. For her part, Leonora saw Isabella as her role model and engaged in the same kinds of intellectual activities, music and sports.

Cosimo was also extremely fond of Leonora, to the extent that he had no desire to see her leave Florence, which was set to happen if her father Garzia found her a husband from elsewhere in Italy or Spain. So Cosimo decided to pre-empt Garzia by arranging, in 1568, a betrothal for Leonora to his son Pietro, who was a year younger than his fiancée. Philip II officially sanctioned the match, for his approval was mandatory where a Spanish noble, such as Leonora, was concerned, even though she had lived all her young life at the Medici court.

In betrothing Leonora to Pietro, Cosimo was also attempting to ensure that his son would receive a wife who had grown accustomed to his aberrations. Francesco might have been disagreeable by nature, but the consensus was that Pietro was emotionally disturbed. He had what would now be called learning difficulties: he was short-tempered and violent, his behaviour, some believed, the result of his mother's death and the subsequent 'liberty with which he grew up'.[4] Nobody, neither Eleonora when she was alive nor his father, had regulated Pietro's life in the way the lives of his older siblings had been. Cosimo thought that, because she and Pietro had known each other for so long, Pietro's issues might be easier for a wife like Leonora to contend with than for a foreign bride brought to Florence as a near adult. Nonetheless, if this reasoning played any part in Cosimo's decision, it was not how his choice was interpreted by the outside world when word reached them of the betrothal. The gossips concluded that Leonora was staying in Florence for the same reason Cosimo had never let Isabella leave: he wanted his wife's pretty niece for himself and she was loved by him in the same shameful way he loved his own daughter.

One result of the betrothal between Leonora and Pietro, and the subsequent realization that Leonora was in Florence to stay, was that the bond between Isabella and Leonora grew stronger. The pair became closer as Leonora reached maturity and she participated in her cousin's more adult-centric activities. Isabella had not been especially close to her own sisters, but Leonora was to become like a younger sister to her.

There certainly was a multiplicity of Eleonoras in Cosimo's life. The woman who became his chief mistress during 1565 was yet another. Eleonora degli Albizzi was, in the words of a contemporary commentator, 'reduced, by the Duke, to his will while she was still at a tender age, and a virgin . . . taken secretly without the knowledge of her father to his villas.' Eleonora was actually about twenty-one when she began her relationship with Cosimo, so although a quarter of a century younger than the duke, she was hardly the *fanciulla* (child) so described. Her father Luigi degli Albizzi, who came from a branch of this long-established Florentine family but was suffering financial difficulties, sanctioned his daughter's relationship with the duke. Everybody in the city knew about it.

Eleonora's tenure as Cosimo's mistress lasted about two years. She quickly became pregnant by him, delivering a baby girl in May 1566. Cosimo, with his particular weakness for daughters, was so thrilled that he declared to one of his servants, Sforza Almeni, his intention to marry Eleonora. Sforza had served Cosimo and his family for several decades. He had been a beneficiary of Cosimo's largesse, receiving, among other things, some of the Salviati properties in the disbursement that provided Isabella with the Baroncelli villa, and had been promoted to gentleman of the bedchamber. However, a few days after the birth of Eleonora's daughter, the diarist Lapini would recount:

> On May 22, on Wednesday, the Eve of Ascension Day, Sforza of Perugia died. He was Duke Cosimo's first gentleman of the bedchamber and his favourite. It is said that it is his master who killed him, for having revealed a secret, I don't know what, of great importance.

It transpired that Sforza had informed Francesco of his father's nuptial plans, 'it is believed with the intention of acquiring the prince's favour' – evidently mindful of the time when the son would succeed his father. Francesco, appalled at the idea of such a marriage, immediately 'expressed his disgust to his father'. Cosimo, realizing the source of the leak, was incandescent with rage. Sforza soon heard of Cosimo's fury and apparently tried to petition both Francesco and Isabella to intervene on his behalf, neither of whom felt inclined to do so. Still believing in Cosimo's affection for him, Sforza rather rashly attempted to mollify the duke in person. However, he did not realize the extent of Cosimo's ire, whose reaction on being confronted by his servant was to run his sword through him, crying, 'Traitor! Traitor!' Reflecting later upon the incident, Cosimo was said only to be sorry about the fact that he had done Sforza 'too much honour' in killing him with his own hand.[5]

Isabella had no more desire than Francesco to see Eleonora marry their father. Still, as mother to a new half-sister she was worthy of attention. When, a few months later, Eleonora fell sick, Isabella went along with Cosimo and a court doctor to visit her. 'I arrived at ten at night,' she reported to Francesco, out at Poggio a Caiano, 'and found Donna Leonora, who was not very well with fever and with discharge . . . but the baby is feeding well . . .' The issue of the child's well-being seems to have been of as great, if not greater, concern for Isabella, because she added in a postscript: 'Now we have been here twelve hours she still seems very poorly to me, but with all that the breast-feeding is going well.'[6] However, while Eleonora recovered, '*la putta*', the little girl, whose name we do not know, died soon after.

Cosimo did not marry Eleonora degli Albizzi, the incident with Sforza Almeni apparently causing her to lose her lustre in his eyes. The following year, 1567, she gave birth to a son, but Cosimo had already made plans for Eleonora's dismissal. He arranged for her to marry Carlo Panciatichi, whose family were among the most loyal to the Medici in Florence. Cosimo arranged for some murder charges against Carlo to be dropped in exchange for his agreeing to marry Eleonora, who would come with a 10,000 *scudi* dowry. The couple married shortly after the birth of her son, and Eleonora would bear Carlo a further three before he shut her up in a convent in 1578, on the grounds of her suspected adultery. The boy Eleonora had with Cosimo did remain with the Medici family. He was christened Giovanni, clearly in memory of the departed favoured son, but Isabella, at any rate, preferred to call him Nanni.

Other babies arrived in the Medici family during the second half of the 1560s. Giovanna quickly proved those who declared her too scrawny to bear children wrong. By September 1566, she was able to announce that she was three months pregnant, a declaration that Isabella used to her own advantage. 'You've been informed', she wrote to Paolo Giordano, who was agitating once more for his wife to come to Rome, 'that I wish to be here for the labour of Her Highness, so I would need to be here until the end of March, because these things can take a long time.'[7] It was actually in February 1567 when Giovanna delivered a baby girl, who became yet another Eleonora to add to the household.

Giovanna produced two more baby girls in successive years, but neither lived more than a few months. As a result, she was even more anxious about the health of her eldest. In September 1570, she was in Siena with Francesco, with three-year-old Eleonora back in Florence in the care of nurses. But when word reached Giovanna that her daughter was sick with chickenpox, she wanted a close family member watching over her. She explained to her father-in-law, 'I have dropped a note to Donna Isabella, who is content to receive her into her house.'[8] Isabella assured Giovanna that she was 'crazy with happiness' to take care of her niece.[9] On another occasion, Isabella wrote to an absent Francesco to let him know that his daughter was very sick, receiving a typically laconic reply from her brother:

> The illness of which Your Excellency writes which has afflicted my baby girl gives me more displeasure than you could imagine. But then there is no other remedy than that which His Divine majesty orders, and we cannot do anything other than conform to his will.[10]

Giovanna had thus far disappointed Francesco in not bearing any sons. His feelings towards his daughters were limited. But although he was displeased at the lack of a male heir, at least his wife was having children, something that Isabella was not. As the 1560s progressed, the issue of Isabella and the bearing of children was one clouded in mystery. Her ability to become pregnant had been proved by the miscarriages she had undergone in 1561 and 1562, but no concrete reports of pregnancy had been reported since that time. In 1564, Ridolfo Conegrano reported that 'everybody says Lady Isabella is pregnant, but she denies it'. Later, she apparently told him 'she does not know if she is or she isn't'.

Isabella did not want to be found pregnant and the date to coincide with a time when Paolo Giordano had not been present in Florence but Troilo had. Such anxieties and uncertainties found some reflection in the stories that circulated about her on the street. One voice claimed: 'She had, not by her husband, two baby girls, who were sent to the Ospedale degli Innocenti [the local foundling hospital].'[11] It is entirely possible that there were medical reasons why Isabella was not announcing any pregnancies, and her fervent partying and hard riding may also have been contributing factors. But if Isabella did not want to become pregnant, she could have turned to substances which had been held to be contraceptives or abortifacients since the Greek Dioscorides had written a herbology treatise, *De Materia Medica*, in the first century AD. In Isabella's time, his work was still the main resource on such matters, and an Italian commentary on the text, written by the Sienese Pietro Mattioli, had been published in Florence in 1547. Mattioli proposed that the herb rue 'moves the urine. In this sense, it extinguishes birth and flatulence.' Ligusticum roots have 'warming faculties, thus they stimulate the menses . . .' Elaterium, a squirting cucumber, 'provokes the menses and kills the foetus', and Mattioli mentioned that a physician of his acquaintance had grown wealthy from its sale.[12] Another herb that was included, pennyroyal, was still used as an abortifacient in the twentieth century.

In 1588, Pope Sixtus V would issue a bull in which he proposed 'the most severe punishments should go to those who procure poisons to extinguish and destroy the conceived foetus . . . who by poisons, potions and *maleficia* induce sterility in women . . . the same penalty should be offered to those who proffer potions and poisons of sterility to women and offer an impediment to the conception of a foetus, and who take pains to perform and execute such acts or in any way counsel them, and to the women themselves who voluntarily take the same potions'.[13] If the Pope was making such a proclamation, it was as a response to the belief that the issue of women seeking contraception or abortion had become prevalent in the previous decades.

The items described by the doctors and herbalists as contraceptives and abortifacients were readily available at a Renaissance apothecary shop, where Isabella was an excellent customer. One of the bills her father paid on her behalf was the substantial sum of 200 *scudi* to 'Stefano Rosselli and company, *speziali*', or apothecaries.[14] Isabella, who had had doctors fussing over her since birth, never missed an opportunity to lament a sore foot, an earache or a toothache, and undoubtedly procured prescriptions to remedy these ailments. But there is no reason to suppose her purchases from the apothecary did not include other 'potions' as well.

When they were betrothed, one exhortation Paolo Giordano made to Isabella was that she should not follow the example of his sister Felice, who 'only knows how to make girls'. Later, he anticipated 'a little body growing in your body' and imagined she was producing a 'Girolamino' (the diminutive of his father's name) or a 'Paolino'. But as the 1560s began to draw a close, with the couple having been married for a decade, he started to give greater voice to his anxiety about his lack of an heir. In August 1569, Paolo was in Tuscany, at the relatively close abbey of Basignano, partaking in hunting excursions and wishing that Isabella join him, 'if you do not have any particular need to remain in Florence . . .' He then indicated that he needed to get her pregnant, and 'it is hard with so many absences'.[15]

Isabella replied to her husband three days later. She said she had read his letter and understood there was something he needed to ask her, 'but I ask you to write to me more clearly so that I can do whatever I can and you know I am always ready to serve you. We are here at Cerreto and we will remain here three or four days, according to what the Duke My Lord says, who is very well, and recommends himself to you. My teeth are better, but I am ill in my soul, as I am without my *dognina* [perhaps sixteen-year-old Leonora] whom I adore. There has been good hunting for partridges and hares and the rest of the time we play piquet [the card game].'[16] By now Cerreto Guidi had become a favourite of Cosimo's, who boasted of it: 'The hunting at Cerreto is so fine and delightful that you could not desire more, and with birds and dogs one can kill so many partridges, hares, stags, small boars that one returns in the evening overloaded with prey . . . I believe that it is perhaps pleasanter than the Roman countryside as one can combine, at one time, the wild, with the domestic.'[17]

One might note that Isabella's response to the most essential part of Paolo's letter was to pretend that she did not understand what he was asking her. Cerreto Guidi was not very far from where Paolo was staying, yet she clearly had no intention of joining him, nor did she invite him to join her. There surely could be no greater sign of a woman trying to avoid getting pregnant by her husband. Absence was, after all, the greatest contraceptive of them all.

CHAPTER 3

Grand Duke

———

In October 1569, Cosimo de' Medici dispatched letters to the dukes of Mantua, Ferrara and Urbino, all of which conveyed the same news, in the same tone. The missives informed his peers that they were, in fact, his peers no longer.

'I have learned', wrote Cosimo, 'that His Holiness the Pope, removed from any thought of my own, or request, has decorated me with the title of Grand Duke of Tuscany, with the most honoured pre-eminence and dignity that I could ever have known, but for which I could never have asked. You know how far removed I am from ambition for such honours,' he continued, with an apparently straight face, 'but to refuse them would be a monstrous insult. I did not desire this splendour, but it is as well that I accept it, for the ornament and for the sake of His Holiness, with whom I have no other interest than love and filial obligation. I know Your Excellency,' he concluded his letter brightly, undoubtedly enjoying the vision of the recipient's face, now tinged with green, 'will be pleased, knowing how sincerely I bear love for you.'

It would be hard to find a more disingenuous letter in the history of diplomatic relations. Cosimo had been manoeuvring to acquire the

Coronation of Cosimo as Grand Duke in the Vatican Palace

title of grand duke, which would assure him pre-eminence and precedence over every ducal family in Italy, for at least a decade. Although
the bequeathal of the title of grand duke to an Italian lord by the Pope
was unprecedented, Cosimo had had good reason to believe that Pope
Pius IV, who had accommodated his Medici 'cousin' in so many
things, would be amenable to his desire. Unfortunately for Cosimo,
Pius IV died before he could grant Cosimo's wishes, and his successor,
Pius V, was not quite as malleable. It took a few years of promises and
concessions to Pius – sending out troops to fight heretics in the Wars
of Religion, supplying galleys to defend the Roman coastline – before
the Pope passed a bull in late August 1569 anointing Cosimo grand
duke.

If Cosimo's letters to the other Italian dukes were outright boasts
about his change in status, he had to be much more careful in how he
informed both Philip II, king of Spain, and Maximilian, the Holy
Roman Emperor, of his news. The conferral of ducal titles was a privilege of those rulers, as well as the Pope, and it was Charles V who had
appointed Cosimo duke over thirty years ago. However, when
Cosimo approached the Habsburgs in the early 1560s about upgrad-
ing him to the title of Archduke, they were heavily disinclined towards
accommodating his request. Others in a similar position to Cosimo
might then demand the same honour, and there were those who would
perceive it as 'the lowering of Habsburg dignity'.[1] Philip II was most
displeased when he learned of Cosimo's plan to bypass himself and his
family in his quest for elevation, stating that no one 'who had been
benefited by him should increase his power without him'.[2]

As such, Cosimo chose his words judiciously in his letters to the
Habsburgs, which he did not send out until November 1569, three
months after the issuing of the papal bull. To Spain he explained he
had been given the title of grand duke, 'with full prerogatives and
precedence not inferior to those of Archduke, with the exception of the
ecclesiastical state and that of His Majesty [Philip II]'.[3] In a more intimate and not entirely truthful letter to Maximilian, with whom he was
more closely related by way of his daughter-in-law, the emperor's sister, Cosimo speculated as to why Pius had chosen to award him the
title: 'I have been alerted by a secret friend, an intimate friend of His

Holiness, that he has seen him sign a bull in which he has bestowed upon me the title of Grand Duke . . . This can only have been through divine inspiration, as this great gift from this rare and holy pope came so spontaneously. I think perhaps he thought to gratify Your Majesty in that the splendour will descend to your own blood . . .'[4]

In other words, Cosimo tried to persuade Maximilian that the grand-ducal title was a good thing for the Habsburgs, as it meant that Francesco and Giovanna's as yet unborn heir, half-Habsburg, would eventually receive the title himself.

Cosimo had timed his letters to the Habsburgs strategically, cognizant that it would take the bureaucracy- and protocol-laden courts a long time to process and respond to his news. On 13 December, he officially received word of the title from the Pope in a formal presentation. Ridolfo Conegrano sent the following report to the Ferrarese duke, who was undoubtedly beside himself with irritation now that Cosimo, in d'Este opinion a mercantile arriviste from a lesser branch of the family, could justly claim to outrank him: 'This morning the duke had from His Holiness the title of Grand Duke of Tuscany. The prince went to the Pitti from where they carried the [now gout-ridden] duke in a sedan chair to the Palazzo Vecchio's great hall, where he remained under a baldachin. His Holiness had sent Signor Michele his nephew to announce the privilege with many loving words in praise of His Highness. That evening,' Conegrano concluded, getting to the part of a day's events he always liked the most, 'there was a little party in the palace, attended by several noblewomen.'[5]

In late January 1570, Cosimo announced his intention of going to Rome, allegedly only to thank the Pope for having presented him with the bull. But this claim merely provided a smokescreen in the face of imperial and Spanish ire for his true purpose. He was really going to Rome to be crowned grand duke, and he had a crown packed, made for this very purpose. For some months Florentine goldsmiths had been at work on a new grand-ducal crown, which incorporated the symbol of Florence, the fleur-de-lys, 'valued, it was said, at 200,000 *scudi*, with 75 precious stones of all sorts, at the peak a garland of the most beautiful and the largest pearls'.[6]

On 3 February, Cosimo set out for Rome. He left Francesco in charge in Florence, and his younger son Pietro stayed behind as well. Isabella, however, did accompany her father, to share his joy and pride in what was to come. They made a fairly leisurely journey south, taking in Tuscan towns en route, reaching Rome's Porta del Popolo on 16 February. There, as was the custom for visiting dignitaries, they stayed over at the Villa Giulia, built by Pope Julius III and to whose design Cosimo's artist Giorgio Vasari had contributed. Cosimo made his formal entry into Rome two days later, processing across the city to the Vatican with the usual sumptuously adorned retinue. He was met by the Pope and his court at the Vatican's great audience hall, the Sala Regia, and it was at this moment that the Habsburg emissaries present had their first clue as to what was actually going to happen. The Pope invited Cosimo to sit down, a privilege only granted to crowned heads of state. The Habsburg ambassadors left in protest at what they perceived as an insult to their masters.

As a woman, Isabella could not attend this event. However, a few days later, 'accompanied by many noblewomen, she went to kiss the feet of the Pope, where she was received with extreme benevolence and courtesy'.[7] She was performing the same role her mother had performed on the last Medici family visit to Rome a decade earlier: acting as the female representative of the Medici.

The real business of the trip did not take place until more than a week later. On 4 March, Cosimo's coronation took place in the Sistine Chapel. He was dressed in a brocade vest 'rich beyond rich', and an overshirt and cloak of ermine. He processed down the chapel's aisle, accompanied by Paolo Giordano, bearing his sceptre, and the other chief representative of the Roman nobility, Paolo's brother-in-law Marcantonio Colonna, holding Cosimo's new crown. Cosimo, however, was also carrying an object. When he reached the altar, where the Pope was standing, he presented him with a present, 'a most beautiful chalice of the finest gold, beautifully worked, with three most beautiful figures, Faith, Hope and Charity . . . the work of Benvenuto Cellini'.[8] At the altar, the Pope instructed Cosimo to 'receive the crown . . . know you are called upon to be the Defender of the Faith . . . bound to protect widows and orphans and whoever is in misery, and may you ever be a ready servant and a notable ruler in the eyes of God'.[9] Once a slighted and seemingly insignificant member of the Medici family, Cosimo had reached heights even his ambitious ancestors might have thought impossible. He was now Grand Duke of Tuscany.

The following week, he and Isabella left Rome together and made another deliberately slow journey back to Florence. Giovanna came out to join them when they neared the city, as Conegrano reported on 22 March: 'His Highness is at San Casciano, with the princess and the Lady Isabella, who came from Rome with His Highness.'[10]

Conegrano knew that the d'Este duke would be interested to learn that Isabella's visit to Rome had been no longer than that of her father's. Many might have supposed that Paolo Giordano would have petitioned his father to have Isabella remain behind, as she had done for a short period at Bracciano on her last visit to Rome. But if he did, he was unsuccessful. Moreover, Isabella did not even stay with her husband while she was in Rome. Instead, she went, as another chronicler noted, 'to lodge in the house of the cardinal her brother', the pretty Palazzo Firenze in the Campus Martius.[11] On other days she went out to the villa Ferdinando had recently acquired and was extending on the Pincian Hill, which, as the Villa Medici, was soon to become his chief residence. For a few days she complained, as a courtier wrote back to Florence, of 'some bother and pain in her kidneys', adding, 'not without hope of pregnancy'.[12] When Paolo questioned her, she responded by letter: 'As to my pregnancy, if I was sure of it, I would immediately let you know . . . as it is, I cannot tell you anything.'[13]

Paolo was, however, dealing with a greater blow to his honour than being deprived of his wife's company and receiving her usual cryptic comments as to whether she was pregnant or not. When he processed down the aisle of the Sistine Chapel with Cosimo and Marcantonio Colonna, he was given an inferior position to his brother-in-law: Marcantonio carried the magnificent new crown, Paolo only the sceptre. In response to his protest at this insult, the master of ceremonies spoke aloud as they processed that the Orsini and Colonna came 'without prejudice to themselves and their families', otherwise, it was understood, 'Paolo Giordano would not give the dignity of the more honoured place to Marcantonio'. In other words, their positions were not to reflect upon which family had precedence in the city. But Paolo knew that such a statement could not disguise the fact that it was his brother-in-law who appeared as the more esteemed individual to those assembled and, even more injuriously, had done so at his own father-in-law's coronation. But the fact remained that it was in both Cosimo's and the Pope's interests to favour Marcantonio over Paolo. Marcantonio was admiral of the papal fleet. Moreover, he had very close ties to Spain: his mother was Giovanna d'Aragona and he had spent a great deal of time there in the previous years. For Cosimo to give him precedence at his coronation could play a small part in smoothing ruffled Iberian–Medici relations. When it came to such affairs, the matter of Paolo Giordano's pride was inconsequential; consider it, Cosimo might have said, part of the interest on all the loans he had advanced his son-in-law.

CHAPTER 4

Cammilla

If Cosimo's successful bid for grand dukedom had caused jealousy and anger in other heads of state, then his next act was to shock and horrify those much closer to home. He had been back in Florence for barely a week after his coronation when dispatches from the city reverberated with the following news: 'On Wednesday, April 5, it was discovered and is now known universally by everybody, how His Most Serene Highness the Grand Duke has taken for his legitimate wife Cammilla, daughter of Antonio di Domenico di Baccio Martelli, known as Balencio.'[1] The Martelli were an old Florentine family, and Cammilla's grandfather Domenico was a particularly loyal supporter of Cosimo. All the same, the Grand Duke of Tuscany was marrying a commoner.

It seems that Cosimo decided not to make the mistake he had made with Eleonora degli Albizzi. He told no one of his plans, and married Cammilla quickly and in secret, only making the announcement after they were married. The explanation he provided to his son Francesco for the marriage was 'God inspired me to do it.'[2] Some have thought that, by fashioning himself as a model Counter-Reformation ruler, the

Return of Cosimo as Grand Duke

marriage was part of Cosimo's payment to the papacy for the grand-ducal crown. By marrying Cammilla, Cosimo was refusing to live in sin and so setting an example to others, thereby endorsing the stricter morals of the Counter-Reformation church. It was at this same time that the new grand duke, who had previously resisted the church's attempts to persecute Jews, issued a proclamation that if Tuscany's Jews wished to remain in the state, they must 'live in the city of Florence in such streets and places, and in that way and with those conditions and obligations that will be declared'.[3] The Medici grand duke established a ghetto in the city, which for the next centuries existed next to the Mercato Vecchio in the streets where second-hand clothes were sold, a key aspect of Jewish trade.

Still, if Cosimo's attitude towards the Jewish population altered in response to the new debt he had to the Pope, his attitude to marriage had not really changed. At one time, Cosimo had been equally keen to marry Eleonora degli Albizzi, Cammilla's predecessor as mistress, and perhaps all that can be said of his decision is that he was the marrying kind. But certainly the news came from out of the blue: Cammilla had been Cosimo's mistress for a little over two years, yet she had not taken a prominent position at the Florentine court. Indeed, it seems that very few people, his children included, actually knew of their relationship.

At the time of the marriage, Cammilla was twenty-five years old, her new husband fifty. Although one courtier expressed the opinion 'in my judgment, she has an unattractive face', he also noted that she was 'tall and well-proportioned'.[4] When Cammilla's daughter Virginia was grown up and about to marry the d'Este heir (she later became Duchess of Ferrara), another remarked that although she was quite good-looking, 'it is the consensus of everyone, her mother is much more beautiful'.[5] And even if Cammilla's face was not to everybody's taste, what she had going for her would blind most to any other flaws, for she was 'fair, and blonde', and the Florentines, more than any other Italians, have always prized '*la bionda*'. A portrait, now widely held to be that of Cammilla, shows a woman with white skin and golden hair. Dripping with jewels, far more than Eleonora da Toledo ever sported in a picture (on their wedding Cosimo provided Cammilla with multiple necklaces and a magnificent emerald), Cammilla appears every inch the Renaissance trophy wife.

Cosimo's adult children Francesco, Isabella and Ferdinando all reeled in disbelief at the news that their father had taken a new bride. After meeting with his father, Francesco reportedly left the room in tears, so humiliated was he that Cosimo, now Grand Duke of Tuscany, had married a woman from one of the less distinguished Florentine families. But outward opposition to Cammilla was not an option for the Medici children. Francesco cautioned Ferdinando down in Rome 'not to give His Highness displeasure and unhappiness at seeing us disobedient and disunited from him'.[6] In his correspondence from Rome, Cardinal Ferdinando was able to temper his response in accordance with the official reaction of the papacy; in other words, he expressed his approval at the morality of his father's actions. He wrote to his father to tell him the marriage was 'greatly endorsed by Our Lord the Pope, who called me yesterday to let me know, with his Christian and judicious thoughts, how he admires the servitude of your soul . . . and I want to let you know in these few lines of my own contentment . . . '[7] To his brother Francesco, Ferdinando wrote: 'I have received many letters from Florence telling me how His Highness my father has married a young Florentine woman, which, like all unexpected things, put me rather in a state of suspended animation, more so for not having received official news. However, yesterday His Holiness called me, gave me confirmation and congratulations on the news, which very much consoled me . . . Given the lengthy and great deeds that his Highness has done for our house and we children,' concluded Ferdinando, 'we would be very ungrateful if we were not content, as well as without love, at what is giving him so much pleasure.'[8]

Cosimo knew very well that his family would not be best pleased with the marriage to Cammilla. In fact, the first of his children he sent for to 'congratulate' him was 'the Lady Isabella, then the Lord Prince'.[9] Breaking with protocol by sending for his daughter before her elder brother suggests that Cosimo thought he would get a more positive reception from Isabella. But while she might have kept her feelings from her father, Isabella was extremely upset at the news. A princess so proud of her Medici name, and with the bluest of Spanish blood in her veins, could only feel it to be tainted by association with the comparatively insignificant Martelli. Isabella was also nervous that Cammilla, now her father's wife, had the potential to dethrone Isabella from her position as first lady of Florence, something Francesco's wife, the daughter of the emperor, had not done. She took the unusual, and potentially risky, step of venting her feelings in a long letter to Ferdinando, which she wrote on 15 April 1570:

I was resolved not to write to you until the displeasure of the new issue had dissipated. However, imagining that you now know everything there is to know, there is nothing else to say than we have to swallow it, there is no other remedy. The Lord Prince, as is prudent, tolerates it in the best way possible. The Grand Duke is out at Poggio with the consort and Don Pietro and Nanni [their half-brother by Eleonora degli Albizzi]. I stayed behind in Florence because I'm not feeling well. The displeasure about this business is great, but without any remedy, so we have to mitigate things and not make such a wound any more painful. She is his wife, he will hold to her, and we, my monsignor, are his children and so must accommodate his will. He says he did it in order to discharge his conscience, and that is certainly true, there are very few people out with them at the villa. She will not hold the rank of Grand Duchess. Nonetheless, she is his wife because she eats with him and he is always with her. They go out in a coach together. I've been to see her as His Highness's spouse, and had imagined the little girl whom my father is calling wife; the Lady Cammilla (as I shall now refer to her) appeared, and was very well-mannered towards me, and told me that although she was my father's wife she wished to be my servant . . . The little sister is called Virginia, she is still in the Montalvo house, where she has been brought up as the daughter of Don Diego . . . Do me the favour of letting my husband know the news, and ensure he does not speak of things, because it would make everything much worse. After having thought I would die, I've calmed down and have comforted myself with the thought that this is God's will. I beg you to burn this, because if it were to be seen, it would be the ruin of me.[10]

Isabella's little brother clearly did not comply with her request to destroy the letter.

Isabella did make allusions to what had happened in her correspondence with Paolo. On 13 April, she told him: 'I am taking advantage of the Cavalier Navarrano [coming to Rome] to give you news of my health. God be praised that I am extremely well in body, but not too well in my soul, the reason for which I will let you know about in another dispatch, but I am afflicted with infinite humours. Tomorrow I am going to Poggio [where Cosimo was with Cammilla] to complete the negotiation of your affairs, which I hope will pass well.' However, two days later, the same day she wrote her missive to Ferdinando, she informed Paolo that she had not been able to assist him with his demands, 'as I am now suffering from fever caused by humours brought on by that which my brother is going to tell you'.[11]

The news might have made her ill; however, Isabella's true feelings about her new stepmother, two years younger than herself, were not revealed to the wider world. Her fears were, as she had hoped, 'mitigated' as it soon became very clear that Cosimo did not intend for Cammilla to take on a public role. As Conegrano reported to the Duke of Ferrara: 'She does not go out in public. I think I have only seen her a few times.'[12] Moreover, Isabella put her true feelings aside and made efforts to befriend Cammilla publicly, knowing it would please her father. Conegrano told his employer: 'I met her on the street with Lady Isabella, I'm not sure what they were doing . . . I understand that at dinner Lady Isabella wishes the bride to have precedence over her, although I do not know how they could do that in public.'[13] In other words, Conegrano intimated, the citizens of Florence would not willingly accept Cammilla Martelli being given a higher place than Isabella de' Medici.

Isabella's apparently warm acceptance of Cammilla and the Martelli was so successful as to make Cammilla's father Balencio ask her to be an agent and advocate for him at her father's court. The letter Isabella wrote to Montalvo, Cosimo's major-domo – who had been Virginia's guardian – on Balencio Martelli's behalf also reveals the continuing strength of her influence upon Cosimo: 'I have always tried to avoid affliction,' she wrote. 'However, I am going to have to annoy you, because you must know how His Highness is most afflicted for having learned that tomorrow Balencio wishes to place above his entrance the coat of the arms of the Grand Duke my lord and those of the Lady Cammilla . . . If His Highness would agree it would be a charitable and kindly thing for him to do. I have told Balencio to delay until the evening while I get a response.'[14]

Cosimo did not want too much public attention drawn to his marriage with Cammilla, and her father displaying a Medici/Martelli coat of arms above his house would do just that. This letter from Isabella let her father know she was agreeable to Balencio doing so, which would reassure Cosimo that she continued to support and endorse his marriage to Cammilla, in the wake of other hostilities. Moreover, Isabella could use Cammilla's presence to her advantage. When Paolo Giordano pressed her about matters she had to present on his behalf, she told him: 'I am treating the matter as if it was an affair of my own, but truly now there's the new bride negotiations are always lengthy.'[15]

If Francesco, Ferdinando and Isabella 'swallowed', in her words, the situation with Cammilla, reacting and adjusting accordingly, there was another in their house who simply could not come to terms with it. Giovanna of Austria was absolutely appalled that her father-in-law had married a commoner. His action was so completely removed from the Habsburg mindset that the imperial princess, not known for excessive egotism, perceived his new union as a direct insult to herself and her family. That it came so soon after his sneakily acquired grand-ducal title made matters worse from the perspective of Giovanna's family. She wrote to her brother, the Emperor Maximilian, expressing her outrage at what had occurred, and he responded in kind: 'I cannot marvel enough', he told his sister, 'at what the duke [Maximilian refused to call him "Grand Duke"] was thinking when he made such a shameful and ugly match, which is degrading to everybody. I'm thinking he is not in his right mind. I encourage Your Highness neither to support this impudent woman who has been so exalted, nor to have any interaction with her, and in this way show your worth, and the greatness of your soul.'[16]

Maximilian's letter to his sister was intercepted at the Florentine court and translated into Italian for Cosimo's benefit. Cosimo then addressed a letter to Giovanna, letting her know he was not to be moved by Habsburg opinion: 'His Majesty says perhaps I am not in my right mind. To which I say that when I need to, I'll show that I am, and what I did was to quiet my conscience, and to render account to God and his Vicar [the Pope] . . . I am not the first prince to take one of his subjects as a wife, and I will not be the last. This lady is my wife, and with the grace of God, will continue to be so . . . Living as a good Christian I will always serve His Majesty and Your Highness, and when I need to be, I will show that I am more in my right mind than ever before.'[17]

Cosimo even mandated that Giovanna was to be given precedence over Cammilla at every Medici function. Giovanna, however, preferred to follow her brother's advice by refusing 'to have any commerce whatsoever with the Lady Cammilla'. Cosimo and Cammilla kept house at the Pitti Palace, and Giovanna would not set foot there. In August 1570, Cosimo decided it was time for the betrothed Pietro and his cousin Leonora to wed, 'but not in the Pitti,' explained Conegrano, 'as the Princess Giovanna does not wish to go there, so they are resolved to have the ceremony in the prince's rooms on the ground floor of the Palazzo Vecchio. So everybody went to the Pitti to fetch the Grand Duke, then they went together for the Mass at the Duomo, and then to those rooms, with the Lady Isabella, the Princess Giovanna, and then came the bride. The Lady Cammilla was not to be found anywhere at any of the ceremonies.'[18] Giovanna had expressly banned Cammilla's presence at events she herself was to attend.

While Isabella was prepared to countenance that Cammilla be a part of the family if it made her father happy, Giovanna used her authority as a Habsburg to ensure she was denied a part in Medici public life. Unfortunately for Giovanna, Cosimo marrying his mistress was to be a comparatively minor humiliation she was to suffer at the hands of the Medici men, and it was not long before she would come to regret isolating herself from her father-in-law. And as for her Habsburg brother, political events would soon demonstrate to the Emperor Maximilian that Cosimo could certainly be in his right mind when he needed to be.

S. PIUS V.O.
Author fœderis Catholici contra Turcas.

CHAPTER 5

'I Turchi'

It did not take very long for the scandal Cammilla Martelli had generated to die down, both in Florence and beyond. Cosimo lived very quietly with his new wife, so it was fairly hard for outrage and gossip to be generated by a woman who was so rarely seen in public. Moreover, as 1570 wore on, there was a far more sinister figure than Cosimo's blonde bride dominating the minds of the Catholic heads of state. They were increasingly preoccupied with the goal of annihilating the looming menace of the Islamic infidel, most frequently referred to in Italy as '*il turco*'.

The year 1453 saw the end of the Byzantine empire, when Constantinople, governed by the last emperor of the 'Greek East', Constantine XI, was besieged and conquered by the Ottoman dynasty. The empire the Ottomans established proceeded to become an increasing threat to the west, to the Habsburg monarchs, their affiliates and their allies. For over a century, the Ottomans had moved steadily west; by 1463, a decade after taking Constantinople, they took Bosnia, then Herzegovina twenty years later. Not only did they cause mounting alarm for the Habsburg Austro-Hungarian empire but for Italian states too, for only a short body of water, the Adriatic Sea, separated the peninsula from this aggressive enemy with a remarkably powerful naval fleet. The Venetian state, with its Adriatic coastline, grew increasingly nervous about its trade and exchange with the Islamic world, and on the other side of Italy Cosimo de' Medici also became anxious. Tuscany had a lengthy coastline, a vulnerable and potentially easy point of entry for the seemingly unstoppable Ottomans. To withstand any such attacks Cosimo had built heavy fortifications on the island of Elba and the port of Livorno. In 1547, he had started assembling a fleet of galleys, made from the trees in the Pisan woods where Cosimo's son Giovanni would contract malaria. As most Tuscans were inexperienced sailors, the galleys were manned by a combination of indentured Greeks and Venetians, the so-called *buonevoglie*, or volunteers. Accompanying them in the rowing galley, that 'last degree of human misery', were the convicts, the *sforzati*, and the slaves, the *schiavi*.[1] The latter were a combination of African blacks, moors and Turks, whose manacles were chained extra tightly when the galley was turned to fight against their countrymen.

The greatest early success Cosimo's little fleet experienced was in 1555, when they routed the Turks, who had attempted, with French backing, an invasion at Piombino on the Tuscan coast. However, it was the possibility of incidents such as this that partly provided Cosimo with the incentive to form a new religious military order. 'If the ancient Etruscans', the English traveller Sir Richard Clayton would later comment, 'were formidable from their piracies to their maritime neighbours, the first Grand Duke had more laudable views, and meant to secure the coasts of Tuscany against such depredations. With this intention he created an order of knighthood like that of St John of Jerusalem.'[2]

This military order, the Knights of Santo Stefano, was founded in 1562. One might recall that Troilo Orsini's younger brother Mario had been eager to join them, an ambition he fulfilled. The first military order of this kind had been the Templars, their original mission to protect Jerusalem against the infidel. When they were suppressed by church and crown in 1312, having been deemed to have grown too autonomously rich and powerful, much of their property was given to a new order, the Knights of Rhodes, who had taken that island as their main military base. They were to act as much like pirates as crusaders, pillaging the Ottoman fleet where they could, but their bravery and military prowess were never questioned. Suffering a major defeat at the hands of the Turks, who took Rhodes from them in 1422, the Knights asked Charles V in 1530 to give them Malta, from which they took their new name. Cosimo modelled his Knights of Santo Stefano upon the Knights of Malta, except the Santo Stefano knights were not bound by rules of celibacy, as the Knights of Malta were, and their base was closer to home, in Pisa. Their name was also redolent of Medici military victory. St Stephen's Day was on 2 August, and it was on that day in 1554 when the battle of Marciano was fought and Cosimo beat the Sienese, the French and the anti-Medici Florentines.

Cosimo anointed himself Grand Master of the order, which soon came to number four hundred, with members such as Giulio de' Medici, Alessandro de' Medici's illegitimate son. Their church in Pisa came 'to be full of standards of horse tails and other trophies taken from the Turks by these valiant champions'.[3] Giorgio Vasari designed their palace in the city. The Knights of Santo Stefano distinguished themselves during the 1565 Siege of Malta, supporting the Knights of Malta as they fended off the Turks. Notably, Spain and the empire provided little assistance at the siege. It took some time for Philip to permit his naval commander, Isabella's uncle Don Garzia di Toledo, to come in to assist in the relief. In fact, the greatest failures Cosimo experienced at sea were when he was lending the Habsburg family support, such as during the botched recovery of Tripoli in 1560. The Ottoman empire was undeterred by its failure at Malta. In February 1570, the Ottomans seized all Venetian ships operating in their waters. The Emperor Selim issued the following dispatch to Venice, stating: 'We demand of you Cyprus [a Venetian possession, along with Crete and Corfu], which you shall give us willingly or by force; and do not arouse our terrible sword, for we shall wage most cruel war against you everywhere.'[4] Venice was prepared to concede Cyprus to the Ottomans, but felt it incumbent upon their honour to at least make some show of defiance, and so asked, somewhat half-heartedly, for Spanish assistance in protecting their interests. With Spanish troops

primarily engaged in supporting their Habsburg cousins in their conflicts with Protestants in the north, there was no great willingness on
the part of Spain to come to Venice's aid.

It was actually Cosimo who urged Pope Pius V to encourage Philip
of Spain to form a Holy League in order to launch an offensive against
i turchi in the southern waters of the Mediterranean. In reality, Cosimo
was less concerned that Venice lose its Mediterranean islands, which
the Venetian themselves were prepared to abandon; rather, he was
afraid that were the Turks not checked, they might once again be on
the shores of Tuscany. Cosimo believed that to fight the Ottomans
should be in every Catholic ruler's interests, for it would curtail
Turkish economic, political and religious expansion. Protestant
nations were now seeking to support the Ottomans – Elizabeth I had
business relations with them – so a blow against the infidel was a blow
against the heretic as well. Still, for the French, presided over by a ruler
traditionally known as 'His Most Christian King' and fighting the
Wars of Religion against the heretic Huguenots, to fight the infidel
would be to lend too much support to the Habsburgs.

Philip was disposed to listen to the arguments in favour of fighting
the Ottomans, as they were presented to him by the Pope. However, he
would not countenance Cosimo as grand duke being a named member of the League, on the grounds that Spain would do 'nothing which
can directly or indirectly confirm the titles given to Your Highness', as
Ferdinando wrote to his father from Rome.[5] But Cosimo's conviction
that fighting the Ottoman empire was the right course of action was
such that he agreed to allow his fleet to sail under the papal flag, with
Marcantonio Colonna as papal commander-in-chief. The overall commander would be the energetic and engaging twenty-four-year-old
Don Giovanni of Austria, the illegitimate son of Charles V. He would
take the place of the increasingly infirm Don Garzia da Toledo, who
was now frequently to be found taking the sulphuric waters near Siena
to relieve his ailments. Don Giovanni was a natural-born fighter. He
had been thwarted by Philip in his attempts to join the relief of Malta
in 1565, but had then earned a reputation for bravery, daring and
mercilessness in the Morisco revolt in Granada. He was close to the
Toledo family and asked for, and listened to, advice from Don Garzia,

who pronounced: 'On the life of St Peter, I swear if I had better health I would ship myself as a soldier as willingly under Giovanni as I would under the King [Philip] himself.'[6]

Also exceedingly keen to go to war and prove his military mettle was Paolo Giordano Orsini. In some ways, it was a good thing that the Medici ships were sailing under the papal flag and the experienced command of Colonna, because otherwise Paolo Giordano would have demanded he be the Medici fleet's commander. His naval experience was limited to a stint in August 1566, when he was placed in charge of a small papal flotilla guarding the Adriatic waters off the port of Ancona in the Marche. The Turkish armada never came remotely near Ancona, and Paolo was back in Rome a month later. As plans for the League's trip south developed further, Paolo petitioned Philip II to be nominated as Don Giovanni's lieutenant. He was informed by way of a Florentine in Madrid, Giovanni Antinori, that there was reluctance to give him the position as his great debts had resulted in 'Your Excellency having little reputation with His Majesty and others in his council'.[7] But there was another equally practical reason for the hesitation in giving Paolo this kind of appointment. A naval commander had to be agile; he needed to manoeuvre across the potentially treacherous rolling decks of his ship, and Paolo's great girth hampered him.

All the same, Paolo was determined to go to war in a position of respect and authority. That his brother-in-law Colonna was papal commander-in-chief was 'ruining my honour', and he demanded some form of compensation.[8] He wanted Cosimo to grant him command of two of the Medici ships, and as usual he pressed Isabella to petition her father on his behalf. Isabella really did not want to touch this issue, as she made clear in a response to her husband: 'I have received one of your letters and understand that you are telling me that you want to command two galleys, but I have not wanted to say anything to His Highness about it, as I think it would be better to broach the subject when you yourself come to Florence.'[9] It was one matter for Isabella to broker loans on behalf of Paolo, but she knew it was quite another to give him a charge upon which so much depended politically and financially, and for which he had so little experience and capability.

It was only in June 1571, when the Holy League had made all other concordats and arrangements to sail south, that the Medici decided to let Paolo Giordano command a single galley of the twelve they were sending to the fight. 'I understand', Ridolfo Conegrano reported back to Ferrara, 'that Signor Paolo Giordano is going to sail for His Highness, I'm not sure to how much satisfaction of these lords.'[10] Moreover, the condition of his command was that he be responsible for all the ship's expenses – furnishings, sailors, galley slaves, soldiers, weapons, food and water, rope, pots of pitch and all other provisions. Of course, Paolo did not command such resources. Cardinal Ferdinando might have been brought up as the son of a duke, but his reactions and responses reveal the extent to which the old Medici banking genes were present in the twenty-year-old. He immediately saw how they could take advantage of Paolo's desires and financial situation, as he conveyed to Francesco: 'As Signor Paolo wishes to sail with Don Giovanni of Austria, and having frittered away what remains of his wealth, he has lent an ear to us buying the holding of Palo, and so I have written to His Highness [their father] that we might buy it for 20,000 ducats. It's a good holding. We can rent it out for 1,500 a year.'[11] In other words, Paolo Giordano could have 'his' ship, and even if it were to be lost, the Medici would still have gained yet another piece of the Orsini property which they had systematically been removing from Paolo's care.

All the same, Paolo felt he had been treated poorly and distrustfully by the Medici, and said as much to Isabella. She told him in reply that she could do very little, that it was impossible for her to take his side against her family, reminding him: 'I am not only your wife, but their daughter and sister.'[12] Moreover, she referred to the entire naval embarkation, which was to see 80,000 men set sail south, as '*vostra gita con Don Giovanni*'. *Gita* is a rather light-hearted word denoting a pleasure trip, 'to go about without concluding that for which one is going'.[13] Isabella clearly deliberately picked this phrase over the more appropriate and momentous-sounding *viaggio* – journey or voyage – to trivialize and dismiss Paolo's preoccupations with naval glory and to show her lack of interest in them.

The Medici galley for his command finally arrived at the Roman port of Civitavecchia in mid-July. Selected – not by Paolo – as its captain was a Genoese from an ancient seafaring family, Pier Battista Lomellini, whose expertise, it was hoped, might compensate for the Roman commander's lack of experience.

The one advantage to giving Paolo a ship was that he brought with him a certain number of seasoned Orsini soldiers. But there was one notable absence from this roll call. In late June 1571, Troilo Orsini sent Paolo Giordano the following note from Florence:

> Despite the accusations of [the Roman noble] Honore Savello, I trust Your Excellency can see my impediments in serving on the *viaggio* [Troilo did not call this trip a *gita*] of the armada, and I know that I would be superfluous. Please accept my good intentions for this endeavour, assuring Your Excellency that I say that there can be nothing better than serving you . . . May God concede to Your Excellency a most fortunate voyage and success in all your actions . . . humbly I kiss your hands.[14]

Troilo had recently taken trips to the French court. His 'impediments' may be a reference to Gallic obligations and loyalty, as the French were not a part of the League against the Ottomans, and Troilo was favoured at that court. But that year Troilo made no further trips to France, and French allegiances notwithstanding it is odd for an Orsini military man not to join a military cause so embraced by his family. Instead, Troilo stayed put in Florence, just as Isabella did, while Paolo Giordano sailed further and further south.

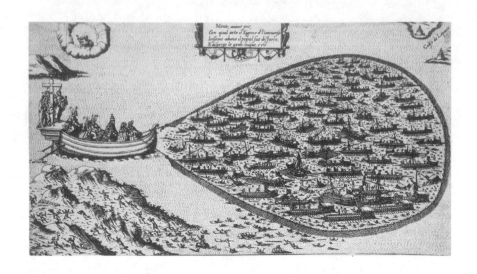

CHAPTER 6

Lepanto and Don Giovanni

The point of assembly for the Spanish, Venetian and papal fleets was Messina in Sicily. All parties convened there in the last week of August 1571, with Don Giovanni arriving with 21,000 men. However, despite this impressive number, Don Garzia di Toledo, taking the waters at the Sienese hot springs, was worried that Philip had endowed Don Giovanni with green, inexperienced men, and that the Spanish king was hoping to avoid the expense of battle entirely. Philip had even sent a letter to Don Giovanni at Messina instructing him to delay fighting until the following year, but his half-brother had already left before the letter arrived. 'The Venetians should not know', Don Garzia cautioned Don Giovanni, 'how much it is in His Majesty's interests that there should be no battle.'[1] Garzia wanted Giovanni to be wary of the Venetians, who in his experience were untrustworthy.

On 17 September, the armada set sail again, landing nine days later on Corfu. The island, a Venetian possession, had recently been sacked by the Ottoman navy, their presence recorded in the chapels in which altarpieces painted by Venetian artists were riddled with Turkish bullet holes, the eyes of the saints depicted in them slashed out with their

Holy League flotilla at Lepanto

scimitars. However, the Corfu natives had captured one Turkish sailor, who gave up the news to the League that his commander-in-chief, the sultan's brother-in-law Ali Pasha, had steered for the Gulf of Lepanto for some respite. Lepanto was an Ottoman naval station on the coast of Greece, about 215 kilometres to the north-west of Athens. It was this gulf that would be the League's final destination in this campaign.

On 5 October, as they prepared for battle, news that was two months old reached the League. The Ottomans had nearly run the Venetians out of Cyprus, but a final surrender had ended violently, when on 5 August negotiations broke down at Famagusta on the Cypriot north-eastern coast, the last bastion of the Venetian hold-out. The Ottoman leader, Lala Mustafa, did not simply kill Famagusta's Venetian captain Bragadino; he had him flayed alive, and then ordered his skin be stuffed with straw and paraded around the town. Don Giovanni was able to utilize this horrific account to galvanize the Venetian fleet, which Don Garzia had advised might not otherwise fight its hardest.

The Ottoman fleet outnumbered that of the Holy League, with about twenty galleys more than the League's two hundred and six, as well as a higher number of smaller ships. But the League's 80,000 soldiers vastly outstripped the 25,000 the momentarily resting Ottomans had stationed in Lepanto. Still, Ali Pasha and his men, flushed with their recent success against the Venetians, were confident that they could once more triumph over their Catholic enemies.

The day of the battle came on Sunday, 7 October, and fighting started at around eleven o'clock in the morning. On every ship was either a Dominican or Franciscan friar or a Jesuit standing with crucifix raised to remind the men they were fighting God's war. Don Giovanni himself went from ship to ship to stir them up further. 'Where is your God?' he asked. 'Fight in His holy name and in death or in victory you will win immortality.'[2] He had arranged the fleet's formation in accordance with advice from Don Garzia, with four divisions on a north–south line. He took one of the central divisions, along with the chief Venetian commander Sebastiano Veniero and Marcantonio Colonna. As the fighting commenced, the Ottomans let out their customary fearsome battle cries, banging and clanging, creating a din that had always frightened their opponents in the past. But Don Giovanni, to show how unperturbed he was by such a display, took his second-in-commands and, as one observer later recorded, 'danced the *gagliardo* on the gun platform to the music of fifes'.[3]

Initially, the League's central division took very hard hits. The Turks took six of its galleys and killed all aboard them. These included two of Cosimo's galleys: the *Florencia*, manned by his Knights of Santo Stefano, which was so wrecked it had to be burned at sea; and the *San Giovanni*, found at the end of the battle with 'rowing benches occupied by corpses'.[4] But eventually the League's superior numbers came into their own and they overwhelmed the Turks. The decisive moment came when Ali Pasha was killed by a bullet to his head. Although Don Giovanni apparently expressed his unhappiness that so worthy an adversary had died in such a way, most accounts agree that he took advantage of the situation and stuck Ali's head on a pike for all to see, which served to spur the League on further and cause the Turks to lose heart.

By four o'clock in the afternoon, the battle of Lepanto was over. Turkish losses have been estimated at thirty galleys and 30,000 sailors and soldiers combined. By contrast, the League had lost comparatively few men – 9,000 – and they were also able to free those Christian prisoners who had been Ottoman galley slaves. It was the first major Ottoman naval defeat since the fifteenth century, and a huge blow to that empire's prestige.

When Cosimo learned of the victory, he informed his envoy Ferrante di Rossi di San Secondo: 'We are sending you to congratulate His Highness [Don Giovanni], as a letter cannot express our consolation, joy and happiness, which you will convey to him, as in one day he has delivered up the spoils and trophies of those Enemies of Christ that for so many years so many potentates have not been able to overcome.'[5] Cosimo knew he could take particular pride in Lepanto, for it had been his prodding that had prompted the initially reluctant participants to form the Holy League in the first place.

Don Giovanni's own inclination was not immediately to inform his 'potentate' Philip of the victory, as, despite providing substantial numbers of troops, the Spanish king had tried to ensure the battle did not take place. He did, however, let Don Garzia know that he felt he owed him the credit for the victory. All the same, on 10 October, his secretary, Luis de Soto, penned the appropriate letter on his employer's behalf citing those who should be commended including: 'The Prince of Parma [the young Alessandro Farnese] was among the first who boarded and took the galley with which his own was engaged; Paolo Giordano Orsini, the Duke of Mondragone, and other lords, vassals and servants of Your Majesty to whom, if Your Majesty pleases, it would be well to order letters of thanks written.'[6]

That same day, Paolo Giordano also sent a letter to Isabella to give the Medici his account of events. Don Giovanni had made Paolo commander of the flagship of the Holy League's left battle wing. With the experienced Lomellini at his side, their ship took that of the Ottoman commander Portù, who was forced to flee on a raft.

I am sending the Cavalier di Fabi to give an account to Their Highnesses [Isabella's father and brother] of the unexpected grace bestowed by Jesus Christ to break the enemy armada and that particularly given to me which allowed me to attack with my ship that of Pasha Portù, and to be the first person in our armada to attack . . . as Don Giovanni knows, as the cavalier will tell. Thanks to God I have no more than a wound from an arrow in my leg of little importance. The Cavalier Orsini is dead . . . and there are many cavaliers and other men of little importance who are dead, as well as many Turks.[7]

Paolo's careless disregard for the deaths of those inferior to him blights his account of himself as the first hero of Lepanto. To Cosimo he wrote that 'I am well, but for a minor blow. I hope that you are satisfied with me as your servant because I fought with Pasha Portù.'[8] The tone of this piece of correspondence seems somewhat truculent; it appears that Cosimo's initial unwillingness to give him a command still rankled with Paolo.

His success at Lepanto earned Paolo a better position in the League's campaigns the following year. Philip appointed him general of the Italian infantry serving the Spanish in an attempt to take back the garrison of Navarino, in the Peloponnese, which the Turks had

seized from the Venetians in 1499. The offence took place in 1572 on
the same date as the Battle of Lepanto a year earlier, 7 October, a date
clearly chosen to bring the League luck. Paolo was now given a much
greater say in the decision-making process, as to when and how to
attack. However, in the aftermath of what was a botched offence, he
became a target for blame. He had held his ships back, the Venetians
complained, been overly hesitant and cautious as a commander. For
others, he was a target of mockery, unable to command his own ship
skilfully, 'revealing himself to be so inept due to his excessive fatness'.[9]
At any rate, Navarino was the final moment in Paolo's naval career.
He would later receive a letter from Spain informing him that he was
'loved and esteemed by the King, but he does not have any need this
present year to inconvenience Your Excellency'.[10]

Paolo Giordano's own inabilities notwithstanding, the 1572 failure
at Navarino was symptomatic of the League's inability to coalesce and
build on the victory at Lepanto. Isabella's assessment of the venture as
a *gita* turned out to be largely correct. The struggles against the
Ottomans continued, although they would be moved to dry land with
the so-called Long Turkish War, begun in 1594 in the Hungarian bor-
der lands.

All the same, the lustre of the victory at Lepanto, considered by
some as the most decisive naval battle since the Battle of Actium in
31BC, remained. The Holy League's success against the infidel was
attributed to the divine intervention of the Virgin Mary, and Pius V
made 7 October a feast day, the day of Our Lady of Victory (now celebrated as Our Lady of the Rosary). And it made a hero out of the
charismatic Don Giovanni, who was extolled as the great warrior of
his age. There was a veritable industry producing statues, portraits,
medals and prints in his image and honour. The Venetian state, once
reluctant to take on the Turks, had over a hundred songs composed in
commemoration of him and his achievements. In Florence, a now
obscure poet, Michele Capri, composed an ode, 'In the Praises of the
Most Serene Lord, Signor Don Giovanni of Austria', which compared
him to gods, emperors and Alexander the Great, and served as fine
military, religious and political propaganda. 'To him whom heaven has
given the grace of seeing the glory of the vanquished Ottomans . . .

who has chased the dogs from the tomb of Christ . . . Europe has faith in you,' Capri concluded enthusiastically.[11]

Capri chose to dedicate the poem not to its subject but to Isabella de' Medici. He declared in the published dedication that the words he had composed in praise of Don Giovanni and 'this triumph of the heavens and the sea' could only be enhanced by association with the 'admirable jolliness and happiness of Your most worthy Ladyship . . . Under the honour of your name . . . I hope you will deign to read it, and keep it in your *studiolo.*' Capri's reference to Isabella's *studiolo* allows him to acknowledge her as a woman of refined learning, like her Medici ancestors.

Isabella may not have met Don Giovanni in person until late in 1574, when she travelled to the port of Livorno with her family to greet him, but she already had a strong connection with him through her Toledo uncles, Luigi and Garzia, to whom he was extremely close and with whom he spent much time at their Neapolitan home. It should go without saying that Don Giovanni was certainly the kind of man who appealed to Isabella. He was a romantic figure, adventurous and brave, lively and daring, a flouter of convention. If Isabella had had Capri's ode to Don Giovanni performed at one of her events, she would have made sure to let the song's protagonist know that she had done so.

One thing Don Giovanni wanted from Florence was some tapestries from the Innocenti workshop, staffed by the specially trained orphans who were by then producing some of the finest quality work in Europe. Don Luigi di Toledo ordered them, bought and paid for them on Don Giovanni's behalf, and then left Florence to go to Naples, expecting the tapestries to be sent on. When they did not arrive, Don Giovanni, at the time also resident in Naples, asked the Medici representative there, Enea Vaini, to write to Francesco, asking him to expedite them as he had authority over export licences: 'Signor Don Giovanni this morning let me know that he is sending a courier to you with a letter begging Your Excellency to release from Florence some tapestries, which have been bought by Don Luigi, and he desired that I also write to you. I replied you would act with great readiness, and thought it would be superfluous, as understanding his wishes, it would be hardly necessary for other intercessions.'[12]

Vaini clearly did not anticipate resistance from Francesco on the matter of Don Giovanni's hangings. As such, it was a very diffident and awkward Vaini who subsequently wrote to Francesco to tell him: 'I presented your letter to Signor Don Giovanni, together with telling him what you ordered me, regarding the export of the hangings belonging to Don Luigi, explaining to him that I cannot violate Your Highness's wishes on this matter . . . Don Giovanni replied to me, smiling that those hangings were his, and that was why he had asked for them . . .'[13] Francesco had evidently blocked the export.

Francesco knew that Don Giovanni had intended to give some of the tapestries to his half-brother Philip. Possibly Francesco pettily resented a Florentine gift being presented to Spain by someone who was not Florentine, and did not mind inconveniencing, not to mention embarrassing, not only Don Giovanni but his own uncle Luigi as well in his embargo. His truculence might have been rooted in even deeper ill will towards the Habsburgs stemming from the period he spent at the Spanish court in the early 1560s. Whatever the reason for Francesco's refusal to part with the tapestries, it was a sign of other rifts in the weave of Medici existence. Cosimo and Isabella might have been proud of Don Giovanni and have enjoyed a warm relationship with the Toledo family. Francesco, however, clearly did not share their regard for their Spanish family and their associates and did not care if he created hostilities between the families.

CHAPTER 7

Putti

As preparations for Lepanto got under way, Isabella readied for an event of her own. On 23 September 1570, Ridolfo Conegrano wrote excitedly to Alfonso d'Este: 'The Lady Isabella is pregnant for certain, she's already showing, and she's being carried about in a litter or a sedan chair.'[1] Isabella did not have to be too diffident about this announcement; although Troilo had been in Florence over the summer, Paolo Giordano had come up for a short time in July as well. However, she had only let Paolo himself know a week or so before. 'You have given me the greatest contentment in the world', he had written to Isabella on 16 September, 'with your certainty that you are pregnant.'[2]

However, Isabella herself was not greatly overwhelmed by the turn of events. A letter she wrote the day Conegrano announced her pregnancy informed Paolo playfully that 'the child sends you a thousand recommendations',[3] but she was more concerned with her husband's request that he borrow her hunting dogs to go out hunting with Cardinal Ferdinando. In the same way she had not wanted to loan her husband her white coach horses, Isabella did not like lending Paolo

Santo di Tito, Head of a small boy

her dogs as she thought he did not take proper care of them and they would end up being gored by a wild boar: 'I am sending you my dogs and I beg that you put them into the hands of the huntsmen to take care of them and make sure they are not killed.'[4]

Still, this was the first time in her life Isabella had carried a pregnancy for more than a few weeks, and she became absorbed, if not appalled, by the changes in her body. 'I must be careful to grow bigger, but not fatter [*ingrossare non ad ingrassare*],' she declared.[5] But by January 1571, she was telling her husband: 'I am so big that I believe that I will make two babies. I can't stand up for long, and I spend so much time in bed that day becomes night and night day. As to your negotiations [Paolo was pressing her in regard to having ships for the League's offence all through her pregnancy], they are as dear to me as they possibly could be. However, I do solicit you to return here in time for my labour, because I'm going to need you to hold my head up, as by that time I will have grown so big that I am going to look like a buffalo.'[6] Isabella's request that Paolo be there at the birth was a joke; men were never present when their wives went into labour.

Despite her proclaimed enormity and inability to get out of bed, Isabella continued to hold events at her house. 'I found myself two days ago at the house of the lady Isabella,' wrote Conegrano to Ferrara on 24 March, 'where all the talk was that there has been found in Bolzano a tomb, 570 years old, inscribed with the Medici coat of arms. These lords have written there to get more information.' Even on the brink of giving birth, Isabella was fascinated by news that could take her family's origins back to the eleventh century and give the Medici the antiquity they lacked. Although rumours spread that the tomb was a fake, Cosimo was not convinced and informed a representative: 'We would dearly like you to send us the stone with the arms, just as it was found, and we will reimburse you for all the expenses in sending it to Florence.'[7]

At other times Isabella's thoughts were centred on the sense of another being growing inside her. 'Your child every day grows stronger,' she informed Paolo.[8] On 13 April 1571, in a letter to Paolo, Isabella referred to the unborn child in a way that would make the man, who had expressed his need and desire for an heir and a 'fine baby boy', uneasy. 'The *nina* is so lively,' she wrote, referring to the child's activities in her womb, 'that I am sure she is going to be the sweetest thing.' But she might have been less than sure she was carrying a girl and was rather, in Isabella's typical epistolary fashion, taking a small measure of revenge on her husband, for the letter goes on to inform him: 'You must know that Bernardo del Riccio [Paolo's estate manager at Bracciano] has been promising your creditors my money and my jewels. But I know', Isabella assured him sweetly, 'that this idea must be devised by your ministers and not by yourself.'9

Nine days later, she wrote: 'The child in my body has for eight days been treating me in the worst way in the world. I cannot eat anything and I feel most troubled.'10 Paolo, however, had not ceased pressing her to expedite the things he would need if he was to go to war, as the rest of her letter to him concerned those issues.11 But as Isabella told him, 'Regarding the weapons, Signor Troilo will immediately send them. It is to him I have left the care of everything.' If Paolo Giordano was not there for Isabella's labour, to help lift her head, then it seems that Troilo was in the vicinity. Not long after, Isabella's first child was born, a little girl named Francesca Eleonora, for both Paolo and Isabella's mothers, but who was immediately called 'Nora' by her own mother.

For a woman who had been so ambivalent about pregnancy and children for so long, the instantaneous bond Isabella had with Nora was notable. She gave birth at the Baroncelli villa outside of the city, and although a wet nurse would have fed the child, Isabella remained with her daughter in the countryside. At just a few days old, 'The *bimba* often has some pains in her body, but it won't be long before she begins to say *babbo*,' Isabella wrote to Paolo in May 1571. But given the proximity of Troilo, one wonders whom Isabella imagined Nora would be addressing as such. Indeed, it was Troilo who stayed with Isabella throughout Nora's first summer.

By June, with Paolo preparing to embark for his journey south, and never having laid eyes on the child, Isabella told him: 'She is more beautiful than ever and already calling for her father.'12 Isabella loved the idea of a precocious child – 'The *pupa* [baby] kisses her hand to her father.' Isabella did lament that the birth had left her physically weakened. 'I have a foot so swollen that I cannot ride a horse,' she complained about three weeks after Nora's birth. 'I believe it is due to liver-related problems.'[13] However, by 7 June, things had improved: 'I am very well, and *la Nora* extremely well, and I believe that she is fattening up [*grassina*] just fine.'[14] Five days later, Isabella was requesting a new hunter so that she could now return to her favourite sport.

Isabella sent Paolo in Rome a portrait of the newborn Nora, and he assured her 'already *tutta Roma* [all of Rome] has come to see it'. But otherwise Paolo made little reference to his daughter in his correspondence with Isabella, often not even sending a greeting to her. He was far more concerned with pressing Isabella to get Cosimo to confirm he would sail with the League as a commander. She found it hard to be patient with him, reminding him that she was preoccupied with 'a daughter, so fine and feminine and born of you', and in any event, she was really 'in the dark about all the goings-on, having as I do a baby on my shoulder'.[15] Such responses did not really satisfy Paolo. 'I have written lengthily and more than once regarding many issues,' he wrote testily to his wife, having not received satisfactory replies. In July, he told her: 'I beg you to write to the Duke of Savoy thanking him for his agreeing to stand as godfather, and confirm that the baptism of the baby will be upon my return.'[16] Paolo would certainly be present at a ceremonial event at which Italy's most illustrious citizens participated, even if he could otherwise wait to see his child.

While awaiting Paolo to return so that she could be baptized, Nora continued to grow. By December, 'She is fussing a bit with her teeth, of which she already has two.'[17] Isabella had returned to fully active post-pregnancy life, travelling to the villa at Cerreto Guidi with the Medici court, 'where we will be for eight days for infinite pastimes, with hunting of every sort, and it is so wonderful'.[18]

By 19 January 1572, Paolo Giordano had made his way to Florence, and Conegrano could report to Ferrara how 'a gentleman from the Duke of Savoy has come to hold as proxy the daughter of Paolo Giordano Orsini at baptism. They did it privately at home, in the chapel of the Palazzo Medici, and gave her the name Leonora. The godmother was the Duchess of Tagliacozza, mother of Marcantonio Colonna [the formidable Giovanna d'Aragona]. The aforementioned gentleman gave the baby girl a jewel of around 2,000 *scudi* in value, and he left two necklaces each worth 70 *scudi* for the *balia* and another lady attendant. In the evening there was a celebration to which twelve noblewomen were invited.'[19]

Most baptisms took place in the Battistero di San Giovanni in front of Florence's Duomo, but a baptism at Isabella's home in the so-called Cappella Medici, if small and private, nonetheless provided the event with a backdrop that allowed family members from the past to be present. Frescoed on the walls by Benozzo Gozzoli between 1458 and 1462 is the 'Adoration of the Magi', a scene which not only includes the three wise men but a cavalcade in which Cosimo Il Vecchio is riding on his brown mule, alongside his son Pietro and grandsons Lorenzo and Giuliano. They are all processing towards the altar, bearing gifts for the Christ child, who is depicted, adored by his mother, in an altarpiece by Filippo Lippi (the original replaced by a copy). But on this occasion, the frescoed figures not only witnessed the Christ child's nativity but Nora's baptism as well.

Carnival in Florence in late February 1572 was, according to Conegrano, 'the most miserable there has been in a long time'. Cammilla Martelli was banned by Giovanna from taking part in public events, so Cosimo did not arrange anything, and Isabella only 'gave a *festino* [a little party] and invited ten noblewomen to her house, and a few other people'.[20] She had other things on her mind, having recently discovered, with Nora little more than nine months old, that she was pregnant once more.

Prevented from pursuing her usual range of physical activities, she asked in March that 'that pair who make carpets could be sent here for my pastime, so that we could make something'.[21] By June, however, 'I find myself in bed plagued by a fall downstairs, which I'm sure affected my kidneys badly, even though now I am so much better that I am out of danger.'[22] And Nora was sick too. 'She has the measles,' Isabella told Paolo, 'but with such little fever that the doctors have said it can't be too dangerous. This year it seems that she's had every illness that she possibly could have . . . I have called for assistance through prayer whenever I can.'[23] Isabella was surrounded by reminders of childhood mortality. Another baby girl had been born to Francesco and Giovanna in August 1571, just a few months after Nora, named after her aunt but known as Isabellina, 'little Isabella'. A year later came the news that 'the fourth daughter of Prince Francesco has died . . . and has been buried in San Lorenzo, without any pomp or formalities'.[24]

Still, it was clear how much pleasure Isabella took in her own daughter: 'I am in the villa where we will stay for the sake of Nora's health, who I am sure does not deceive me in her love, but it truly is the sweetest thing in the world. In fact, it is such that I feel I will make another baby girl, even though this pregnancy feels very different from the other one.'[25]

One can imagine how delighted Paolo Giordano was by Isabella's beliefs about the sex of the child. But in the event, 'Last Thursday,' Conegrano wrote to Ferrara on 13 September 1572, 'at 15 hundred hours, the lady Isabella gave birth to a big and beautiful baby boy to the great contentment of the Lord Duke and of all these lords. And when His Excellency heard she was in labour, he was out in his coach, and immediately went to her, but he was not in time, because the lady had just a short time before delivered. She is very well, thanks to God, she does not have any sort of a fever. A courier was immediately sent to Signor Paolo to tell him this good news.'[26]

Isabella's baby boy was Cosimo's first grandson and his portrait would soon hang in what was now Cosimo's full-time residence, the Pitti Palace, as a testament to his grandfather's pride. After fourteen years of marriage between Isabella and Paolo, the Medici–Orsini union had finally achieved its purpose. It was a small thing then to allow Paolo to endow the boy with an Orsini family name. He was called Virginio, after his great-great-grandfather, one of those able *condottieri* which the Orsini had once produced so easily.

However, ten days after this moment of triumph for the Medici and the Orsini, a strange and tragic event occurred, vividly recounted by Ridolfo Conegrano:

Lady Isabella lives in the Medici palace with all her *famiglia*, where she gave birth. Wednesday night, at four in the morning, a fire was started in a room where one of the slaves lived, who had gone to sleep in a room keeping a light in a box, which she knocked over in such a way that the fire multiplied with incredible rapidity. The slave was overcome by smoke, could not be saved and burned to death. The Lady Isabella, having given birth a fortnight ago, was alerted to the fire, immediately got up and had time to escape with her children and her other ladies to the neighbouring houses. Then the prince came, and he took them to the Palazzo Vecchio, where they awaited the fire being put out with all diligence possible. The palace has not been burned very much, less than half, although many of her ladyship's things have: all of her dresses and linens, among other things, and infinite other items, to the extent that they say His Excellency will have to give her more than 10,000 *scudi* to replace them. And this will come out of an inheritance he would otherwise have bequeathed to Signor Paolo, so we will see what he is going to have to say about that.[27]

Paolo might have gained a son, but it looked like he had lost 10,000 *scudi*.

Veduta della Piazza di S. Marco
1 Chiesa e Convento delle Monache di S. Caterina 2 Casino di S.M.I 3 Compagnia detto Scalzo 4 Chiesa di S. Marco de PP. Domenicani e Convento de
dette PP. 5 Cappella di S. Antonino 6 d.° Chiesa de SS. Duchi Salviati 7 Stalle di S.M.I 8 Serraglio delle Fiere 9 Chiesa detto S. Annunziata. 10 Spedale di S. Matteo
11 Monache di S. Lucia

CHAPTER 8

Bianca

In May 1572, Ridolfo Conegrano wrote to Ferrara to impart the most
recent bit of scandal regarding the antics of the Medici family: 'Signor
Mario Sforza has returned here and they say that Prince Francesco is
annoyed with him and equally so with his wife [Fulvia], who has told
Her Highness [Giovanna] that the lord prince has been making love
with the Venetian lady Bianca Cappello. What I don't know', smirked
Conegrano, 'is how she could not have seen it for herself.'[1]

   Bianca Cappello was born in 1548, not long after Cosimo's new
wife Cammilla. She was the archetypal Venetian beauty, possessed,
her portrait indicates, with copious amounts of Titianesque reddish
blonde hair. With her white skin and a seriously impressive bosom,
she was a Venus or a Flora come to earth. She had pedigree as well,
belonging to a venerable Venetian family who had housed the young
Cosimo when his mother sent him to Venice to protect him from the
invading imperial troops following his father's death late in 1526. But
it was not a Medici connection that had brought Bianca to Florence.
She had arrived in the city in 1563, having scandalized her family and
Venice at large by eloping with the Florentine Pietro Buonaventura. He

Piazza di San Marco, Florence

had been working as a clerk for his uncle, who was the manager of the Venetian branch of the Florentine Salviati bank, whose offices were just opposite the Cappello family palace. Bianca, who later said her home life had been miserable due to her stepmother's meanness, also insisted that Pietro had been able to seduce her in part by claiming he was a Salviati family member. It was only when they arrived in Florence and moved into his parents' small rented home on the Piazza San Marco, not far from the Palazzo Medici in which Isabella lived, that she learned he was not what he had pretended to be.

Thus, life in Florence for Bianca showed no indications of being any more agreeable than her life back in Venice. She did not join the ranks of the Florentine nobility as she imagined she would. Her movements were also extremely restricted. Notwithstanding the birth of a daughter, Pellegrina, her family wanted her back in Venice, and there was the fear that they might abduct her, incarcerate her in a convent or even kill her for besmirching the Cappello honour. Pietro, whose uncle back in Venice had been imprisoned in retaliation, had to go about Florence carefully for fear of assassination. Needless to say, the marriage on both sides began to suffer under these strains. With the romance dwindling, Bianca was to prove receptive to outside offers.

There are conflicting accounts of how Francesco met Bianca. He could have first encountered her at the Medici court itself, for both Pietro and Bianca had to appear there in regard to the Venetian petitions to extradite Bianca from Florence. In February 1564, Pietro began to work at the Medici court in the *guardaroba*, best described as the court's provisions office, which paid a reasonable, but not lavish, six *scudi* a month. Other stories are more colourful. Celio Malespini, the author of the *Duecento Novelle*, which includes the tale of Isabella, Troilo and the slave in Ridolfo Conegrano's bed, seems to have been privy to a good deal of Bianca's chronicles. He reports that she had originally caught Francesco's eye as she leaned over the balcony of the Buonaventuras' sad little home, in which she was more or less a prisoner. Francesco passed by the house on his way to the laboratory he kept at the Casino adjacent to the church of San Marco for his experiments in alchemy, porcelain- and poison-making. The prince subsequently arranged for her to be invited to the neighbouring home of close Medici associates the Spanish Mondragone family in order to declare himself to her and woo her in such a way 'that the lady was in the end pleased to give her love to the enamoured [Francesco]'.[2] But whatever the circumstances of their meeting, one thing is certain: Bianca Cappello proved to be the only human being to succeed in arousing in Francesco the kind of obsessive devotion he had previously demonstrated only towards the study of chemistry and alchemy.

Once her relationship with Francesco had begun, both Bianca and Pietro's standard of living improved considerably. By 1566, Pietro had begun to make property purchases vastly out of the league of his seventy-two *scudi* a year income, buying land out in the Mugello for 1,650 *scudi*. The following year he spent 1,800 *scudi* on a house on the Via Maggiore in the Oltr'arno, not far from the Ponte Santa Trinità. Described by Malespini as 'a most beautiful palace in which they [Pietro and Bianca] lived most happily with so much abundance of everything in the world', it was also convenient to the Pitti Palace.[3] It was here Francesco would visit his lover, with her husband relegated to an apartment downstairs. The River Arno provided sufficient distance from the Palazzo Vecchio, where Giovanna resided, for Francesco to conduct his relationship with Bianca with some discretion.

By 1569, Pietro had been promoted to head of the *guardaroba,* with his salary more than doubled and 'extremely contented by the great luck and fortune that the great Prince's love for his wife had brought'.[4] Pietro's elevated status ratified Bianca's attendance at court. She was no longer a gullible fifteen-year-old who had believed her boyfriend when he told her he belonged to one of Florence's elite families; instead, Bianca was now practised in the art of deception herself. Brazenly, she made overtures of friendship to a clueless Giovanna and, more remarkably, was successful in her attempts. In July 1571, Bianca's cousin Andrea Cappello received the news that Bianca was 'to be found in great happiness close to the Princess in Florence. She is always with her in her room or out with her in her coach.'[5]

As Conegrano observed, it is difficult to understand how Giovanna could not see what was so plain to everybody else around her. However, the Habsburg princess's obsession with protocol meant she would not countenance being approached uninvited with such news by an inferior at court, and her rather limited Italian meant she did not pick up easily the gossip around her. Nor did anybody want to alert her and risk Francesco's anger, as Giovanna's ignorance was of great convenience to him. When Fulvia Sforza told Giovanna who Bianca really was, she and her husband had perhaps calculated beforehand that Francesco's ire could be offset by gratitude from the Emperor Maximilian. As thanks for enlightening the emperor's sister, Mario, a career soldier, might obtain imperial military appointments.

Not that learning about Bianca did Giovanna any good, the revelation only serving to make her exceedingly unhappy. 'Just when I thought I might be the happiest woman in Italy, I find myself to be the unhappiest who ever lived,' she wrote to her brother the emperor in a letter that was intercepted and translated at the Medici court. 'I thought I had won in my husband a lord and patron who would offer me protection and be Your Majesty's most devoted and attentive servant. I now see the opposite is true . . . and it is clear I am not loved by him.'[6]

Giovanna's misery had been exacerbated by having gone to Cosimo to protest at Bianca's place at court and being met with little sympathy by the grand duke. 'Every one of Your Highness's upsets troubles me greatly,' Cosimo informed his daughter-in-law by way of a letter. 'However, you do not need to believe everything you are told at courts where everyone delights in disseminating scandal. I know that the prince wishes the best for you and you for him, but it is necessary to concede to each other some things, and to let youthful things run their course, to bear with prudence that which time will eventually correct, otherwise you will ignite bit by bit a disdain and hatred that can never be extinguished. I do not believe that the prince lets you want for anything. He gives you constant company and he will always be content to supply whatever you and your household need . . .'[7]

It would have been little trouble for Cosimo to instruct Francesco to keep Bianca away from the court so that Giovanna might at least save face. But Giovanna's treatment of Cammilla and her family's refusal to acknowledge his status as grand duke made Cosimo, if not spiteful, at least outwardly indifferent to his daughter-in-law's plight. Certainly, enduring Bianca's presence now made that of Cammilla seem like a very minor ordeal for Giovanna by comparison.

Giovanna attempted a rally of sorts. Convinced that part of her problem with Francesco lay in her inability to bear him a son, she undertook a pilgrimage to Loreto. She went to pray, as other women anxious for sons had done before her, at the shrine which contained, it was believed, the house in which Mary had conceived Christ. She 'invited the lady Isabella to go with her, but she is not resolute about going, and says she would need first to write to Signor Paolo in Rome', reported Conegrano.[8] Given that this would have been the first time Isabella asked Paolo's permission to do anything, it was more likely that she did not feel like going all the way to Loreto with a doleful Giovanna. However, having been so bitterly hurt and humiliated by Bianca, Giovanna now felt that Isabella was her only friend. But even had she felt so inclined, Isabella could not reciprocate such loyalty.

Like everybody else at court, Isabella had known all along about her brother's affair with Bianca. She was also cognizant of her hold over Francesco, as was her brother Ferdinando, who asked Isabella, in a letter from January 1572, to 'make my recommendations to the lady Bianca' on his behalf.[9] However, it definitely was not in Isabella's interests to reveal the matter to Giovanna, regardless of the extent to which she had courted and cultivated her sister-in-law on behalf of herself and Troilo. While her father was Isabella's primary facilitator, the one who sanctioned her activities and bestowed money upon her when she was short of cash, Isabella could not deny the extent of her brother's power and influence. She and Francesco were not naturally close, and she did not want to go out of her way to alienate him. Isabella also perceived the potential power of twenty-four-year-old Bianca after Cosimo had made it clear to Giovanna that he would do nothing to preclude Bianca's presence at court. Isabella could see in Bianca a rival as the pre-eminent female in Florence, in the same way she had initially feared Cammilla, until it became clear that her father was going to ensure his new wife kept a low profile and would be no threat to her. But it was evident that Bianca was much more aggressive than Cammilla, and, as her false friendship with Giovanna revealed, she was clever. Francesco's obsession with his mistress was only going to render her ascent to the top all the faster. Isabella needed to find a way to neutralize Bianca, but to do so she required leverage as well as opportunity.

CHAPTER 9

An Assassination

Pietro Buonaventura enjoyed the benefits of his wife's relationship with Francesco. He had a good job and lived in a magnificent house, but Florence perceived him as a cuckold nonetheless. There were plenty of jokes made about the 'golden horns' he wore, and piles of antlers sometimes found their way to the Via Maggiore's doorstep. At least in part to restore a sense of his own masculinity, he began to pursue other women, and one in particular: a young widow, Alessandra de' Ricci Bonciani, sometimes known, appositely, as Cassandra. Her own relative, the diarist Giuliano de' Ricci, claimed that her extramarital activities had resulted in '12 homicides being carried out because of her' by her jealous husband before he passed away.[1]

The Ricci were one of Florence's illustrious families. Closely associated with the Medici, they owned a big bank and included archbishops and a commissioner general of the Tuscan naval fleet among their number. They were infinitely superior to Pietro in status; Bianca's affair with Francesco afforded him no elevation in rank, and Alessandra's association with Pietro was as deeply offensive to the Ricci as Bianca's had been to her family back in Venice. However, no

View to Ponte Santa Trinità, Florence

Ricci family member reacted more strongly to the liaison between Pietro and Alessandra than her nephew, Roberto, who in 1570 had been part of the cortège that accompanied Cosimo to Rome to receive the grand-ducal crown. Roberto went to Francesco to ask him personally to put a stop to Pietro's relationship with his aunt. Pietro evidently chose not to heed Francesco's words of admonition and carried on the relationship. Increasingly vexed, Roberto paid a visit to Isabella, after whom he had named his eldest daughter. 'Being the most faithful servant of the lady Isabella,' Celio Malespini would later recount, 'he took recourse in her because he had to react to the insolence and temerity of Buonaventura, telling her he could no longer bear the scorn which had arisen [from the affair] and that he would do whatever he could to see its end, with no fear of anything, neither loss of possessions, nor anything else. Thus heard by that great lady, she went to find the prince, and made him understand the total ruin this affair was about to bring. Hearing of this new state of the matter, he told her he would try again.'[2] This time Francesco advised Pietro to get out of Florence, as his life was in danger. Pietro's only reply was that 'he was certain he would prevail, and he was not changing his life and habits'.

What Malespini does not reveal in his story is that Isabella's involvement went far beyond just petitioning her brother to speak with Pietro. Other sources reveal that by August 1572, a heavily pregnant Isabella would be complicit in helping Roberto assemble a group of assassins, who gathered on 28 August to take out Pietro. 'They say among these was Carlo Fortunati,' noted one account written just after the event.[3] Carlo, one might recall, was Isabella's indentured servant, largely unemployable and a recipient of her charity. But he had form for murder from as far back as 1560, when Isabella had petitioned her father to allow him safe conduct back to Florence so he could see his mother. According to this same account, another in this group was Celio Malespini, which would explain how he came by such a graphic and explicit description of how Pietro met his end.

The band of assassins had lain in wait for Pietro as he was crossing the Ponte Santa Trinità at around one in the morning, reputedly on his return from an assignation with Alessandra. 'Ricci,' narrated

Malespini, 'the leader, began to cry, "Kill, kill this traitor . . ." He [Pietro] was extremely well armed, defended himself courageously, and struck down two of them. Ricci advanced on him, intending to kill him, but Pietro saw him, gave him a blow from the right, which slowed him down, and then gave him a wound to his head. Then Ricci's cousin threw a reverse thrust into poor Pietro, which opened up his chest, and at the same time he redoubled, and struck him in the head, completely split it open, leaving part of his brains attached to the wall . . . and thus they saw the unlucky Pietro dead, with more than 25 mortal wounds.'

The wounded Ricci had a predetermined destination as a safe house. Any officer of the law making late-night enquiries into the whereabouts of Pietro's assassins would not enter into the palace of a Medici princess, so Ricci had headed 'straight for the palace of Lady Isabella, where he was visited by surgeons, as although the wound was dangerous and mortal, they brought him back to health'. Roberto thereafter fled to Venice to avoid prosecution for the crime, but he did not remain there very long.[4]

As for Alessandra, her part in the shaming of her family was not forgotten. Malespini concluded: 'The following night, two masked men entered into the house of the miserable Bonciani and they cut her windpipe from her throat, leaving her bathed and dying in her own blood.'

Isabella's collusion in the murder of Pietro, supplying at least one of the assassins, Ricci, with a sanctuary after the deed, is proof of her interest in the removal of Bianca's husband. But other than helping a loyal servant assuage his honour, what did she have to gain by Pietro's demise? Isabella had calculated that Bianca as a widow was a much more vulnerable and potentially malleable creature, even as the prince's mistress, than she was a married one. Pietro, while he was alive, had offered her protection as a husband that she could not be certain her relationship with Francesco might afford her. That she had a legal husband was what had largely precluded her Venetian relatives from forcing her back to Venice. Isabella was sure that the potential isolation she faced now would make Bianca grateful for any protection Isabella might offer her. Isabella presented herself as Bianca's benefactress, her *patrona*, and Bianca received the offer of Isabella's protection with apparent delight.

Isabella had a very busy few weeks in the aftermath of Pietro's death. Two weeks later she gave birth to Virginio, and shortly afterwards the mysterious fire at her house occurred. But Bianca was very much on her mind, for this was the moment when Isabella felt she could insert herself into the Venetian's life and turn it in the direction she wanted. She wrote to Bianca the very day after the conflagration, any distress it might have caused her clearly secondary to other issues preoccupying her.

My most magnificent sister, As I am experiencing 1,000 travails due to the great fire in which I found myself yesterday evening, we cannot talk in person, as would be my desire, and which we could have done had I found myself in my own house, because I would have sent a closed coach for you, and we could have talked more elaborately than I can in these few verses addressed to you. You know very well that I love you, and that I would not advise you on anything that would not be for your benefit and honour. I have been told that your father has sent someone here with the intention of taking you back to Venice. I don't want to be remiss in reminding you of the little regard in which he has held you these past eight years, and that his strange way of proceeding has caused all the world to wonder, seeking to take what is yours, and to show no pity to you whom he gave life, for an error committed by others rather than yourself. Now think about what will happen if you put yourself in his hands, and how you will be treated. I remind you, as your loving sister, that you are in your own house as mistress, and you should not give that over to your father, who past indications have shown loves you little, as neither does your brother nor cousin. You will get little satisfaction from such a resolution. Think well about things and consider everything I am telling you, I am only telling you because I love you, and remember that I swore to be your sister, and you gave me your promise that you would not do anything without my knowledge. And if I could talk to you in person I could prove to you that how your father is behaving towards you is more for show than love. If it was true paternal love, I would have heard of it by now . . .[5]

Isabella kept herself very close to Bianca, publicly attending any number of events with her. 'I will write no more now,' Bianca, who had now entered into negotiations with her family back in Venice, wrote on 9 January, 'because I was in a hot church with the Lady Isabella on Epiphany, and going out into the frigid air, I caught a cold.'

Isabella did not want Bianca to go back to Venice so soon after the murder of Pietro because she knew how angry her brother would be. He might have sanctioned Pietro's death, but Isabella was also implicit in his demise, and she did not want Francesco to hold her responsible for Bianca's departure. So she devised what might be thought of as Plan A and Plan B. In Plan A, Bianca remained in Florence, but only in a way that stood to benefit Isabella.

'If I wanted,' wrote Bianca to her cousin Andrea in March 1573, 'in these months my Illustrious Lady Isabella would give me to a lord of the house of Orsini, a Roman gentleman with an income of 4,000 *scudi* a year: he is a most princely man and a distant relative of the aforementioned lady.'[6]

It seems more than likely that this Orsini, a distant relative of Isabella's, was none other than Troilo. They were cousins after all, both having Clarice Orsini as an ancestor. In Isabella's eyes, such a match resolved any number of issues and satisfied all parties concerned. With Troilo occupied with Isabella, Bianca would be free to continue her relationship with Francesco, respectably married again but with a husband who would take no issue with her extramarital relationship. The marriage secured Troilo a permanent place in Florence and, Isabella envisioned, future benefits from Francesco of the kind he had given Pietro, only better. It also took Troilo off the marriage market, should his thoughts stray that way. If Isabella could not marry him herself, this situation was as near ideal as possible.

But Bianca, after Pietro's death, was now worth 30,000 *scudi* thanks to the property and possessions the couple had acquired by way of Francesco. She knew she could aim higher than Troilo should she wish to. So Plan B for Isabella, if she could not convince Bianca of the Troilo match, was to persuade her to return to Venice in triumph with a new husband. Isabella told Bianca that remarrying would ensure the Cappelli would not attempt to avenge themselves upon her by taking her wealth and sticking her in a convent. For Isabella, a married Bianca in Venice was hardly likely to return to Francesco in Florence.

'Even should I wish to depart for Venice,' Bianca told her cousin, 'Lady Isabella, my benefactress, would never permit it, for she fears I would come to harm. But if I were married, that would content her.'[7]

All year long, Bianca behaved rather as Isabella did in dealing with Paolo Giordano's requests that she come to Rome: with obfuscation, procrastination, telling everybody – her family in Venice and Isabella herself – what they wanted to hear. In August, she told her brother: 'The lady Isabella will be ruined when she sees that I am making provisions to return to Venice.' But no such journey occurred. The fact was that no matter how quiet Francesco may seem to have been, seemingly unconnected to the murder of Pietro Buonaventura and never mentioned in Bianca's correspondence with her family back in Venice, his presence in her life is undisputed. And no amount of scheming on the part of Isabella was going to alter Bianca's situation as long as Francesco was in love with her. Bianca knew that too, the proud exclamations about the protection she enjoyed from Isabella as much a facade as her avowal of friendship to Giovanna had been. As 1573 progressed, she married no one, went nowhere. Bianca was in Florence to stay. The murder of Pietro had benefited no one but herself, for she was now autonomously wealthy, able to enjoy the privilege of her own Venetian nobility without being associated with a former bank clerk. In the first half of the seventeenth century, the Jacobean playwright Thomas Middleton would dramatize Bianca's story as *Women Beware Women*, in which Bianca evolved from an innocent into a power-crazed expert manipulator. Isabella, for all her brilliance, had been outmanoeuvred by a woman for whom scheming had been for a long time her means of survival. Moreover, her power, unlike that of Isabella, did not stem from Isabella's father but from his heir.

CHAPTER 10

The Best of Times

Despite her inability to neutralize Bianca, the period following the birth of Isabella's son Virginio was in many ways a very good time for the Medici princess. She continued to play an active role in the lives of her children. They were with her constantly and Isabella spent far more time with them than her own mother had with her. Nora and Virginio's development delighted and fascinated her. In fact, they revealed what would otherwise be a hidden interest and talent of Isabella's, painting. 'The children are well,' Isabella wrote to her husband on 6 April 1573, with Virginio not yet seven months old, 'and today I have begun the portrait of both of them together, which I shall send you.'[1] Although some instruction in drawing and painting was the norm for the female nobility when they were young, this is perhaps the only document indicating a noble mother actually making a picture of her children. Isabella could have called upon any number of artists at court, who would have undoubtedly done a better job than she, but she evidently wanted to experience the pleasure of recording her children's likenesses herself.

The portrait certainly took some time. More than a month had

Festival float

passed when she avowed: 'The portrait I am doing I will send you immediately when I've finished it. I've put the feet on the baby, who now has two teeth and is the most rambunctious son you could ever see.'[2] Only by June was the portrait ready, and whether it reached Paolo remains unknown, for his correspondence to Isabella from this period makes no mention of it. Virginio at this time 'is boiling over with so much energy that I believe within the year he will be walking; he is already by himself standing up on his feet by way of holding onto a stool'.[3] At this point, Isabella might well have put Virginio into a *girello*: like a modern-day baby walker, it was a round frame on casters to give him further confidence on his feet.

In other households, the arrival of the male heir would marginalize the existence of any elder sister, but not in Isabella's. She continued to be as charmed by Nora's antics as she was by Nora's lively younger brother. And if Virginio had inherited her energetic high spirits, it seemed Nora had her ready tongue. Isabella took her daughter personally to church – in fact, to Santa Trinità, which she herself had attended as a little girl and where a less melancholic Francesco had imitated the priest, giving blessings to his sisters with holy water. On 17 May, as she told her husband, 'I took her to Mass at Santa Trinità, where they were celebrating the feast day. Then returning home my nurse asked her who was beautiful in church. She with great *sossiego* ['gravity of manner', a word long since out of usage in Italian] replied, "The lady mother" . . . which for a little girl of 26 months seems much too sharp a response! If I write to you sounding like an old dote, then the guilt lies with being a mother.'[4]

Although Isabella defined herself as a mother to her children 'who has no other end but theirs and of that they can be certain', her prominent position in Florentine life and culture did not diminish. In her twenties, her primary commissions and sponsorships had been within the realm of music and theatre, but as she entered her thirties, these expanded into different areas. As a child, she had had some basic instruction in astrology and astronomy: she had an understanding of how an astrolabe or an armillary sphere functioned, and the loggia at Castello was adorned with the alignment of the stars which had brought Isabella's father to power. Cosimo was fascinated by the cosmos, and in 1571 appointed the mathematician, cartographer and cosmographer Egnazio Danti, a Dominican friar, as 'Cosmographer to the Grand Duke of Tuscany'.[5] Cosimo very much enjoyed spending time with his new appointee studying the night sky. Isabella was also interested in what Danti had to impart. If she was not much concerned with the earthly world beyond Florence, the idea of what the heavens had to offer was certainly intriguing. While Cardinal Ferdinando in Rome was also interested in cosmography, Francesco, back in Florence, was hostile to both the discipline and Danti. As such, Danti turned to Isabella as a patron second only to her father. He dedicated two of his books to her: two treatises on the spheres, one published in 1571 and the other in 1573. He peppered the dedications with his appreciation for 'how much she delighted in this most noble and pleasing science', and how she was 'most knowledgeable in this discipline' and gave him 'infinite benefices, which I receive continuously from her'.[6]

It was also during this period that Isabella sponsored a reading of Torquato Tasso's epic poem, *Gerusalemme Liberata*, recently composed but not published until 1581. One might think that the humid month of July would be a deterrent to heavy intellectual discourse, but it did not preclude such discussion between Isabella and her friends out at the Baroncelli. On 20 July 1573, Isabella adjudicated a debate between two young men who formed part of her summer company.

'We, Lady Isabella Medici Orsina, Duchess of Bracciano, elect to decide and determine the dispute which has arisen in the days past between Don Pietro della Rocca from Messina on one side and Cosimo Gaci on the other, regarding the interpretation of the use of the word "never", as to whether in our Tuscan language its use affirms or denies that to which it has been conjoined . . .' Isabella's verdict was: 'We declare that the cavalier Don Pietro della Rocca who holds that "never" negates without the negative [i.e. a negative adverb creates a negative meaning in a sentence without the use of no/not/neither/never constructions] has understood and holds well, according to common and good use in Tuscan parlance, while the aforementioned Cosimo Gaci, who holds that without the negative it does not, has not understood matters well, as it is contrary to good and common use in Tuscan parlance.'[7] Ironically, it was Cosimo Gaci, who had just been appointed as gentleman of the bedchamber to Isabella's brother Pietro, who would go on to have a career as a poet. Pietro della Rocca, a Knight of Malta, would eventually become the grand admiral of his order.

The basis for Isabella's judgement in favour of Pietro came, as she explained, from 'the *Decameron* of Sir Giovanni Boccaccio, which highlights that in common Tuscan parlance 'never' will be adopted for a negative without "no(ne)" as one will also read in those good texts, penned by hand during the times in which the Tuscan Language flourished and our own Sir Giovanni Boccaccio in his *Decameron* used "never" as a negative without "no", as one can read in the text written 8 or 9 years after the death of that Sir Giovanni, copied from the true original, which is to be found in our house of Medici . . . In faith,' Isabella concluded, 'that what we have written is our praise, declaration and sentence, this shall be affirmed by our hand, and signed with our usual seal. Given in our palace at the Baroncelli.' To make her decision official, Isabella had the declaration witnessed by two of her companions: her neighbour in Florence Giovanna Antinori and one 'Sir Roberto de' Ricci'. Less than a year ago, Roberto had been bludgeoning the life out of Pietro Buonaventura; now he was out at Isabella's villa listening to a disquisition on the finer points of the Tuscan language.

Troilo also played a prominent role in Isabella's social scene during this period. 'As I hope to live in the good graces of their Excellencies Lady Isabella and Donna Leonora,' wrote the Count of San Andrea to Troilo from Naples, in June 1573, 'I humbly beg you to kiss their illustrious hands on my behalf, as those princesses have all the virtues and beauty of this world accompanied by otherworldly grace.' The count added: 'And to Signor Bardi, the Cavalier Conegrano and all the other gentlemen of that noble company, kiss their hands as well.'[8] But Troilo was not just part of the crowd. His closeness to Isabella afforded him an increasingly prominent role in Florentine society. The soldier who liked to travel with a violin began to put on theatrical entertainments at his own home in Florence, such as a Christmas 1572 performance by the 'Commedia di Zanni'. The Zanni, better known as the 'Commedia dell'Arte', were troops of clownish actors who would trick and mock each other, play practical jokes and make sarcastic asides. In October 1573, Giovanna honoured Troilo when she held a wedding dinner at the Palazzo Vecchio for one of her ladies-in-waiting, inviting Troilo to come as the representative of her brother the Duke of Bavaria. Her own husband was conspicuous by his absence from this event.

In fact, Francesco appeared to participate only reluctantly in social activities involving his family. On 10 October 1573, as Conegrano described, 'Lady Isabella gave a banquet with His Highness, Lady Leonora, the Cardinal de' Medici, Don Pietro, and myself, as well as the ladies of her house, of which there were about thirty. She also invited six noblewomen from the city, and there was the most beautiful music and there was dancing until the early hours of the morning. The prince came before dinner, then he went away, and he did not return.'[9] Conegrano observed that only turning up for the serving of the meal was a pattern for Francesco: 'he is not be found at those dances and games that they put on'.[10] Now that his relationship with Bianca was out in the open, Francesco had no need to keep secret where he preferred to spend his time.

Ferdinando, however, 'goes willingly' to his sister's events. At this point in time, he and Isabella were friendly towards each other, united at least in part by their mistrust of Bianca. Nor did Isabella have any problem with her brother's open disdain towards her husband. In February 1573, she assisted Ferdinando with a favour to the family of the new pope, Gregory XIII, the former Ugo Boncompagni of Bologna. Gregory, although renowned as an instigator of Catholic reform, would also be the last pope to have a child, whom he acknowledged openly and promoted heavily: a son, twenty-five-year-old Giacomo. On 27 February 1573, 'A natural born son of Signor Giacomo Boncompagni, Castellan of Castel San Angelo and Governor of the Holy Church, was baptized and given the name Gironomo. The godfather was Cardinal Ferdinando de' Medici, the godmother Lady Isabella. The mother from whom the child was born was Beatrice de Garze, a Spaniard, who gave birth to the said child on the last night of Carnival in the house of Ruoti da Campestri in the Mugello, where she had been taken, pregnant on June 25, by order and commission of said Cardinal Ferdinando.'[11] So Ferdinando removed Giacomo's mistress from Rome, while Giacomo's father, Gregory XIII, set about initiating a prestigious marriage for his son. At the same time, Ferdinando also endowed the baby boy with Medici validation, aided by Isabella, the two serving as his godparents.

In early February of the following year, Ferdinando was in Florence when he fell ill 'with a throat infection, which the doctors call *sprimantia*, which has brought no small danger to his life'.[12] *Sprimantia*, or quinsy, was a severe and potentially fatal form of tonsillitis, and Isabella came in from the Baroncelli 'to nurse him, although he left still feeling ill'. While she was in Florence, she hosted a dinner on 8 February at the Palazzo Medici for the influential Spanish cardinal Francesco Pacheco of Toledo and Count Clemente Pietra, who had recently served as a Florentine envoy to Spain. Pacheco and Pietra were due to travel to Genoa together for talks with Isabella's cousin, the great Spanish general Fernando Álvarez di Toledo, the Duke of Alba. But Pietra, 'a little while after leaving the palace, going towards his home on the Via San Gallo, was about halfway up the Via Larga, when he was met and assaulted by Francesco Somma of Cremona, who wounded him in the leg, from which he died two days later'.[13] It was reported that Pietra had attempted to sort out a quarrel between Somma and another man, and Somma resented his interference. Yet anybody hostile towards Florentine/Spanish relations and negotiations might have hired Somma for the assassination.

Isabella subsequently 'came down with a bit of fever and has left the city. Carnival', Conegrano wrote glumly, 'is going to be really chilly. The lady Princess [Giovanna] will put on the comedy . . .'[14] The idea of the increasingly melancholic Giovanna hosting the playful spectacles everybody was anticipating was too much to bear. But Isabella stepped in to save the day. On 20 February, she returned to Florence to give a party, 'and we danced the whole night', cheered Conegrano. A few days later, Carnival was rounded off with a joust.[15] The participants were Troilo and another of Isabella's courtiers, Bellisario Simoncello from Orvieto, both men enjoying reputations for their weaponry skills. Most of Florence turned out to watch, but Francesco 'was nowhere to be found'. That month, Troilo and Isabella were truly the Carnival king and queen of Florence. If there was any moment in Isabella's life when she could feel like a heroine in *Orlando Furioso*, then this would have been it, watching her lover joust as if he was a hero from those chivalric times.

Isabella's position in her city and as her father's daughter received further ratification during this time when the Bolognese Mario Matasilani dedicated his *La Felicità del Serenissimo Cosimo Medici, Granduca di Toscana* to her. The subject of the dedication was the reasons for the fortune and happiness of Florence. Given, however, that the subject and object of the dedication were female, in praising Florence the author praised Isabella, the city's first lady, regardless of the other pretenders to that throne. 'Florence', wrote Matasilani, 'is fortunate for the fertility of her gracious lands, fruitful and abundant in all things that humankind could need, for the sweetness of those delightful places, which provide every sort of honest pleasure, decorated by countryside, rivers, hills situated within a temperate climate and good air . . . all the provinces of Italy look to her, revere her and honour her as their Patroness, Lady and Queen.'[16]

Following the dedicatory passages, Matasilani's oration compared Cosimo to the Emperor Augustus, proclaiming the grand duke's fortune had been predetermined by the stars. Florence had been waiting for centuries for Cosimo, as her ruler, to bring the city to the pinnacle of achievement. For many today, the pre-ducal Medici – Lorenzo the Magnificent and Cosimo the Elder – are the truly illustrious members of the family, under whose auspices the Florentine Renaissance flourished and things were never really the same after their demise. But without Grand Duke Cosimo the reputation of the Medici would have died with Lorenzo. It is this younger Cosimo who resuscitated the family, and indeed Florence – 'finding a chaos, he left to his successors a well-ordered state'.[17] Almost half a millennium after his rule, Cosimo's stamp on the city he loved is still visible; it is arguably his hand that shapes any visitor's Florentine itinerary. Without him there would be no Uffizi and no Boboli Gardens in which to stroll; nearly every church in Florence contains an altarpiece from his time. His reach went far beyond the city walls, for it was Cosimo who made Tuscany Medici – the villas, the countryside, the sea. Under his rule the once fiercely proud and independent Siena and Pisa became mere satellites.

It is very clear that it was Cosimo who instilled an equally fierce sense of pride in being Medici, in what it meant to be Florentine as outlined by Matasilani, in Isabella. Throughout her life, her passion was underscored in different ways: in her anxiety to prove the depth of the Medici roots, her belief they were first in Italy 'after the Pope'; and in her satisfaction in her family's possession of such treasures as the manuscript of Boccaccio, the father of modern Italian. And it was Cosimo who had devised a means by which his daughter had not had to leave the family and the city that was her everything, permitting her to taste pleasures and independence to an extent denied to every other woman of her time. Isabella fulfilled her part of the bargain too: she produced the son needed to make her aberrant marriage to an Orsini spendthrift worthwhile.

Inevitably, however, there was a shadow to Isabella's life, a truth implicitly acknowledged but perhaps rarely and unwillingly examined by the Medici princess. The freewheeling nature of her life, her ability to live apart from her husband, the permissiveness she enjoyed – all were permitted by way of her father's sanction. What would happen without it? 'Isabella,' some liked to claim Cosimo cautioned his daughter, 'I will not live for ever.'[18] But life without Cosimo must have seemed inconceivable, as he had been a young father to his elder children, just turned twenty-three when Isabella was born. Was there any reason for Isabella truly to fear she would ever have to live without the endorsement and blessing of her *babbo*?

PART V

The Troubles of a Medici Princess

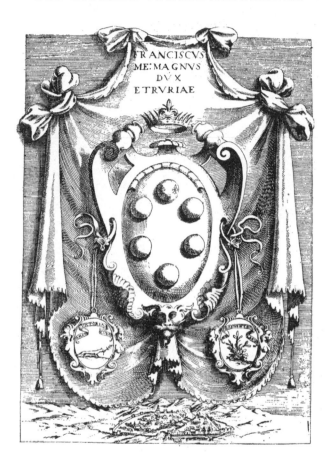

FRANCISCVS
ME: MA GNVS
DV X
ETRVRIAE

Grand Duke Francesco de' Medici's coat of arms

CHAPTER 1

The Decline of Cosimo

As the Medici *capofamiglia*, Cosimo's health and well-being were of the utmost importance and subject to minute discussion and attention. If ever her father was feeling poorly, Isabella would drop everything and rush to be by his side. The greatest scare had occurred at her house during the Carnival of 1568, when after a day and night of parties at the palazzo on Via Larga, he got hit by 'a drainpipe falling on him. It was thought he might be dead . . .' But he suffered from more than concussion; he experienced a small stroke, which resulted in 'his arm being impeded and also his speaking'.[1] He was in a rather weak state for some time afterwards, although he forbade anyone to say anything about his condition. Even after Cosimo recovered, he preferred to be carried in a sedan chair. But any apparent decline in health had not prevented him from his successful campaign for grand dukedom, marriage to his mistress and serving as a critical instigator in the Holy League against the Turks. Rather, Cosimo seemed to use ill health when it suited him, as an excuse to retire from public life and enjoy his time with Cammilla.

Indeed, for somebody who had allegedly passed over governance of

Grand Duke's catafalque

the state to his son, Cosimo continued to be as involved as ever in a plethora of wide-ranging issues concerning Florence and the Tuscan state. Over the course of 1572, he dedicated himself to a vast array of matters. With Pope Pius V dead, Cosimo wanted to see yet another lesser cardinal made pontiff, one whom he could influence, and so he became instrumental, by way of support and bribes, in the election of the Bolognese Ugo Boncompagni as Pope Gregory XIII. He was equally concerned about the development of fortifications, weapons, galleys, bridge construction and mechanical tools in Tuscany. He demanded to know why the quality of lead being mined in Tuscany had deteriorated in quality. He continued to haggle with Catherine de' Medici about the estate of Alessandro de' Medici, who had now been dead for thirty-five years. Cosimo had always mistrusted the Jesuits. He feared their fervour and charisma could usher in a new Savonarolan-like era into Florence, and he was dismayed to learn they wanted to take over the highly fashionable church of Santa Trinità from the Vallombrosan monks who occupied it. He immediately blocked the move, informing the Pope that 'those monks there live religiously and without scandal . . . moreover, the church is a most ancient one in the city, built by Florentine gentlemen, who have tombs and chapels there, and they have always been content with those monks'.[2] Cosimo proposed the Jesuits take over the monastery of San Frediano, safely far away on the other side of the Arno in a more shabby part of town, where their influence would be diminished. He showed himself as merciless to anti-Medicean rebels as ever, instructing the local government in Lucca to take the hanged corpse of the rebel Giovanni Catasta and display it publicly, 'so that it can be seen from all the land around as an example to others'.[3] Yet he wanted to pardon one Fornaino, caught stealing valuable coral decorating Florentine fountains, 'because he's old and poor, and further punishment won't help him any more'.[4]

Nonetheless, the embellishment of his Florentine world was still a great priority for Cosimo. He was pleased for Giorgio Vasari, who had been invited to decorate the Sala Regia at the Vatican Palace, but asked that he 'expedite the work so that you can return and finish the painting on the cupola' of Florence's Duomo.[5] Before sending some newly acquired slaves to the galleys at Livorno, he noted, 'we have destined them for work on the building at the Pitti'.[6] Despite the fact that Francesco had long since held the title of regent, Cosimo still did not find his son sufficiently proactive in the government of the state he would one day inherit. Cosimo would send Francesco instructions such as to familiarize himself with the issues surrounding the Florentine apothecaries' dispute over selling a new kind of balm from India. He also had him read a 'little book' detailing the reorganization of the Monte dei Paschi bank in Siena.

However, early in 1573, Cosimo began to ail again. He suffered from lengthy periods of partial paralysis and agitation. Moreover, his trophy wife was beginning to show distinct signs of tarnishing. In February, Francesco sent his personal secretary Antonio Serguidi out to Pisa, where Cosimo was staying with Cammilla. Ostensibly Serguidi was there to transact the usual court business, but in reality he was there to spy on Cammilla and report back to the chief secretary of state, Bartolomeo Concino, which Serguidi did with glee. Referring derogatorily to Cosimo's wife as 'La Cammilla' (he should respectful-ly have called her 'the Lady Cammilla'), Serguidi filled his colleague's ears with tales of Cammilla's dreadful behaviour: 'It's always been known that Cammilla has been vain and unloving, but these days she is worse than ever. She won't move a step for His Highness, she won't feed him any more, as she used to, she leaves that to Madonna Costanza [her chief lady-in-waiting], and at night, if she hears him complain, she won't go to him, and she adorns herself in clothes and vanity more than ever before. Even this morning she wanted to go to Mass all adorned with a golden veil on her head in the Roman style, and when His Highness saw her, his pulse increased. He did not want to go back to sleep until she had returned, and while she was gone he did nothing but cry.'[7]

According to Serguidi, Cammilla withheld her attention from Cosimo if he did not give in to her wishes. 'Yesterday,' he reported to Florence, 'Cammilla went to His Highness, and very insistently begged him to make her cousin Domenico Martelli a gentleman of the bedchamber for Don Pietro. His Highness replied that the Prince dealt with those matters, and he did not want to alter that arrangement. She got down on her knees to insist again, and he still rebuffed her. That evening she did not want to go to feed His Highness dinner, even though he asked for her.'[8]

Cammilla also alienated other family members. By March, Serguidi reported, 'The Grand Duke proceeds in his improvement, and domestic displeasures proceed as well, for Cammilla has exchanged words with the Lady Leonora [Isabella's cousin], whom His Highness wished to have come visit, and she did not want to come, so His Highness was obliged to go and fetch her.'[9] 'And', Serguidi added, 'she persecutes the servants.' But whatever disruptions she caused and however disagreeable she might have been, Cammilla had her own hold over Cosimo. On one bad night, Cosimo's doctors brought a separate bed into Cosimo's chamber for Cammilla. Cosimo 'flew into a rage, he made them take the bed away, as he wished to have his wife right next to him'.[10] His doctors, for the sake of his health, wished for him to abstain from sexual intercourse with Cammilla, which Cosimo had no intention of doing. 'Having done with the wife that which he is not supposed to do, he has returned to the same state of ill health,' reported Serguidi. 'If he does not abstain from the acts of Venus, the same will happen again.'[11] Word leaked out that Cosimo had bequeathed Cammilla an annual pension of 4,000 *scudi* in his will.

Everyone felt easier when Cosimo returned from Pisa to Florence, and 'the Prince and the Cardinal go every day to visit him, as do the Ladies Isabella and Leonora. But', Conegrano added, 'the Princess Giovana never, on account of Cammilla.' Cosimo went out as well, going to Isabella's house for her parties and dances, but his condition worsened as he lost the power of movement and speech. 'He appears to me', observed Conegrano in January 1574, 'like an immobile statue on his sedan chair, although he does eat and sleep well.'[12] The Venetian ambassador went even further, commenting: 'he has lost all his senses, and lives more like a plant than a man'.[13]

Mercifully, for someone who had lived with such vigour and energy, the Grand Duke of Tuscany was spared too prolonged an existence in such a state. His health deteriorated further in early April, and towards the end of the month it was public knowledge that his death was imminent. 'On 20 April, around midnight, those last pains which finish everything began,' wrote one observer, 'and word went out around Florence that he was dead . . . but moving his left arm a little he gave hope to those around him when he took the hand of the Lady Cammilla his wife . . .'[14] But this gesture was to be the grand duke's last. The following day, 'His most serene and invincible Highness Cosimo de' Medici, Grand Duke of Tuscany, at seven in the evening, passed to the next life at the Pitti Palace.'

Francesco was summoned and arrived an hour later, where he carried out his first order of business as the new ruler of Tuscany. Five hours later, 'at one in the morning, the Lady Cammilla Martelli was sent to the convent of the Murate with four female attendants and two servants . . . and with her went her chief lady, [Costanza] Pitti'.[15] The Murate was a strict, severe institution, and Cammilla's outbursts of hysteria at being placed so unexpectedly in such an environment resulted in her being moved that August to the less spartan setting of Santa Monica in the Oltr'arno. Nonetheless, the next time Cammilla would travel beyond those walls was twelve years later, when she was allowed out for the marriage of her daughter by Cosimo, Virginia, to the Duke of Ferrara.

Having disposed of his stepmother, the more elaborate disposal of Francesco's father had to take place. On 22 April, 'the Pitti Palace was opened up, all the churches began to ring the death toll, and in the palace the corpse of the Grand Duke was on view, his crown on his head, his sceptre in his hand, and the uniform of a Knight of Santo Stefano at his feet. The palace was covered entirely with black satin, which began outside at the palace's main gate. Around his body were posted 18 or 20 German armed guards.'[16] Cosimo's body was displayed on a quickly assembled catafalque, upon which 'a master upholsterer worked night and day making the pillows, the hangings for the catafalque and its baldachin, and the black taffeta fly swatters'.[17] Cosimo's body had yet to be embalmed, and maggots have no respect for grand-ducal status.

The next day, the body was taken for embalming to the church of San Lorenzo. The funeral itself was delayed to allow time for dignitaries across Europe to be informed of Cosimo's death and for their representatives to arrive at the funeral. Francesco sent Troilo Orsini to the Emperor Maximilian, and then sent him even farther afield to Poland, where Catherine de' Medici's younger son Henri had recently and unwillingly taken the throne.

In the meantime, the planning for a funeral as opulent and lavish as any of the more recent wedding ceremonies went ahead. Notably, Giorgio Vasari, who had been Cosimo's right-hand man in almost everything the grand duke had envisioned for his city, was not involved in the funeral's design, although several of his students were. Vasari himself was failing, and he would be dead by June of that same year. Cosimo's funeral took place on 17 May. The ritual began in the Palazzo Vecchio, where an effigy of Cosimo had been laid upon the catafalque, the face and hands made of wax, with the coffin below. The catafalque was then carried in a procession to San Lorenzo. The cortège began with six trumpeters dressed in scarlet and black on horseback, followed by a hundred torch-bearers surrounding one carrying a great cross, a group carrying thirteen banners and 'six great and most beautiful horses, who used to serve as mounts for the person of the dead Grand Duke, covered in black velvet with great trains and plumes on their heads, lead riderless and in line by their groomsmen'.[18] Also in the funeral train were representatives of all the Tuscan towns and the university at Pisa, all of the Florentine guilds, the Knights of Santo Stefano, the magistrates of Florence and ambassadors. The Florentine nobles included members of the Strozzi, Albizzi, Machiavelli, Capponi, Rucellai, Pucci and Frescobaldi families. Roberto de' Ricci, the assassin of Bianca's husband Pietro, was there as well. Accompanied by the papal nuncio and his brother Pietro, Francesco marched in procession and cut a sinister figure dressed in a *gramaglia* – a long mourning robe – and with his face concealed by a peaked hood. Paolo Giordano marched in the group directly behind the Medici brothers.

In the piazza in front of San Lorenzo, barricades were erected to hold back the crowds. The interior of the church was decorated with black drapery, and the adornments included banners with the Medici coat of arms, Medici mottoes and skeletons in mourning carrying scrolls. The coffin was set beneath a baldachin in front of the high altar, surrounded by hundreds of flickering candles, and then the funeral Mass was performed. At the service's end, the coffin was removed, to be taken to San Lorenzo's Old Sacristy, where Cosimo's body was laid next to his wife Eleonora, in whose absence from the world Cosimo had led such a different way of life. When the funeral was over, Francesco de' Medici threw back his peaked hood, and the cortège returned to the Palazzo Vecchio, where the dark decorations of mourning had been removed, as had Cosimo's coat of arms. In their place were those of Francesco, the new grand duke. A new era had formally begun.

As had been with the case with her brother Giovanni's funeral, Isabella, as a woman, was denied formal participation in her father's. However, she gave voice to her sense of loss in a letter she composed to the Duke of Mantua regarding her father's death, two weeks after his demise. The words Isabella chose seem to take their cue from the lyrics of the madrigals sung at her house, the songs where lovers express their grief at abandonment:

> We cannot escape death, and these accidents that occur are as intolerable for those who have had similar losses as they are for me. Nonetheless, it is with every bitterness and disembowelled pain that I find myself deprived of the Serene Grand Duke my lord and father – *sopra tutti gli alti amori* [above all other loves] . . .[19]

Cosimo had been Isabella's constant, the one man who had been with her at every step of her thirty-one years. It was over eleven years since Giovanni had left her, while the vagaries of Troilo's livelihood, dependent as he was on opportunities and favours from others, meant Isabella could never be entirely sure that he would stay by her side. But Cosimo had always protected his daughter, allowing her her charmed and glittering life in Florence and shielding her from a life and a husband she did not want in Rome. Now, with Cosimo's passing, she was not only deprived of a father whom she loved, and who had loved her too. For when she spoke of being disembowelled, Isabella knew that the core of her very existence was now threatened, the guts of her way of life in danger of evisceration.

CHAPTER 2

The Children's Negotiation

In the wake of Cosimo's death, all of Florence was keen to learn how he had distributed the Medici inheritance. According to some reports, 'In addition to the State of Tuscany, he [Francesco] has been left the Palazzo Pitti, the villas of Poggio a Caiano and Castello.' Ferdinando was to receive a yearly income of 80,000 *scudi*, Pietro 30,000. 'To the Princess Isabella his daughter he has provided an income of 7,000 *scudi* a year, in addition to income from the proceeds of the customs from Siena, along with the Villa of the Baroncelli.'[1] Although what he left Isabella might seem less than what he left her brothers, her out-goings should be less, so Cosimo intended to leave her very well provided for indeed.

Moreover, recognizing the vicissitudes of Paolo Giordano's 'fortune', Cosimo had taken the most unusual step of providing for Isabella's children, a duty which was usually the sole province of their father. Cosimo wanted to leave 30,000 *scudi* for his grand-daughter Nora's dowry, which was 10,000 more than he was endowing his own daughter by Cammilla, Virginia. The problem was, Cosimo's will had never been formalized, and it was in

View of the Villa of Artimino

Francesco's power to carry out Cosimo's wishes as he himself, and not his father, saw fit.

Ownership of the Baroncelli villa was in Isabella's name. It was her autonomous possession, so that property should not be contested by Francesco, however irritated he might be that his sister had secured it in the first place. However, Isabella was greatly concerned about her children's welfare and financial future. The Medici had no legal obligation to Nora and Virginio, who bore the name of Orsini and were their father Paolo Giordano's fiscal responsibility, even though they lived in Florence. As early as 1573, when Isabella saw her father begin to decline, she thought it would be wise to begin discussion with Francesco regarding what monetary bequests Nora and Virginio could expect and how they could be secured. A certain amount of what should have been their Orsini patrimony had been acquired by the Medici family, as Paolo Giordano had been obliged to part with it to pay his debts or purchase military commissions. Isabella would have no problem with such acquisitions on the part of the Medici, but she did want to make sure that one day Virginio and Nora would be the eventual beneficiaries. As such, in the spring of 1573, Isabella began what she would refer to in her correspondence as '*il negotio degli putti*' 'the children's negotiation'. What Francesco was willing to entertain was a proposal in which 'Signor Paolo donates to his son all of his possessions before he destroys them completely. The plan seems good and useful for the boy . . .'[2] However, Isabella knew that Paolo would not countenance being dispossessed in such a way. What she hoped to achieve was a resolution which ensured an inheritance for her children, under terms to which her husband would agree. 'In regard to the negotiation for our children,' wrote Isabella to Paolo, 'you should know that it is better to discuss things with me and not with the Prince directly, and that I am doing everything I can for them. Don't marvel if I am late in responding because this negotiation is so important.'[3] Isabella's words indicate that she did not trust her husband to broker things with her brother in a way that would be satisfactory to her. However, the negotiation clearly entailed promises and paperwork from Paolo, possibly with regard to providing rents or other monies. Yet, in May, she wrote to tell him: 'I have not received papers of any

sort as you said. Have them sent to me so that we are not in a bad situation as I am looking to end this as soon as possible.'⁴

By the time of Cosimo's death, however, matters had not been
resolved. Nothing had been produced in writing which would con-
tractually bind the Medici to providing for Isabella's children. The
funeral, the subsequent period of mourning and the time to allow
Francesco to become accustomed to the grand-ducal mantle meant it
was not until June 1574 when Isabella was able to resume the negotiations with her brother. 'I feel like a ship battered by the winds who
has no hope of seeing port,' she told her husband in early July, imply-
ing that her discussions with the new grand duke were proving troublesome. In mid-July, however, she seemed happy about the way
things were going. 'Our negotiation is well, the path is showing the
way to resolution,' she pronounced.⁵ But by the end of the month,
things had not turned out the way she had anticipated, as she
explained to her husband:

> The disbursement is difficult for many reasons. First of all, there are
> the debts from our father the Grand Duke which reach 270,000
> *scudi* and which he is forced to pay from here until next May . . .
> truly these are difficult things, and they are urgent things, so in this
> way the negotiation must take their lead, and take what time con-
> cedes . . . we must be patient and hope that God does not abandon
> these children . . . we have to do the best we can in the service of
> our children.⁶

Isabella's tone is unusually stoic for her, and in this letter to Paolo
she plays the part of a good Medici princess for whom resolving any
problems in the Tuscan state must come first. She urges patience on
Paolo, who was clearly anticipating some kind of personal payout with
the resolution of the settlement for the children, and Isabella's stress on
the 'service of our children' is an indication of her fear that, in the
meantime, Paolo would strip away further assets. But Isabella was not
telling her husband the whole story. She had apparently come to some
private arrangement with Francesco, but at some point during these
protracted negotiations, the brother double-crossed the sister.
Francesco went back on an accord Isabella had personally signed, one

she believed would secure her children's future in a way that would satisfy Paolo and also be of benefit to her. A loose, unsigned letter is to be found in the Florentine archive, tucked into the Medici secretaries' correspondence. It can only be from Isabella, and it indicates that she had agreed and signed her name to an arrangement that Francesco had subsequently altered. The letter reads:

> It is with my great displeasure that I understand that Your Majesty's letter with my undersigning has been altered. If I had thought that would be done, I would never have signed, my sole intention having been only to serve you, and to do the right thing. But as I had thought that this negotiation had been concluded through Your Majesty's good grace, not having heard any more spoken of it, I signed because I was persuaded that it provided every augmentation of my honour, and of this house, my children, nephews and nieces and servants, of whom Your Majesty is the patron. Nor should it be said to me that Your Majesty feels the pleasures of ensuring my well-being, that of my husband and children, which should render me certain that as your sister you bear me that fraternal love that comes through blood, and which merits the will that I have, together with all of this house, in serving you, and of seeing your supreme exaltation. I shall not go any further in expressing my distaste except to say that Your Majesty has seen me condemned. You should remember well that I am also the daughter of the glorious memory that is our Father, and that great princes, who have estates and servants for their devotion, have procured them with every skill and expense, while Your Majesty has his house without such expense . . . I assure you that you will never find satisfaction and contentment.[7]

The precise nature of Francesco's betrayal of Isabella is unclear. At the very least, one can surmise that he was reneging on this promise of funds for Isabella's children and income for Isabella herself, as well as Paolo. Without the money promised her by the 'glorious memory' of her father, Isabella's ability to live well in Florence was endangered to a certain degree. She had the Baroncelli, with its working farm, and she had her part of the Palazzo Medici, from which Francesco could not forcibly evict her. All the same, he had evidently just made her life a lot more difficult. There had never been much love between Isabella and Francesco, who loved only Bianca, as her reference in one letter she wrote to Troilo referring to Francesco's 'miserable ways' makes clear. But it is one thing to say such things in an ostensibly secret letter to another. The letter to Francesco, which notably Isabella chose not to sign, is remarkable for its demonstration of her anger. Gone is any attempt at courtly diplomacy. Instead, Isabella's use of 'Your Majesty' seems replete with mockery, for the letter drips with sarcasm. And there is a not so subtle subtext suggesting that it is Isabella who is their father Cosimo's true child, Francesco being only the passive beneficiary of inherited wealth and privilege, which will never bring him any pleasure and which he will squander. It is a letter in which Isabella identifies her adversary, and that adversary is her brother. She might not have declared all-out war with Francesco, but this letter certainly serves to mark out enemy lines between them.

Isabella's letter to Francesco contained truths to which she could not sign her name. In the past, she had used songs to relieve her feelings, to express herself by way of half-truths, to make allusions to herself and those around her that could be interpreted in more ways than one. In this new period of her life, she seems to have turned to painting, commissioning from the Florentine painter Giovanni Maria Butteri an image that might seem an icon to family piety, but one with an emphatic subtext. It is a picture of the *Holy Family with Saints*, who are portrayed by members of Isabella's family.[8] Her mother Eleonora appears as the Virgin Mary, her grandmother Maria Salviati as St Anne. The baby Jesus has the reddish hair Isabella had as a child and may well be Isabella's son Virginio. If no member of the Medici family is immediately recognizable in the infant John the Baptist, then the fact that in Italian he is Giovanni might be an indication of who Isabella intends him to represent in the painting.

However, it is among the saints surrounding this central group where the real drama of the painting is played out. Three figures are depicted on the right-hand side of Christ. Cosimo de' Medici appears, as he does in other paintings, as his namesake St Cosmas, while Ferdinando, in clerical robes, is depicted behind his father portraying Cosmas's companion, St Damien. The Medici family had long ago adopted these martyred third-century saints as their own, for both Cosmas and Damien had been doctors, *medici*. Seated at her father's feet is Isabella, playing the part of St Catherine, the symbol of her martyrdom, the broken wheel, by her side. This positioning makes clear the bond between father and daughter, and they are linked further, for Cosimo and Isabella both hold leather-bound books emblazoned with the Medici coat of arms, as if the wisdom and inheritance of the father is being passed on to the daughter. They also hold ink pots and quills, as if they are not only the recipients but the writers of Medici history too. Catherine, a saint with no particular connection to the Medici family, is one whom Isabella would have felt suited her quite well. According to legend, the early fourth-century saint was a young noblewoman of great learning and bravery who confronted the Emperor Maximinus to condemn him for his cruel persecution of the Christians. Neither the emperor nor the scholars he called on to debate with her could defeat her in argument, and Maximinus's response was to condemn her to death. Catherine, then, is the scholarly female saint, and the intellectual superior of her male peers.

If Isabella had no argument with those with whom she posed on the right-hand side of the painting, then what about the left? There, Francesco and Paolo Giordano stand together, dressed as unidentifiable warrior saints. It is difficult not to perceive Francesco, who, unlike the other figures, makes no outward gestures to the viewer, as lurking sinisterly in the background. As for Paolo, the artist has disguised his corpulence to some degree by way of a strategically positioned cape. But one might note the spatial and psychological distance between himself and his wife, and the way that San Giovanni, seated like Isabella/Catherine, comes between them.

On the surface this painting might appear to be a remarkably pious gesture on the part of Isabella, venerating her family as saints. But Isabella seems to have viewed faith as something to be called on to help her out as the occasion demanded: relics might be venerated to cure an ailment, while confession was a good way of clearing out a week's worth of sin. Her life had not been marked by spiritual fervour, and she did not need the church as a means of self-expression as other women of her standing did. In this instance, then, the painting allowed

Isabella the opportunity to make a statement about her family life and her allegiances. The arrangement of the figures in the painting is no coincidence. The figures to whom she is closest are Giovanni and Cosimo, and her connection with her father is underscored by way of those books emblazoned with the Medici emblem. She has put Ferdinando, who, if not her strongest ally, was not her enemy either, on the same side. The central figures of Eleonora, the Virgin Mother, Maria Salviati, the holy grandmother St Anne, baby Virginio, the Christ child, and Giovanni, John the Baptist, are benign influences, but they are also either dead or too young to be of any help to her. It is the figures on the other side of the painting – dressed to go to war, regardless of their halos – who are not her allies: her husband and brother, whom Isabella will have to fight, just as Catherine took on the emperor. Would Isabella be victorious where Catherine failed, or was she to be another learned noble martyr?

CHAPTER 3

'My Coming'

Fighting Francesco to secure an inheritance for her children was not Isabella's only problem. In losing her father, she had not only lost the individual who wanted to ensure Nora and Virginio were well provided for, she had also lost the man who for almost two decades had ensured that Isabella had been able to live her life as a Medici in Florence and not undergo an enforced transplant to Rome. The last time Isabella had gone to the Eternal City – for her father's coronation in 1570 – she had contrived to stay at Ferdinando's cardinalate residence. She had apparently not set foot in her husband's house of Monte Giordano, and she certainly had not gone near the gloomy, draughty castle of Bracciano.

But now, 'after the death of her father, there was no reason for her to remain in Florence'.[1] This recent assessment of the relationship between Paolo and Isabella, relying upon the 'flood of love' apparent in their supposedly private, yet in reality public, letters, proposes an Isabella desperate to be united with her husband in Rome. This version of Isabella sees her prepared to abandon the life she had cultivated and adored in Florence: her home at the Palazzo Medici, her villa at

View of the River Arno and Ponte Santa Trinità

the Baroncelli, her friends, her family, never mind her romantic life. She was willing to relinquish all this, not to mention her autonomy, to live in Rome under Paolo Giordano's rule. Her husband might be the leader of the Orsini family, but Isabella knew just how well-regarded he really was by the Roman court. The Orsini and Colonna might be ranked equally as families, but on a personal level Paolo Giordano fell far short of his counterpart Marcantonio Colonna. Isabella was accustomed to being the first lady of Florence. How, then, could she take on a secondary position in a foreign town, a town with the well-known proverb '*In Roma vale più la puttana che la moglie*' – 'In Rome the whore is worth more than the wife'?[2] Moreover, she could not but consider something far more unpleasant: what punishment might be meted out to her for her involvement with Troilo?

In July 1574, Isabella informed Paolo: 'The beauty that caused you to fall in love with me is no more because it has gone with the years. However, I congratulate myself that you love me with that love that exists between husband and wife.'[3] 'She felt ugly and old, and was now afraid she would no longer please her husband,' is a recent interpretation of Isabella's self-appraisal.[4] In this scenario Isabella was anxious that she would no longer appeal to the man who during this period confessed that 'due to the heaviness and condition of my body, no horse is any good'.[5] He had become too fat for any regular horse to carry him. And while it is true that painted portraits can deceive, pictures of Isabella from this time, including her image in the *Holy Family*, suggest she had not lost her appeal. She might, then, have uttered such a comment to dampen her husband's enthusiasm at the prospect of their being reunited in Rome. But Isabella's looks would be immaterial to Paolo, and not because of the 'love that existed between them as husband and wife'. A wife at his side, or rather kept at Bracciano while he continued to play as he always had in Rome, would restore Paolo's honour. He would not have to contribute to the support of a separate household in Florence, and he could appropriate for the Orsini any income from the Baroncelli, now that Isabella was no longer occupying it.

All the same, if Isabella was going to stall, if not outright prevent herself from ever being transported to Rome, she had to tread very carefully indeed and give at least no written indication of any reluctance on her part. She no longer had Cosimo to deflect and delay Paolo's requests that she come to Rome. Francesco did not have the authority over his sister to force her to go, but nor was he going actively to facilitate her staying in Florence either. In one letter from the summer of 1574, Isabella told Paolo that 'I promise you I felt so much desperation this last time after your departure from here.' Still, she had obviously said something she regretted, had been a bit too honest, perhaps, with her husband, as she continued: 'God be thanked I have recovered my brain in my head, as what I said was not in my interests.'[6]

Through the summer, Isabella had the excuse of having to attend to the '*negotio degli putti*' to delay her coming. In late August, she sent Paolo a directive that makes it appear as if she was indeed planning on leaving Florence: 'The children are well, even though the son in my arms is tormenting me. I ask you to send me the measurements of the little chamber and bedroom where I would be staying so that I can have two black hangings made,' suggesting that she would be hanging her chambers with drapes in mourning for her father.[7] Still, it seems as if this was another stalling technique, or else why would she not simply instruct her husband to adorn her rooms appropriately? Moreover, Isabella was not behaving like someone preparing for an imminent departure. Two days later, Carlo Fortunati, last seen among the party murdering Bianca Cappello's husband, wrote to Paolo to tell him: 'My lady has gone with the Cardinal and Don Pietro and the lady Leonora to the mountains of Pistoia for the coolness, and has left the children in the care of my mother, who adores them, and as this morning there are certain ladies of the household who have contracted smallpox, as a precaution my mother has gone with them to the gardens of Don Luigi [di Toledo].'[8] Isabella's uncle's vast gardens, adorned with an enormous pergola and huge fountains, were located just to the east of the Piazza San Marco and were subsequently demolished to make way for Florence's nineteenth-century urban expansion. The epidemic, as reported by the diarist Bastiano Arditi, particularly affected 'children of a young age' and was so virulent and deadly that in the small town of Borgo San Lorenzo they buried nine in one day.[9] One Medici child was lost – the youngest of Francesco and Giovanna's daughters, Lucrezia – meaning that out of the five daughters Giovanna had borne three were now dead.

The Medici adults did not escape sickness either. Pietro and Leonora fell ill, although both recovered. Isabella, returning to Florence, apparently escaped the pox, although she did experience what the court doctor described as '*un gran flusso di sangue*', a heavy menstrual haemorrhage, which he attributed to 'an intemperate stomach, and cold and damp liver'.[10] At the same time, Paolo Giordano himself became gravely ill with a viral infection that was also suffered by others around him. In late September, Isabella wrote to him to tell of her 'greatest contentment at your great improvement . . . I have not lacked saying prayers for you . . . I promise you being deprived of you would be impossible.' She assured her husband that she hoped 'my own illness will improve, as there is nothing I desire more than to serve you and see you'.[11]

And yet, in the following months of October and November, it was as if Cosimo had never died. Letters from Paolo contain very familiar refrains. On 28 October 1574, he wrote: 'I understand you are resolved about your coming here . . . I shall prepare the house of Monte Giordano and hope you will be comfortable, and the children as well.'[12] But there was apparent silence from Isabella. The following month, he told her: 'I do desire to know about your coming here, and I beg you to let me know.'[13] Isabella gave him one of her classically vague replies: 'In regard to my coming, I can't say anything else than above all it depends on the Cardinal, who has arrived here right at this very hour.'[14] Exactly what Ferdinando had to do with or say about her departure for Rome is not clear, but it does cause one to reflect that if it had been Giovanni who was the Medici cardinal in the city, Isabella would have left for Rome with much greater alacrity. Perhaps she herself recognized this to be true; in the aftermath of Cosimo's death she refers, for the first time in a long time, to the 'happy memories I hold of my brother the cardinal'.[15]

By December, Paolo was too distracted by the 'needs of my affairs being so very great' – which resulted in him having to sell yet another piece of Orsini land, the farmlands of Galera – to make enquiries as to why Isabella had yet to turn up in Rome.[16] Isabella took this opportunity to offer to enter into negotiations once more with Francesco on his behalf, promising him in January that 'I will not lack in treating your negotiations as if they were my own.' Then she went on to say that 'truly, in regard to my coming, as I have already written I have to deal with certain of my affairs regarding things that belong to me . . . but I cannot say exactly when'. She ended with a familiar refrain: 'Your Excellency should be certain that there is nothing more I desire than to see and serve you.'[17] Over the previous six months, Isabella had promised to come on at least two occasions: once in early September, when she was put off by apparent illness; then again in November, but she never materialized in Rome then either. Now she was delaying once more in order to put some apparently previously unanticipated affairs in order.

The following month, the Roman Cardinal Savelli received a letter from Paolo, to which he sent the following response: 'I am replying to your letter of 2 February which you wrote to me to recommend the case of Lorenzo di Giovanni Bolognese, on account of his wife who escaped from him. I am convinced that it is well that the said wife, together with her mother, are imprisoned. They have been very obstinate about not wishing to return to her husband, her mother in particular, due to many mistreatments that they assert they have received from the husband . . . Nonetheless, when they leave prison . . . if it pleases you along with the aforesaid Lorenzo, his wife shall be made to return to him.'[18] Paolo Giordano was not endowed with a great deal of instinctive sympathy and sensitivity to others, but if ever he could empathize with an individual, it would be with the condition of Lorenzo. What he needed was someone who could force Isabella to come to him, the way Lorenzo's unhappy wife was to be returned to her spouse.

CHAPTER 4

The New Ambassador

It was not only her father's death in 1574 that signified the end of an era for Isabella. In July of that year, Alfonso d'Este had to recall that key member of her merry company, his ambassador Ridolfo Conegrano, back home to Ferrara. Ridolfo had got into some trouble regarding the arrival in Florence of a young Ferrarese noble, who had come to the city in order to kill two other Ferrarese. 'It appears', wrote Giuliano de' Ricci in his diary, 'that the ambassador who is here on behalf of the Duke of Ferrara had invited him, but the Grand Duke had not conceded he come, so it has tacitly been decided that he, the ambassador, should leave Florence . . .'[1]

Isabella and Ridolfo exchanged letters, of which only part of his side of the correspondence is extant. He wrote his letters in an amorous yet platonic style, perhaps deliberately recalling the letters the poet Pietro Bembo sent Lucrezia Borgia, Alfonso's grandmother. Ridolfo very much missed 'Florence, that magical, beautiful city, full of so many genteel and loving noble people'.[2] But it was Isabella whom he declared he missed the most. He wrote to her in November 1574:

Santi di Tito, Gentlemen at court

My lady, so meritorious and so revered, regarded and loved by me, how many virtues and qualities do I know in you, the singular affection I bear for you. I have your beautiful image sculpted in my heart, and the portrait of you I keep close to me, those objects that I once referred to in those improvisatory stanzas . . . I assure Your Excellency that in regard to your welfare I find myself so afflicted that I cannot do everything I should be able to . . . Whether I live or die it shall be in contemplation of your beauties, and I believe my spirit shall depart me in not being able to see you. I am beginning to shorten the evening so that I can go and dream that I might awaken in Your Excellency's house, enjoying the sweetness of your conversation, and that beautiful music, lovely games and those sweetest temptations. You were my sun . . .

You may remember that you lent me a quarter of a thousand *scudi*. With the occasion of Signor Alessandro [Strigio, a musician] returning to Florence, I did not wish to delay paying this debt any longer. I am returning the debt as a sign of the memory I hold of you, as well as a velvet hat, worked in black, embroidered with little black pearls and with a plume of four crowns to signify that you are Queen of four kingdoms. I kiss your honoured and beautiful hands.[3]

Isabella's response to Conegrano was so 'full of courtesy and lovingness, brought me so much content reading that I enjoyed myself more than I could possibly understand. But I derived greater contentment from hearing that the hat is entirely to your taste.' Ridolfo was in the process of renovating his house, asking Isabella to 'do me the favour of coming as if it were your own', if she wished 'to flee from ceremonies'.[4] By April 1575, he told her about his plans to 'build a house for Your Excellency, which I hope you can still come to see one day. I beg you to give an order that I should be sent a coloured sketch of your coat of arms which can be painted on this house.'[5]

Isabella and Ridolfo both knew that her visiting him, especially at this complicated time in her life, was a near impossibility. But while what she wrote to the former ambassador remains unknown, one senses that he recognized she was in need of a means of escape from her troubles. And his willingness to pay a monetary debt to her suggests he knew she was in a degree of financial difficulty.

The former ambassador was also able to tell Isabella in his December letter the name of his replacement in Florence – 'Ercole Cortile, Ferrarese gentleman, a young man of thirty and married' – and he promised Isabella that he would let their mutual friend Alessandro Strigio fill her in on what Ridolfo knew about his successor. Ridolfo implied that while his loyalty had in fact been first and foremost to 'my lords and patrons' in Florence, his successor would put Ferrara first and was unlikely to be as discreet as Ridolfo himself had been about what he had seen and in what he had participated.

Cortile arrived just after New Year in 1575. 'At this time there came to Florence to live the ambassador for the Duke of Ferrara, not him who was here such a long time,' commented Bastiano Arditi, who noted the change. 'He moved into the Botti house on the Via Chiara [now part of Via dei Serragli on the Oltr'arno]. He was young with a wife and family.'[6] On 15 January 1575, Cortile sent a dispatch back to Ferrara to let the d'Este duke know how he had been getting on. The Grand Duchess Giovanna had received him with much kindness, he said, but 'I have not been able to visit the Lady Isabella yet, despite using much diligence, because she has excused herself as being somewhat indisposed. However, other people used to the situation have clarified that she does not wish to be visited unless she feels in total perfection.'[7] It took another week before Isabella would agree to see her friend's successor.

By the end of the month, Cortile's dispatches make it very clear that if Ridolfo Conegrano's long tenure in Florence had meant he had, in diplomatic parlance, 'gone native', then Ercole Cortile was a very fresh pair of eyes and ears. By 29 January, he had established by talking with the fashionable preacher and Franciscan friar Francesco Panigarola, who was very close to the devout Giovanna, that she 'was deeply troubled and remains extremely unhappy'.[8] A week later, Cortile had befriended a real insider, the Marchesa of Cetona, Eleonora Cibò, who was a granddaughter of Lorenzo the Magnificent. 'The Marchesa', Cortile explained, 'speaks very freely, partly because it is her nature, and partly because she feels dissatisfied with these lords.' The Marchesa underscored Giovanna's unhappiness regarding Bianca Cappello and also told him that 'the lady Isabella rides about a great deal in a carriage with "BC"'.[9] Isabella had clearly decided to attempt to continue to keep close to Bianca, whose ascendancy prevailed under Francesco's reign.

The Venetian's sway over the otherwise misanthropic Francesco never ceased to fascinate those around them. Cortile noted to the d'Este duke that 'they are like children together . . . it causes not only us ambassadors to laugh but also the people to see this great Prince, so great and wise, to become more like a child than a man' in Bianca's presence.[10] Her existence became more and more public, and her behaviour more like that of a duchess than a mistress. In December 1574, she went, along with her daughter Pellegrina, on a pilgrimage to Loreto, which contemporaries described as seeing her 'accompanied in a similar fashion as the Grand Duchess had been the previous year'.[11] Such a journey made two very important statements. Bianca was attended on her journey by Florentine nobles provided by Francesco, just as Giovanna had been, which meant he had sanctioned that she make her trip in the same style as his wife, thereby setting up an evident parity between them. Moreover, everybody would understand why she was going to Loreto. Bianca, like so many women before her, was visiting the shrine to pray for a baby. Perhaps, unlike Giovanna, her prayers would be answered and she would give Francesco a son.

No pregnancies resulted from the pilgrimage, although at least one end was achieved: the further humiliation of Giovanna. She 'grows ever more melancholic' was an eternal refrain from Cortile. A diplomatic incident almost occurred when she and Bianca attempted to cross the Ponte Santa Trinità simultaneously in their coaches. Neither was prepared to stand down, although in the end it was Bianca who blinked first. Giovanna's only response to Bianca was, as she had done with Cammilla, to refuse to participate in any events which included her. But while Cosimo had accommodated Giovanna's honour by keeping Cammilla to the Pitti Palace and had ensured Bianca was excluded from events, as decorum dictated, Francesco had no such intentions.

Bianca's political clout became even more evident when a Venetian emissary who came to express condolences on Cosimo's death and congratulations on Francesco's elevation to grand dukedom occupied Bianca's house while she was absent in Siena. Bianca was turning the house on the Via Maggio into a high-profile piece of self-advertisement. Using funds from Florence's mint, she commissioned the Medici court artist Bernardo Buontalenti to decorate its facade with a monochromatic *sgrafitto* decoration still visible today. Her personal device, the *cappello*, hat, features prominently in the design.

The tables really were turned for Isabella and Bianca. Now it was not Isabella's goodwill that Bianca might find useful; instead, Isabella really needed that of Bianca as a line of influence to Francesco, who was 'like a child' in the Venetian's hands. However much she might despise her brother, however much she might feel him to be an enemy, it was in her interests to have him sufficiently well-disposed towards her. She clung, therefore, to the hope of support from Bianca. In the summer of 1575, Bianca's brother Vittorio visited Florence, and Isabella made a point of making him feel welcome. 'I am continuously aware of the effects of Your Ladyship's affection towards our house,' he wrote to her on his return to Venice. 'I see that you procure with every readiness of soul, with so much care of the spirit, benefits for my sister, not only in regard to her own person, but also in regard to the marriage of her daughter, and in so doing become her protectress as well.'[12] So it seems that Isabella, if she could not dictate whom Bianca might have taken as a second husband, could invest in promoting a marriage for Pellegrina into a family with whom she might have influence. Despite her mother's relationship with Francesco de' Medici, Pellegrina was still the daughter of a commoner, who had only three years previously been murdered for overstepping his social boundaries. Her marriage prospects were still not what the Cappello family might desire, and Vittorio might have believed that Isabella's goodwill might prove beneficial to his niece.

Still, if Vittorio noted his appreciation of Isabella's apparent benevolence, his sister appeared to take it as part of her due. Bianca was unstoppable. A critical marker came in October 1575: the inaugural event at the villa not far from Poggio a Caiano Francesco had given her. 'There was a meal at the villa of Madonna Bianca,' recounted the diarist Arditi, 'most beautifully appointed to receive every great lord, and these were the personages: the Cardinal de' Medici, Don Pietro and his lady [Leonora], the Lady Isabella and Signor Paolo her husband, the Count of Bagno and his lady, that is his bride, as well as many other lords. It was an extraordinary thing.'[13] Although it took place in the country and not the town, the fact that all the Medici went officially to visit Bianca as a hostess was a sign of her sanctioned status.

If any exchange regarding this event passed between Isabella and Cardinal Ferdinando, it was perhaps the tacit acknowledgement that the party was a clear manifestation that Bianca had won. If anybody was there to stay in the grand dukedom of Francesco de' Medici, it was Bianca Cappello.

CHAPTER 5

Leonora

Isabella de' Medici was not the only woman at the Medici court for whom Cosimo's death had brought anxiety, if not downright misery. Cammilla Martelli railed futilely against convent captivity, and Giovanna von Habsburg was more tortured than ever before by her humiliation at the hands of Bianca. Isabella's young cousin Leonora di Toledo, married to her brother Pietro, was unhappy too. Cosimo had arranged the marriage in part to keep the charming Leonora in Florence, not to mention the substantial dowry she brought with her – 40,000 gold ducats and 5,000 in jewellery. But he had also perhaps hoped that a bride who had known Pietro since childhood might help with the mental problems he seemed to be facing. If, of Cosimo's surviving sons, Francesco could be described as misanthropic and Ferdinando as pragmatic, then Pietro was downright disturbed. He had been only six when his mother had died, had grown up with untrammelled freedom, and was 'now fed by the riches left him by his father . . . every day shaping him into the most dissolute youth in the State'.[1]

Whatever Cosimo had hoped, marriage to Leonora proved not to be Pietro's cure. An indication of his disturbance occurred on the

Villa of Poggio a Caiano

occasion of the official consummation of Pietro and Leonora's marriage. On 26 April 1572, Conegrano reported back to Ferrara that 'Don Pietro has consummated his marriage with Donna Leonora.'[2] The couple had actually married two years earlier. This, then, was a peculiarly lengthy gap. The bride was now nineteen, the groom eighteen, and both had long been mature enough to enter into official marital relations. Moreover, word got out that even at this point Pietro had been extremely reluctant to take his wife and 'had to be forced to penetrate her', as the ambassador to Urbino later commented.[3]

Given that Pietro was less than physically prepossessing, while Leonora was the acknowledged young beauty of the Medici court, such unwillingness on Pietro's part to have sexual intercourse with his wife could only be regarded as very strange. Pietro's activities with other women are documented, so he clearly had his own reasons for his aversion to Leonora. Nonetheless, in early February 1573, Leonora did give birth to a son, whom they named Cosimo and who became known as 'Cosimino'. Pietro asked for Francesco's advice on the choice of godparents (Don Giovanni of Austria and the Duchess of Savoy): 'so as not to make a mistake I anxiously await the most serious judgement of your more mature deliberation'.[4] Even when his father was still alive, it was to Francesco, thirteen years his senior, whom Pietro turned first for counsel, and if he was guided by anybody, it was his elder brother.

Just prior to the birth of his son, Pietro had been appointed General of the Seas of Tuscany, so he was given the naval career that would have been his elder brother Garzia's but for his death in 1562. Pietro embarked on missions that took him away from Florence. During those periods, Leonora spent increasing amounts of time in the company of Isabella, and while Isabella was indisputably the chief hostess to her group, Leonora sat at her right hand, praised and admired by those who visited. If she did not have Isabella's depth of education and erudition, she still wanted to follow her cousin in intellectual pursuits. Isabella's court was an academy of sorts in its own right. Leonora, resident at the Palazzo Vecchio with her brother- and sister-in-law, without such a seat of her own, came to serve as the patron of the literary academy, the Accademia degli Alterati. The Alterati met twice weekly to discuss poems, prose, plays and the promotion of pure Tuscan, that regular topic of conversation at Isabella's own home.

But there were differences between Isabella and Leonora other than the eleven-year age gap. Isabella conducted her life with a certain degree of prudence and caution. The songs sung at her court appeared to be lamentations to a beloved absent husband. She did not sign or even write in her own hand a potentially damaging letter. She would take pains not to say anything deleterious about Paolo Giordano or anyone else in front of the wrong people, nor to be caught outright in any kind of compromising behaviour that might be the subject of gossip. She also accepted that her married life and her romantic life were two separate entities; preserving that latter part of her existence was very important to her and she did not want to jeopardize it. By contrast, Leonora seems to have taken an unhappy marriage much more personally and, as a consequence, reacted much less cautiously. In late February 1573, Cammilla Martelli had tried to get Leonora into trouble by gossiping about a flirtation she claimed to have witnessed between Leonora and a servant in her and Pietro's retinue, Alessandro Gaci, when they were in Pisa.[5] It was this indiscretion which was believed to be the cause of Cammilla and Leonora 'exchanging words', as Francesco's secretary Antonio Serguidi reported back to Florence.

Alessandro was the brother of Cosimo Gaci, to be seen arguing the use of the word '*mai*', 'never', up at the Baroncelli in Isabella's presence. It was at Isabella's house where Leonora's troubles really began to escalate. There was an astonishing amount of temptation for a lonely girl in the presence of the array of sympathetic males assembled there, from the pretty pageboys through to their older cavalier brothers. Unlike her husband, they wanted her, to play with her, flirt with her, to go wherever she was prepared to go and willing to listen to whatever she had to say. But there was no more avid pair of ears than the new Ferrarese ambassador Ercole Cortile, who did not hesitate to report back to his boss on the conversations he had with Leonora. On 22 January 1575, he wrote to Alfonso d'Este: 'I was invited to the house of Signora Isabella, and Donna Leonora asked me to perform in a comedy. There was a bit of partying in the room, and I took up dancing with Leonora, who, teasing me, asked me if I had seen an old and enamoured ambassador dancing without his hat and sword, and if I had seen the Papal nuncio without his Beretta doing the *gagliardo*.'[6] Having joked over the nuncio together, Leonora took a very ill-advised further step: she brought a foreign ambassador, whom she barely knew, into her confidence. She let Cortile know that 'she is very unhappy, and the reason is her husband. He will not sleep with her, he attends only to whores and matters of vice. And she began to cry. Truly,' remarked Cortile, 'she really is the most unfortunate and unhappy princess who ever lived, especially for being one so beautiful and accomplished.'[7] But Cortile's sympathy to this princess's plight did not extend to keeping Leonora's confidence a secret.

Now the discord between Leonora and Pietro de' Medici was not simply gossip and rumour; word of it from her very mouth was recorded in an ambassadorial dispatch. If Isabella had not been so caught up in her own troubles, she might have been quicker to instruct Leonora not to air her dirty laundry so publicly, to ease whatever pain she felt more quietly. Instead, Isabella effectively authorized the breakdown of Medici family relations. In allowing her house to be the locus of Leonora's lament, she was siding with her Toledo cousin over her Medici brothers. Perhaps for the first time in her life, simply being a Medici did not come first for Isabella.

CHAPTER 6

The Duelling Season

Francesco de' Medici served as prince regent of Tuscany for almost a decade before he came to power as the state's grand duke. If he did not have the power Cosimo liked to claim to the outside world was invested in his son, his period as regent was one in which Francesco was supposed to be in training for the day he would become the ruler of the state of Tuscany. But Francesco was only a diligent pupil in matters that really interested him. Unlike his father, he was not a natural statesman; he had no care for military matters or concern for the Florentine social institutions his father had promoted. He did not have Cosimo's head for business. In terms of the further embellishment of his city, Francesco's interests did not extend much beyond the sciences and the support of intellectual academies. Otherwise, he accepted his inheritance as his due, seeming to have no interest in the fact that his state was a garden which he had been entrusted to tend. Isabella recognized this lack of care in her brother and had not been afraid to tell him there was no comparison between him, who had inherited all he had, and those like his father, who had fought and campaigned for what was theirs. Others would later try to account for Francesco's

Jousting

sullen, misanthropic disposition and conclude it was perhaps a matter of diet. He preferred dishes of a tepid temperature, he 'drank too much distilled water', he disdained meat and had what was perceived as an excessive fondness for vegetables, of which he ate almost any kind.[1] In other words, he did not eat as a real man should.

But the critical difference between the first grand duke of Tuscany and the second is that Cosimo cared for Florence and Tuscany as if it was an extension of himself in a way that Francesco did not. There is no question that after the death of Eleonora, Cosimo's court was a libertarian one in many respects. However, all the evidence refutes eighteenth-century English claims that 'plunging into dissipation, he [Cosimo] renounced that sober and active life to which he had hitherto accustomed himself, and passed from unexampled activity to the most lethargic indolence. His infatuation for pleasures of every species led him into actions which disgraced him and were totally inconsistent with the prudence for which he was so admired . . . '[2] As long as Cosimo was alive there was no sense that Florence was an anarchic city, one that was out of control. But those conditions did begin to prevail the moment the thirty-three-year-old Francesco came to the ducal throne. 'Florence had become a city full of murderers,' railed Bastiano Arditi. 'Every night there were injuries and death and other various and awful incidents. And from the day that Duke Cosimo died, which was 18 April [sic] 1574, until 12 July 1575, there were 186 cases of death and injuries.'[3] Ample proof indeed that Francesco, whose major interests were Bianca and discovering the secret to the manufacture of porcelain (then known only to the Chinese), had little concern about the state of the city he was meant to be ruling. Florence became 'a cave and forest for assassins from Rome and Naples and Genoa and Milan, and above all Venice and Ferrara and Lucca and Urbino and other places'.[4] Despite this influx of foreign cut-throats, they were not the only ones responsible for the rise in the murder rate. The young male elite, without fear of the kind of authoritarian repercussions that would have occurred while Cosimo was alive, were acting on their natural bellicose tendencies and obsession with honour to duel, fight and kill like never before.

Many of the incidents reported in Arditi's diary and those of his counterparts involve the young men associated with Isabella's circle. In 1568, she had written to Paolo in Rome, telling him that 'the bearer of this letter will be Luigi Bonsi, who has come to serve Your Excellency . . . I would be obliged if you would favour him in taking him into your service as there is an issue with Cornelio Altoviti [from the important Florentine banking family], who spoke words to his own wife that were hardly becoming to a gentleman, and this young man rushed to defend her honour and struck blows on Cornelio.'[5] However, as Altoviti was not armed, Bonsi was in danger of being charged with assault for the attack, so Isabella wanted to keep him out of Florence for the time being. But several years later, the issues between the two men had not been resolved. On 19 April 1574, 'with licence from His Highness the Prince', reported Giuliano de' Ricci, 'the Cavalier Luigi di Matteo Bonsi and Cornelio di Francesco Altoviti had their fight. Altoviti received two very major wounds in the leg. He died.'[6] The fight having been legally sanctioned, Bonsi became a Knight of Santo Stefano and died of disease in 1579 at sea, going to war in Portugal.

Bonsi and Altoviti's fight was followed by one involving Bellisario Simoncello, who earlier that year had participated in a jousting display with Troilo Orsini. 'A cavalier of Santo Stefano,' Ricci recounted, 'Jacopo di Domenico Bartoli, affronted Signor Bellisario Simoncello of Orvieto . . . striking the first blow to his head . . . They each had their weapons in hand, in which time Bartoli fell, having received several wounds in the face and legs and several others which would have finished him off had he not called for his life for the love of God. Finally, they put down their swords and daggers, and decided it would be better if they went home, Simoncello with one wound and Bartoli with many.'[7]

The autumn and winter of 1574 saw further fights. Two Sienese, Leandro Berti and Jacopo Federighi, fought on 16 October, the latter dying of his wounds a few days later. At the end of November, Jacopo Mannucci, who had gone from wool manufacturer to Cosimo's majordomo, was wounded by an unknown assailant. On 22 December, Niccolai Carducci died at the hands of an unknown assailant. 'There have been many homicides and woundings,' Ricci remarked, 'and never is the offender found or punished.'[8] It seems that the grand duke simply did not care about the perception of justice in his town.

Ricci did, however, have very precise information about the killing he described in this entry in his diary: 'On December 28,' he wrote, 'wounded with acceptance and death at 2.30 outside the Stinche [the old Florentine prison] was Signor Torello de' Nobili da Fermo, a young man of 20, presently serving as a gentleman of the bedchamber to Signor Don Pietro de' Medici. This Torello was armed with every weapon: chain-mail shirt and sleeves, sword, dagger and a thin steel skull cap.'[9] Despite such body armour, 'he was killed by Signor Troilo Orsini because of the Lady Isabella de' Medici, with whom both men were in love'.[10]

Ricci's diary is regarded as one of the more cautious chronicles of its time, as he was reluctant to report anything he did not know to be true or had not heard on good authority. His entry indicates that knowledge of Isabella and Troilo's affair had long gone beyond the walls of her establishments. It also suggests that if young men in their twenties were still finding her appealing and were prepared to declare themselves to her, Isabella's claim to her husband that the beauty she had had as a young woman was gone was not quite accurate.

Troilo had had an eventful existence since the death of Cosimo, having undertaken the long journey to Poland. He had spent some weeks in June and July in Krakow at the court of Henri de Valois, as the bearer of the news of Cosimo's death. From there he sent reports to Francesco whose informal tone he perhaps should have rethought. 'The King made some apology to me that he did not speak Italian well enough, and then mysteriously ignoring the fact I understood French [Troilo was a frequent visitor to Paris], turned to his Vice-Chancellor to reply to me, who used terms and phrases that I could have desired should be more loving. They were in a tone that all the neighbouring lords could hear, and of substance which Your Highness will understand better on my return.'[11] Relations between Florence and France were increasingly chilly, and Troilo intended to indicate they had not thawed. By 24 August 1572, Huguenots thronged Paris to celebrate the marriage of the Protestant Bourbon prince Henri de Navarre to Catherine de' Medici's daughter Marguerite. Subsequent events left thousands of them dead at the hands of the French crown, in the city as well as beyond, the events for ever after known as the St Bartholomew's Day Massacre. Catherine consequently accused her cousin Cosimo of colluding with the Huguenots, perhaps unjustifiably. Nonetheless, it is true that Cosimo did wish to cultivate Henri de Navarre, believing that he would be the future of the French monarchy once the impotent Valois flame burnt itself out.

In a subsequent letter from Poland, Troilo advised Francesco that if Florence were to establish a full-time ambassadorial presence in Poland, 'see that you choose a handsome and well-dressed man, and you will be treated honourably. Everybody in these parts takes great care of their appearance.' Troilo also provided unsolicited advice about Francesco's friendship with François, Duke of Montmorency, the commander of the French armies: 'I know that you don't need any advice; however, Your Highness should not warm up in favour of Montmorency. I really believe that to be true, and pardon me if I am too presumptuous.' Montmorency had been associated with Joseph de la Môle, beheaded that same year for his part in a plot to put Catherine de' Medici's youngest son, the Duke of Alençon, on the throne. Still, the tone Troilo used in his letters to Francesco was not really appropriate for correspondence with a grand duke. It is a bit too casual and familiar, the tone of a rather arrogant and self-confident man, one who was accustomed privately to mocking and disparaging the addressee, most likely in the company of his sister. Like Isabella, Troilo often won over those he met by way of his charm, but at the end of the day he always had the instincts of a soldier, a cavalier, and not of a career diplomat.

In Krakow, those instincts emerged when he got into a fight with the ambassador from Ferrara, who did have a full-time presence in Poland. The exchange took place before a royal Mass was about to be celebrated on 9 June and was over that ever-contentious issue between Florence and Ferrara as to whose representative should have precedence at ceremonial events. The Ferrarese ambassador, Battista Guarini, had not yet arrived and Troilo had taken his seat, which was close to the king. Guarini showed up and, according to one observer, said to Troilo, 'That's not your place, get up.' Troilo replied, 'It is my place.' Henri de Valois offered another place to Guarini, who said, 'Your Majesty, I do warn you not to do this to my Duke, who has sent me here to honour you.' Troilo's response was that the place should be his because '"his duke was Grand Duke." To which Ferrara responded that his duke had been one for 150 years.' Troilo later admitted that 'I would have taken a sword to Ferrara,' but he decided to resolve the situation by ceding the seat to Ferrara, 'as Troilo Orsini and not as an ambassador'. Troilo had been merely doing his job, for he had been instructed on previous occasions not to cede to Ferrara. Still, the incident, in front of an entire congregation, was distasteful, and Troilo had hardly put Florence in a good light by his actions.

Five days later, the news arrived that King Charles IX of France was dead. His younger brother Henri de Valois could give up being king of Poland – for which he had no enthusiasm in the first place – and take up the French crown that his mother Catherine de' Medici had long desired for him. The Polish court was disbanded and Troilo made his way back to Italy. A little more wary and unsure what or where his next position would be, he thought it prudent to write to Paolo Giordano in much more humble terms than he had three years previously when he told him he was not going to Lepanto. In early September 1574, he told his Orsini cousin: 'I come to Your Excellency who is my prince. I beg you to believe that there is nothing that moves me more . . . always it has been my desire to serve Your Excellency.'[12] But if Troilo was hedging his bets, attempting to ingratiate himself with the man whose wife he'd been involved with for the best part of a decade and more, his subsequent activities belied any new loyalty to his cousin. His killing, just over three months later, of Torello de' Nobili is proof that the relationship between Isabella and Troilo was very much alive and well. Troilo's presence in Florence could only have fuelled her fervour and desire to stay in her city, but his action, at such a delicate moment in Isabella's life, was foolhardy. It drew attention to them at a time when discretion would have had a greater premium. But Troilo was thinking with his sword. He had taken advantage of the anarchic and violent environment Francesco had allowed to flourish in order to fell a small-town boy who he must have known was no real rival for Isabella's affection. But young Torello had overstepped a boundary that his Florentine counterparts knew not to cross. Even at this precarious point in time, when all was said and done, Isabella was still Troilo Orsini's woman.

CHAPTER 7

The Pucci Conspiracy

Troilo's murder of Torello de' Nobili might have rounded off 1574, but the fights and murders carried on into the next year. In late February, a worker at gold-cloth manufacturers the Ricasoli killed the firm's lawyer after 'certain disputes'. On the first day of March, Agnoletta, 'a public prostitute', was killed by her French client and found 'in her undershirt, with stab wounds, in the church of San Lorenzo'.[1]

It was a bitter winter. 'Carnival is as cold as it could possibly be,' Isabella wrote to Paolo Giordano on 3 March, 'although I have taken much pleasure from Carnival activities.'[2] She perhaps realized she had made a mistake in sounding as if she was enjoying herself, and two days later composed a much longer letter, explaining that 'I have had tertian fever [a type of malaria] for two weeks, and I was without fever for three days, but now it's come back . . . I am ashamed to say I have been negligent about the negotiations.'[3] Still, tertian fever had not prevented Isabella from receiving an ambassador from Philip of Spain, who, she explained to Paolo, 'was sent here to send condolences on the death of the Grand Duke in the king's name, and who came the other

The Bargello, Florence

day to visit me and after discharging his ambassadorial mission entered into a discussion in which he asked me if this year you would want to take on a foreign embarkation. I replied I did not know but I did know that you would desire to serve our king.'[4] Clearly, if Paolo could be persuaded to go on any kind of expedition away from Italy, he would not be around to press Isabella to leave Florence.

In addition to the tertian fever, Isabella told Paolo that 'the doctors have told me that all my illness must be related to the liverishness which began last August, and that I must take exercise. They have taken 18 ounces of blood through my feet, and I am going to the villa to exercise.'[5] Isabella did have some kind of foot problem, never fully specified beyond a reference to her having a lump.

On 20 April 1575, a year after their father's death, her brother Pietro wrote to her from Naples in response to correspondence she had sent him, although he made no mention of the anniversary. 'Your letter gave me much happiness', he told her, 'to learn of your good health, as much as it greatly displeased me to learn of my consort's illness.' So now Isabella was well, but Leonora was not.

This letter is a rare piece of correspondence between Isabella and her younger brother, and it contains some quite interesting information. Pietro went on to tell her: 'I read Your Excellency's letter in which you let me know that the lady Cammilla has asked that on my return to Florence I would secretly send her the fourteen pieces of gem stones and other things. Please do me the favour of letting me know what I should do.'[6] One can surmise from Pietro's words that Cammilla was hoping he would use his authority to acquire things she had left in the Pitti Palace and send them to her. Isabella had clearly left a line of communication open with Cammilla, who was permitted visitors at the convent of Santa Monica, which was not very far from the Baroncelli villa. Cammilla knew better than to ask Francesco to send her possessions, but Isabella was prepared to ready the way for her younger brother to assist Cammilla, otherwise she would not have sent her letter on to him.

It might seem odd that Isabella should be prepared to help Cammilla, to whom she had only extended goodwill during Cosimo's lifetime because it was the politically prudent thing to do. Cammilla was now less than influential, but with Cosimo's death Isabella and the younger woman who was technically her stepmother had more in common than they had during his lifetime. They had a common enemy: Francesco, the son-in-law who had enclosed his father's former wife in a convent, the brother who was blockading the money his father had promised his grandchildren. If nothing else, the pair could sit in Santa Monica's *parlatorio* and rail in private against the grand duke.

Railing against the grand duke had become a commonplace activity in Florence. It was not only diarists like Giuliano de' Ricci or Bastiano Arditi who were shocked and appalled at the murder rate or rising taxes. Francesco became a greater target of animosity for the populace at large as well because it could be seen that there was no longer a united front to the Medici family. With Cosimo alive, even after incidents such as Giovanna's refusal to talk to Cammilla or her outrage at the presence of Bianca Cappello, the family could be seen to move as one. Now there was no such sense of unity. Instead, there was a miserable Giovanna, an unhappy Leonora, an anxious Isabella, an absent Ferdinando and a dissolute Pietro. The only unity Francesco projected, the only bond with another human being about which he cared was with Bianca, sneered at by many as a *puttana*, a whore.

What also resurfaced were those rebellious anti-Mediccan sentiments that those families who had once been peers of the Medici felt. In the spring of 1575, a group of young Florentine nobles began to spend nights 'in the company of several noblewomen' conspiring as to how they could bring down the despised grand duke, and indeed kill his brothers as well. They centred around Orazio Pucci, whose own father had been executed on grounds of treason against Cosimo back in 1560. His band of co-conspirators included members of the Capponi, Machiavelli and Alamanni families, as well as a cousin of Cammilla Martelli's, Cammillo. Given the hardly secret circumstances of their discussions, the plotters did not get very far before they were discovered. Such sloppiness was perhaps due to what they perceived as the lax state of the law in Florence, a belief that little would befall them if they were uncovered. But they reckoned without one thing: that when it came to personal revenge, Francesco revealed the tenacity and obsessiveness which thus far he had reserved for his mistress and his scientific experiments. He was very, very good at revenge, the major characteristic he had inherited from his father. The difference between them, though, was that Cosimo was not necessarily interested in the personal. There had to be a point to it, something worthwhile, like the Baroncelli villa, which had belonged to the Salviati family and had to be confiscated. Francesco, on the other hand, would pursue vengeance as an end in itself. Satisfaction could only come to him once his target had been eliminated. One can see how quickly he banged Cammilla Martelli up in a convent, attending to that before the business of Cosimo's funeral. Similarly, Francesco had Orazio Pucci, the ring-leader of the conspiracy, executed on 22 August, although Cammillo Martelli was not beheaded until 1578. As for Piero Capponi, who managed to flee Florence, Francesco patiently tracked down and had assassinated in Paris in 1582, seven whole years after the original plot.

The Capponi were a family who had had a close alliance with Isabella. All the same, if she did have knowledge of the plot, she managed to keep her name out of it. The same could not be said of her cousin Leonora. On 25 July, Ercole Cortile reported to the Duke of Ferrara: 'Pierino Ridolfi has been accused of plotting to kill Don Pietro while he was in a whorehouse, to murder his son and poison Cardinal Ferdinando. He is in the service of Donna Leonora and the duke is in a great rage with her for having given Pierino a necklace worth 200 *scudi* and a horse on which to escape.'[7]

The charges seem excessive. It is unlikely that Ridolfi did plan to kill Leonora's son if she was prepared to come to his aid. However, killing her husband could only have been of benefit to Leonora. Undoubtedly, both she and Ridolfi saw his plan as full of chivalry and gallantry, rescuing her from a cruel and unloving husband. No doubt Leonora saw romance in providing him with jewellery and a getaway steed. What must have vexed Francesco was that Leonora was successful in her bid to free Ridolfi, who fled to Germany, only to be captured some time later and imprisoned. Small wonder Francesco, Cortile reported, was 'prepared to wash his hands of his sister-in-law'.[8]

Leonora's public complaints about Pietro were dangerous enough. Now, in aiding and abetting Pierino, she had got herself involved in treason, she was as good as implicated in the Pucci plot. All the same, Francesco was impeded in how he could deal with her by one very important issue. Leonora di Toledo was Spanish nobility of the highest rank. As ambivalent as his relationship was with Spain, Francesco still needed the ratification of his grand-ducal title from the Habsburgian crowns. He needed to proceed very carefully with his Spanish relations, and washing his hands of a troublesome sister-in-law was not quite so easy.

Just a couple of weeks after Pierino Ridolfi's escape, Leonora was attending a meeting of her literary academy, whose minutes read that she 'would like to have judgement made on Maestro Alessandro Piccolomini's book on Aristotle's poetics', which had been recently published.[9] For the time being at least, life appeared to continue apace in this now fractured Medici family.

CHAPTER 8

Troilo, Bandito

———

Through the spring of 1575, Isabella continued to renegotiate on Paolo Giordano's behalf loan terms and repayments with Francesco, as well as the settlement for the children. But it could be said that she was dragging things out. 'The lady Isabella has sent me a very old letter, dated the 14th of last month,' Ferdinando wrote to Francesco in late March, 'regarding the business with Signor Paolo Giordano together with the new statutes.' Ferdinando stated that he did 'not see how these statutes can be of benefit to his children', although he did admit that there would come a time when they would need 'to provide for them and help them, given their father's irreparable shamelessness'. Still, the Medici brothers were certain they were in control of Paolo. 'You know the way', continued Cardinal Ferdinando, 'that together we can break him *presto presto* . . .'[1]

On 28 April, Paolo wrote to Isabella to thank her 'for the efforts you are making on my account . . . I beg you to try to bring things to a conclusion . . . I am putting the rooms in my castles into order, and making a garden.'[2] He appeared to be indicating Bracciano was awaiting Isabella. Five days later, Isabella wrote to Paolo to lament the fact that

View of the Stinche, old Florentine prison

'my indisposition' in regard to her health had delayed the negotiations, but that she was using all due diligence.[3] Two weeks later, 'with the opportunity of the Cavalier Beccaria [being in Rome] I did not want to be remiss in kissing your hands, and giving you news of my improvement. I do hope to recover my health with a bit of patience. Here everyone is well, and Friday the Duke of Parma [Ottavio Farnese], that most courteous and handsome cavalier, is coming to dine with me.'[4] It seems Isabella could not resist making a mention of his Farnese cousins, of whom Paolo was envious. Otherwise, the negotiation and her health, the only issues that justified her staying in Florence, are practically the sole matters about which she writes. Sometimes issues concerning the children arose. In January 1575, Isabella had one of her servants write to Paolo to ask if he would send to Florence 'the ring and reliquary of Santa Brigida to help Virginio, who is a little ill, the cause of which cannot be determined . . . as Her Excellency has such faith in holy relics she is resolute in having it sent'.[5] Isabella's religious faith did extend to belief in the power of relics; one might recall how the previous decade she had badgered her father to make the friars at Santissima Annunziata let her see the miraculous painting of the Annunciation. The fourteenth-century Swedish Santa Brigida spent the last twenty years of her life in a convent she founded in Rome's Piazza Farnese, which nuns still run as a hotel. The Orsini family possessed a fragment of her clothing, set into a ring, which was believed to have healing properties. It was one of his family's most treasured possessions, but Paolo could not refuse to let it travel to Florence to aid his only son. In due course, Virginio recovered, and by the end of May 1575 Isabella could report that 'Virginio [not quite three] is riding, as if he was born knowing how to.'[6]

That summer, Troilo Orsini returned from Naples, where Francesco had sent him as an envoy to Don Giovanni. At this point, Isabella went silent on Paolo, although she was active in Florentine social life and cultivating Bianca's brother Vittorio. She knew that Paolo was in financial talks with her brother Ferdinando in Rome, and as such there was no 'negotiating' she was required to do on his behalf in Florence. Silence, then, was a good policy, for it allowed her to avoid the issue of when she was coming to Rome. She received a letter from Paolo on 3

September, in which he railed: 'I have sent you six letters and not had a response to one. I've heard about Nora's illness and that she has been quarantined, and it displeases me that I should have to learn that my daughter has been at death's door from others. Madam, I beg you to remember that I am your husband, and if myself or my letters bother you I will write no more.'[7]

On 17 September, Isabella made contact with Paolo: 'I have received two bills and I have signed an acceptance to pay them in mid-October, and I will do that through a loan from the Monte di Pietà, otherwise to do so would be impossible. I have been looking for an architect and I have found more than one who might serve you [Paolo was planning renovations on his properties]. I will continue to get progressively better, like the rain, for until now it has not rained here in three months.' Isabella concluded in her letter to Paolo: 'I hope to finish getting back to health, because I am much better, were it not for a bad leg that does not let me exercise. The children are well, God be praised, and continue to grow. I desire nothing more than to serve you, so order from me the things you want.'[8]

The night before Isabella wrote to Paolo, two more murders took place in Florence. One death was that of an unnamed spy working for the 'Ufficio dell'Onestà', the bureaucratic office set up in 1415 to invigilate wrongdoings and nefarious activity, including prostitution, in the city, whose headquarters were in the Uffizi. The other murder was that of Cammillo Agnolanti, whose father had worked in purchasing at the Medici court. He was killed by another member of the Martelli family, Orazio. While Orazio's motives for the murder of Cammillo remain unknown, after the crime he sought, and received, refuge at Troilo Orsini's house.

A few days later, Giuliano de' Ricci reported: 'For the murder of Cammillo Agnolanti . . . on suspicion of having been involved, the servants of Signor Troilo Orsini were taken into custody, along with his brother, who was ill in his house.' Troilo did not hesitate to react immediately to the arrests. 'He went to see the Grand Duke, who was at Pratolino [his new villa], and made a complaint to Corbolo, the secretary of the Eight [the '*magistratura degli otto*', the top judicial body in Florence], demanding that they be released. [Corbolo] replied in the negative, saying they could not be freed, as the rules of justice needed to be followed.'⁹

Troilo knew very well just how many crimes and murders had been carried out in the city in the past eighteen months without any intervention from city officials. Harbouring a murderer, even if the victim was the son of a Medici employee, hardly constituted a crime which warranted the arrest of his servants and brother. Standing before Corbolo, it would not have taken him long to realize that the arrest of his household was only a preliminary to what would be the major arrest: that of himself. He turned to the secretary and told him, 'As I can have from you neither grace nor favour, I shall take my leave.' 'And without turning back for Florence,' Ricci recounted, 'he went [north] in the direction of Bologna.'

Troilo's suspicions proved correct. On 22 September, he was 'cited in the piazzas [a warrant for his arrest was put out], along with his *maestro di casa* and a servant. It is believed', Ricci explained, 'the grounds are the murders of that spy from the Ufficio dell'Onestà, or for having harboured Orazio Martelli, who killed Cammillo Agnolanti, or in truth for having in those months past killed Torello de' Nobili da Fermo.'¹⁰ These were grounds aplenty for putting a warrant out for Troilo, except that, relatively speaking, they were quite minor infractions. There was nothing to connect him with the murder of the Onestà's spy and he had not been directly involved in the murder of Agnolanti. Torello de' Nobili was an individual of little importance by comparison with Troilo, who had served regularly as Medici ambassador. Moreover, that murder had taken place ten months previously, so why prosecute Troilo now for it? The real reasons for this action against Troilo must therefore lie elsewhere. Given Troilo's fairly high rank, nothing would have been done without the authority of Francesco. It was he who had planned to have Troilo arrested, with punishment to follow. It has been suggested that Troilo was another part of the Pucci conspiracy, even if his name does not appear among the others, and that was what precipitated Francesco's move. It is perfectly plausible that he was involved in or at least knew about the plot. However, it is as likely that Francesco, whose taste for revenge had been aroused by the Pucci conspiracy, had decided to apprehend Troilo because he had been his sister's lover, and the murders with which he was associated were a useful pretext on which to do so. Troilo was a critical component in Isabella's world, one in which she had fashioned Leonora, her younger and now treasonous cousin, in her image and of whom Francesco also wished to 'wash his hands'. Francesco had just waited for the appropriate moment to deal with Troilo. This was his particular talent; he was always prepared to wait for what he saw as the opportune time to enact revenge.

He might have managed to escape prison, but Troilo could not return to Florence without being arrested. He had to well and truly disappear from the city. The accounts by the diarists Ricci and Arditi of Troilo's departure from Florence are supported by Cortile, who admitted not knowing the exact reason why he has gone, but that he had heard 'he caused the death of one of the spies of these lords'. There are no surviving comments from the Medici about his departure and nothing from any Orsini sources. But if there are no recorded sentiments from Isabella, it does appear that she reacted very violently to the news and its implications. For if Troilo was to be persecuted, what, then, might happen to her?

That very same week, Isabella de' Medici, denied the opportunity to say goodbye to her lover, went into a major decline. On 26 September, six days after Troilo's departure, her brother Ferdinando wrote to Paolo Giordano telling him that 'she cannot get out of bed for fear of dropsy' and suggested that he come to Florence.[11] Up until this point, any references to Isabella's ill health primarily come from her alone, but this time she manifested such a complex range of symptoms that two Medici court doctors, Francesco Ruggiero and Baccio Strada, went out to stay at the Baroncelli to tend to her.

On 8 October, a rather baffled Strada sent a report to Francesco: 'We have found Her Excellency, in addition to her old ailments, to be unable to keep food down, along with a bit of fever, and we think this flux might have been caused by two days before it started her going fishing out at Galluzzo [one might remember that on 17 September Isabella had told Paolo she could not exercise because of a sore leg, but here her doctor indicates she was well enough to go fishing not long after] . . . where she ate a lot of eggs in the house of a peasant . . . we have endeavoured to soothe her stomach a bit with oil of mastic [from the shrub of the same name, believed to help indigestion] . . .'

Strada had also written to colleagues 'in Rome and Pisa to confer the opinion that the lumps on her feet that she once had, the fever, the heart palpitations, and the other ailments derive from the same source . . . phlegmatic and raw humours generated by an intemperate stomach, a cold liver, and the damp acquired a year ago from that haemorrhage she had when she came back from the mountains of Pistoia . . . This morning we found her with a high fever, and I told her that I did not want to leave her until she was better . . . For now we are attending to the care of the fever, and to alter the remedies as the occasion seems to require. And what we do we will let Your Highness know.'[12]

It has been suggested that it was 'very probably Paolo Giordano who was giving orders to the doctor', who 'lied about the reason for her symptoms [eating eggs] in order not to worry her husband'.[13] But overconsumption of eggs was certainly a more neutral cause of illness than having been driven into a frenzy by the departure of her lover under very alarming circumstances. If it was Paolo giving Strada orders, the doctor makes no mention of Paolo's presence at Isabella's side in his report to Francesco. But he was in Florence by the end of October, when Isabella's condition had improved so greatly that in a report on the twenty-seventh on the health of the court, Strada noted: 'The lady Isabella can be considered as having got better because she no longer has any fever, and it does not show any sign of returning.'[14] Cortile wrote to Ferrara that 'The Lady Isabella, who had been very swollen corporally, is no longer puffed up, and she has returned to a state of well-being following a major purge.'[15] During this time he got to know Paolo Giordano a little and got the impression, as he told the d'Este duke in the same letter, that judging by his words and 'a little bit of conversation' there was a great deal of ill will between the couple. Not long after, Cortile wrote to say that Paolo had told him that 'he will be leaving Florence in six to eight days, not liking his rooms here very much, from what I could understand from his words'.

Paolo's apparent discontent may lie in his supposition that when Troilo fled Florence, Isabella would reconcile herself to leaving her city. But the Medici princess had other intentions. Back in Rome,

Paolo received a letter from her on 13 December: 'I remain as you know not too well, and so I am with fever, and when I attempt as usual to get out of bed, neither my legs nor head will let me. Your departure caused my decline.'[16]

There was another bit of scandal brewing for Cortile to report home. On 19 December, he told of how Francesco 'threw out at three in the morning one of those German ladies who came with Her Highness. The lady Duchess is of very ill will and has said to the Marchesa of Cetona that the only reason for this is to cover up the dishonour of the lady Isabella, and that these are lies.'[17]

This story is somewhat cryptic, but Troilo had spent a certain amount of time in the company of Giovanna and her ladies-in-waiting. He had gone with them to Loreto as part of Giovanna's retinue, and he had been at the wedding banquet she held for one of the *tedesche*. From Francesco's perspective, if he sent one of them away on the grounds she had been having an affair with Troilo, it might deflect outside attention and conversation away from what his sister had been doing with the Orsini cavalier. Such a move was less to conceal Isabella's dishonour than to promote Medici honour in the wider world.

For a woman apparently unable to rise from her bed, Isabella was quite busy the following week. On 22 December, Ercole Cortile wrote to tell the Duke of Ferrara that 'The Lady Isabella gave a party for Christmas. She put on a comedy, and invited the duchess and Donna Leonora.'[18] This party appears to be the only Isabella-sponsored event Giovanna is recorded as having attended. Inviting her might have been a gesture of goodwill on Isabella's part. She must have heard that in Giovanna's eyes she was the reason why she had lost one of her ladies-in-waiting, the only women in Florence with whom Giovanna was really in sympathy. Giovanna, for her part, may have chosen to go to refute the stories Cortile was hearing about the animosity that existed between her and her sister-in-law. Possibly, appalled as she was to be a part of a family that had humiliated her in ways both real (Bianca) and imagined (Cammilla), it was Christmas after all and she wanted some company. Beneath the elaborate rituals of polite behaviour Isabella's Christmas festivities required were three troubled women:

Giovanna was scorned by her husband, whose mistress was succeed-
ing in taking her place; Leonora was implicated in a plot to wipe out
all three Medici brothers; while Isabella had a lover on the run from
her brother's ire and a husband trying to extract her from her city for
an undetermined fate in Rome.

Still, Isabella remained undeterred. Her hostess duties done for the
Christmas season, she held fast to her strategy of not moving for anyone. Four days after her party, Paolo Giordano heard from her: 'I am
still so very weak, I go between the bed and the litter. Three days ago
I had to be carried in a sedan chair to Don Luigi's garden. My troubles
are such that I have to go to bed for at least ten or twelve days . . .'[19]

PART VI
Final Acts

Hunting stag

CHAPTER 1

The New Year

New Year's Day 1576 saw Troilo Orsini pen the following letter to
Francesco de' Medici from Paris: 'I understand that after my departure
from Florence, I have been the subject of many citations, which leads
me to understand that a prosecution is being formed against me which
would eventually see a condemnatory sentence.' Troilo continued:
'This appears to me to interrupt many years of my good and faithful
service to Your Highness and your most serene house, and forces me
to absent myself from your lands in order to avoid being charged with
an official sentence of banishment . . . I have chosen to pass into France
. . . I do desire not to be impeded by a public banishment from
Florence, which many have here, and which makes me appear as a
fugitive.'[1]

One might have thought that on fleeing Florence the Roman Troilo
would go south. Even if he did fear a ban from Tuscany, he was not
banned from Rome, and as an Orsini he should have had the protection of his own family. Unless, of course, protection was not on offer
because Troilo had done something which alienated him from his clan.
Having a long-standing affair with the clan leader's wife would proba-

Villa of Cafaggiolo

bly fall into that category. The Orsini had tolerated it as long as the Medici, bankrolling their leader Paolo Giordano, permitted it. Now that Francesco had put a plan of prosecution against him into action, Troilo was on his own. There was nothing he had to offer his Roman family in return, and they were not going to protect him.

Troilo fled to France partly because he had personally got on well with the two key members of the royal family, King Henri III and Catherine de' Medici. But Paris had for a long time been a refuge for anti-Medici Florentines, whose numbers were on the increase now that Francesco was on the throne. Their welcome in Paris became even warmer as relations between Francesco and Catherine and Henri deteriorated. Francesco, in his bid to ensure that the Habsburgs in Spain and Germany recognized his grand-ducal title, had decided to make an all-out show of loyalty to them and enmity to France. When Henri became king of France, Francesco refused to send a congratulatory emissary to him. His father would never have been so foolish, knowing the importance of the outward show of courtesy and friendliness, no matter how one felt inside.

So it was clear that in Paris Troilo would be among friends. In case he was in any doubt about his status in Florence, the next month the following sentence was issued: 'Signor Troilo Orsini, Roman, and Giovan Maria Santa Croce, known as Trionpho, of Fabriano, for having in the month of December, 1574, outside of the Stinche, wounded with many blows and brought death to Signor Torello de' Nobili da Fermo, have been condemned for their disobedience to banishment and confiscation of property.'[2] Such property would include anything that had been in his house, such as Troilo's letters, including the correspondence Isabella had sent him, which helps explain why letters belonging to this Roman noble should come to be in the Medici archive. Isabella could be somewhat reassured that her letters did not bear her name and nor were they in her hand, but were they really cryptic enough to fool anyone that they were not from her?

As January came to an end, Francesco could feel that making an enemy of France to secure a Habsburg blessing had been justified. On 26 January, the Emperor Maximilian, the misery and unhappiness of his sister Giovanna at Francesco's hands notwithstanding, agreed to acknowledge the Medici grand-ducal title. On 13 February, formal ceremony took place in the Palazzo Vecchio to celebrate the announcement. The proclamation was read out that: 'The Emperor Maximilian, moved by the virtues and merits of His Most Serene Highness Francesco de' Medici, his brother-in-law . . . and by the authority of the Holy Roman Empire makes, creates, and constitutes him Grand Duke of Tuscany . . . wishing and declaring that he must be called and recognized as such by the other princes of the Christian Republic, decorating him with all dignities, honours and privileges that such a name accords.'³ His virtue and merits aside, Francesco had certainly paid for the ratification, having made long-term loans of 200,000 *scudi* to Maximilian and a further 100,000 to the dukes of Bavaria, into whose family Maximilian's sister Anna had married. Francesco, along with the papal nuncio on his right, his brother Pietro on his left, an armed guard and forty-eight members of the council of Florence, then processed to the Duomo to hear Mass. The following day was deemed a public holiday and the shops were shut.

There is no mention in the accounts of the ceremony of any Medici women being present, the way they so often had been during Cosimo's time. Still, at the end of February, Isabella reprised a familiar role, acting as first lady of Florence. She provided the formal greeting to Costanza Sforza of Santa Fiore, a close maternal cousin of Paolo Giordano who was travelling from Parma to Rome to marry Pope Gregory XIII's son Giacomo. Just two years previously, Isabella had stood at the baptism of Giacomo's own illegitimate son out in the Florentine countryside. She went out to meet Costanza, who was 'accompanied by many cavaliers. The bride came down from her litter and got into the Lady Isabella's coach.'⁴ Isabella saw her off the next day, as did her brother Pietro. Leonora, however, did not, on account of having suffered 'some accident', reported Ercole Cortile.

Another February event that caught Florence's attention was the murder of Orso Orsini. Orso was the Count of Pitigliano, an estate in the far southern reaches of Tuscany. He had been a Knight of Santo Stefano, although Cosimo had always been somewhat suspicious of his motives and had sent one of his servants to the galleys for spying on behalf of his master. Orso had taken as a wife Eleonora degli Atti, from the tiny fiefdom of Sismano in the Lazio. But in October 1575, he had killed his wife and absconded to Florence, where Francesco agreed to protect him from the anger of his wife's family, who had entreated the Colonna, their relatives and Orsini rivals, to bring them satisfaction against Orso. However, when Orso killed a young Colonna boy, the boy's uncle Prospero, a son of the family's leader Marcantonio who was serving as a Medici major-domo, intervened. On 15 February, Prospero, 'in the company of six or seven of his servants confronted Count Orso Orsini, and between his legs, face and head gave him 14 or 16 wounds that were impossible for him to overcome'.[5] Orso hung on for two weeks before he finally passed away. Prospero went uncastigated by Francesco, but the Medici family stepped in to take care of Orso's children. Cardinal Ferdinando took one as a page, Pietro another. Isabella, however, took in two of these Orsini boys, once again expanding her household.

It was now Carnival time. In past years, it had been Isabella's party which got everybody excited. When Giovanna had been the host one year, everyone was disappointed with the festivities. But now there was a new Carnival queen. Bianca 'is in charge of the Carnival celebrations', Cortile informed Ferrara on 4 March, 'and today she gave an absolutely superb banquet'.[6]

Isabella chose to make a public appearance not at Carnival, but at Lent. She took Leonora, and the pair 'went around through the city with boxes collecting for charity'.[7] Piety and altruism might have played a part in the cousins' motives for such activity, but their actions also served to contrast with the ostentation of Bianca, to differentiate themselves from her. It was a good public-relations exercise for Isabella and Leonora. Rattling their collection boxes out on the street might have gone some way, in their minds at least, to dispelling their image as adulterous party girls. There was plenty of talk in the street now about what the cousins had been up to. Word had apparently even reached Rome, where they had become the subject of pasquinades, the ribald satirical poems pinned to the statue of Pasquino near the Piazza Navona. The one Medici pasquinade that survives from this time is, however, about Isabella's brother Ferdinando. He had taken as his mistress Clelia, the illegitimate daughter of Cardinal Alessandro

Farnese. 'The doctor [*medico*] rides the Farnese mule' was the doggerel written in Cardinal Ferdinando's honour.

On 2 April, Isabella received a letter from Paolo, noting in her response to him that 'you lament that I have not written'. She pleaded fatigue and preoccupation, but informed him: 'I am very well. I want to take a purge this week, and then go to the villa and take some exercise.' The following week she wrote again: 'I am well, although troubled a bit by the new spring weather, so they [the doctors] want to give me a bit of medicine.' She had also taken on a commission to get shirts made for her husband, which, at the end of April, 'I am sending to Your Excellency, and handkerchiefs, and if they are not as fine as you deserve the fault is in the linen that was brought to me.'[8] The children continued to flourish, even if Nora had what Isabella herself sometimes suffered from – 'a deaf ear, brought on by catarrh'.

The Medici court saw the publication of a collection of pastoral poems by Felice Faciuta. He wrote two in praise of Isabella, one extolling her 'angelic deportment, divine steps' and imagining the 'happy painter by whom the holy image is embellished . . . O happy is the one who stretched out the ivory fingers for the hands.' 'I shall write', Felice declared, 'about the deeds of your most esteemed life, and while I live I shall write the praise concerning your breasts.' Isabella's breasts were 'two fruits, and they lend grace to your white neck'.[9]

Collecting for the poor, taking in the children of a murdered man, greeting visiting dignitaries, sending her husband shirts, reading poems dedicated to her: these are the kinds of events that seemed to occupy Isabella during the first few months of 1576. They give no hint of any particular turbulence in her existence, and on some levels perhaps Isabella could let herself believe that she had arrived at a new modus vivendi, albeit a fragile one. She had not been brought up as a long-term strategist. She was a princess who had been born and grew up with immense privilege, never having to think about the very nature of survival, the art of which was difficult to learn almost from scratch for a woman in her early thirties. Isabella had never had to rely upon her wits the way Bianca Cappello had when she was a teenager in Florence, with a family out to reclaim and possibly kill her. Paolo

Giordano's grandmother Felice della Rovere may have ended up as Rome's most powerful woman, but she began life as a cardinal's marginalized daughter and, unlike her cousin Cathérine de' Medici, Isabella had not spent the early years of her womanhood bitterly humiliated while her husband treated his mistress as if she was queen of France. She had always thought in the short term; if she had money, she spent it, sure in the knowledge that she would in due course receive another remittance from her father. When Paolo wanted her to come to Rome while Cosimo was alive, she could always put him off and wait for another issue to materialize to preoccupy her husband, as it always did. Now she was still employing these same techniques to stay in Florence, using the excuses of financial negotiations and of her ill health to avoid leaving her city.

Isabella knew that Paolo was not her strongest enemy, that she would always defeat him with the right ally. The problem was the only individual whom she really needed to be her ally, Francesco, was, in fact, her enemy. She knew perfectly well that in making Troilo an outlaw from Florence, he had struck a blow against her as well, taking from her an individual who could do little to protect her but whom she loved. The strength of Francesco's animosity towards Isabella might seem surprising, but one must recall that for many years now there seemed to have been little love lost between the siblings. When Giovanni died, he berated her for her grief, which he told her was bestial. Francesco also tried to impede his sister from getting the villa she wanted. Isabella, in turn, wrote disparagingly about her brother to Troilo. When she felt Francesco had betrayed her regarding settlements from their father, she wrote to him in no uncertain terms expressing her contempt for him. Francesco could now lay the blame at Isabella's feet for the way their cousin Leonora had turned out; without Isabella as her model Leonora might have caused a lot less trouble. Moreover, did Francesco wish that there be no rival in Florence to his Bianca? Bianca had vanquished the ever more melancholic and reclusive Giovanna, but as long as Isabella existed in Florence Bianca could never truly claim total pre-eminence over every other woman in the city. Isabella would still stand as first lady of Florence in the eyes of its citizens. Bianca knew that too, which was why she was prepared to play Isabella along. For her part, Isabella thought if she could bring Bianca over to her side, she had a potential mediator between herself and Francesco, but she reckoned without Bianca's own understanding that Isabella could do little for her but ultimately impede her rise, not to mention Francesco's desire to see his mistress reign supreme.

So Bianca was no ally to Isabella, and it is hard to see who she did have on her side. She could discount any assistance from Cardinal Ferdinando, who might have shared her disdain of her husband, but whose self-interest, which grew ever clearer, would not allow him to give support to his sister. While Isabella, on her own like this, had little political influence, there are two letters to her from correspondents in Spain and France whose opacity suggests that she had entered into private dealings, separate from either overarching Medici or Orsini interests. Both letters are written in the authors' native tongues, indicating Isabella's facility with languages, and in the French letter the writer chooses not to sign his name. He wrote, on 18 May 1575: 'Madame, I received the letter it pleased you to send by way of the Cavalier Petrouche and I thank you humbly for your kind regards. If it pleases you, you have in me a very humble servant who will do anything it pleases you to command of me . . .'[10] This Petrouche was Giovan Maria Petrucci, who had been Medici ambassador in France until 1572. After the St Bartholomew's Day Massacre, Catherine de' Medici accused him of mixing with Huguenots, compromising his position and forcing Cosimo to have him withdraw. But Petrucci still had French connections, which three years later were of apparent interest to Isabella.

The Spanish letter, written by the 'Belprior Don Pedro' in Barcelona on 11 July 1576, was in response to a letter and gift Isabella had sent him on 28 February by way of a Florentine envoy, Roberto Ridolfi. Once again, the author assures Isabella that 'anything you want in the world, if I have the means to acquire it I will'.[11] Neither letter employs the appropriate protocol of sending greetings to her brothers or husband, suggesting that whatever Isabella wanted from them was personal. At this point, Francesco's relations with France and Spain were tense, if not hostile, so was Isabella looking for some degree of private leverage, a means of escape for the time when she had exhausted the excuse of the *letto* and *lettica?* Yet on 17 April of 1576, Isabella communicated with a friend, suggesting a new optimism about her outlook. 'If I can keep the place where I have focused all my hopes I will be content,' she wrote. 'Place' is a little ambiguous, but it could refer to the Baroncelli, for as long as she had her own place in Florence she would not need to go anywhere. Moreover, she also wrote 'of the favours I have received from the Grand Duke, which are many . . .' Could it be that she had somehow extracted an agreement from Francesco to her advantage? Had indeed her finessing of Bianca achieved results after all?[12]

But it was not very long after this communication that rumours about Isabella began to spread again that would once more have renewed her brother's anger. On 13 May Ercole Cortile reported: 'Lady Isabella has been these past five days staying at Cafaggiolo, and there are some saying that a previous time when she went, it was to let her body swell, and that it will be like that other time, when she was healthy again after nine months.'[13] Cortile's cryptic little missive appears to be a reaction to stories about mysterious disappearances and reappearances of Isabella's, the clues of course being the reference to the swelling of her body and that nine-month time period. Such tales Cortile might have heard in taverns, but equally likely in court circles. His predecessor, Ridolfo Conegrano, had undoubtedly been privy to the same tales and might even have had first-hand information as to what going on. But given that he had become so entrenched in Isabella's court, he would be less quick to pass on what he heard to the d'Este duke. Cortile, on the other hand, with no such allegiance to the Medici princess, was extremely intrigued by her departure for this Medici villa, which he saw as curious and which apparently fitted an earlier pattern of behaviour.

Cafaggiolo was fifteen miles north of Florence, in the foothills of the Apennine mountains. Lying in the heart of the Mugello, from which the Medici came, the property had been acquired by Cosimo Il Vecchio in 1443. When Cosimo's architect Michelozzo undertook the renovation of the fourteenth-century castle, he was instructed to enhance its castellated appearance in order to make it look as if it was the Medici titular home, which had been in their family for centuries.

Despite its place in her family history, it was not one of the Medici villas Isabella visited regularly, and why she chose to go there now, when she had a more accessible villa of her own, is as intriguing today as it was then for Ercole Cortile. One should not dismiss his not-so-subtle bit of gossip to Alfonso d'Este entirely out of hand. It is not impossible that Isabella was carrying an unwanted pregnancy. Troilo had left Florence in late September of the previous year, meaning Isabella could have been by now about eight months pregnant. She had gone months without seeing Paolo Giordano, and when he did appear at the end of September she was on her sickbed and not likely to permit conjugal relations. If she were pregnant now it would be difficult to suggest Paolo was the father of any child she was carrying. If she had not grown too large and had ample skirts to disguise her body, she could have concealed a pregnancy up until this point and deliver in secrecy. Other than Cortile's comment, however, there is a veil of silence over most of the month of May 1576. There is no surviving correspondence from her from this period, to anybody, and certainly no references to further favours from Francesco.

But whatever Isabella was doing apparently alone in Cafaggiolo, if all she was doing was choosing to be by herself with her thoughts in the heart of Medici country, her solitude was fast coming to an end. Paolo Giordano decided, at the end of May, that he would come to Florence. 'The signora', one of Isabella's servants assured him in a letter, 'awaits you with every desire, and so does all of Florence.'[14]

Paolo took his time getting to Florence, and did not appear until the first week of July. Cortile reported to the Duke of Ferrara: 'Signor Paolo Giordano Orsini is awaited and he is coming to take the Lady Isabella back to Bracciano, if he can. But', added Cortile, 'it is believed that he's not going to be able to, because the aforesaid lady does not want to leave here for anything.'[15] Isabella's horror of being made to leave for Bracciano was now public, made official even by ambassadorial dispatch.

CHAPTER 2

A Trip to Cafaggiolo

If Isabella's June was spent in gloomy contemplation of her husband's imminent arrival in Florence, then her cousin Leonora's was no less troubled. Ercole Cortile, who had made a point of telling the d'Este duke the previous summer that Francesco de' Medici wished to be done with her, now began to report on the spates of ill health that had begun to afflict the twenty-three-year-old redhead. She had had bouts of illness in February and April, and, on 3 June, Cortile reported 'the Lady Leonora is very ill from incidents and many doctors say that they are doubtful that she is ill naturally'.[1] Florence, then, had its suspicions that the princess was being poisoned. But if she was not sick of natural causes, then her husband apparently was, having, as Bastiano Arditi claimed, 'the French disease [syphilis] caught from cavorting with so many whores in Florence, when he had the most beautiful girl in the city for a wife!'[2] By early July, Cortile did report, in the letter regarding Isabella's reluctance to go to Bracciano, that 'the lady Leonora is better, but unhappy as usual', and he added, 'the Duchess is more melancholic than ever'. However, if Leonora's health was better, what had transpired in June was enough to make her very unhappy indeed.

Statues of Knights of Santo Stefano

No matter how many got themselves killed in duels or by assassins or found themselves on the run, Florence was still full of ardent, hot-headed cavaliers, of whom Bernardino Antinori was one. Bernardino and his family had long been connected to Isabella's household, and his mother Regina had petitioned Isabella personally to extend her patronage to him in the 1560s. He was a Knight of Santo Stefano who had conducted himself well at the battle of Lepanto but less so in his native city. In February 1576, he had got into a fight after a football match with one Francesco Ginori, allegedly because both saw themselves as rivals for Leonora's affections. Bernardino was arrested, imprisoned in the Bargello and then subsequently released. Leonora, apparently oblivious to the trouble in which her aiding and abetting of Pierino Ridolfi's escape after the Pucci conspiracy had landed her, readily took up with Bernardino. 'He appeared frequently as a courtier in the Lady Leonora's coach,' wrote Giuliano de' Ricci.[3] Such a public display of flirtation could not possibly go unnoticed, least of all by Francesco de' Medici, who was on the lookout for any transgressive behaviour by his sister-in-law. Bernardino had been writing love letters and poems to Leonora that were 'found, hidden in her foot stool'.[4] In late June, he took a trip to the island of Elba, where, 'invited by Count Lionello delli Oddi to dine, he was, after eating, imprisoned on the order of His Most Serene Highness'.[5] Then, on 9 July, 'he was strangled at five in the morning' in Elba's prison.[6]

As word spread of Bernardino's rearrest on the grounds of his affair with Leonora, it would seem apparent to all that this young woman had learned nothing from her involvement with the Pucci conspirators and instead had moved on to a new lover. There was no question that she was disrespecting the Medici, her husband Pietro and the grand duke himself, whether they deserved it or not. Her behaviour was a symbol of everything that was wrong with Francesco de' Medici's governance. If he could not control the women of his family, then how could he control the states that he ruled? Cosimo de' Medici might have run an equally libertarian court, but it was obvious to all that he was a highly competent ruler. Adultery and anarchy had not gone hand in hand at Cosimo's court the way they did at Francesco's. Francesco had not proved himself a worthy successor to his father, and the situation was one which Medici enemies could use to their advantage. He had been lucky with the Pucci conspiracy, but he might not be as lucky next time. The time for him to act had come now. To preserve himself he had to restore the appearance of balance and order to the Medici family.

Renaissance Florence was physically a rather small city but with a large and consequently dense population. As ambassadorial dispatches and the diaries of Florence's citizens make clear, anything that went on in the city, any incident that occurred, would be uncovered quickly and news would travel fast. Therefore, if one was planning a murder, especially of someone whose death would be of great interest to many Florentines, it would be best if it could be carried out some way from the city. That way, word would be slower in reaching concerned parties, and the distance could provide distortion and spin as to what had really happened, allowing the perpetrator greater control of events. Using distance as a temporal buffer is an especially prudent strategy if the victim in question is a high-ranking woman in one's family in whose movements everyone is keenly interested.

In the second week of July 1576, Pietro de' Medici and Leonora da Toledo travelled due north to the castellated villa of Cafaggiolo, the same Medici property where Isabella had spent some time in May. Leonora's family knew she was in deep trouble because of the Pucci and Antinori affairs. Down in Naples, her father Garzia and uncle Luigi were making plans for her to leave Florence before she landed herself in deeper waters. Nonetheless, the trip to Cafaggiolo did not necessarily suggest anything particularly untoward, such villa peregrinations were after all the norm for the Medici family. However, shortly after their arrival at Cafaggiolo, on the morning of 11 July, Pietro de' Medici sent this short note to his brother Francesco: 'Last night, at seven o'clock, an accident and death came to my wife, so Your Highness can take peace, and write to me about what I should do, if I should come back or not.'[7]

Pietro might have used the word 'accident', but the fact that Leonora's death should bring peace to Francesco is a strong indication that both brothers had known exactly what was to happen to her once she arrived at the villa. A plan had been executed, and it was now Francesco's turn to go into action. The next day, he sent a more detailed account of Leonora's death to Cardinal Ferdinando in Rome: 'Last night, around five o'clock [time was already being dissembled], a really terrible accident happened to Donna Leonora. She was found in bed, suffocated, and Don Pietro and the others were not in time to revive her, which has given no small trouble. Last night she was taken from Cafaggiolo to the church of San Lorenzo, where the necessary burial will take place.'[8] That burial, Bastiano Arditi would record, had her 'deposited, in a box, in San Lorenzo, without any other ceremonies'.[9] There was no Mass said, nothing more to mourn the most beautiful girl in Florence with eyes like two stars in her head.

That Leonora's death had taken place some distance from Florence was already working in Francesco's favour, buying him time to embellish and reshape the events that had occurred. But Pietro and Leonora had not gone to Cafaggiolo alone and, in a world in which it was very hard to keep a secret, alternative accounts to that of Francesco were soon to emerge. 'Universally, it is said that she has been killed,' wrote the diarist Agostino Lapini. All that Giuliano de' Ricci would commit to was: 'She was found dead in bed.'[10] However, he bookended his entry of her death with one on the strangulation of Antinori in prison and another on the discovery of Antinori's letters to Leonora in her stool, leaving the reader to draw their own conclusions as to how she died. The avowedly anti-Medici Arditi was much bolder. In his account, 'The duke determined and advised that her departure had to be effected, executed in Cafaggiolo. And so, violently, was the said Leonora deprived of life.'[11] He also took this opportunity to note that her marriage to Pietro should never have been allowed in the first place, given that they were first cousins and 'such alliances are contrary to holy doctrine'.[12]

A few weeks later, Ercole Cortile sent the Duke of Ferrara the detailed account he had uncovered of how Leonora had died. The missive was sent by way of a complex cryptogram, a code that Cortile would be using more and more over the coming months to let the d'Este know of what was going on in Florence without detection. 'She was strangled by a dog leash by Don Pietro,' he wrote, 'and finally died after a great deal of struggle. Don Pietro bears the sign, having two fingers on his hand injured from the bite of the aforesaid lady. He might have come off worse were it not that he called for help from two villains from the Romagna, who they say had been called there for that purpose. The poor lady, it is understood, put up the greatest defence, as was seen from the state of the bed, found all tumbled up, and from the voices heard throughout the house.'[13]

Where was Isabella when word of Leonora's death broke? The last news of her movements had come from Cortile on 8 July, saying she expected Paolo Giordano in Florence to take her away to Bracciano. But Isabella was away from her city, deeper into the Tuscan countryside than Leonora had been, to the west at the villa of Cerreto Guidi. Just as Leonora had gone to Cafaggiolo in the company of Pietro, so too had Isabella gone to Cerreto with her own husband.

CHAPTER 3

A Trip to Cerreto Guidi

Shortly after Paolo Giordano had arrived in Florence in July, he sent a note to the Duke of Urbino. 'Finding myself here in Florence,' he wrote, 'without any other pleasure but a bit of hunting, and finding myself without either dogs or birds, I ask Your Excellency if you could provide me with ten hounds bred by Leonardo of Gubbio, a pair of harriers, and a pair of extra slaves.'[1] The letter is somewhat puzzling. The Duke of Urbino does not appear to be an individual who features greatly in Paolo's correspondence, which makes one wonder why he should now be asking him for hounds. And why could the Medici not provide him with any from their extensive kennel? It suggests that Paolo had no idea he was going to be hunting when he came to Florence, or else he wanted to establish a hunting trip as a pretext for his being there in the mind of an important outside party. Or somebody had told him to do so.

Isabella had no reason not to agree to go on a hunting expedition to Cerreto Guidi. Indeed, her reaction to the proposed excursion was surely relief at yet another opportunity presented to her to buy time. There seems to be no question in the minds of the participants that she

Fishing at the Villa of Ambrogiana

was well enough to go to this isolated hamlet, despite Paolo having recently sent two mules to Florence to pull his apparently frail wife's *lettuccio*. Perhaps it was in Isabella's head that she could go into another decline once the trip was over; perhaps Paolo really would be obliged to leave for Rome without her once more.

It was a big party that went out to Cerreto. In fact, were it not for the absence of her father, it might have seemed like old times to Isabella. Paolo's retinue included his Roman neighbour, a Massimo family member who was a Knight of Malta, while Isabella brought her ladies-in-waiting and her singing poet priest Elicona Tedaldi. Even Morgante the dwarf accompanied them.

That Leonora was sent out with Pietro to Cafaggiolo just as Isabella went to Cerreto with her husband would not have necessarily alarmed Isabella, Antinori's arrest notwithstanding. In all likelihood she was preoccupied by the issue of getting out of going to Bracciano. To the extent that her deep reluctance was now public knowledge, her cousin's problems were a lesser priority for her. But nor did Isabella necessarily have reason to fear death being meted out to Leonora. The Antinori incident was really a lot less serious than the one with Pierino Ridolfi from a year ago, and in any event Leonora was a Spanish grandee by birth and a Medici princess by marriage. No matter how things had developed with Francesco as grand duke, in Isabella's mind this status surely offered its own protection. However things had turned out for Troilo or Bernardino Antinori, she perhaps nursed the hope that surely the worst that could happen to Leonora or herself was enclosure in a convent or, in Isabella's case, at Bracciano, which for her would have amounted to the same thing. Isabella knew perfectly well that wives were killed for transgressions every day in Italy. She herself was tacitly implicated in the killing of Cassandra de' Ricci, whose lover Pietro Buonaventura's death Isabella had helped to engineer. But Isabella thought the rules did not apply to herself and Leonora. Princesses, she could reason, unless they became queens of England, did not, as a rule, get killed.

But some time on 14 July, three days after Leonora's demise, any such belief that she and Leonora would be protected was shattered completely. That was the day when a letter arrived from Francesco –

addressed, interestingly enough, to his brother-in-law – informing the hunting party of the death of Leonora. Paolo Giordano's ensuing response on that day to his brother-in-law survives:

> I learned with extreme sorrow, as Your Excellency rightfully sup-
> posed, in the letter it pleased you to write to me, of the strange and
> unexpected [*improvviso*] accident that Donna Leonora has suffered.
> The Lady Isabella has suffered no less sorrow. If pain could restore
> the loss we would grieve to the heart to bring her back . . . as it is we
> shall console and comfort ourselves that it is Divine vocation.*

Isabella's sorrow would have been for the loss of her younger cousin, to whom as a child she had given coins to practise charitable giving and with whom, only a few months previously, she had roamed Florence, surprising its citizens that Medici women would be out on the streets collecting for the poor. Leonora, Florence's prettiest girl, admired by everybody except Isabella's own brothers, had looked up to Isabella, emulated her intellectual interests and followed her down other paths as well, paths which Isabella could now see had led to Leonora's death. She could not possibly have believed that Leonora accidentally suffocated in bed, an implausible death at the best of times, assuming that Francesco had written the same news to Paolo that he did to Ferdinando. And the quick and lively mind that was Isabella's would very quickly have turned to this question: if Leonora had been sent to her death at the country villa at Cafaggiolo, what was she, Isabella, really doing at Cerreto Guidi?

It seems strange as well that Francesco wrote directly to Paolo Giordano and not Isabella, who was the one closest to Leonora. Was such a letter a prearranged signal to his brother-in-law? Learning of Leonora's death would have caused great distress to Isabella, as well as a burgeoning fear. But she could not be allowed too much time to act on her fear. Cerreto Guidi was as close to Pisa as it was to Florence. From Pisa it was easy to get to the port of Livorno, and if Isabella could make it there, there were boats to Naples, to the protection of her Toledo uncles, who had yet to learn of Leonora's death. But more dangerous for Francesco was the chance that Isabella could get to Paris, that haven for anti-Medici exiles and where, of course, Troilo now resided. Cathérine de' Medici would have been delighted to welcome Francesco's sister into Paris, regardless of her sins. To do so would shame him, turning what was still relatively private Medici business into an international scandal. Isabella could then become a rallying point against Francesco. She could be used in any way that Cathérine, possessed of all the cunning that Isabella had never learned to develop, thought would be useful to her. As for Isabella, she might have disdained the French on many an occasion in the past, but if Cathérine and Henri offered her the chance to be free of Paolo and the threat of Bracciano and to be reunited with Troilo, then she would take it. Such a scenario was almost straight out of the verses of *Orlando Furioso*, a dreamily romantic solution to the grief and difficulties of the past two years since Cosimo, Isabella's protector and champion, had left her. Small wonder that in the decades to come it would be claimed that Isabella was indeed planning an escape to France.[3]

Still, to come to such a decision, to make preparations for this break for freedom, would take time. Isabella had two children. To escape immediately from Cerreto Guidi would be to abandon them to an unknown fate. Would threats against them be used against her? Were instructions issued to the grooms not to give her a horse so that she wouldn't escape? Was she paralysed with fear at a time when quick decisive action was called for? It is even possible that Isabella still refused to believe that she would receive the same punishment as her cousin, that her life, albeit one lived on a knife edge of uncertainty, would go on as it had before. But time for Isabella de' Medici, mistress of prevarication, had just run out.

CHAPTER 4

'As If She Imagined What Was in Store for Her'

On 16 July, just forty-eight hours after Paolo Giordano had written to him expressing regret at the death of Leonora, he sent Francesco another letter. The following, penned by Francesco's secretary and only signed by the grand duke, was issued in return:

> With so much sorrow I have heard in your letter about the death of the Lady Isabella, your wife and my sister. You can judge it so, because this lady remained the last of this house, and was loved by me so tenderly. I believe you did not lack any diligence or remedy in attempting to save her from the accident which took her life, and if Your Excellency has any need of anything at this time, I will send whatever I have in store. Well, seeing as how God has pleased to take her to him, I exhort you, as I do myself, to accept in peace that which comes from His Divine Majesty. You can have her brought tomorrow morning or the next in a box to outside the Porta San Frediano, where the monastery of Monticello or of Monte Oliveto will take care of all the formalities for taking her to bury her in San Lorenzo with the honours that merit such a lady, and Your

Alessandro Allorí, Skeleton

Excellency can, at your convenience, come either before or after her, whatever pleases you.[1]

Despite the declarations of the tenderness of his love for his sister and the intention that she have a fitting burial, there is no escaping the business-like tone of Francesco's letter to Paolo. No shock is expressed, especially in light of the supposedly equally *improvvisata* death of Leonora less than a week before. It is almost as if Francesco anticipated Isabella's death in advance. Also of some interest is the fact that Paolo Giordano, after he arrived back in Florence following the death of Isabella, wrote a note to the Duke of Urbino to inform him that 'on the 16th the Lady Isabella my wife passed suddenly and repentantly to another life'.[2] This letter to the Urbino duke seems to dovetail with the one Paolo wrote to him less than a fortnight previously, as if he was putting the finishing touches on an alibi and confirming that nothing nefarious had occurred. All that had happened was Paolo's wife had died 'suddenly' on a planned hunting trip. That Paolo should use the word 'repentantly' would suggest to the Urbino duke that Isabella had received last rites. This, however, conflicts with Francesco's words that she was found dead, all attempts to revive her having failed. Three days after her death, Francesco reported the death of his sister to the Holy Roman Emperor: '[Isabella] died unexpectedly [*improvvisa* is used again, as Paolo used it for Leonora's death] while she was washing her hair in the morning at Cerreto. She was found by Signor Paolo Giordano, on her knees, having immediately fallen dead.'[3]

Rather like Leonora suffocating in bed, Francesco leaves the precise cause of death ambiguous. It has been suggested that his account indicates she suffered an epileptic fit or a heart attack, or that she hit her head on the basin in which she was washing her hair. That was to be the official Medici line. But once again Ercole Cortile, on learning of her death, left no stone unturned in attempting to piece together the circumstances, relying on what those who were present at the villa were prepared to tell him. Again in a cryptogram, he let the Duke of Ferrara know what he had learned 'from those willing to talk':

Lady Isabella was strangled at midday. The poor woman was in bed when she was called by Signor Paolo. Immediately she rose, wrapped a robe around her, for she was only in her chemise, and went to the said Signor Paolo's chamber, passing through a room where there was the priest Elicona and others of her servants. They say that she turned to them and shrugged her shoulders, as if she imagined what was in store for her. And so she went into the chamber. Morgante was there behind her and another of her women, but Signor Paolo chased them away and locked the chamber door with a great fury. Hidden under a bed was the Roman Cavalier Massimo, who helped him to kill the lady. They had not been locked in that room for more than a third of an hour when Signor Paolo called another one of her ladies, named Madonna Leonora, saying that she should bring some vinegar because the lady had gone into a faint. And when the lady entered, with Morgante right behind her, she saw the poor woman on the ground, leaning against the bed, and overcome with the love she bore her she said, 'You have brought her to her death, what do you need vinegar or anything else for?' Signor Paolo threatened her, and said she should keep quiet or he would kill her.[4]

What is so interesting about Cortile's account is that he invokes the names of witnesses who are known to us to be part of Isabella's circle – Elicona and Morgante – which endows his tale with greater authenticity. Even without threats of violence, these individuals were powerless to make any protest about what had happened. They were indentured to the Medici, and for them there was no life without the family. It did not matter to Francesco, or even to Paolo, that they had witnessed what had occurred. The worst they could do was to let what had occurred slip out in 'secret', but there would still be no repercussions for the perpetrators. In fact, their presence was necessary, as Isabella would have been highly suspicious if her retinue had not been permitted to accompany her to Cerreto as it usually did.

Cortile did not conclude his dispatch with the death of Isabella. Instead, he went on to tell the Duke of Ferrara:

The said lady was placed in a coffin for that very purpose and taken at night into Florence, and placed in the church of the Carmine [not far from the Porta di San Frediano] and the coffin opened up so

325

whoever wanted to see her could do, and those that did said that they had never seen such an ugly monster. Her head was huge beyond measure, fat lips as big as two sausages, eyes big like two wounds, breasts swollen, one split open, because, they say, Signor Paolo threw himself upon her so as to make her die more quickly.[5]

If the Duke of Ferrara was aware of Paolo's large size, he would recognize its effectiveness as an instrument of death. Cortile continued: 'The body was so putrid that no one could stand to be near it.' One can imagine how just a day or so of a Tuscan July would contribute to the swelling and stench of a corpse. Yet the opportunity to view the Medici princess's body was too much for some to resist, such as a compatriot of Cortile's, who let him know that Isabella's body 'was black in its upper half, but completely white below, as Niccolò da Ferrara told me, who lifted her clothes, as did several others, and could see everything'. This blackness, it has been suggested, came from the corpse or the coffin having been upside down, causing the blood to settle in the upper body parts. So much, then, for Francesco's promise that he would honour his sister's remains as she merited. Instead, he let Isabella's body be placed on display for its ghastly appearance to be commented upon, her clothes lifted up and her rotting flesh examined. He thereby ensured that the last sight the people of Florence had of the woman who was once the ebullient star of the Medici court was that of a monster. The woman who had barrels of water brought to her home so that she might bathe now festered, emitting that very particular odour of death in the hot sun: the sickly sweet odour of cheese left to ripen in hell. To leave Isabella's rotting corpse on display in such a way was rather like leaving the bodies of executed traitors hanging on the gibbet as a warning to others not to emulate the behaviour that had brought them to where they were now.

Cortile's friend Niccolò's evidence is corroborated by the account of the diarist Agostino Lapini, who wrote: 'She appeared to those who saw her like a monster, so black and ugly.' As to the cause of her death, he had heard 'that she had been poisoned, and it is said that she had been, like her relative, killed'.[6] Ricci, in his account, is rather more circumspect. In July, he writes in his diary:

In these days the Signora Isabella de' Medici went about, a young woman of about 33, most beautiful in her body, as splendid and free-spirited as she could possibly be, the daughter of the Grand Duke Cosimo of blessed memory and wife of the most illustrious Signor Paolo Giordano Orsini, who had not a week since returned from Rome, where he spent most of his time far away from his wife. The Lady Isabella and her husband went for fun to Cerreto Guidi, where, having drunk too much cold liquid and from the sickness that had been in her for a few months, they discovered a slow and aggravating illness in her, and seeing that she could not stay at the villa any longer, they resolved to return to Florence. And on the way she was assailed by the illness most ferociously at Empoli, where she died at 1800 hours on 16 July to the great sorrow of everyone who knew her, as other than being most beautiful in her body, she was most beautiful in her soul, a true *virtuosa*, splendid, a free spirit.

The writer does admit that this is only one version he heard of how she died, and he goes on to record a different set of circumstances for her death: 'She died in the manner above, or she died at Cerreto Guidi, after having dined and playing games, she was called by Signor Paolo to a chamber below, where immediately an accident occurred and she passed from this life.'[7]

It is obvious from Francesco's letters that the story of Isabella falling sick en route home is highly unlikely and may have been disseminated to the Florentine populace to stop speculation as to how Isabella died, unsuccessful though such an attempt may have been. Ricci was evidently uneasy about what he had been told, and added an account which more closely matches Cortile's, in which Isabella de' Medici was called to a room by her husband and never came out alive.

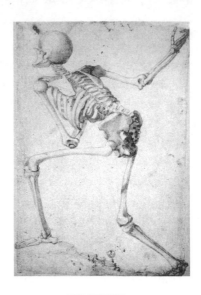

CHAPTER 5

Post-Mortem

It has been easy to see the murders of both Leonora and Isabella as crimes of honour in a country that was perceived by a generation of seventeenth-century English dramatists as 'rich in blood, unequalled in revenge'.[1] Both women had had extramarital relations, and their deaths at the hands of their husbands are justifiable within the context of their time. They join a murder roll of other adulterous women in Renaissance Italy, the stories of the majority lost for ever. Some do emerge from the archive, like Vittoria Savelli, from the Roman noble family, who was married to a cousin, Gian Battista of the same name. He cut her throat in July 1563 when he found her in bed with his half-brother Troiano, who was simultaneously stabbed to death by Gian Battista's henchmen.[2] Others, such as the widowed Duchess of Malfi, did not even have to commit adultery to meet what was perceived as a justifiable end. She was killed by her brother Cardinal Luigi d'Aragona after she married her steward and bore him children, defiling and besmirching the family honour by her ignoble association.

Although that particular event, famously recounted by John Webster in his eponymous play published in 1613, fascinated the

Alessandro Allori, Skeleton

English, it barely raised an eyebrow in Italy, where adultery laws allowed for such vengeance killings. This helps to explain why Florence's diarists express apparent sorrow at the deaths of Leonora and Isabella, eulogizing their beauty, charm, charisma and intelligence, but accepting the murders with little sense of outrage.

There was always a double standard for adulterous men and women; women were supposed to pay a price for any sort of infidelity. In Boccaccio's *Decameron* tale of Nastagio degli Onesti, a young man, scorned by the woman he loves, walks through the woods in despair. He spies a ghastly scene; a young woman pursued by a man with his dogs, who catch her and tear out her heart. He learns they are the ghosts of a couple who were in a similar predicament to himself and his own love. To win her back, he stages a banquet out in the woods to which he invites her and her family. The scene repeats itself in front of them. Horrified, she agrees to marry him, lest such a fate befall her.

Francesco de' Medici, whose bloodlust might seem deranged to a modern observer, was able to use Leonora's correspondence with Antinori to justify her death and to admit to Philip II that she had actually been killed by Pietro. 'I have to say', Francesco wrote, 'that Lord Pietro our brother took her life for the treason she committed with her conduct unbecoming to a noblewoman.' The phrasing is suitably ambiguous; the treason could refer to her adultery or to her part in the escape of the conspirator Pierino Ridolfi. 'We want His Majesty to know the real truth,' Francesco went on to say, 'having decided that he should know the reason for every action of this house, particularly this incident, because if veils are not lifted from eyes, we cannot serve His Majesty honourably and well, and so at the first opportunity he will be sent the documents [Antinori's letters and poems], so that he should know with what just cause Lord Pietro was moved to act.'[3] The king of Spain could accept Leonora's death under these conditions.

All the same, Francesco moved slowly in letting the Spanish court know everything that was happening in Medici circles. On 7 August, the Tuscan ambassador to Spain Bartolomeo Orlandini had his first meeting with Philip regarding the death of Leonora. At the meeting's end, another courtier present, Isabella's cousin the Duke of Alba, asked if the rumours of Isabella's death were true. The ambassador said he knew nothing about that, but he wrote straight away to Florence: 'Please assure me that the death of Signora Isabella has not taken place. We are at present in continual agony.'⁴

But if Leonora was to die, then so was Isabella. It was a double murder, the killings separate yet inextricably linked. Isabella could be seen, in Francesco's mind at least, as being responsible for what Leonora had become. Leonora had been formed in Isabella's image, emulating her older cousin's liberality, only with a little less sense, being more indiscreet, reckless and dangerous. Isabella's death was in part punishment for not reining in Leonora as she should have done. Moreover, she became a liability in the wake of Leonora's death. She was close to Leonora's father Garzia and their uncle Luigi, who were both incandescent with rage and anguish at the loss of their girl. Realizing that Leonora's marriage to Pietro was no longer tenable, they had actually wanted to take Leonora away from Florence and 'to take care of her in Naples'.⁵ They still did not know of her death by 20 July and had sent an envoy up to Rome to discuss the matter with Ferdinando, who informed his brother he had said nothing about Leonora's death and 'I persuaded him [the envoy] to turn around.'⁶ Francesco, for his part, was desperate to prevent Don Garzia registering a protest to Philip, which he would do all too soon. Had Isabella joined her uncles in condemning her brothers for what had happened to Leonora, her voice would give strength to theirs, causing further trouble for Francesco, who was still awaiting ratification from Spain for his grand-ducal status. As it was, Francesco ended up paying out what amounted to blood money for Leonora's death, disguised in the form of loans to Spain that would amount to almost one million *scudi* over the next decade. He also handed over straight away what was arguably the most beautiful crucifix to be found anywhere in Renaisssance Italy: Cellini's white marble *Crucified Christ*, still in the monastery of San Lorenzo del Escorial near Madrid. Pietro was also sent as a hostage of sorts to the Spanish court, the Toledo brothers doing what they could to make sure he had an unpleasant reception at court.

The death of Isabella did not involve such post-mortem negotiation and damage control. It is more than possible that Paolo Giordano had simply been waiting for word from Francesco to kill Isabella, which was what he had wished to do for a long time now. Cortile would describe Isabella as Paolo's '*moglie tanto odiato*' – 'wife so hated' – and he had clearly seen and heard enough during his tenure in Florence to recognize the tension between them. Isabella had contributed to his peers' contempt for Paolo Giordano. Regardless of both Paolo's and Isabella's adultery, Isabella had lived separately and autonomously, beyond Paolo's command and control, thus demeaning his masculinity. To kill her would bring him satisfaction. But Paolo was so dependent upon Medici funds that his personal opinion of Isabella did not matter. If Francesco ordered him to kill his wife, then he would follow that command. Conversely, she stayed alive as long as it was Francesco's will. Of course, inasmuch as Isabella's death was related to that of Leonora, there were additional motives for him to have her killed. Isabella's affair with Troilo and Troilo's own behaviour have long been understood as major factors in her death.

The baroque expressions of affection in their letters and Isabella's sporadic and sometimes apparently grave illnesses in the wake of Cosimo's death have been invoked to declare that Paolo did not kill his wife and that she in fact died of natural causes, meaning that Paolo has been unjustly cast as a monster. Ricci's remark that Isabella had been in ill health for some months is used as further supporting evidence. The fact that in the same passage he also suggests that she died of drinking too much cold liquid and, most concretely, that she died after being called by Paolo into another room and suffering an accident is ignored. Bastiano Arditi's tale of her death makes reference to a handsome young gardener at the Baroncelli and is dismissed as the ramblings of an anti-Medici septuagenarian tailor, a man so low down the social scale that he could hardly have been privy to accurate information. On the other hand, the high-ranking ambassador Ercole Cortile's very detailed account of how Isabella met her end is seen as the malicious gossip of an equally hostile Ferrarese, jealous of the Medici. Only in this case it is Paolo Giordano and another Roman, the cavalier Massimo, who are the villains in Cortile's account to Alfonso d'Este. He makes no mention whatsoever of any other Medici family members' complicity and makes no derogatory statements about them.

Cortile may have willingly listened to gossip and he might have exaggerated, but he could only do so in the context of his time and of what he had seen for himself. On 1 September, he wrote to the Duke of Ferrara regarding the division of Isabella's estate, for Isabella, as a document signed by Francesco makes clear, had died intestate:[7] 'They have given the Lady Duchess guardianship of the children of the Lady Isabella. It has been said that Signor Paolo does not want them, claiming that they are not his children, although I have not had confirmation of this. They are selling up all of her possessions. La Bianca has taken a great many of her underclothes and other things. His Highness has taken her jewels in order to pay her debts.' It had become public knowledge that Isabella's debts amounted to more than 2,500 ducats. Her creditors wanted to be paid in cash, not jewellery, but Francesco told them they had to 'take what they could'.[8] Cortile went on to say that 'Lord Paolo has taken the Baroncelli, which was the Lady Isabella's and in which she lived her life. He went up there with four or five prostitutes and they have come and gone publicly riding in her carriage . . . Yesterday,' he concluded this dispatch to Ferrara, 'Signor Paolo came to visit and begged me to kiss your hand on his behalf.'[9]

Her rotting body on display for all to see and even touch should they care to; her husband's whores roaming her property: these were not the only ways to defile Isabella's memory. On 22 September, Paolo sent Francesco a long letter regarding the management of his debts. His creditors were on the point 'of sequestering all my things', and he was clearly hoping for, if not actually expecting, Francesco's continued aid. 'In regard to the tomb for the Signora,' he continued, 'I do know well that its expense should fall upon me and not Your Highness, so I wanted to write to you to present the argument that it is not because I lack soul nor willingness to do so, but because of these debts that I cannot.'[10] In other words, Paolo Giordano, who had always bought whatever he wanted regardless of how much debt he was in, was claiming he could not afford a proper tomb for his wife. Of particular interest is that he only refers to Isabella as '*la signora*'. The conventional and appropriate way to refer to the dead is to say '*di felice memoria*', 'of happy memory', which is what Italians used in place of 'God rest her soul'. Francesco does the same. In fact, it has been proposed that he issued a *damnatio memoria* against his sister to expunge her identity from the history of the Medici family. Such an act would have destroyed portraits of her, her writings and her letters, and it is true that her portraits lie scattered, her writings fragmented. Denying her, in correspondence, the title *di felice memoria* could be seen as another method of *damnatio*.[11]

The letter from Paolo to his brother-in-law certainly attests to the fact that whatever sweet words they used in their letters, Paolo and Isabella's relationship had always been fundamentally transactional. From the very moment when he as a sixteen-year-old had told his creditors that he would pay them back with her dowry, and even now that she was dead, Paolo's greatest concern had always been how Isabella could facilitate his existence financially. Yes, perhaps his honour was assuaged when he killed her, but if it had been in his financial interests to let her live – in other words, if his source of revenue, Francesco de' Medici, had commanded it – then he simply would have had to acquiesce. Francesco might have been at some distance, but it was he who in effect killed his sister Isabella, because he no longer wished for her to live. In fact, his key role in the demise of both Isabella and Leonora came to be recognized. As Mark Noble would write in the eighteenth century: 'He [Francesco] gave them [their husbands] full permission to punish the fair culprits with death, a proposal they received with avidity.'[12] Isabella was a liability whom he saw as threatening his rule as Medici grand duke. The 'Orsini' of Isabella's name had always been an afterthought. She never lived as an Orsini and she did not die as an Orsini. It might have been, metaphorically speaking, an Orsini sword that slew her, but it was a Medici hand on the hilt.

The Culling Continued

Francesco de' Medici's vengeance against his sister and her world did not cease with Isabella's death. He next turned his attention to arresting those within her circle who had served her and whom he pinpointed as prime movers in the enabling of her existence. Such arrests would initiate a culture of fear in those who had been close to her. Who might be next, and for what reasons might they be detained? In the weeks after her demise, Florence's chroniclers recorded the names of those he arrested. 'There were taken in different places and at different times', wrote Ricci, 'Bernardo di Giovannbattista [a prominent Florentine merchant] de' Servi, a man of arms very close to the Lady Isabella de' Medici, and Carlo di Jacopo Fortunati.'[1] If Bernardo's name is unfamiliar within the well-documented life of Isabella, that of Carlo certainly is, as he had been associated with Isabella for over fifteen years. Bastiano Arditi adds that his mother, 'an attendant of the said Isabella', was also imprisoned at this time. Isabella had sometimes entrusted the care of her children to Carlo's mother. If the ultimate fates of Carlo and his mother are unknown, both writers mention that Bernardo died – 'violently in prison,' wrote Arditi; 'secretly beheaded,'

Torture at the Bargello

recorded Ricci. Cortile mentions the same arrests. Bellisario Simoncello, who two years before had jousted with Troilo and duelled with another adversary, now 'was taken . . . he had also attended this lady in her coach', noted Ricci. Ricci mentions the arrest of her gardener at the Baroncelli, a young man of twenty-four from Montevarchi who under Isabella's employ, Arditi had heard, had gone from wearing 'the clothes of a labourer to much finer ones'.

Arditi continued to track those arrested in connection with 'the Lady Isabella, daughter of Duke Cosimo, already killed [*già uccisa*]'.[2] Just over a year later, in August 1577, he added more names to the list of Isabella-related arrests: 'a certain *votapozzo* [well or cesspit cleaner] was taken away, put there [in jail] on her account after her death. As was a certain Maestro Paolo, surgeon, who had taken a baby that the said Lady Isabella had acquired from the handsome young Signor Troilo and who, not having revealed what had occurred to the duke, was put in prison after her death, and there he still is.' One might dismiss this news as spurious gossip, although it is odd that such gossip was still being spread a year after Isabella's death when by rights, interest should have died down. Moreover, it is not beyond the realms of credulity to tie Arditi's comment to Cortile's not-so-cryptic hint to the d'Este duke that the reason for Isabella's retreat to Cafaggiolo in May 1576 was that she was about to deliver a baby. Was such a baby born dead and given to the *votapozzo* for him to dispose of the little corpse?

Some employed by Isabella during her lifetime clearly felt they could rest easy in regard to their former association with her. The musician Stefano Rossetti, who had composed 'Olimpia's Lament' for Isabella, was now stationed at the Habsburg court of Innsbruck. Dissatisfied with the quality of musical instruments available to him in Austria, he wrote to Francesco in March 1577 to see if he could provide Rossetti with the 'six viols and a Neapolitan clavichord that the Illustrious and Excellent lady your sister, of happy memory, Lady Isabella' had once possessed.[3] Others were decidedly more circumspect. Fausto Sozzini, Isabella's secretary and sometime legal adviser with heretical tendencies, wrote cautiously to Francesco from Basel, where he had gone in 1574 to undertake theological training. 'While she lived, the lady Isabella de' Medici, Your Highness's sister, was my benefactress . . . While her death is very bitter, giving me reason to weep, hope has been raised in me, and that same desire to serve is now turned towards Your Highness, and this letter, full of good faith, is to beg you to condescend to believe that throughout your great dominion you have no more faithful subject than myself, nor one who has any greater desire than to spend his life in the service of Your Highness.'[4] What Fausto was clearly hoping for was a guarantee of safe passage from Francesco, a pledge that he would not be arrested when he entered Florence, as was clearly happening to so many of Isabella's employees and associates. In the event, Fausto never did return to Italy. He ended up in Poland, where his protestant anti-Trinitarian principles would later be embraced by such founding fathers of America as Benjamin Franklin and Thomas Jefferson. It is hard to imagine a world farther removed from grand-ducal Medici Tuscany than the republicanism of the new United States.

But there were associates of Isabella's in whom Francesco was far more interested than Fausto. The one whom he was desperate to annihilate was, of course, Troilo Orsini. On 21 July, Cortile wrote to Ferrara that Francesco had sent out 'Bellisario Simoncello with his men to kill Troilo Orsini.' That Bellisario was unsuccessful in this mission may have been an underlying cause of his subsequent arrest. On 14 August 1576, less than a month after Isabella's death, Troilo wrote to Francesco from Paris: 'Most serene Lord, most worshipful patron,' Troilo began,

> The lamentable case of the death of my Excellent lady cousin and sister to Your Serene Highness has filled all your subjects with sadness and myself in particular, as I must participate in any joys and sorrows which affect Your Highness. May God have accepted her in glory and bring to an end every incident that could perturb Your Highness. You may deign to be pleased to hear that the King [of France] has news that Casimir with all his people is now outside his kingdom.[5]

Casimir, the son of the count palatine of the Rhine, was a Calvinist possessing crack mercenary troops who had been helping France's Huguenots, and who would not leave France until Henri III paid him

off. Troilo proceeded to give Francesco other up-to-the-minute information about France's current political negotiations.

The letter, written as if it was from a Medici envoy dispatching the
latest news from the French court rather than from someone last
known writing to Francesco to confirm there was a ban against him in
Florence, was a deliberate taunt from Troilo to Francesco. Unlike
Fausto Sozzini, he knew he could not test the waters to see if a return
to Florence was feasible. Instead, Troilo wanted Francesco to know
that he was well ensconced at the French royal court, right at the centre of things, and that Francesco should consider him well protected by
Henri III, not to mention Cathérine de' Medici. And Troilo possessed
Cathérine's ear, the original *intrigante* who liked nothing more than to
hear of the scandalous affairs of the cousins she so disdained back in
her native Florence. On 11 September 1576, the Florentine ambassador at the French court sent the following note to Francesco:

> I have to give Your Highness an account of what is going on here, so
> I must warn you for your own interest about the envy brought
> about by your greatness, and the other malignity and most false
> inventions and calumnies against you. These, poisonously slithering
> from one mouth or another, have entered in such a way into the soul
> of the Queen Mother . . . I have been told that she has taken to dis-
> cussing at length the deaths of those ladies of *felice memoria*, showing
> herself disposed to believe certain revelations that their deaths were
> violent ones, and she feels herself confirmed in this erroneous opin-
> ion because in succession came the death of Signor Don Cosimo.[6]

Leonora's son, three-year-old Cosimino, the only other boy
fathered by one of the Medici brothers, died in August, just a few
weeks after his mother, apparently of dysentery. Almost simultaneously, Bianca Cappello bore Francesco a son, Antonio, whom it would
later be claimed was a child smuggled in in a warming pan. Continued
the ambassador:

> She evidently marvels at how these strange accidents could cumu-
> late together in such a way, and the greater marvel is that Your
> Highness has not sent her any account of the incidents. I would

have willingly avoided writing such things, increasing the infinite sorrow that I am certain accompanies such disgrace. Nonetheless, it seems my duty to urge Your Highness with the depth of his wisdom to dissuade Her Majesty from these false impressions . . .[7]

Medici ambassadors everywhere were certainly having a difficult time spinning the deaths of Leonora and Isabella. His ambassador in Vienna told Francesco quite bluntly that nobody there was inclined to believe 'one death was from apoplexy, and the other from epilepsy'.[8] But only Paris had Troilo, whose closeness to Isabella and first-hand knowledge of what had really been going on at the Medici court gave his accounts an authenticity which clearly enraptured Cathérine de' Medici. Of all those individuals associated with Isabella, Troilo was at the top of Francesco's most-wanted list. The problem for Francesco was that Troilo was prey which, unlike Isabella and Leonora, was on the loose. He was not so easily trapped and disposed of in a remote country villa, and he continued to elude the Medici grand duke.

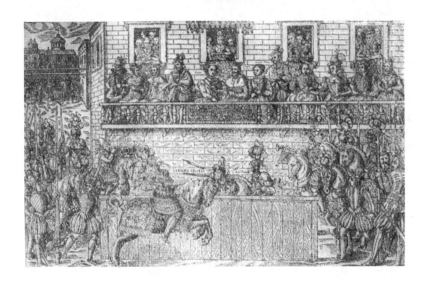

CHAPTER 7

The Assassin's Tale

According to Ercole Cortile's account of the killing of Leonora, Pietro de' Medici had been aided in the murder by 'two villains from the Romagna'. The province of the Romagna, immediately to the north of Tuscany, was sufficiently distant from Florence that such a pair would not have had local family and friends to whom they would repeat their story. Leonora's death was better publicized than Francesco would have liked, but still he was satisfied enough with this Romagnan duo's work that when over a year after Isabella's death Troilo continued to elude him, he turned again to one of their countrymen. However, in this instance the assassin he hired, Ambrogio Tremazzi, left behind a remarkable document for a contract killer: a written account of more than five thousand words of his mission to Paris. He sent it to Francesco's secretary, Antonio Serguidi, its length and style conditioned by Ambrogio's desire that 'His Highness should favour me, as he has verbally promised me'.[1]

Ambrogio began by revealing that he was solicited for the job by Ridolfo Isolani. Ridolfo was a nobleman from Bologna, Emilia Romagna's largest city, possibly the recruiter of Leonora's killers as

Joust at the French court

well. He was related by marriage to Ciro Alidosi, lord of the Romagnan town of Imola and a member of what constituted Francesco's inner circle. Later, Ridolfo would become Bolognese ambassador to Florence, perhaps a reward for past favours to the grand duke. Ridolfo arranged for Ambrogio to come to Florence. 'I came', Ambrogio recalled,

> because I understood that His Highness would be pleased if Signor Troilo Ursini was killed. The Lord Count Isolani let me know that this was something very dear to him indeed. One morning then, I found myself in the Grand Duke's palace, in Don Pietro de' Medici's rooms, who said to me: 'Well, Ambrogio, have you thought about how much money you need for this endeavour?' I said no. He said, 'Would you be satisfied with 200 *scudi*?' I replied that the journey was long, and I was going in search of someone I did not know. He replied, 'Do you think 300 would be enough?' I replied yes. And this lord said to me: 'Tomorrow come find me, and I will have taken the money out of a bank and I will give it to you.' According to the order given me I went to find him at the house of his chamberlain Piro on the Via Larga, and he gave me the 300 *scudi*.

Ambrogio asked if they would accept his twelve-year-old son as a hostage to his completing the mission. They acquiesced, so the contract killer returned to his home town of Modigliana to fetch the boy. On his return to Florence, 'I asked that I should speak with His Highness to tell him that I was that Ambrogio who had been recommended by Count Ridolfo. They told me that there was not time for such a proposition, that when His Highness left the palace, he was always accompanied by 2 or 3 lords in a carriage, that if I were to talk to him these gentlemen would overhear us, and that in no way did he want this negotiation to be known to many people.'

Ambrogio continued: 'I won't bother with the details of my journey day by day, but I will tell you that I arrived in Paris on the 12th of this past August, 1577.' He got to work straight away, assembling information on Troilo's movements. He learned Troilo 'was in great credit with His Majesty. He was currently to be found with the court at

Pontier, but having been wounded out there by an harquebus, it was thought he would return to Paris.' Ambrogio was clearly not the only assassin in France with Troilo as his target. 'This was the first time I had news of Signor Troilo, and so the time passed from week to week. Because I heard that most of the Italians lived outside of Paris in the faubourg of Saint Germain, it occurred to me that Signor Troilo might also have his house there. And so I resolved to leave Paris and to install myself in Saint Germain.' Ambrogio ingratiated himself with the Saint Germain Italians: 'One day, finding myself in the house of Signor Pietro Paolo Tosinghi, and speaking with Signor Camillo Tolomei, I asked him, "Signor Camillo, who is that young ruddy fellow whom I have not seen before?" He replied that he was a soldier whom Signor Troilo kept close by him. He had had another *bravo*, but he had died when Signor Troilo was wounded. "From what place is that lord?"' Ambrogio casually asked. 'He replied to me, "Roman, from the house of Orsini."'

On Halloween, Ambrogio found himself invited to a party given by an actor named Claudio, who also hailed from the Romagna. As he was standing near the doorway, he noticed the arrival 'of a gentleman on a black horse with a docked tail, with a companion, who was that young man with the ruddy skin. And I asked Claudio, "Who is that lord?" He replied to me, "That's Signor Troilo." And I fixed him with a look, and saw that by the left part of his nose, up towards the eye, there was a little black hole, about the size of a *quatrino*.' Ambrogio watched while Troilo mingled for a while and then departed in the direction of the Louvre. The assassin from the Romagna followed in his wake. 'And so I came to know the desired house' in which his target lived. But still Ambrogio could not get a fix on him, although he was tantalizingly close. One time Ambrogio saw him at the house of an actress named Vittoria, in the company of two Florentines. Another time he attempted to stalk him in the 'Palace of the King, and his antechambers, as well as other places, to my great peril'. Once he caught sight of Troilo hearing Mass in the Chapelle Royale, on his way to dine with the king. Although there were balls at court every Thursday, Troilo chose to stay away when large crowds like that gathered. He also spent quite a bit of time in the company of Cathérine de' Medici.

Then 30 November arrived, St Andrew's Day, 'which is a very lucky day for me', explained Ambrogio. 'I got up and took myself to the palace, and the moment I arrived I saw him.' Ambrogio lost him, but then caught sight of him again leaving a game of tennis. 'I saw him go up towards the King's apartments, and pass a bit of time in the rooms of the Queen Mother. Then he left the Queen Mother's rooms, and entered into those of Monsieur Montmorençy, where he heard the Ave Maria.' After the Hail Mary, Troilo left the Louvre. It was early evening by this time. He first went home, and then visited the home of Monsieur de la Chapelle. Still Ambrogio could not get a fix on him. 'Troilo left Chapelle's house, I followed behind him at a gallop, he dismounted and went into a house whose name I don't know.' Troilo spent ten minutes in this house, perhaps aware he was being followed and attempting to throw his pursuer off his trail. But the assassin finally had Troilo in his sight. 'I took my harquebus from my side, and fired it with as much force as I could.' Troilo fell from his horse, and as he fell 'he uttered nothing other than oh, oh'.

Ambrogio's account of how he killed Troilo is corroborated independently by the letter Francesco's ambassador sent to him: 'The evening of St Andrew's Day, around eight o'clock in the evening, Signor Troilo was leaving the house of the cousin of Monsieur de la Chapelle, and firing a pistol into his stomach, [the assassin] completely ran him through.'[2] On 19 December, a Florentine Knight of Santo Stefano was arrested in connection with the murder. It appeared that Ambrogio's luck held, and his success in killing Troilo where others had failed persuaded Francesco to hire him to assassinate other Florentine exiles in Paris.

Francesco seemed oblivious to the rising anger of the French crown, and to Cathérine de' Medici in particular, who even as late as 1581, four years after the death of Troilo, declared: 'The Grand Duke does not take account of me, as to the displeasure of myself and the king, and in front of our very eyes he had Signor Troilo Orsini and others killed.'[3] The Florentine response to her protest was: 'Even if the lives of Signor Troilo and the others were taken in your kingdom, what they had done meant they did not deserve life.'

What ensued was a complete breakdown in diplomatic relations between France and Francesco, which were finally repaired when in 1600 Francesco's daughter Maria married King Henri IV of the Bourbon line, the former Henri de Navarre. The De Valois became extinct in 1589 with the death of Henri III.

It seems that Ambrogio Tremazzi's luck eventually ran out as well. On 5 December 1578, a representative of the German Fugger bank in Paris sent the following report back home: 'Of news we have none, save that on the last day of November the secretary of the Duke of Florence, who together with the ambassador has been here a year or two, was taken into custody by the court provost by the order of the king.' Perhaps coincidentally – or not – 30 November was the anniversary of Troilo's death. 'It is supposed that this was done because of several murders which the Duke of Florence is said to have instigated. Not long since he caused Don Troilus d'Orsini to be shot at night by his [Francesco's] servants between the hours of 8 and 9. Suspicion falls upon him because the said Troilus stood in too close a friendship with the duke's sister. Some 14 days ago, a Florentine of the name of Captain Bernardo was shot in the suburb of Saint Germain. The culprit was caught and put on the rack. After all his members had been broken, he was given water to drink twice as he lay on the wheel. It was only then much information was gained from him, and it is said that he confessed that he had taken money from the said secretary to commit this and the other crime. The culprit was an Italian who had already done 6 people to death.'[4]

Alla Illustriſsima, & Eccellentiſsima Signora
D. ISABELLA de MEDICI
Orsina, Ducheſſa di Bracciano.

From the frontispiece to Michele Capri's *Delle lodi del Serenissimo*
Signor Don Giovanni d'Austria, 1571

Isabella Eterna

The deaths of Isabella, Leonora, Troilo and those associated with them did not put an end to scandal, drama and trouble for the Medici family. Francesco de' Medici made the assumption that if he continued to support Paolo Giordano financially, then he would be able to control him and make him do exactly as he chose. In 1579, Francesco wished to reward Ciro Alidosi, related by marriage to Ridolfo Isolani, the Bolognese procurer of assassins, for his faithful service. The reward would be that his daughter would become Paolo's new bride. But the Duke of Bracciano refused to comply, writing to Francesco, 'I know that I owe you everything, without you my life would be nothing. But I ask you, please do not make me make love to the daughter of Signor Ciro.'[1] Paolo's pleading and craven tone, hardly that of one ducal brother-in-law to another, is testament to the extent to which he was still dependent upon Francesco's patronage. Nonetheless, he was resisting Francesco's command because, in the aftermath of Isabella's death, and perhaps even before, Paolo had fallen in love with the most beautiful woman in Rome, Vittoria Accoramboni.

The affair between Paolo and Vittoria set off its own chain of events

Parnassus, in a Florentine setting

and even more murders, beginning with that of Vittoria's husband in order that Paolo might marry her. But the worst aspect of this relationship from the Medici perspective was how Paolo, anticipating others from Vittoria, treated his children by Isabella, Nora and Virginio. The siblings, in the wake of Isabella's death, had remained in Florence, as Ercole Cortile indicated they would. Every so often Paolo sent stipends for their upkeep, stipends that were invariably late and which always required multiple demands from the Medici court before the children received them. In the meantime, Paolo only increased his spending in Rome, massively enlarging the Monte Giordano palace and the Bracciano castle, buying paintings and furniture and showering Vittoria with gifts. The word Cortile had heard in the aftermath of Isabella's death, that Paolo did not believe Nora and Virginio were his children, seems to be confirmed not only by this neglect of them but also by the fact that he was prepared to all but disinherit his son. When he died in 1585, Paolo left 60,000 *scudi* to Vittoria, a sum whose disbursement would have required the virtual dismantling of the Orsini estate, given its great debts, thereby depriving Virginio of his inheritance. In the aftermath of Paolo's death, Vittoria refused to concede in negotiations with Medici representatives on what she held to be hers. Not long after, she was stabbed to death by another Orsini family member, Ludovico. However, it was widely believed that Francesco de' Medici sponsored the assassination in order to ensure that his nephew got what was his. Thus he preserved the patrimony of what had always been the real purpose of his sister's marriage to Paolo Giordano: the production of a Medici–Orsini heir.

The Paolo and Vittoria affair became the first international *cause célèbre* and was the basis for the Jacobite dramatist John Webster's 1612 play *The White Devil*. Details of events emerged in the *avvisi*, newsletters reporting Roman happenings, and in pamphlets disseminated across Europe. However, the Medici had largely managed to suppress the true story of Isabella, and as such the Isabella who appears in Webster's play is really a fictional character. Isabella would hardly have recognized herself in the play as the rather drippy individual who is steadfastly and pathetically in love with her husband. This Isabella does not dance and play music; instead, every night before she goes to bed this worshipful wife kisses a portrait of her husband, which he has had poisoned and which causes her demise. The real Isabella might have laughed at the macho and masterful creature her husband becomes in the play, for in Webster's hands Paolo is quite the alluring villain. She herself was disdainful and contemptuous of Francesco, but there is no doubt that Webster's sinister Duke Francesco does capture the disposition of the real-life model.

In other aspects of real life, had she lived Isabella would also undoubtedly have been annoyed at Bianca's rise to power. In 1578, Bianca achieved the ambition she had long nursed, when the melancholic Giovanna died. It was an end to a life in Florence that had been lived largely without joy, although Giovanna did briefly see some satisfaction after giving birth in 1577 to a son, Filippo, named to honour the man to whom Francesco was now political hostage, Philip II of Spain. At least Giovanna was spared the pain of that boy's death in 1582. With Giovanna dead, Francesco quickly married Bianca and, to Florence's horror, gave to the woman they called the Venetian *puttana* the official title of Grand Duchess, honouring her publicly in a way Cosimo never did Cammilla. Later, he legitimized their natural-born son Antonio as Medici heir.

The sense that in some ways it was Isabella whom Bianca aspired to be seems confirmed by the way she appropriated her underclothes, intimate apparel, in the aftermath of her death. She also took as her own Isabella's courtier poets, such as Elicona Tedaldi, present at Isabella's death, who would write and publish sonnets in Bianca's honour. But even Bianca's triumph was relatively shortlived. In 1587, nine years after her marriage to Francesco, the grand duke and duchess died, just a few days apart, apparently of malaria. Currently, a debate is raging among pathologists who have disinterred their remains as to whether or not they died of deliberate arsenic poisoning. If they did, the finger has been pointed at Cardinal Ferdinando as a possible culprit.

In the wake of his brother's demise Ferdinando lost no time in travelling back to Florence from Rome. He divested himself of his cardinal's robes and fully revealed all the cunning that his years as the younger Medici brother had only hinted he possessed. Ferdinando declared Antonio illegitimate and encouraged the doubts that he was

Francesco's son at all. He took the grand-ducal crown for himself and a wife in the form of Christina di Lorena, who proved as fertile as Eleonora '*La Fecundissima*' by bearing him nine children. The very last Medici grand duke, Gian Gastone, who died in 1737, was one of Ferdinando's descendants. Ferdinando was described by the English traveller Robert Dallington in 1598 as 'of stature meane, of colour by complexion browne, of body corpulent. His government was merely despoticall.'[2] Nonetheless, he succeeded in operating a government that was far more in keeping with his father's competent style than that of his brother. It was Ferdinando who arranged the marriage between Francesco's daughter Maria and Henri IV of France, thus allowing Florentine–French relations to resume and ensuring his father's prophecy that Henri de Bourbon was the one to watch would come to pass. And if Ferdinando had offered his sister no useful support during her final years, she would have found satisfaction in that he did thwart Francesco and Bianca's plans to allow their son to take the grand-ducal throne. Nor would Isabella have raised any objections if indeed it was Ferdinando who poisoned the couple.

Isabella would have been proud of how her children, who continued to be raised in the Medici court, turned out. Virginio took up the Orsini dukedom on his father's death, but having grown up at the Florentine court he was always more Medici than Orsini, spending, by choice, as much time in Florence as Rome. In the late autumn of 1600, he arrived at the court of Queen Elizabeth I for an extended stay. This young and gracious nobleman proved popular with his English counterparts. On 6 January, Epiphany of 1601, the Queen's players performed William Shakespeare's *Twelfth Night*, a light-hearted comedy composed especially for the feast. One of the play's principal characters, Duke Orsino, took his name from the Italian visitor seated as guest of honour in the audience. As for Nora, she had her mother's cultural interests and, like her, enjoyed composing music. She was married for twenty years to her cousin Alessandro Sforza and bore him numerous children, but it was not a happy marriage. Nonetheless, Nora proved to be a woman of self-conviction and, in 1621, she separated from him and installed herself in a convent of her own founding, a somewhat different and undeniably less risky response to an unsatisfactory marriage than that of her mother.

Isabella herself largely disappeared from the record at the Florentine court. In the early seventeenth century, a portrait of her was described in an inventory as being of 'the mother of Signor Virginio when she was a young girl', her name never mentioned. However, her memory was revered by others. When the great Medici sculptor Giambologna died in Florence in 1608, his bedchamber was adorned with a portrait of Giovanna, the virtuous and wronged Medici Grand Duchess, and one of Isabella, not so virtuous but equally, if not more so, wronged. Still, in knowing so little about her, the Elizabethan and Jacobean dramatists, avid for all things Italian, were denied the opportunity to use her as a character in the way she deserved. Even then, Isabella's personality, which one might say combines Juliet with Rosalind, with just an undercurrent of Lady Macbeth, might have been too much for them. In the eighteenth century, Isabella appears to have bewildered the English curate Mark Noble, who declared her to be 'one of the most profligate princesses that ever disgraced the Christian profession', as well as 'the patroness of Socinus, and as long as she lived all the endeavours of the Inquisition to confiscate his effects were ineffectual'.[3] The fact is that Isabella possessed a remarkable mix of qualities that even today would be hard to find. Today's high-profile society girls, to some extent the descendants of Isabella, do not care about language, the ancient world, astrology or the discussion of heresy in the way that those subjects mattered to Isabella and informed her life.

The nineteenth century, with its taste for tragic heroines, invested in that aspect of Isabella's existence: as the woman forced into the arms of another by her husband's neglect. Isabella, an avid consumer of romances like *Orlando Furioso*, might have enjoyed Francesco Guerrazzi's melodrama *Isabella Orsini, Duchessa di Bracciano* (even if he omitted Medici from her name), all the more as a lyric opera in 1921. But the fact remains that for much of her life this tragic heroine was anything but tragic. She not only played and partied; she had the opportunity to think and create, to love and be loved at a time when many women were valued as little more than dowry-bearing vessels. It seems important to celebrate the laughing, high-spirited, liberal Isabella, as much as one might lament her fate. There was never another Medici woman like her, although the resolve of Francesco's daughter Maria, queen and subsequently regent of France, might have impressed her. But Isabella's brilliance, daring and passion were never to be replicated, either in the daughters of the family or in the wives, largely imported from the north. The 'fall' of the Medici family is often seen as beginning in the late sixteenth century, but that is not strictly true. The Medici hung on and prospered while their Italian counterparts and rivals – Gonzaga, d'Este and della Rovere – declined. But what is true is that the Medici really became rather dull, worthy and stolid, whereas Isabella, 'star of the Medici court', sparkled and shone. There are many characters from Renaissance Italy whom one might wish to meet, but few, I think, would be as much fun as Isabella as a companion. Her playfulness, vibrancy, often sarcastic sense of humour, sharpness and interest in a huge variety of topics – not to mention the great parties she held – all suggest an individual very much to modern tastes.

The tragedy of Isabella's life lies in the fact that ultimately she was punished for being female. Had she been male her life would not have ended as it did. A comment put into the mouth of a late sixteenth-century noblewoman by the writer Torquato Tasso in a dialogue on games he published in 1582 does come to mind when thinking about Isabella. In his book, Margherita Bentivoglio complains that when playing competitive games, men will let women win, a situation she abhors because it does not reflect true life, in which a woman was always in a weaker position than a man. The same might be said of Isabella's existence. She seemed to win on so many occasions on the gilded game board her father helped her create, but in the harsh light of reality she was the loser.

It is difficult not to be tempted to envision 'What if?' scenarios in the life of Isabella. What if Giovanni had not died so young? What if Cosimo had lived and Paolo had died? How would Isabella's trajectory have altered? She was really quite young when she died. An older Isabella, with a diminished taste for parties and lovers but still with a position of power in Florence, could have become a more political creature or one even more invested in her native city's development and progress. Or what if she had managed to escape to France and be united with Troilo? What political explosions might then have been ignited?

More recently, popular culture and folklore have embraced Isabella and she now enjoys a reputation as a ghost. The *commune* of Bracciano have adopted her, and guided tours of the castle feature lurid and entirely invented tales of how she lived there, taking lover after lover, whom she then had killed by throwing them into a knife-filled well. Recently she featured in the tabloid press, where it was speculated she might be haunting the wedding which took place at Bracciano of one of Hollywood's golden couples. Given that Isabella could not bear the idea of living in Bracciano when she was alive, it seems unlikely she would choose to haunt the castle dead. Cerreto Guidi claims her presence too. She would be annoyed at the deforestation that has taken place since her demise, ruining the *spassi*. Still, it seems likely that Cerreto would be her more likely haunt of choice, especially if she could select her company of fellow ghosts. There is no question that Isabella would choose her *babbo* Cosimo and her brother and near twin Giovanni to join her. There would be some companions to make her laugh: the Ferrarese Ridolfo Conegrano and the tiny but bellicose Morgante, who faithfully tried to follow her into the room where Paolo was preparing to kill her. There would be musicians, poets and playwrights to entertain. Isabella's cousin Leonora would be there, with whom she could have a girlish laugh, generated by the presence of a few ardent pages and *cavalieri*, who could join her in the hunts that would take place every day. Such companions would need to be careful because undoubtedly Isabella would have Troilo Orsini make the journey back from Paris to Cerreto, reuniting her with a lover from whom she was forced apart. In this new celestial world Isabella, the goddess, could reign eternal, as the poet Felice Faciuta promised she would: 'Always beautiful, she is made ever more beautiful . . . she will delight the deities with the sweet sound of song. And when Apollo's chariots expand their lights, they show you good Isabella.'

umil.ma S.va et sorella
dognia Isabella
Medici Orsina

Bibliography

ARCHIVAL AND MANUSCRIPT SOURCES

Florence
Archivio di Stato (ASF): *Mediceo dopo il Principato* (MDP)
Carte Strozziane
Settimani, *Diario*, Manoscritti, 128
Miscellanea Medicea
Ducato d'Urbino
Online database, Medici Archive Project (MAP): http://www.medici.org

Mantua
Archivio di Stato di Mantova (ASM): Archivio Gonzaga (AG)

Modena
Archivio di Stato di Modena (ASMo), *Ambasciatori a Firenze*

Rome
Archivio di Stato Capitolino (ASC)
Archivio Orsini (AO)

London
British Library (BL): Sloane, H., 'Tragico fine della signora Eleonora di Toledo moglie di Cosimo primo de' Medici e dell' Isabella figlia d'ambedue, moglie del signor Paolo Giordano Orsini e di molti altri cavalieri, li 11 Luglio 1567', 1930, ff. 27–40

Los Angeles
UCLA, Special Collections, Orsini Family Papers

PRINTED SOURCES

Acidini, Cristina Luchinat, *Taddeo e Federico Zuccari, fratelli pittori del cinquecento*, Milan, 1998–9
—— *The Medici, Michelangelo and the Art of Late Renaissance Florence*, London/New Haven, 2002
Adriani, Maurilio, *Arti magiche nel Rinascimento a Firenze*, Florence, 1980
Ajmar, Marta Wollheim, and Dennis, Flora, *At Home in Renaissance Italy*, London, 2006
Allegri, Ettore, *Palazzo Vecchio e i Medici*, Florence, 1980
Arditi, Bastiano, *Diario di Firenze e delle altri parti della cristanità (1575–1579)*, ed.
    Roberto Cantagalli, Florence, 1970

Ariosto, Ludovico, *Orlando Furioso*, ed. Guido Waldman, Oxford, 1999

Anderson, Jaynie, '"A most improper picture": Transformations of Bronzino's erotic allegory', *Apollo*, 384, 1994, 19–28

Atti della Pontificia Accademia Romana di Archeologia, 1923

Avery, Charles, 'The Gardens called "Bubley": Foreign Impression of Florentine Gardens and a New Discovery Relating to Pratolino', in Charles Avery, *Studies in Italian Sculpture*, London, 2001

Bargagli, Girolamo, *Dialogo di guochi che nelle vegghie sanesi si usano di fare (1572)*, Siena, 1982

Barocchi, Paola, and Giovannna Gaeta Bertela (eds), *Collezionismo mediceo: Cosimo I, Francesco I et il Cardinale Ferdinando: Documenti 1540–1587*, Modena, 1993

—— *Collezionismo mediceo: Da Cosimo I a Cosimo II, 1540–1621*, Florence, 2002

—— and Giovanna Ragionieri (eds), *Gli Uffizi. Quattro secoli di una galleria. Atti del convegno internazionale di studi*, 2 vols, Florence, 1983

Belmonte, Pietro, *L'institutione della sposa*, Rome, 1587

Berti, Luciano, *Il principe dello studiolo. Francesco I de' Medici e la fine del Rinascimento fiorentino*, Pistoia, 2002

Bicheno, Hugh, *Crescent and Cross; The Batle of Lepanto, 1571*, London, 2003

Bini, Pietro di Lorenzo *et al.*, *Memorie dello calcio fiorentino*, 1688, Florence, 1991

Blunt, Anthony, 'A Series of Paintings Illustrating the History of the Medici Family Executed for Maria de' Medici', *Burlington Magazine*, 109, September 1967, 492–8 and October 1967, 560–6

Boase, T. S. R., 'The Medici in Elizabethan and Jacobean Drama', *Journal of the Warburg and Courtauld Institutes*, 37, 1974, 373–8

Boccini, Floriano, *Fonti per la storia della malaria in Italia*, Rome, 2003

Boiardo, Matteo, *Orlando Innamorato*, trans. W. S. Rose, Edinburgh/London, 1893

Bonora, Elena, *Ricerche su Francesco Sansovino, imprenditore, libraio e letterato*, Venezia, 1994

Booth, Cecily, *Cosimo I, Duke of Florence*, Cambridge, 1921

Borsini, Francesco, *Firenze del cinquecento*, Rome, 1974

Borsook, Eve, 'Art and Politics at the Medici Court: The Funeral of Cosimo de' Medici', *Mitteilungen des Kunsthistorisches Instituts in Florenz*, XII, 1965, 1–2, 31–54

Bresnaham Menning, Carol, 'Loans and Favors, Kin and Clients: Cosimo de' Medici and the Monte di Pietà', in *The Journal of Modern History*, 61, 3, September 1989, 487–511

Brunelli, Giampiero, *Soldati del papa, politica militare e nobilità nello Stato della Chiesa (1560–1644)*, Rome, 2003

Buckley, Wilfred, 'Six Italian Diamond Engraved Glasses', *The Burlington Magazine*, 61, 355, October 1932, 158–61

Capri, Michele, *Delle lodi del Serenissimo Signor Don Giovanni d'Austria*, Florence, 1571

Cardamone, Donna G., 'Isabella Medici-Orsini: A Portrait of Self-Affirmation', in Todd M. Borgerding (ed.), *Gender, Sexuality and Early Music*, London, 2002, 1–25

Caroso, Fabritio, *Courtly Dance of the Renaissance; A New Translation and Edition of the Nobiltà di dame*, 1600, trans. and ed. Julia Sutton, New York, 1986

Castiglione, Baldessar, *Book of the Courtier*, trans. Charles Singleton, New York, 1959

Casulana, Maddalena, *Il primo libro di madrigali a quattro voci novamente posti in luce, e con ogni diligentia corretti*, Venice, 1568

Catena, Gian Battista (ed.), *Lettere del Cardinale Giovanni de' Medici, figlio di Cosimo I, Gran Duca di Toscana, non più stampate*, Rome, 1752

Celletti, Vincenzo, *Gli Orsini di Bracciano; glorie, tragedie e fastosità della casa patrizia più interessante della Roma dei secoli XV, XVI, e XVII*, Rome, 1963

Cellini, Benvenuto, *The Life of Benvenuto Cellini written by Himself*, trans. J. Symonds, Garden City, NJ, 1975

Chiarini, Marco (ed.), *Palazzo Pitti, l'arte e la storia*, Florence, 2000

Ciappelli, Giovanni, *Carnevale e Quaresima: comportamenti sociali e cultura a Firenze nel rinascimento*, Rome, 1997

Clayton, Richard, *Memoirs of the House of Medici from its Origins to the Death of Garzia and of the Great Men who flourished in Tuscany within that period. From the French of Mr Tenhove, notes and observations by Sir Richard Clayton*, II, Bath, 1797

Cochrane, Eric, *Florence in the Forgotten Centuries, 1527–1800*, Chicago, 1973

Cohen, Thomas V., *Love and Death in Renaissance Italy*, Chicago, 2004

—— and Elizabeth S. Cohen, *Words and Deeds in Renaissance Rome: Trials Before the Papal Magistrates*, Toronto, 1993

Conti, Cosimo, *La prima reggia di Cosimo I nel Palazzo già della Signoria di Firenze*, Florence, 1893

Conti, Ginori, *L'apparato per le nozze di Francesco de' Medici e di Giovanna d'Austria*, Florence, 1936

Corti, Gino, 'Two Early Seventeenth-Century Inventories Involving Giambologna', *Burlington Magazine*, 118, no. 882, September 1976, 629–34

—— 'Cinque balli toscani del cinquecento,' *Rivista italiana di musicologia*, 12, 1977, 73–82

Cox Rearick, Janet, *Dynasty and Destiny in Medici Art: Pontormo, Leo X and the Two Cosimos*, Princeton, 1984

—— *Bronzino's Chapel of Eleonora in the Palazzo Vecchio*, Berkeley, 1993

D'Accone, Frank A., 'Corteccia's Motets for the Medici Marriages', in David Rosen and Claire Brook (eds), *Words on Music: Essays in Honor of Andrew Porter on the Occasion of His 75th Birthday*, Hillsday, NY, 2003

Dallington, Robert, *A Survey of the Great Duke's State of Tuscanie, 1598*, Amsterdam, 1974

Desjardins, Abel, *Négociations Diplomatiques de la France avec la Toscane*, IV, Paris, 1859–86

Dumas, Alexandre, *Les Médicis*, Brussels, 1845

Edelstein, Bruce, '"Acqua viva e corrent": private display and public distribution of fresh water at the Neapolitan villa of Poggioreale as a hydraulic model for sixteenth-century Medici gardens', in Stephen J. Campbell, *Artistic Exchange and Cultural Translation in the Italian Renaissance City*, Cambridge, 2004

Eisenbichler, Konrad (ed.), *The Cultural Politics of Cosimo I de' Medici*, Aldershot/Burlington, 2001

—— *The Cultural World of Eleonora di Toledo*, Aldershot/Burlington, 2004

355

BIBLIOGRAPHY

Faciuta, Felice, *Foelicis Faciutae melphitani pastorali. Eiusdem divers poemata*, Florence, 1576

Fanfani, Tommasso (ed.), *Alle origini della banca: etica e sviluppo economico*, Rome, 2003

Fantoni, Marcello, 'The Grand Duchy of Tuscany: The courts of the Medici 1532–1737', in John Adams (ed.), *Princely Courts of Europe, 1500–1750, Ritual, Politics and Culture Under the Ancien Régime*, London, 1999, 255–75

Ferri, Marco, *I medici riesumano I Medici*, Florence, 2005

Fiorani, Francesca, *The Marvel of Maps: Art, Cartography and Politics in Renaissance Italy*, New Haven/London, 2005

Fleming, Touba Ghadessi, *Identity and Physical Deformity in Italian Court Portraits 1550–1650: Dwarves, Hirsutes, and Castrati*, PhD thesis, Northwestern University, 2007

Foster, T. F., and K. J. P. Lowe (eds), *Black Africans in Renaissance Europe*, Cambridge/New York, 2005

Furlotti, Barbara, *Baronial Identity and Material Culture in Sixteenth-Century Rome: Paolo Giordano I Orsini and his Possessions, 1541–1585*, PhD thesis, University of London, 2008

—— 'Collezionare antichità al temp di Gregorio XIII: Il caso di Paolo Giordano I Orsini', in *Unità e frammenti di modernità, arte e scienza nella Roma di Gregorio XIII Boncompagni (1572–1585)*, Rome, 2008

Fusai, Giuseppe 'Un litigio fra due ambasciatori alla Corte di Polonia', in *Archivio storico italiano*, V, serie XL, 1907, 118–22

Galluzzi, Riguccio, *Istoria del Granducato*, Florence, 1781, reprinted 1974

Garfagnini, Gian Carlo (ed.), *Firenze e la Toscana dei Medici nell' Europa del Cinquecento*, Florence, 1983

Gaye, Johann, *Carteggio inedito degli artisti del secolo XIV, XV, XVI*, III, Florence, 1840

Giaccone, Carla Micheli, *Bracciano e il suo castello*, Rome, 1990

Ginori, Gino, *Descrittione della pompa funerale fatta nelle essequie del Serenissimo Signor Cosimo de' Medici*, Florence, 1574

Giovio, Paolo, *Lettere*, ed. G. G. Ferrero, Rome, 1956

Gnoli, Domenico, *Vittoria Accoramboni; storia del secolo XVI,* Florence, 1870

Grendler, Paul F., *Schooling in Italy, Literacy and Learning 1300–1600*, Baltimore, MD, 1991

Grieco, Allen J., 'Les plantes, les régimes végétariens et la mélancolie à la fin du Moyen Age et au début de la Renaissance', in A. J. Grieco *et al.* (eds), *Le monde végétal (XII–XVIIIe); savoirs et usages sociaux*, Saint Denis, 1993, 11–29

Grisone, Federico, *Gli ordini di cavalcare*, Naples, 1550

Haar, James, 'From Cantimbanco to Court: The Musical Fortunes of Ariosto in Florentine Society', in Massimilliano Rossi and Fiorella Giofreddi Superbi (eds), *L'arme e gli amori, Ariosto, Tasso and Guarini in Late Renaissance Florence*, II, Florence, 2003

Hale, J. R., *Florence and the Medici: The Pattern of Control*, New York, 1983

Hatfield, Rab, 'Some Unknown Descriptions of the Medici Palace in 1459', *Art Bulletin*, 52, September 1970, 232–49

Hibbert, Christopher, *The Rise and Fall of the House of Medici*, New York, 1979

Keutner, Herbert, 'The Palazzo Pitti "Venus" and Other Works by Vincenzo Danti', *The Burlington Magazine*, 100, 669, December 1958, 426–431

Kirkham, Victoria, 'Laura Battiferra degli Ammannati's First Book of Poetry: A Renaissance Holograph Comes out of Hiding', in *Rinascimento*, 35, 1996, 351–91

–– (trans. and ed.), *Laura Battiferra and Her Literary Circle: An Anthology*, Chicago and London, 2006

Kisacky, Julia, *Magic in Boiardo and Ariosto*, New York, 2000

LaMay, Thomasin, 'Maddalena Casulana; my body knows unheard of songs', in Todd M. Borgerding (ed.), *Gender, Sexuality and Early Music*, London, 2002

–– *Musical Voices of Early Modern Women: Many-Headed Melodies*, Aldershot, 2005

Langdon, Gabrielle, *Medici Women: Portraits of Power, Love and Betrayal from the Court of Duke Cosimo I*, Toronto, 2006

Langedijck, Karla, *The Portraits of the Medici, 15th–18th Centuries*, 3 volumes, Florence, 1981–87

Lapini, Agostino, *Diario Fiorentino d'Agostino Lapini*, G. O. Corazzini (ed.), Florence, 1900

Lazzaro, Claudia, *The Italian Renaissance Garden*, New Haven/London, 1990

Leuzzi, Maria Gubini, 'Straniere a corte. Degli epistolari di Giovanna d'Austria e Bianca Cappello', in Gabriella Zarri (ed.), *Per lettera. La scrittura epistolare femminile tra archivio e tipografia, secoli XV–XVIII*, Rome, 1999, 413–44

Lisci, Leonardo Ginori, *The Palazzi of Florence. Their History and Art*, Florence, 1985

Lorenzetti, Roberta, *L'antropologia filosofica di Fausto Sozzini*, Milan, 1995

Lorenzetti, Stefano, *Musica e identità nobiliare nell' Italia del Rinascimento: educazione, mentalità, immaginario*, Florence, 2003

Macdougall, Elizabeth (ed.), *Renaissance Garden Fountains*, Washington DC, 1978

Malespini, Celio, *Duecento novelle*, Venice, 1608

Manni, Domenico Maria, *Lezioni di lingua Toscana*, Florence, 1737

Martini, Magna, *Fausto Socino et la pensée socienne: un maître de la pensée religieuse (1539–1604)*, Paris, 1967

Masi, Maria, *Bianca Cappello*, Milan, 1986

Matasilani, Mario, *La felicità del Serenissimo Cosimo Medici Granduca di Toscana*, Florence, 1572

McClure, George, 'Women and the Politics of Play in Sixteenth-Century Italy: Torquato Tasso and His Theory of Games', *Renaissance Quarterly*, 2008

Mellini, Domenico, *Le dieci mascherate della bufole mandate in Firenze il giorno di Carnevale l'anno 1565*, Florence, 1566

Meloni Trkulja, Silvia (ed.), *I Fiorentini del 1562*, Florence, 1991

Minor, Andrew C., and Mitchell Bonner, *A Renaissance Entertainment; Festivities for the Marriage of Cosimo I, Duke of Florence in 1539*, Columbia, MO, 1968

Morandini, Antonietta, 'Una Missione di Troilo Orsini in Polonia per il Granduca di Toscana (maggio–luglio 1574)', *Testi e documenti*, CXXIII, 1965, 94–112

Mori, Elisabetta, 'L'onore perdute del duca di Bracciano: dalla corrispondenza di Paolo Giordano Orsini e Isabella de' Medici', *Dimensioni e problemi della ricerca storica*, 2, December 2004, 135–74

–– 'La malattia e la morte di Isabella Medici Orsini', in Maura Picciauti (ed.), *La sanità a Roma in età moderna*, XIII, I, January–March 2005

Mulcahy, Rosemarie, 'Two murders, a crucifix and the Gran Duke's "serene highness". Francesco I de' Medici's gift of Cellini's "Crucified Christ" to Philip II', in *Philip II of Spain: Patron of the Arts*, Dublin, 2004

Musacchio, Jacqueline Marie, 'Weasels and Pregnancy in Renaissance Italy', *Renaissance Studies*, 15, 2, June 2001, 172–87

Mutinelli, Fabio (ed.), *Storia arcana e aneddotica d'Italia raccontata dai veneti ambasciatori*, I, Venice, 1855–8

Nagler, A. M., *Theatre Festivals of the Medici 1538–1637*, New Haven/London, 1964

Najemy, John M., *A History of Florence, 1200–1575*, Oxford, 2006

Noble, Mark, *Memoirs of the Illustrious House of the Medici*, London, 1797

Orsi Landini, Roberta, and Bruna Niccoli, *Moda a Firenze: Lo stile di Eleonora di Toledo e la sua influenza*, Florence, 2005

Ovid, *Metamorphoses*, Arthur Golding trans. (1567), New York, 1965

Palandri, Eletto, *Les négotiations politiques et religieuses entre la Toscane et la France a l'époque du Cosme Ier et de Cathérine de Médicis (1544–1580)*, Paris, 1908

Park, Katharine, *Doctors and Medicine in Early Renaissance Florence*, Princeton, NJ, 1985

Picinelli, Roberta (ed.), *Le collezioni Gonzaga: Il carteggio tra Firenze e Mantova, 1554–1626*, Milan, 2000

Pieraccini, Gaetano, *Le Stirpe de' Medici di Cafaggiolo*, 3 volumes, Florence, 1986

Pietrosanti, Susanna, *Le cacce dei Medici*, Florence, 1992

Plaisance, Michel, *L'Accademia e il suo principe: cultura e politica a Firenze al tempo di Cosimo I e di Francesco de' Medici*, Rome, 2004

Pronti, Stefano (ed.), *Le carrozze: La raccolta di Palazzo Farnese a Piacenza*, Milan, 1998

Razzi, Silvano, *La Gostanza*, Florence, 1565

Reiss, S., and D. Wilkins (eds), *Beyond Isabella: Secular Women Patrons of Art in Renaissance Italy*, Kirksville, MO, 2001

Ricci, Giuliano de', *Cronaca (1532–1606)*, ed. Giuliana Sapori, Milan/Naples, 1972

Riddle, John M., *Contraception and Abortion from the Ancient World to the Renaissance*, Cambridge, MA, 1992

—— *Eve's Herbs: A History of Contraception and Abortion in the West*, Cambridge, MA, 1997

Ringhieri, Innocenzo, *Cento guochi liberali*, Bologna, 1551

Romoli, Domenico, *La singola dottrina di M. Domenico Romoli sopranominato Panunto dell'ufficio dello scalco*, Venice, 1560

Saltini, Guglielmo, *Tragedie Medicee domestiche, 1557–87*, Florence, 1898

—— *Bianca Cappello e Francesco de' Medici*, Florence, 1898

—— 'Due Principesse Medicee del secolo XVI', *Rassegna Nazionale*, 1901–2

Sansovino, Francesco, *La Storia della Famiglia Orsini*, Venice, 1565

Siegmund, Stefanie B., *The Medici State and the Ghetto of Florence: The Construction of an Early Modern Jewish Community*, Stanford, 2006

Spini, Giorgio, *Cosimo I de' Medici: Lettere*, Florence, 1940

—— 'The Medici Principality and the Organization of the States of Europe in the Sixteenth Century', *Journal of Italian History*, 2, 3, 1979, 420–47

—— *Cosimo I de' Medici*, Florence, 1980

Stirling Maxwell, William, *Don John of Austria*, London, 1883

Tasso, Torquato, *Il Gonzaga secondo over del giuoco*, Venice, 1582.

Thomas, William, *The History of Italy,* 1549, Ithaca, NY, 1963

Tognaccini, Laura, 'Il guardaroba di Isabella de' Medici' in Isabella Bigazzi ed., *Apparir con stile: Guardaroba aristocratici e di corte, costume teatrali e sistemi di moda,* Florence, 2007, 51–68.

Tosi, C. O., 'Cosimo I e la r. villa di Castello', *L'illustratore fiorentino,* 1908, 33–47

Varchi, Benedetto, *Storia fiorentina*, Florence, 1857–8

Vasari, Giorgio, *Le vite de' più eccellenti pittori, scultori ed architettori,* 1568 edn, Florence, 1878–88

Vives, Juan Luis, *The Instruction of a Christian Woman*, Chicago, 2002

Von Klarwill, Victor, *The Fugger News Letters*, trans. Pauline de Chary, New York, 1925

Von Reumont, Alfred, *Geschichte Toscanas seit dem Ende des Florentinischen Freistaates,* Gotha, 1876

Weaver, Elissa, *Convent Theatre in Early Modern Italy: Spiritual Fun and Learning for Women*, Cambridge, 2002

Weinberg, Bernard, 'Argomenti di discussione letteraria nell'Accademia degli Alterati, 1570–1600', in *Giornale storico della letteratura italiana,* 131, 1954

Winspeare, Fabrizio, *Isabella Orsini e la corte medicea del suo tempo*, Florence, 1961

Wittkower, Rudolf, and Margaret Wittkower, *The Divine Michelangelo: The Florentine Academy's Homage on His Death in 1564*, London, 1964

Notes

I A MEDICI CHILDHOOD

1 The New Medici
1 ASF, MDP, 1170, 2.
2 Giorgio Spini, *Cosimo I de' Medici*, Florence, 1980, 36.
3 Janet Cox Rearick, *Dynasty and Destiny in Medici Art; Pontormo, Leo X and the Two Cosimos*, Princeton, 1984, 238
4 Cecily Booth, *Cosimo I, Duke of Florence*, Cambridge, 1921, 11.
5 Ibid., 18.
6 Ibid., 31.
7 Ibid., 61.
8 Ibid., 79.
9 Janet Cox Rearick, *Bronzino's Chapel of Eleonora in the Palazzo Vecchio*, Berkeley, 1993, 23.
10 Spini, 135.
11 Gaetano Pieraccini, *Le Stirpe de' Medici di Cafaggiolo*, Florence, 1986, II, 56.
12 Cox Rearick, 1993, 23.
13 Andrew C. Minor and Bonner Mitchell, *A Renaissance Entertainment; Festivities for the Marriage of Cosimo I, Duke of Florence in 1539*, Columbia, MO, 1968.
14 Booth, 102–3.
15 Cox Rearick, 1993, 33.
16 Ibid., 354, note 36.
17 Chiara Franceschini, 'Eleonora and the Jesuits', in Konrad Eisenbichler (ed.), *The Cultural World of Eleonora di Toledo*, Aldershot/Burlington, 2004, 185.
18 Cox Rearick, 1993, 35.
19 Minor and Mitchell.
20 Bruce Edelstein, 'La fecundissima Signora Duchessa', in Eisenbichler, 2004, 71–97.
21 Winspeare, *Isabella Orsini e la corte medicea del suo tempo*, Florence, 1961, 13.
22 Pieraccini, II, 79.
23 Ibid., 78.
24 Paolo Giovio, *Lettere*, ed. G. G. Ferrero, Rome, 1956, I, 295.

2 'I Have Never Seen a More Beautiful Baby Girl'
1 ASF, MDP, 5926, 30.
2 Pieraccini, II, 173.
3 Ibid., 172.
4 Ibid., citing ASF, MDP, 358, 627, 163.
5 Winspeare, 18.
6 ASF, MDP, 1171, 285.

7 Giorgio Vasari, *Le vite de' più eccellenti pittori, scultori ed architettori*, 1568 edn, Florence, 1878–85, VI, 251–2.

8 ASF, MDP, 1170, 77.

9 Booth, 121.

10 Pieraccini, II, 483.

11 Cosimo Conti, *La prima reggia di Cosimo I nel Palazzo già della Signoria di Firenze*, Florence, 1893, 275–6.

12 ASF, MDP, 1171, 285.

13 Ibid., 1173, 25.

14 Ibid., 1176, 23.

15 Ibid., 1173, 211.

16 Conti, 32

17 Ibid.

18 William Thomas, *The History of Italy* (1549), Ithaca, NY, 1963, 95.

19 Conti, 72–78.

20 Charles Avery, 'The Gardens called "Bubley": Foreign Impression of Florentine Gardens and a New Discovery Relating to Pratolino', in *Studies in Italian Sculpture*, London, 2001.

21 ASF, MDP, 4, 15. From MAP.

22 Ibid., 195, 9. From MAP.

23 Ibid., 411. From MAP.

24 Domenico Romoli, *La singola dottrina di M. Domenico Romoli sopranominato Panunto dell'ufficio dello scalco*, Venice 1560, 33ff.

25 Ibid.

26 ASF, MDP, 1170.

27 Roberta Orsi Landini and Bruna Niccoli, *Moda a Firenze; Lo stile di Eleonora di Toledo e la sua influenza*, Florence, 2005, 55.

28 ASF, MDP, 1170, 417.

29 Landini and Niccoli, 63, cited in ASF, Medici Guardaroba 34, c. 27 v, 46 v.

30 ASF, MDP, 453, 146.

31 Winspeare, 20.

3 Growing up Medici

1 Some of these assessments are made on the basis of relations between the Medici siblings as young adults, presumably based on bonds formed in infancy, and discussed further along in the book.

2 C. O. Tosi, 'Cosimo I e la r. villa di Castello', *L'illustratore fiorentino*, 1908, 42.

3 ASF, MDP, 1172, I, 27.

4 Ibid., 1175, 45.

5 Winspeare, 20–1, citing ASF, MDP, 358, 412.

6 ASF, MDP, 1172, 37.

7 Ibid., 1171, II, 62. From MAP.

8 Ibid., 1171, III, 147. From MAP.

9 Maurilio Adriani, *Arti magiche nel Rinascimento a Firenze*, Florence, 1980, 79.

10 ASF, MDP, 1172, IV, 39.

11 Matteo Boiardo, *Orlando Innamorato*, trans. W. S. Rose, Edinburgh/London, 1893, 184ff.

12 Pieraccini, II, 88.

13 Fabritio Caroso, *Courtly Dance of the Renaissance; A New Translation and Edition of the Nobilità di dame,* 1600, trans and ed. Julia Sutton, New York, 1986, 89.

14 Ibid., 125.

15 Guglielmo Saltini, *Tragedie Medicee domestiche, 1557–87,* Florence, 1898, 5.

16 Vasari, VIII, 89.

17 Ibid., 187.

18 ASF, MDP, 1171, VI, 270. From MAP.

19 Baldessar Castiglione, *The Book of the Courtier*, New York, 1959, 55–7, 76–7.

20 Stefano Lorenzetti, *Musica e identità nobiliare nell' Italia del Rinascimento; educazione, mentalità, immaginario,* Florence, 2003, 93.

4 Approaching Adulthood

1 Thomas, 97.

2 Juan Luis Vives, *The Instruction of a Christian Woman*, Chicago, 2002, 14.

3 Ibid., 23.

4 Ibid., 25.

5 Pieraccini, II, 89.

6 Ibid., 166.

7 Candace Adelson, 'Cosimo I and the Foundation of Tapestry Production in Florence', in Gian Carlo Garfagnini, ed., *Firenze e la Toscana dei Medici nell' Europa del Cinquecento*, Florence, 1983, III, 910.

8 Laura E. Hunt, 'Cosimo I and the Anglo French Negotiations of 1550', in K. Eisenbichler (ed.), *The Cultural Politics of Cosimo I de' Medici*, Aldershot/Burlington, 2001, 29.

9 Pieraccini, II, 109.

10 Maria Masi, *Bianca Cappello*, Milan, 1986, 37.

11 Bruce Edelstein, 'Bronzino in the Service of Eleonora di Toledo and Cosimo de' Medici', in S. Reiss and D. Wilkins (eds), *Beyond Isabella; Secular Women Patrons of Art in Renaissance Italy*, Kirksville, MO, 2001, 229.

12 Ibid., 252.

13 Pieraccini, II, 116.

II A MEDICI PRINCESS GROWS UP

1 A Bridegroom for Isabella

1 Pieraccini, II, 170.

2 Domenico Gnoli, *Vittoria Accoramboni; storia del secolo xvi,* Florence, 1870, 44–5.

3 Benvenuto Cellini, *The Life of Benvenuto Cellini Written by Himself,* trans. J. Symonds, Garden City, NJ, 1975.

4 Thomas, 50.

5 Thomas V. Cohen and Elizabeth S. Cohen, *Words and Deeds in Renaissance Rome; Trials Before the Papal Magistrates*, Toronto, 1993, 64.

6 ASC, AO, I, 157, 6.

7 Ibid., 9.

8 Gnoli, 44.

9 Carol Bresnaham Menning, 'Loans and Favors, Kin and Clients: Cosimo de' Medici and the Monte di Pietà', in *The Journal of Modern History*, 61, 3, September, 1989, 487–511.

10 Robert Dallington, *A Survey of the great Duke's State of Tuscanie*, 1598, Amsterdam, 1974.

11 Giorgio Spini, *Cosimo I de' Medici; Lettere*, Florence, 1940, 165–9.

2 Medici Weddings

1 Saltini, *Tragedie Medicee,* 1898, 26.

2 Settimani, *Diario*, vol III. 117v: Manoscritti, 128, ASF.

3 Ibid.

4 Agostino Lapini, *Diario Fiorentino d'Agostino Lapini*, ed. G. O. Corazzini, Florence, 1900, 121.

5 Frank A. D'Accone, 'Corteccia's Motets for the Medici Marriages', in David Rosen and Claire Brook (eds), *Words on Music: Essays in Honor of Andrew Porter on the Occasion of His 75th Birthday*, Hillsday, NY, 2003, 48.

6 D'Accone, 65–6.

7 Ibid., 66.

8 Victoria Kirkham, 'Laura Battiferra degli Ammannati's First Book of Poetry: A Renaissance Holograph Comes out of Hiding', in *Rinascimento*, 35, 1996, 364.

9 Settimani, *Diario*, III, 123.

3 Zibellini and a Hat Full of Musk

1 See in particular ASMo, *Ambasciatori a Firenze*, 21.

2 Gino Corti, 'Cinque balli toscani del cinquecento', in *Rivista italiana di musicologia*, 12, 1977, 73–82.

3 ASF, MDP, 210, 33. From MAP.

4 Settimani, III.

5 Stefanie B. Siegmund, *The Medici State and the Ghetto of Florence; The Construction of an Early Modern Jewish Community*, Stanford, 2006, 55.

6 Cohen and Cohen, 62–4.

7 ASC, AO, I, 157, 42.

8 Victoria Kirkham (trans. and ed.), *Laura Battiferra and Her Literary Circle: An Anthology*, Chicago and London, 2006, 99.

9 Johann Gaye, *Carteggio inedito degli artisti del secolo XIV, XV, XVI*, III, Florence, 1840, 26.

10 Gian Battista Catena (ed.), *Lettere del Cardinale Giovanni de' Medici, figlio di Cosimo I, Gran Duca di Toscana, non più stampate*, Rome, 1752, 106.

11 Ibid., 68.
12 Ibid., 79.
13 Ibid., 101.
14 Ibid., 106.
15 Settimani, III, 180 r.

4 The Duke and Duchess of Bracciano
1 Catena, 108.
2 UCLA, Special Collections, Orsini Family Papers.
3 Lapini, 121.
4 Catena, 273.
5 Ibid., 202.
6 ASF, MDP, 328, 8.
7 ASC, AO, I, 157, 216.
8 Settimani, 180.
9 ASC, AO, I, 487, 596.

5 'My Brother and I'
1 MDP 1212a, 26.
2 Vasari, VII, 703.
3 Pieraccini, II, 101.
4 ASC, AO, I, 157, 56.
5 Ibid.
6 Ibid., 50, 51.
7 Ibid., 158, 7.
8 Ibid.
9 Ibid., 157, 211.
10 Ibid., 203.
11 Ibid., 212.
12 Ibid., 54.
13 ASM, AG, 1112, 290.
14 ASC, AO, I, 157, 50.
15 Janet Cox Rearick, 'The Posthumous Eleonora', in Eisenbichler, 2004, 227.
16 ASC, AO, I, 157, 52.
17 Ibid., 59
18 Pieraccini, II, 20–2.
19 ASF, MDP, 5095, 28v.
20 Pieraccini, II, 110–11.
21 ASC, AO, I, 157, 52.
22 Catena, 202.
23 Ibid., 294.
24 Ibid., 450.
25 ASC, AO, I, 157, 62.
26 Ibid.

6 Overcome by Sorrow

1 ASC, AO, I, 157, 49.
2 ASMo, *Ambasciatori a Firenze*, 21. February 8, 1562.
3 Ibid., January 20, 1562.
4 ASC, AO, I, 157, 77.
5 ASF, MDP, 6366, 210.
6 ASMo, *Ambasciatori a Firenze*, 21. May 22, 1562.
7 Settimani, III, 219r.
8 ASC, AO, I, 157, 73.
9 ASF, MDP 5095, 148v.
10 Ibid., 208.
11 Ibid., 159 v.
12 Ibid., 160v.
13 Ibid.
14 ASF, MDP, 211, 44. From MAP.
15 Saltini, *Tragedie Medicee*, 127.
16 Cellini, Book CXIII.
17 ASMo, *Ambasciatori a Firenze*, 21. November 23, 1562
18 Saltini, *Tragedie Medicee*, 127–8.
19 ASMo, *Ambasciatori a Firenze*, 21. December 10, 1562.
20 Ibid., December 12, 1562
21 Saltini, *Tragedie Medicee*, 149.
22 Pieraccini, II, 121.
23 ASMo, *Ambasciatori a Firenze*, 21. December 12, 1562.
24 Saltini, *Tragedie Medicee*, 138.
25 Ibid.
26 ASMo, *Ambasciatori a Firenze*, 21. December 17, 1562
27 Mary Westerman Bulgarella, 'The Burial Attire of Eleonora di Toledo', in Eisenbichler, 2004, 222.
28 Saltini, *Tragedie Medicee*, 140.
29 Ibid., 130.
30 Ibid., 131.
31 ASC, AO, I, 158, 79.

III THE FIRST LADY OF FLORENCE

1 After Eleonora

1 ASF, MDP, 6366, 244.
2 ASM, AG, 1097, 6.
3 MDP 219, 333. From MAP.
4 Ibid., 34. From MAP.
5 Settimani, III, 261r.
6 MDP, 219, 70. From MAP.

7 Ibid., 224.

8 Ibid.,153.

9 Ibid.,17.

10 Ibid., 224.

11 ASMo, *Ambasciatori a Firenze*, 21. December 20, 1562.

12 Ibid., 22 (no date).

13 Ibid., January 14, 1563.

14 ASF, MDP, 6366, 244.

15 ASMo, *Ambasciatori a Firenze*, 22. January 14, 1563.

16 Ibid., October 23, 1563.

17 ASC, AO, I, 157, 80.

18 Silvia Meloni Trkulja (ed.), *I Fiorentini del 1562*, Florence, 1991.

19 Winspeare, 59.

20 BL, Sloane, H., 1930, *Tragico fine della signora Eleonora di Toledo moglie di Cosimo primo de Medici . . .*

21 Settimani, III.

22 Mark Noble, *Memoirs of the House of Medici*, London, 1797.

23 Alexandre Dumas, *Les Médicis*, Brussels, 1845, 165.

24 ASC, AO, I, 157, 231.

25 ASMo, *Ambasciatori a Firenze*, 22. October 21, 1563.

26 BL, Sloane, 1930.

2 At Home with Paolo and Isabella

1 Catena, 292.

2 Vasari, II, 433.

3 Rab Hatfield, 'Some Unknown Descriptions of the Medici Palace in 1459', *Art Bulletin*, 52, September 1970, 246.

4 Rudolf and Margaret Wittkower, *The Divine Michelangelo; The Florentine Academy's Homage on His Death in 1564*, London, 1964, 16.

5 Ibid., 16.

6 ASF, MDP 6375, 6376.

7 ASF, Guardaroba, 79.

8 ASC, AO, I, 157, 263.

3 Debt

1 ASC, AO, I, 152, 17.

2 Ibid., 90.

3 Ibid., 337, 249.

4 Ibid., 316.

5 Ibid., 156, 237,

6 ASF, MDP, 221, 29 and 31. From MAP.

7 ASC, AO, I, 157, 298.

8 Ibid., 235–6.

9 Ibid., 324.

10 ASF, MDP, 6374a.
11 ASF, Miscellanea Medicea, 508, 22r.
12 ASMo, *Ambasciatori a Firenze*, 22. February 4, 1563.
13 ASC, AO, I, 157. Ibid., 336, 303

4 Conflict

1 ASC, AO, I, 268.
2 Ibid., 226.
3 Ibid., 264
4 Giampiero Brunelli, *Soldati del papa, politica militare e nobiltà nello Stato della Chiesa (1560–1644)*, Rome, 2003, 43 and note 70. Cited in Elisabetta Mori, 'L'onore perdute del duca di Bracciano: dalla corrispondenza di Paolo Giordano Orsini e Isabella de' Medici', *Dimensioni e problemi della ricerca storica*, 2, December 2004, 135–74.
5 ASC, AO, I, 157, 215.
6 Ibid., 269.
7 Ibid., 158, 20.
8 Francesco Sansovino, *La Storia della Famiglia Orsini*, Venice, 1565, Book VI, 91 ff.
9 Saltini, 'Due Principesse Medicee del secolo XVI', *Rassegna Nazionale,* 1901–2, 605–6.
10 ASC, AO, I, 157, 98.

5 The Baroncelli

1 Lapini, 152.
2 ASM, AG, 1087, 48.
3 Cited in Winspeare, 82.
4 ASC, AO, I, 157, 121.
5 ASF, Miscellanea Medicea, 360, 88.
6 *Atti della Pontificia Accademia Romana di Archeologia*, 1923, 118.
7 Ovid, *Metamorphoses*, Arthur Golding trans. (1567), Book X, New York, 1965.
8 Borghini, *Riposo*, Florence, 1730, cited in Herbert Keutner, 'The Palazzo Pitti's "Venus" and Other Works by Vincenzo Danti', *Burlington Magazine*, 100, 669, December 1958, 428, note 8.
9 ASC, AO, I, 157, 299.

6 The Theatre of Isabella

1 ASC, AO, I, 157, 121.
2 ASC, AO, I, 57, 12
3 Silvano Razzi, *La Gostanza*, Florence, 1565.
4 Elissa Weaver, *Convent Theatre in Early Modern Italy; Spiritual Fun and Learning for Women*, Cambridge, 2002, 132.
5 ASC, AO, I, 1572, 323.
6 Ibid., 205.
7 Langdon Gabrielle, *Medici Women: Portraits of Power, Love and Betrayal from the Court of Duke Cosimo I*, Toronto, 2006, 163.
8 Maddalena Casulana, translated in Thomasin LaMay, 'Maddalena Casulana; my

body knows unheard of songs', in Todd M. Borgerding (ed.), *Gender, Sexuality and Early Music*, London, 2002, 41–2.

9 Thomasin LaMay, 'Composing from the Throat: Maddalena Casulana's "Primo libro de madrigali, 1568"', in LaMay (ed.), *Musical Voices of Early Modern Women; Many-Headed Melodies*, Aldershot, 2005, 382

10 Ibid., 384.

11 Ibid.

12 Donna G. Cardamone, 'Isabella Medici–Orsini: A Portrait of Self-Affirmation', in Borgerding (ed.), 2002, 8–9.

13 ASC, AO, I, 157, 222.

14 Settimani, III, 325 v.

15 Celio Malespini, *Duecento novelle*, Venice, 1608, 149.

16 ASMo, *Ambasciatori a Firenze*, 22. May 24, 1567.

17 Torquato Tasso, *Il Gonzaga secondo over del giuoco*, Venice, 1582. Also see George McClure, 'Women and the Politics of Play in Sixteenth-Century Italy: Torquato Tasso and His Theory of Games', *Renaissance Quarterly*, 2008.

7 Fidelities

1 Winspeare, 61–2.

2 Fabio Mutinelli (ed.), *Storia arcana e aneddotica d'Italia raccontata dai veneti ambasciatori*, I, Venice 1855–8, 61.

3 ASC, AO, I, 157, 213.

4 ASF, MDP, 6375, 11.

5 ASC, AO, I, 157, 220.

6 Ibid., 263.

7 Ibid., 222.

8 Ibid.

8 Troilo

1 Bastiano Arditi, *Diario di Firenze e delle altri parti della cristanità (1575–1579)*. Roberto Cantagalli (ed.), Florence, 1970, 70.

2 Mutinelli, 61.

3 ASF, MDP 6373, insert 1.

4 Ibid.

5 Ibid.

6 Ibid.

7 ASMo, *Ambasciatori a Firenze*, 22. July 1, 1564.

9 A 'Clandestine' Affair

1 Malespini, 124ff.

2 Casulana, unpublished, trans. T. LaMay.

3 James Haar, 'From Cantimbanco to Court: The Musical Fortunes of Ariosto in Florentine Society', in Massimilliano Rossi and Fiorella Giofreddi Superbi (eds), *L'arme e gli amori, Ariosto, Tasso and Guarini in Late Renaissance Florence*, II, Florence, 2003, 196.

4 Kirkham, 2006, 107

5 Some of the portions of the correspondence between Troilo and Isabella, described below, are published in Winspeare. Others are unpublished and can be found in ASF, MDP, 6373, ins. 1.

6 Winspeare, 97, from ASF, MDP, 6373, ins. 1.

7 ASF, MDP 6373, ins 1.

8 Ibid.

IV MEDICI MACHINATIONS

1 The Imperial Sister-in-Law

1 Settimani, III, 312r.

2 ASF, MDP, 6366, 270.

3 ASC, AO, I, 157, 171.

4 ASF, MDP 5094, I, 103. From MAP.

5 Saltini, *Bianca Cappello e Francesco de' Medici,* Florence, 1898, 99.

6 Vasari, VII, 619.

7 Pieraccini, II, 129.

8 Ibid.

9 ASC, AO, I, 157, 234.

10 ASF, MDP, 6366, 371

11 Ibid., 372

12 Ibid., 371.

13 ASC, AO, I, 157, 297.

14 Ibid., 297.

15 ASM, AG, 112, 317.

16 ASF, MDP, 6373, I.

17 Eletto Palandri, *Les négotiations politiques et religieuses entre la Toscane et la France a l'époque du Cosme Ier et de Cathérine de Médicis (1544–1580),* Paris, 1908.

2 Family Lives

1 ASMo, *Ambasciatori a Firenze,* 22. April 27, 1569.

2 ASC, AO, I, 157, 240.

3 ASF, MDP, 6375.

4 Saltini, 'Due Principesse', 571.

5 Booth, 222.

6 ASF, MDP, 522, 733.

7 ASC, AO, I, 157, 211.

8 ASF, MDP, 5926, 104. From MAP.

9 Ibid., 6366, 396.

10 ASC, AO, I, 157, 267.

11 BL. Sloane, 1930.

12 John M. Riddle, *Contraception and Abortion from the Ancient World to the Renaissance,*

Cambridge, MA, 1992, 148–9.

13 John M. Riddle, *Eve's Herbs: A History of Contraception and Abortion in the West*, Cambridge, MA, 1997.

14 ASF, MDP, 221, 31. From MAP.

15 ASC, AO, 157, 320.

16 Ibid., 295.

17 ASF, MDP, 211, 81. From MAP.

3 Grand Duke

1 Booth, 229.

2 Ibid., 228.

3 ASF, MDP, 321, 1. From MAP.

4 Ibid., 2.

5 ASMo, *Ambasciatori a Firenze*, 22. December 13, 1569.

6 Lapini, 167.

7 Settimani, III, 486 v.

8 Lapini, 167.

9 Booth, 238.

10 ASMo, *Ambasciatori a Firenze*, 22. March 22, 1570.

11 Settimani, III, 477 r.

12 ASF, MDP, 1177, 16, from MAP.

13 AO, ASC, I, 158, 90.

4 Cammilla

1 Lapini, 169.

2 Saltini, *Tragedie Medicee*, 240.

3 Siegmund, xv.

4 Picraccini, II, 73.

5 Pieraccini, II, 215.

6 Saltini, *Tragedie Medicee* (citing Galluzzi), 245.

7 Ibid., 245.

8 Ibid., 246.

9 ASMo. *Ambasciatori a Firenze*, 22. April 8, 1570.

10 Saltini, *Tragedie Medicee*, 247–9.

11 ASC, AO, I, 158, 80.

12 ASMo, *Ambasciatori a Firenze*, 22. April 27, 1570.

13 Ibid.

14 ASC, AO, I, 158, 43.

15 Ibid., 61.

16 Saltini, *Tragedie Medicee*, 356.

17 Ibid., 357–8.

18 ASMo, *Ambasciatori a Firenze*, 22. August 26, 1570.

5 'I Turchi'

1 William Stirling Maxwell, *Don John of Austria*, London, 1883, 97.
2 Richard Clayton, *Memoirs of the House of Medici from its Origins to the Death of Garzia and of the Great Men who flourished in Tuscany within that period. From the French of Mr Tenhove, notes and observations by Sir Richard Clayton*, II, Bath, 1797, 463.
3 Ibid., 464.
4 Hugh Bicheno, *Crescent and Cross: The Battle of Lepanto, 1571*, London, 2003, 185.
5 Booth, 255, citing C. Manfroni, 'La Marina di Guerra del Granducato Mediceo', in *Rivista Marittima*, May, 1895, 29.
6 Stirling Maxwell, 358.
7 Mori, 2004, citing ASC, AO, I, 152, 142.
8 ASC, AO, I, 158, 71.
9 Ibid., 59.
10 ASMo, *Ambasciatori a Firenze*, June 8, 1571.
11 ASF, MDP, 5085, 471.
12 ASC, AO, I, 158, 101.
13 *A New Dictionary of the Italian and English Languages*, London, 1854, I, 274.
14 ASC, AO, I, 146, 2.

6 Lepanto and Don Giovanni

1 Stirling Maxwell, 375.
2 Ibid., 407.
3 Ibid., 411.
4 Ibid., 420.
5 ASF, MDP, 2636, 31. From MAP.
6 Stirling Maxwell, 434.
7 ASC, AO, I, 158, 102.
8 Gnoli, 56.
9 Ibid., 57.
10 Mori, 2004, 148, citing ASC, AO, I, 146, 84.
11 Michele Capri, *Delle lodi del Serenissimo Signor Don Giovanni d'Austria*, Florence, 1571.
12 ASF, MDP, 4153. From MAP.
13 Ibid.

7 Putti

1 ASMo, *Ambasciatori a Firenze*, 22. September 23, 1570.
2 ASC, AO, I, 158, 168.
3 Ibid., 91.
4 Ibid.
5 Ibid., 79.
6 Ibid., 119.
7 ASF, MDP, 241, 41, from MAP.
8 ASC, AO, I, 158 107.

9 Ibid., 109.
10 Ibid., 111.
11 Ibid.
12 Ibid., 123.
13 Ibid., 127.
14 Ibid., 125.
15 Ibid., 101.
16 Ibid., 135.
17 Ibid., 120.
18 ASC, AO, I, 158, 126.
19 ASMo. *Ambasciatori a Firenze* 22., Jan 19, 1572.
20 Ibid. Feb 23, 1572.
21 ASC, AO, I, 158, 147.
22 Ibid., 146.
23 Ibid.
24 Settimani, III, 575v.
25 Ibid.
26 ASMo, *Ambasciatori a Firenze*, 22. Sept 13, 1572.
27 Ibid., Sept 27, 1572.

8 Bianca

1 ASMo, *Ambasciatori a Firenze*, 22. May 1, 1572.
2 Malespini, Book II, 278r.
3 Ibid.
4 Ibid.
5 Saltini, *Bianca Cappello*, 127.
6 Saltini, *Tragedie Medicee*, 359–60.
7 Saltini, *Bianca Cappello*, 133.
8 ASMo, *Ambasciatori a Firenze*, 22. April 4, 1573.
9 ASC, AO, I, 158, 63.

9 An Assassination

1 Giuliano de' Ricci, *Cronaca (1532–1606)*, ed. Giuliana Sapori, Milan/Naples, 1972, 42.
2 Malespini, Bk II, 279r.
3 Saltini, *Bianca Cappello*, 156, citing Biblioteca Nazionale di Parigi, cod. 10074, *Lettere, istruzioni, Orazione e alti scritti, pressochè tutti concernenti la famiglia de' Medici, inserto XV e ultimo.*
4 Saltini, *Bianca Cappello*, 160, citing ASF, MDP, 5101, 322.
5 Ibid., 170–1.
6 Arditi, citing ASF, MDP, 5947b, 9v.
7 Ibid., 175.

10 The Best of Times

1 ASC, AO, I, 158, 184.
2 Ibid., 188.
3 Ibid., 183.
4 Ibid., 188.
5 Francesca Fiorani, *The Marvel of Maps; Art, Cartography and Politics in Renaissance Italy*, New Haven/London, 2005, 42.
6 Ibid., no. 88, 287.
7 Domenico Maria Manni, *Lezioni di lingua Toscana*, Florence, 1737, cited in Winspeare, 86–8.
8 ASF, MDP, 6373, ins.
9 ASMo, *Ambasciatori a Firenze*, 22. October 10, 1573.
10 Ibid., January 8, 1574.
11 Settimani, III, 615 v.
12 Ricci, 75.
13 Ibid., 77–8.
14 ASMo, *Ambasciatori a Firenze*, 22. February 12, 1574.
15 Ibid., February 20, 1574.
16 Mario Matasilani, *La Felicità del Serenissimo Cosimo Medici Granduca di Toscana*, Florence, 1572.
17 Alfred von Reumont, *Geschichte Toscanas seit dem Ende des Florentinischen Freistaates*, Gotha, 1876, I, 293.
18 BL, Sloane 1930.

V THE TROUBLES OF A MEDICI PRINCESS

1 The Decline of Cosimo

1 Pieraccini, II, 40.
2 ASF, MDP, 238, 78. From MAP.
3 Ibid., 60.
4 Ibid., 74.
5 ASF, MDP, 241, 84. From MAP.
6 Ibid., 19. From MAP.
7 Saltini, *Tragedie Medicee*, 261–2.
8 Ibid., 262–3.
9 Ibid., 263.
10 Pieraccini, II, 42.
11 ASF, MDP, 1212, 1, 103. From MAP.
12 ASMo, *Ambasciatori a Firenze*, 22. January 8, 1574.
13 Pieraccini, II, 45.
14 Ibid.
15 Ricci, 85.
16 Ibid.

17 Eve Borsook, 'Art and Politics at the Medici Court: The Funeral of Cosimo de' Medici', *Mitteilungen des Kunsthistorisches Instituts in Florenz*, XII, 1965, 1–2, 36.

18 Gino Ginori, *Descrittione della pompa funerale fatta nelle essequie del Serenissimo Signor Cosimo de' Medici*, Florence, 1574.

19 ASM, AG, 1112, 403

2 The Children's Negotiation

1 Settimani, III, 620r.

2 ASF, MDP, 5088, 45r.

3 ASC, AO, I, 158, 185.

4 Ibid., 188.

5 Ibid., 198.

6 Ibid., 200.

7 ASF, MDP, 1170, loose leaf.

8 Barbara Furlotti originally proposed Isabella as the patron of this work in *Baronial Identity and Material Culture in Sixteenth-Century Rome: Paolo Giordano I Orsini and his Possessions, 1541–1585*, PhD thesis, University of London, 2008.

3 'My Coming'

1 Mori, 2004.

2 Thomas, 50.

3 ASC, AO, I, 158, 198.

4 Mori, 2004, 160.

5 Gnoli, 44.

6 ASC, AO, I, 158, 198.

7 Ibid., 201.

8 Ibid., I, 152, 191.

9 Arditi, 16.

10 Pieraccini, II, 175.

11 ASC, AO, I, 158, 197.

12 Ibid., 206.

13 Ibid., 199.

14 Ibid., 203.

15 Ibid., 199

16 Ibid., 191.

17 Ibid., 225.

18 Ibid., 146, 289.

4 The New Ambassador

1 Ricci, 114.

2 ASC, AO, I, 158, 194.

3 Ibid., 193.

4 Ibid., I, 146, 10.

5 Ibid., I, 158, 237.

6 Arditi, 35.

7 ASMo, *Ambasciatori a Firenze*, 24. January 15, 1575.

8 Ibid., January 29, 1575.

9 Ibid., February 8, 1575.

10 Saltini, *Bianca Cappello*, 180.

11 Settimani, IV, 15v.

12 ASC, AO, I, 337, 8

13 Arditi, 74.

5 Leonora

1 Riguccio Galluzzi, *Istoria del Granducato*, Book IV, Florence, 1781, reprinted 1974, 246.

2 ASMo, *Ambasciatori a Firenze*, 22. April 26, 1572.

3 Saltini, 'Due Principesse', 570–1.

4 ASF, MDP, 5154, 21. From MAP.

5 Saltini, 'Due Principesse', 629.

6 ASMo, *Ambasciatori a Firenze*, 24. Jauary 22, 1575.

7 Ibid., February 8, 1575.

6 The Duelling Season

1 Luciano Berti, *Il principe dello studiolo. Francesco I de' Medici e la fine del Rinascimento fiorentino*, Pistoia, 2002, 22.

2 Clayton, 457.

3 Arditi, 57.

4 Ibid., 83.

5 ASC, AO, I, 157, 299.

6 Ricci, 85.

7 Ibid., 118.

8 Ibid., 137.

9 Ibid.

10 Ibid.

11 For the cited extracts from Troilo's Polish experience, see Antonietta Morandini, 'Una Missione di Troilo Orsini in Polonia per il Granduca di Toscana (maggio–luglio 1574), *Testi e documenti*, CXXIII, 1965, 94–112, and Giuseppe Fusai, 'Un litigio fra due ambasciatori alla Corte di Polonia', in *Archivio storico italiano*, V, serie XL, 1907, 118–22.

12 ASC, AO, I, 152, 189.

7 The Pucci Conspiracy

1 Ricci, 140.

2 ASC, AO, I, 146, 229.

3 Ibid., 158, 232.

4 Ibid.

5 Ibid.

6 ASC, AO, I, 158, 202.

7 ASMo, *Ambasciatori a Firenze*, 24. July 25, 1575.

8 Ibid.

9 Bernard Weinberg, 'Argomenti di discussione letteraria nell'Accademia degli Alterati, 1570–1600', in *Giornale storico della letteratura italiana*, 131, 1954, 182–3.

8 *Troilo, Bandito*

1 ASF, MDP, 5088, 160r.

2 ASC, AO, I, 158, 235.

3 Ibid., 224.

4 Ibid., 245.

5 Ibid., 146, 42.

6 Ibid., 228.

7 Ibid., 239.

8 ASC, AO, I 158, 231.

9 Ricci, 176.

10 Ibid.

11 Elizabetta Mori, 'La malattia e la morte di Isabella Medici Orsini', in Maura Picciauti (ed.), *La sanità a Roma in età moderna*, XIII, I, January–March 2005, 92.

12 Pieraccini, II, 175.

13 Mori, 2005, 92.

14 Pieraccini, II, 175.

15 ASMo, *Ambasciatori a Firenze*, 24. October 29, 1575.

16 ASC, AO, I, 158, 230.

17 ASMo, *Ambasciatori a Firenze*, 24. December 19, 1575.

18 Ibid., December 22, 1575.

19 ASC, AO, I, 158, 227.

VI FINAL ACTS

1 The New Year

1 ASF, MDP, 681. Cited in Arditi, 69.

2 ASF, Bandi, 2696, 46. Cited, ibid.

3 Ricci, 185.

4 ASMo, *Ambasciatori a Firenze*, 24. February 22, 1576.

5 Ricci, 186.

6 ASMo, *Ambasciatori a Firenze*, 24. March 4, 1576.

7 Arditi, 91.

8 ASC, AO, I, 158, 251.

9 Felice Faciuta, *Foelicis Faciutae melphitani pastorali. Eiusdem divers poemata*, Florence, 1576, 77–8. Translated by Stephen D'Evelyn.

10 ASC, AO, I, 146, 120.

11 Ibid., 17.

12 ASF, Carte Strozziane, I, Fa. 338, 292 r+v.

13 ASMo, *Ambasciatori a Firenze*, 24. May 13, 1576.

14 Mori, 2005, 93.

15 ASMo, *Ambasciatori a Firenze*, 24. July 9, 1576.

2 A Trip to Cafaggiolo

1 ASMo, *Ambasciatori a Firenze*, June 3, 1576.

2 Arditi, 93.

3 Ricci, 193

4 Ibid., 197.

5 Ibid., 193.

6 Ibid., 196.

7 Pieraccini, II, 185, citing ASF, MDP, 5154, c. 86.

8 Ibid., citing ASF, MDP, 5088, c. 34.

9 Arditi, 107.

10 Ricci, 197.

11 Arditi, 105.

12 Ibid., 106.

13 Saltini, 'Due principesse', 6, 188–9. From ASMo, *Ambasciatori a Firenze*, 24. July 1576.

3 A Trip to Cerreto Guidi

1 ASF, Ducato d'Urbino G 236, 1350.

2 ASF, MDP, 6366, 585.

3 See, for example, BL, Sloane, 1930.

4 'As If She Imagined What Was in Store for Her'

1 Winspeare, 170, from ASF, MDP, 245, 247.

2 ASF, Ducato d'Urbino G 236, 1351.

3 ASF, Miscellanea Medicea, 12, ins. 6.

4 Arditi, 292. From ASMo, *Ambasciatori a Firenze*, 24. July 29, 1576.

5 Ibid.

6 Lapini, 192.

7 Ricci, 198.

5 Post-Mortem

1 John Marston, *Antonio's Revenge*, London, 1602, cited by T. S. R. Boase, 'The Medici in Elizabethan and Jacobean Drama', *Journal of the Warburg and Courtauld Institutes*, 37, 1974, 374.

2 Thomas Cohen, 'Double Murder in Cretone Castle', in *Love and Death in Renaissance Italy*, Chicago, 2004.

3 Galluzzi, 267–8.

4 ASF, MDP, 4902, 84r. See Rosemarie Mulcahy, 'Two murders, a crucifix and the Gran Duke's "serene highness". Francesco I de' Medici's gift of Cellini's

"Crucified Christ" to Philip II', in *Philip II of Spain; Patron of the Arts*, Dublin, 2004, 91–114.
5 ASF, MDP, 5089, 146.
6 Ibid.
7 ASF, Carte Strozziane, Serie I, 369, 75.
8 Arditi, 128–9.
9 ASMo, *Ambasciatori a Firenze*, 24. September 1, 1576.
10 ASF, MDP, 6373, 587.
11 See in particular Langdon, 165–70.
12 Noble, 271.

6 The Culling Continued
1 For these deaths, see Ricci, 200 and Arditi, 114–5.
2 Arditi, 164.
3 ASF, MDP 695, 5. From MAP.
4 Ibid., 688, 6.
5 Ibid., 4.
6 Abel Desjardins, *Négociations Diplomatiques de la France avec la Toscane*, IV, Paris, 1859–86, 81–2.
7 Ibid.
8 Winspeare, 173.

7 The Assassin's Tale
1 This account of Tremazzi's is to be found in ASF, Carte Strozziane, I, 97, published by Gnoli, 404–14.
2 Desjardins, 131–2.
3 Palandri, 196.
4 Victor Von Klarwill, *The Fugger News Letters*, trans. Pauline de Chary, New York, 1925, 29–30.

Epilogue
1 ASF, MDP, 5367, 3.
2 Dallington, 39.
3 Noble, 270–1.

List of plates

1 Agnolo Bronzino, *Eleonora di Toledo*, 1543, Národní Gallery, Prague.
2 Agnolo Bronzino, *Cosimo de' Medici*, 1543–44.
3 Agnolo Bronzino, *Bia*, circa 1542, Galleria degli Uffizi, Florence.
4 Agnolo Bronzino, *Isabella de' Medici*, circa 1549, National Museum, Stockholm.
5 Agnolo Bronzino, *Isabella de' Medici*, circa 1558, Galleria Palatina, Florence.
6 Anon., *Francesco de' Medici*, late 1560s, Galleria Palatina, Florence.
7 Agnolo Bronzino, *Saint John the Baptist*, circa 1561, Galleria Borghese, Rome.
8 Detail of Cardinal Ferdinando de' Medici from Jacopo Zucchi, *Mass of St Gregory*, 1575, Church of Ss. Trinità dei Monti dei Pellegrini, Rome.
9 Agnolo Bronzino, workshop, *Pietro de' Medici*, 1560s, Galleria degli Uffizi, Florence.
10 Alessandro Allori att., *Isabella de' Medici*, circa 1565, Private Collection, United Kingdom.
11 Paolo Giordano as illustrated in Francesco Sansovino, *La Storia della famiglia Orsini*, Venice, 1565.
12 Anon., *Calcio in Piazza Santa Croce*, 1589, John and Mable Ringling Museum of Art, Sarasota, Florida.
13 Anastagio Fontebuoni, *Troilo Orsini bringing aid to Cathérine de' Medici*, circa 1626, Mari Cha Collection.
14 Anon., *Giovanna of Austria*, Museo Storico della Caccia e del Territorio, Cerreto Guidi.
15 Alessandro Allori, *Cammilla Martelli*, circa 1571, Galleria Palatina, Florence.
16 Alessandro Allori, *Leonora di Toledo*, circa 1568, Kunsthistorisches Museum, Vienna.
17 Anon, *Bianca Cappello*, circa 1584, Galleria Palatina, Florence.
18 Giovanni Stradano, 'Betrothal of Lucrezia de' Medici to Alfonso d'Este', 1558, Palazzo Vecchio, Florence.
19 Vincenzo Danti, *Venus*, circa 1570, Palazzo Pitti, Florence.
20 Vincenzo de' Rossi, *Adonis*, circa 1570, Palazzo Pitti, Florence.
21 Agnolo Bronzino, *Double Portrait of Morgante*, circa 1550, Galleria degli Uffizi, Florence.
22 Sandro Botticelli, *Scene from the Story of Nastagio degli Onesti*, 1487, Prado Museum, Madrid.
23 Giovanni Maria Butteri, *The Medici depicted as the Holy Family*, 1575, Museo del Cenacolo del Andrea del Sarto a San Salvi, Florence.

Acknowledgements

I never expected I would write a book about the Medici and I could not have done it without a lot of assistance. I've profited from exchange, advice and support from Guendalina Ajello, Kathy Bosi, Jacki Mussachio, Touba Ghadessi Fleming, George McClure, Flora Dennis, Bruce Edelstein, Sara Matthews Grieco, Deanna Schemek, Suzanne Cusick, Thomasin LaMay, Sheila ffoliott, Rupert Sheperd, Beryl Williams, Stephen D'Evelyn. Olwen Hufton gamely took train after bus with me on a rainy Saturday to Cerreto Guidi. Sabine Eiche has my eternal gratitude for emergency and meticulous document transcription in Florence. Ed Goldberg, former director of the Medici Archive Project was extremely generous and I cannot praise enough MAP's online database, from which many of the archival sources cited here emerged. I have especially enjoyed exchange with Barbara Furlotti, proof historians can climb two sides of the same tree, and I look forward to seeing her own work on Paolo Giordano's consumption appear in print. As usual, I've appropriated quite an array of ideas from the lively mind of Henry Dietrich Fernández. All errors are my own.

At Faber, it was Julian Loose who first figured out this was Isabella's story, and he has been as meaningful an editor as ever. Thanks also go to Henry Volans, Kate Murray Browne, Kate Ward and copyeditor Ian Bahrami. In New York at Oxford University Press, Tim Bent has been a wonderful adopter of Isabella, as have all the staff at OUP. I'm very fortunate to have Gill Coleridge as an agent and Melanie Jackson.

I conducted research at the Archivio di Stato in Florence, Mantua, Modena, Rome, the Archivio Capitolino, Rome, the British Library, the Warburg Institute, London, the Fine Arts, Widener and Houghton Libraries, Harvard University, the Getty Research Library and the Special Collections, UCLA, Los Angeles. Thank you to the staff of those institutions.

My father, Brian Murphy died as I was revising the manuscript, and the ghost of his presence permeated that process. To those who knew him, he and Isabella might not seem at first glance to have much in common, but in fact they both had a lot of charm, liked a party, had an impressive range of intellectual interests and loved a lively debate. Like Isabella, he would have been perfectly happy spending the afternoon discussing the correct use of *mai* and I miss him.

Index